Praise for David E. Hoffman's

# THE BILLION DOLLAR SPY

'An astonishingly detailed picture of espionage in the 1980s, written with pacey journalistic verve and an eerily contemporary feel. Essential reading for anyone who wants to know how the spy mind works.'

Ben Macinytre, *The Times*

'It is the human factor that elevates *The Billion Dollar Spy* to a different level: non-fiction as rich and resonant as a spy novel by John Le Carré or Graham Greene.'

*Mail on Sunday*

'*The Billion Dollar Spy* is one of the best spy stories to come out of the Cold War and all the more riveting ... for being true. It hits the sweet spot between page-turning thriller and solidly researched history ... and then becomes something more, a shrewd character study of spies and the spies who run them, the mixed motives, the risks ... This is a terrific book.'

*Washington Post*

'*The Billion Dollar Spy* reads like the very best spy fiction yet is meticulously drawn from real life. It is a gripping story of courage, professionalism, and betrayal in the secret world.'

Rodric Braithwaite,
British Ambassador in Moscow, 1988–92

'In an era of suicide bombers and ISIS beheadings, the spy dramas of the Cold War can seem tame, almost polite affairs. Central Intelligence Agency officers who worked in the Soviet capital complained about operating under Moscow rules, meaning the relentless scrutiny of the K.G.B. And they knew that any Soviet citizen caught spying faced certain execution. Still, there were rules. Those rules may actually be a reason that David Hoffman's [book] about Adolf Tolkachev, a Soviet radar expert who spied for the C.I.A., is such an engrossing tale. The story played out over several years, almost entirely on the streets of Moscow, in a twilit chess game that pitted American intelligence officers against their Soviet counterparts.'

*New York Times*

'A fabulous read that also provides chilling insights into the Cold War spy game between Washington and Moscow that has erupted anew under Vladimir Putin ... It is also an evocative portrait of everyday life in the crumbling Soviet Union and a meticulously researched guide to CIA sources and methods. I devoured every word, including the footnotes.'

Michael Dobbs, author of
*One Minute to Midnight: Kennedy, Khrushchev, and Castro on the Brink of Nuclear War*

'A true-life tale so gripping at times it reads like spy fiction.'
*Los Angeles Times*

'Engrossing ... Mr Hoffman's book particularly shines in cinematic accounts of ... anxious encounters.'
*New York Times*

'A rare look at the dangerous, intricately choreographed tradecraft behind old-school intelligence gathering … What [Hoffman]'s accomplished here isn't just a remarkable example of journalistic talent but also an ability to weave an absolutely gripping nonfiction narrative.'

*Dallas Morning News*

'Hoffman excels at conveying both the tradecraft and the human vulnerabilities involved in spying.'

*The New Yorker*

'Gripping and nerve-wracking … Human tension hangs over every page of *The Billion Dollar Spy* like the smell of leaded gasoline … [Hoffman] knows the intelligence world well and has expertly used recently declassified documents to tell this unsettling and suspenseful story. … *The Billion Dollar Spy* reads like the most taut and suspenseful parts of *Tinker Tailor Soldier Spy* or *Smiley's People*. It's worth the clenched jaw and upset stomach it creates.'

*USA Today*

'Hoffman viscerally evokes the secret, ruthless Cold War battle between the American Central Intelligence Agency and the Soviet KGB in his true-life espionage thriller … An exciting, revealing tale with a courageous, sympathetic protagonist.'

*Tampa Bay Times*

'The fine first sentence of *The Billion Dollar Spy* could almost have been written with an icicle. A work of painstaking historical research that's paced like a thriller.'

*Departures*

'Hoffman [proves] that nonfiction can read like a John le Carré thriller … This real-life tale of espionage will hook readers from the get-go.'

*Publishers Weekly* (starred review)

'Fascinating … Hoffman's revealing of [Adolf Tolkachev] as a person and a spy is brilliantly done, making this mesmerizing true story scary and thrilling.'

*Booklist* (starred review)

'Hoffman ably navigates the many strands of this complex espionage story. An intricate, mesmerizing portrayal of the KGB-CIA spy culture … A thoroughly researched excavation of an astoundingly important (and sadly sacrificed) spy for the CIA.'

*Kirkus Reviews*

'This riveting drama … packs valuable insights into the final decade of the cloak-and-dagger rivalry between the United States and the former Soviet Union … A must-read for historians and buffs of that era, as well as aficionados of espionage.'

*Christian Science Monitor*

'One of the best real-life spy stories ever told. This is a breakthrough book in intelligence writing, drawing on CIA operational cables—the holy grail of the spy world— to narrate each astonishing move. Hoffman reveals CIA tradecraft tricks that are more delicious than anything in a spy novel, and his command of the Soviet landscape is masterful. Full of twists so amazing you couldn't make them up, this is spy fact that really is better than fiction.'

David Ignatius, author of *The Director*

David E. Hoffman

# THE BILLION DOLLAR SPY

David E. Hoffman is a contributing editor at *The Washington Post* and a correspondent for PBS's flagship investigative series, *Frontline*. He is the author of *The Oligarchs* and *The Dead Hand* (Icon, 2011), about the end of the Cold War arms race, and winner of a Pulitzer Prize. He lives with his wife in Maryland.

www.davidehoffman.com

Also by David E. Hoffman

*The Oligarchs: Wealth and Power in the New Russia*

*The Dead Hand: Reagan, Gorbachev and the
Untold Story of the Cold War Arms Race*

# THE BILLION DOLLAR SPY

# THE
# BILLION
# DOLLAR
# SPY

## A True Story of
## Cold War Espionage
## and Betrayal

David E. Hoffman

ICON

This edition published in the UK in 2018
by Icon Books Ltd, Omnibus Business Centre,
39–41 North Road, London N7 9DP
email: info@iconbooks.com
www.iconbooks.com

Previously published in the UK in 2017 by Icon Books Ltd

First published in the USA in 2015 by Doubleday,
a division of Penguin Random House LLC

Sold in the UK, Europe and Asia
by Faber & Faber Ltd, Bloomsbury House,
74–77 Great Russell Street,
London WC1B 3DA or their agents

Distributed in the UK, Europe and Asia
by Grantham Book Services,
Trent Road, Grantham NG31 7XQ

Distributed in Australia and New Zealand
by Allen & Unwin Pty Ltd,
PO Box 8500, 83 Alexander Street,
Crows Nest, NSW 2065

Distributed in South Africa by
Jonathan Ball, Office B4, The District,
41 Sir Lowry Road, Woodstock 7925

Distributed in India by Penguin Books India,
7th Floor, Infinity Tower – C, DLF Cyber City,
Gurgaon 122002, Haryana

ISBN: 978-178578-352-4

Author photograph © Carole F. Hoffman
Book design by Michael Collica
Maps © 2015 by Gene Thorp

Printed and bound in the UK by Clays Ltd, Elcograf S.p.A.

*To Carole*

Everything we do is dangerous.

*—Adolf Tolkachev, to his CIA case officer*
*October 11, 1984*

# CONTENTS

# THE BILLION DOLLAR SPY

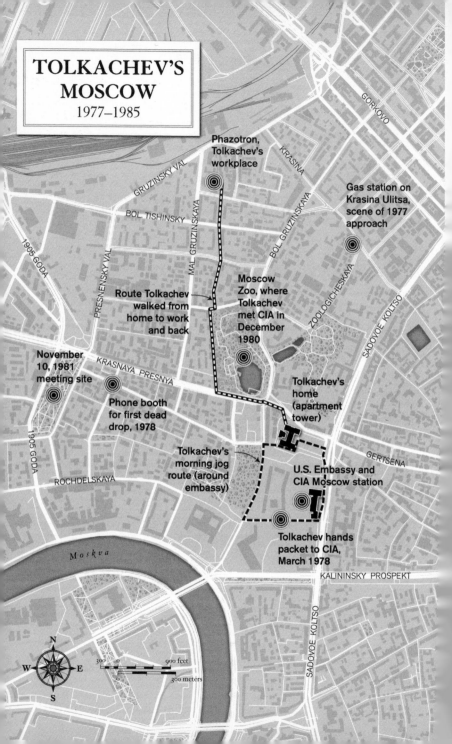

# TOLKACHEV'S MOSCOW
## 1977–1985

Phazotron, Tolkachev's workplace

Gas station on Krasina Ulitsa, scene of 1977 approach

Route Tolkachev walked from home to work and back

Moscow Zoo, where Tolkachev met CIA in December 1980

November 10, 1981 meeting site

Phone booth for first dead drop, 1978

Tolkachev's home (apartment tower)

Tolkachev's morning jog route (around embassy)

U.S. Embassy and CIA Moscow station

Tolkachev hands packet to CIA, March 1978

GORKOVO

KRASINA

GRUZINSKY VAL

BOL. TISHINSKY

MAL GRUZINSKAYA

BOL GRUZINSKAYA

ZOOLOGICHESKAYA

1905 GODA

PRESNENSKY VAL

KRASNAYA PRESNYA

1905 GODA

ROCHDELSKAYA

GERTSENA

SADOVOE KOLTSO

Moskva

KALININSKY PROSPEKT

SADOVOE KOLTSO

N W E S

300    0              900 feet
300 meters

# TIMELINE

**Jan. 12, 1977**
Adolf Tolkachev approaches CIA officer at gas station

**Feb.–May, 1977**
Tolkachev makes three more attempts

**March 1, 1978**
Tolkachev identifies himself in note to CIA

**March 5, 1978**
CIA officer phones Tolkachev from Bolshoi Theater

**Aug. 24, 1978**
CIA first dead drop

**Jan. 1, 1979**
Tolkachev meets CIA first time

**Feb. 17, 1979**
CIA emplaces dead drop including camera

**April 4, 1979**
Tolkachev gives CIA film, long letter

**June 6, 1979**
Film, notes passed to CIA at meeting

**Oct. 15, 1979**
Tolkachev meets CIA, wants suicide pill

**Dec. 27, 1979**
Tolkachev gives CIA electronics, gets 150,000 rubles

**Feb. 11, 1980**
Tolkachev meets CIA, suicide pill refused

**June 17, 1980**
Tolkachev gives CIA 179 rolls of film

**July, 1980**
Air Force says material worth $2 billion

**Oct. 14, 1980**
Tolkachev meets CIA, wants Western music for son

**Dec. 9, 1980**
CIA relents, gives Tolkachev suicide pill

**March 10, 1981**
CIA gives Tolkachev device "Discus"

**Nov. 10, 1981**
Tolkachev meets in car with CIA

**Dec. 8, 1981**
Tolkachev helps CIA fake building pass

**Feb. 15, 1982**
Tolkachev gives CIA circuit board

**May 24, 1982**
CIA gives Tolkachev razor blades, Walkman

**Dec. 7, 1982**
CIA officer uses "Jack in Box" to evade KGB, meet Tolkachev

**March 16, 1983**
Tolkachev asks for Solzhenitsyn, other books

**April 23, 1983**
Tolkachev rejects CIA exfil plan

**April 26–27, 1983**
Fearing discovery, Tolkachev destroys CIA materials

**Nov. 16, 1983**
Tolkachev tells CIA of security scare

**April 19, 1984**
Tolkachev meets CIA, says all quiet

**Oct. 11, 1984**
Tolkachev says documents photographed in toilet stall

**Jan. 18, 1985**
Tolkachev meets CIA, photos unreadable

**June 13, 1985**
CIA officer arrested on way to meet Tolkachev

# PROLOGUE

The spy had vanished.

He was the most successful and valued agent the United States had run inside the Soviet Union in two decades. His documents and drawings had unlocked the secrets of Soviet radar and revealed sensitive plans for research on weapons systems a decade into the future. He had taken frightful risks to smuggle circuit boards and blueprints out of his military laboratory and handed them over to the CIA. His espionage put the United States in position to dominate the skies in aerial combat and confirmed the vulnerability of Soviet air defenses—that American cruise missiles and bombers could fly under the radar.

In the late autumn and early winter of 1982, the CIA lost touch with him. Five scheduled meetings were missed. Months had gone by. In October, an attempt to rendezvous with him failed because of overwhelming KGB surveillance on the street. Even the "deep cover" officers of the CIA's Moscow station, invisible to the KGB, could not break through. On November 24, a deep cover officer, wearing a light disguise, managed to call the spy's apartment from a pay phone, but someone else answered. The officer hung up.

On the evening of December 7, the next scheduled meeting, the future of the operation was put in the hands of <u>Bill Plunkert</u>. After a stint as a navy aviator, Plunkert had joined the CIA and trained as a clandestine operations officer. He was in his mid-thirties, six feet two, and had arrived at the Moscow station in the summer for a tour devoted to handling the spy. He pored over the files, studied maps and photographs, read cables, and talked to the case officers. He felt he knew the man, even though he had never met him face-to-face. His mission was to give the slip to the KGB and make contact.

In the days before, using the local phone lines they knew were tapped by the KGB, a few American diplomats had organized a birthday party at an apartment for Tuesday evening. That night, around the dinner hour, four people walked to a car in the U.S. embassy parking lot, under constant watch by uniformed militiamen who stood outside and reported to the KGB. One of the four carried a large birthday cake. When the car left the embassy, a woman in the rear seat behind the driver held the cake on her lap.

Driving the car was the CIA's chief of station. Plunkert sat next to him in the front seat. Their wives were in back. All four of them had earlier rehearsed what they were about to do, using chairs set up in the Moscow station. Now the real show was about to begin.[1]

Espionage is the art of illusion. Tonight, Plunkert was the illusionist. Under his street clothes, he wore a second layer of clothes that would be typical for an old Russian man. The birthday cake was fake, with a top that looked like a cake but concealed a device underneath created by the CIA's technical operations wizards. Plunkert hoped the device would give him a means of escape from KGB surveillance.

The device was called the Jack-in-the-Box, known to all as simply the JIB. Over the years, the CIA had learned that KGB surveillance teams almost always followed a car from behind.

They rarely pulled alongside. It was possible for a car carrying a CIA officer to slip around a corner or two, momentarily out of view of the KGB. In that brief interval, the CIA case officer could jump out of the car and disappear. At the same time, the Jack-in-the-Box would spring erect, a pop-up that looked, in outline, like the head and torso of the case officer who had just jumped out.

To create it, the CIA had sent two young engineers from the Office of Technical Service to a windowless sex shop in a seedy area of Washington, D.C., to purchase three inflatable, life-sized dolls. But the dolls were hard to inflate or deflate quickly. They leaked air. The young engineers went back to the shop for more test mannequins, but problems persisted. Then the CIA realized that given the distance from which the KGB followed cars in Moscow, it wasn't necessary to have a three-dimensional dummy in the front seat, only a two-dimensional cutout. Illusion triumphed, and the Jack-in-the-Box was born.[2]

The device had not been used before in Moscow, but the CIA had grown desperate as weeks went by, with no contact with the agent. A skilled disguise expert from headquarters was sent to the Moscow station to help with the device and to bring Plunkert some "sterile" clothing that had never been worn before, to avoid any telltale scents that could be traced by KGB dogs or any tracking or listening devices that could be hidden inside.

As the car wound through the Moscow streets, Plunkert took off his American street clothes and put them into a small sack, typical of the kind Russians carried about. Wearing a full face mask and eyeglasses, he was now disguised as an old Russian man. At a distance, the KGB was trailing them. It was 7:00 p.m., well after nightfall.

The car turned a corner, briefly out of view of surveillance. The chief of station slowed the car with the hand brake to avoid illuminating the rear brake lights. Plunkert swung open the passenger door and jumped out. At the same moment, the chief of station's wife took the birthday cake from her lap and laid it on the front passenger seat where Plunkert had been sitting. Plunkert's wife reached forward and pulled a lever.

With a crisp whack, the top of the cake flung open, and a head and torso snapped into position. The car accelerated.

Outside, Plunkert took four steps on the sidewalk. On his fifth step, the KGB chase car rounded the corner.

The headlights caught an old Russian man on the sidewalk, then sped off in pursuit. The CIA car still appeared to have four persons inside. With a small handle, the station chief moved the head of the Jack-in-the-Box back and forth, as if it were chattering away.

The JIB had worked.

Plunkert felt a momentary rush of relief, but the next few hours would be the most demanding of all. The agent was extraordinarily valuable, not just for the Moscow station, but for the entire CIA and for the United States. Plunkert shouldered a heavy personal burden. One small error, and the operation would be forever lost. The spy would face execution for treason.

No one at the CIA knew why the spy had disappeared. Was he under suspicion? He was not a professional intelligence officer; he was an engineer. Had he made a careless mistake? Had he been arrested and interrogated and his treason revealed?

Alone, Plunkert walked the Moscow streets, a frigid tableau of slick ice and inky shadows. He thought it was just about perfect for espionage. He talked to himself a lot. A practicing Catholic, Plunkert prayed—little, short prayers. Every time he exhaled under the mask, his eyeglasses fogged up. He stopped after a while, removed the mask, and donned a lighter disguise. He took public trolleys and buses in a roundabout route to the rendezvous point. He watched for KGB surveillance but saw none.

He had to find the spy. He could not fail.

# 1

# OUT OF THE WILDERNESS

In the early years of the Cold War between the United States and the Soviet Union, the Central Intelligence Agency harbored an uncomfortable secret about itself. The CIA had never really gained an espionage foothold on the streets of Moscow. The agency didn't recruit in Moscow, because it was just too dangerous—"immensely dangerous," recalled one officer—for any Soviet citizen or official they might enlist. The recruitment process itself, from the first moment a possible spy was identified and approached, was filled with risk of discovery by the KGB, and if caught spying, an agent would face certain death. A few agents who volunteered or were recruited by the CIA outside the Soviet Union continued to report securely once they returned home. But for the most part, the CIA did not lure agents into spying in the heart of darkness.

This is the story of an espionage operation that turned the tide. At the center of it is an engineer in a top secret design laboratory, a specialist in airborne radar who worked deep inside the Soviet military establishment. Driven by anger and vengeance, he passed thousands of pages of secret documents to the United

States, even though he had never set foot in America and knew little about it. He met with CIA officers twenty-one times over six years on the streets of Moscow, a city swarming with KGB surveillance, and was never detected. The engineer was one of the CIA's most productive agents of the Cold War, providing the United States with intelligence no other spy had ever obtained.

The operation was a coming-of-age for the CIA, a moment when it accomplished what was long thought unattainable: personally meeting with a spy right under the nose of the KGB.

Then the operation was destroyed, not by the KGB, but by betrayal from within.

To understand the significance of the operation, one must look back at the CIA's long, difficult struggle to penetrate the Soviet Union.

The CIA was born out of the disaster at Pearl Harbor. Despite warning signals, Japan achieved complete and overwhelming surprise in the December 7, 1941, attack that took the lives of more than twenty-four hundred Americans, sunk or damaged twenty-one ships in the U.S. Pacific Fleet, and thrust the United States into war. Intelligence was splintered among different agencies, and no one pulled all the pieces together; a congressional investigation concluded the fragmented process "was seriously at fault." The creation of the CIA in 1947 reflected more than anything else the determination of Congress and President Truman that Pearl Harbor should never happen again. Truman wanted the CIA to provide high-quality, objective analysis.[1] It was to be the first centralized, civilian intelligence agency in American history.[2]

But the early plans for the CIA soon changed, largely because of the growing Soviet threat, including the blockade of Berlin,

Stalin's tightening grip on Eastern Europe, and Soviet acquisition of the atomic bomb. The CIA rapidly expanded far beyond just intelligence analysis into espionage and covert action. Pursuing a policy of containment, first outlined in George Kennan's long telegram of 1946 from Moscow and later significantly expanded, the United States attempted to counter Soviet efforts to penetrate and subvert governments all over the world. The Cold War began as a rivalry over war-ravaged Europe but spread far and wide, a contest of ideology, politics, culture, economics, geography, and military might. The CIA was on the front lines. The battle against communism never escalated into direct combat between the superpowers; it was fought in the shadows between war and peace. It played out in what Secretary of State Dean Rusk once called the "back alleys of the world."[3]

There was one back alley that was too dangerous to tread—the Soviet Union itself. Stalin was convinced the World War II victory over the Nazis demonstrated the unshakability of the Soviet state. After the war, he resolutely and consciously deepened the brutal, closed system he had perfected in the 1930s, creating perpetual tension in society, constant struggle against "enemies of the people," "spies," "doubters," "cosmopolitans," and "degenerates." It was prohibited to receive a book from abroad or listen to a foreign radio broadcast. Travel overseas was nearly impossible for most people, and unauthorized contacts with foreigners were severely punished. Phones were tapped, mail opened, and informers encouraged. The secret police were in every factory and office. It was dangerous for anyone to speak frankly, even in intimate circles.[4]

This was a forbidding environment for spying. In the early years of the Cold War, the CIA did not set up a station in Moscow and had no case officers on the streets in the capital of the world's largest and most secretive party-state. It could not identify and recruit Soviet agents, as it did elsewhere. The Soviet secret police, which after 1954 was named the KGB, or *Komitet Gosudarstvennoi Bezopasnosti*, was seasoned, proficient, omnipotent, and ruthless. By the 1950s, the KGB had been hardened by three decades of experience in carrying out the Stalin purges, in eliminating threats to Soviet rule during and after the war, and in stealing America's atom bomb secrets. It was not even possible for a foreigner to strike up a conversation in Moscow without arousing suspicion.

The CIA was still getting its feet wet, a young organization, optimistic, naive, and determined to get things done—a reflection of America's character.[5] In 1954, the pioneering aviator General James Doolittle warned that the United States needed to be more hard-nosed and cold-blooded. "We must develop effective espionage and counter-espionage services and must learn to subvert, sabotage and destroy our enemies by more clever, more sophisticated and more effective methods than those used against us," he said in a top secret report to President Eisenhower.[6]

The CIA faced intense and constant pressure for intelligence on the Soviet Union and its satellites. In Washington, policy makers were on edge over possible war in Europe—and anxious for early warning. Much information was available from open sources, but that wasn't the same as genuine, penetrating intelligence. "The pressure for results ranged from repeated instructions to do 'something' to exasperated demands to try 'anything,'" recalled Richard Helms, who was responsible for clandestine operations in the 1950s.[7]

Outside the Soviet Union, the CIA diligently collected intelligence from refugees, defectors, and émigrés. Soviet diplomats, soldiers, and intelligence officers were approached around the world. From refugee camps in Europe, the CIA's covert action unit recruited a secret army. Some five thousand volunteers were trained as a "post-nuclear guerilla force" to invade the Soviet Union after an atomic attack. Separately, the United States dropped lone parachutists into the Soviet bloc to spy or link up with resistance groups. Most of them were caught and killed. The chief of the covert action unit, Frank G. Wisner, dreamed of penetrating the Eastern bloc and breaking it to pieces. Wisner hoped that through psychological warfare and underground aid—arms caches, radios, propaganda—the peoples of Eastern Europe might be persuaded to throw off their communist oppressors. But almost all of these attempts to get behind enemy lines with covert action were a flop. The intelligence produced was scanty, and the Soviet Union was unshaken.[8]

The CIA's sources were still on the outside looking in. "The only way to fulfill our mission was to develop inside sources—spies who could sit beside the policymakers, listen to their debates, and read their mail," Helms recalled. But the possibility of recruiting and running agents in Moscow who could warn of decisions made by the Soviet leadership "was as improbable as placing resident spies on the planet Mars," Helms said.[9] A comprehensive assessment of the CIA's intelligence on the Soviet bloc, completed in 1953, was grim. "We have no reliable inside intelligence on thinking in the Kremlin," it acknowledged. About the military, it added, "Reliable intelligence of the enemy's long-range plans and intentions is practically non-existent." The assessment cautioned, "In the event of a surprise attack, we could not hope to obtain any detailed information of the Soviet military intentions."[10] In the early years of the agency, the CIA found it "impossibly difficult to penetrate Stalin's paranoid police state with agents."[11]

"In those days," said Helms, "our information about the Soviet Union was very sparse indeed."[12]

For all the difficulties, the CIA scored two breakthroughs in the 1950s and early 1960s. Pyotr Popov and Oleg Penkovsky, both officers of Soviet military intelligence, began to spy for the

United States. They were volunteers, not recruited, who came
forward separately, spilling secrets to the CIA largely outside
Moscow, each demonstrating the immense advantages of a clandestine agent.

On New Year's Day 1953 in Vienna, a short and stocky Russian handed an envelope to a U.S. diplomat who was getting into
his car in the international zone. At the time, Vienna was under
occupation of the American, British, French, and Soviet forces,
a city tense with suspicion. The envelope carried a letter, dated
December 28, 1952, written in Russian, which said, "I am a Soviet
officer. I wish to meet with an American officer with the object
of offering certain services." The letter specified a place and time
to meet. Such offers were common in Vienna in those years; a
horde of tricksters tried to make money from fabricated intelligence reports. The CIA had trouble sifting them all, but this
time the letter seemed real. On the following Saturday evening,
the Russian was waiting where he promised to be—standing in
the shadows of a doorway, alone, in a hat and bulky overcoat. He
was Pyotr Popov, a twenty-nine-year-old major in Soviet military intelligence, the *Glavnoye Razvedyvatelnoye Upravleniye*, or
GRU, a smaller cousin of the KGB. Popov became the CIA's first
and, at the time, most valuable clandestine military source on the
inner workings of the Soviet army and security services. He met
sixty-six times with the CIA in Vienna between January 1953
and August 1955. His CIA case officer, George Kisevalter, was
a rumpled bear of a man, born in Russia to a prominent family in St. Petersburg, who had immigrated to the United States
as a young boy. Over time, Popov revealed to Kisevalter that he
was the son of peasants, grew up on the dirt floor of a hut, and
had not owned a proper pair of leather shoes until he was thirteen years old. He seethed with hatred at what Stalin had done
to destroy the Russian peasantry through forced collectivization
and famine. His spying was driven by a desire to avenge the

injustice inflicted on his parents and his small village near the Volga River. In the CIA safe house in Vienna, Kisevalter kept some magazines spread out, such as *Life* and *Look,* but Popov was fascinated by only one, *American Farm Journal.*[13]

The CIA helped Popov forge a key that allowed him to open classified drawers at the GRU *rezidentura,* or station, in Vienna. Popov fingered the identity of all the Soviet intelligence officers in Vienna, delivered information on a broad array of Warsaw Pact units, and handed Kisevalter gems such as a 1954 Soviet military field service manual for the use of atomic weapons.[14] When Popov was reassigned to Moscow in 1955, CIA headquarters sent an officer to the city, undercover, to scout for dead drops, or concealed locations, where Popov could leave messages. But the CIA man performed poorly, was snared in a KGB "honeypot" trap, and was later fired.[15] The CIA's first attempt to establish an outpost in Moscow had ended badly.

In 1956, Popov was transferred to East Germany and resumed spying for the CIA, traveling to West Berlin for meetings with Kisevalter at a safe house. He again proved a remarkably productive agent. His intelligence take included the text of a revealing speech in March 1957 by the Soviet defense minister, Marshal Georgy Zhukov, to troops in Germany about the use of nuclear weapons in war. In 1958, Popov was abruptly recalled to Moscow and interrogated, and his treachery was discovered. However, the KGB kept this under wraps and used Popov to occasionally pass misleading information to the CIA. On September 18, 1959, Popov slipped the CIA a message written in pencil on eight strips of paper and rolled into a cylinder about the size of a cigarette. The message told the CIA what had happened, a courageous last act of defiance by a doomed spy. The message was rushed back to headquarters, where Kisevalter read the penciled Cyrillic on the tiny strips of paper and broke down in sobs. Popov was tried in January 1960 and executed in June by firing squad.

The second breakthrough began to unfold just two months later in Moscow, on August 12, at about 11:00 p.m.

Two American student tourists, Eldon Cox and Henry Cobb, strolled across Red Square cobblestones, still wet from a light rain, heading back to their hotel after seeing a performance of the Bolshoi Ballet, when a man came up behind them and pulled at Cobb's sleeve, holding a cigarette and asking for a light. The man was of medium build, wearing a suit and tie, with reddish hair showing gray at the temples. He asked if they were Americans, and when they said yes, he began to speak rapidly while looking around to make sure they were not being observed. He pressed an envelope into Cox's hands and pleaded with him to take it immediately to the American embassy. Cox, who spoke Russian, took it to the embassy that night. Inside was a letter. "At the present time," said the writer, "I have at my disposal very important materials on many subjects of exceptionally great interest and importance to your government." The writer did not identify himself, but enclosed a hint that he had once been stationed in Ankara, Turkey, for Soviet military intelligence. He gave precise instructions for how to contact him—with messages in a matchbox concealed behind a radiator in the entrance hall of a Moscow building. He included a diagram for the dead drop.[16]

The writer of the letter was Oleg Penkovsky, a colonel in the GRU, an imaginative, energetic, and self-confident officer who served with distinction in the artillery during World War II. He was now working at the State Committee for Coordination of Scientific Research Work, a government office that oversaw scientific and technical exchanges with the United States, Great Britain, and Canada and provided cover for Soviet industrial espionage and clandestine acquisition of technology in the West.

The letter was delivered to the CIA, which was suspicious at first. They knew the Soviets had been deeply embarrassed by the Popov case. Was the letter a trap? A decision was made at headquarters to contact the writer, but at the time the CIA did not have a streetwise operative in Moscow. The U.S. ambassador in Moscow, Llewellyn Thompson, was adamantly opposed to the assignment of any CIA personnel to the embassy. Eventually, in the autumn of 1960, an arrangement was worked out to send a young officer from the Soviet division at headquarters to Moscow, expressly to make contact with Penkovsky. The officer did not speak Russian very well. The CIA gave him a code name: COMPASS. He screwed up, drank heavily, and failed to make contact.[17]

Penkovsky was frustrated. He had written his first letter to the Americans in July 1960, and he spent weeks looking for someone to deliver it. "I stalked the American Embassy like a wolf, looking for a reliable foreigner, a patriot," he recalled.[18] After he handed the letter to Cox on Red Square in August, Penkovsky waited and waited for the CIA to respond. He heard nothing. He tried to pass his information through a British businessman, then a Canadian, without success. He was growing desperate.

Finally, on April 11, 1961, Penkovsky slipped a letter to a British businessman that was addressed to the leaders of the United States and the United Kingdom. The businessman, Greville Wynne, shared the letter with the British Secret Intelligence Service, or MI6, which provided the letter to the CIA. The American and British services decided to work together to run Penkovsky as a spy.

Nine days later, Penkovsky came to London as head of a six-man Soviet trade delegation shopping for Western technology—steel, radar, communications, and concrete-processing techniques. It was a tense time; the CIA's Bay of Pigs invasion in Cuba had just failed. On arrival, Wynne met Penkovsky at the airport, and Penkovsky immediately handed an envelope to him. It included descriptions and diagrams of the latest Soviet missiles and launchers. Later that evening, Penkovsky left his room at the sprawling

Mount Royal Hotel on Oxford Street in London and walked to room 360. He knocked on the door, wearing a business suit, white shirt, and tie. When he entered the room, he was greeted by two British and two American intelligence officers. "You know now that you are in good hands," a rumpled, heavyset American reassured Penkovsky. He was Kisevalter. Penkovsky replied, "I have thought about this for a long time."

In the conversations that followed, Penkovsky told the American and British officers that his career as a Soviet intelligence officer had gone off the rails, and he was bitter. His father died when he was only four months old, and his mother had told him it was from typhus. But papers had been found about a year earlier showing that his father had served as a first lieutenant in the White Army, fighting against the Bolsheviks, which threw Penkovsky's loyalty into doubt. He was accused of covering it up. An assignment to India fell through, and he was shunted aside. He loathed the KGB.

On two extended visits to London, first in April and May and then in July and August, and one trip to Paris in September and October 1961, Penkovsky spoke to the British and American intelligence officers for 140 hours in smoke-filled hotel rooms, which produced twelve hundred pages of transcripts. Penkovsky also delivered 111 rolls of exposed film. In Moscow, he used a tiny Minox commercial camera to photograph more than five thousand pages of secret documents, almost all of them about the Soviet military and taken from the GRU and military libraries. Penkovsky was filled with zeal and took risks, once photographing a top secret report right off the desk of a colonel who had momentarily stepped out of his Moscow office.

Not all the conversations with the American and British officers went smoothly. In one of the early sessions at the Mount Royal Hotel, Penkovsky presented a bizarre plan to hold Moscow and the entire Soviet leadership hostage. He wanted to deploy twenty-nine small nuclear weapons in random fashion throughout Moscow in suitcases or garbage cans. The United States was to provide the weapons, instruct him on welding them into the bottom of garbage cans, and provide him with a detonator. With difficulty, he was talked out of the fantasy.[19]

But Penkovsky took his espionage mission seriously and demonstrated to the CIA how a single clandestine agent could produce volumes of material. When asked if he could obtain copies of the Soviet General Staff journal *Military Thought* and urged to look for the secret version, Penkovsky asked if the CIA also wanted the top secret version. The CIA didn't know there was one. Penkovsky provided almost every copy of the journal, in which Soviet generals debated concepts of war in the nuclear age.[20] His reports provided critical insights into Soviet intentions during the 1961 Berlin blockade, informed the West for the first time about the existence of the all-important Military Industrial Commission, which made decisions about weapons systems, and provided key technical details of the R-12 medium-range missiles that the Soviet Union sent to Cuba in the fall of 1962, especially the range of the missiles and time required to make them operational. Penkovsky's intelligence, code-named IRONBARK and CHICKADEE, was a key ingredient in decision making as President Kennedy stood up to Khrushchev during the Cuban missile crisis.[21] Penkovsky's information on the Soviet medium-range missiles was included in the President's Daily Brief in the third week of October 1962. Additionally, Penkovsky's information, along with the first reports from the new Corona spy satellite, debunked the myth that the Soviet Union was churning out intercontinental ballistic missiles like sausages, as Khrushchev had boasted. The "missile gap" didn't exist.

Penkovsky was, at the time, the most productive agent ever run by the United States in the Soviet Union.[22] The CIA and MI6 agreed to pay him $1,000 a month for intelligence worth millions.[23] After the meetings in the hotel rooms in London and Paris, the operation moved into a second phase in which Penkovsky was run in Moscow. The British businessman Wynne, who visited the Soviet Union periodically, met with Penkovsky, collecting intelligence and passing it to MI6. But Penkovsky was eager to deal directly with the American and British intelligence services in Moscow.

The CIA was not ready. Ever since the disaster of COMPASS, a replacement officer had been in training, but the replacement pulled out at the last minute, leaving the CIA empty-handed at a critical juncture. "We had an increasingly desperate and very valuable agent out there and no one in a position to contact him," recalled a CIA officer who was involved at the time.[24] The agency also still lacked suitable spy gear for the operation.[25]

While the Americans had played the preeminent role in the meetings in London and Paris hotel rooms, the British came to dominate the operation in Moscow. According to the CIA officer, "MI6 was able to do what we could not—devise and carry out a cover operational plan for the case." The British chose Janet Chisholm, wife of the MI6 station chief, to be Penkovsky's case officer. She met with Penkovsky a dozen or so times, at British embassy receptions and a cocktail party, at the nearly empty delicatessen shop of the Praga restaurant, at a secondhand shop, in a park, and in apartment building foyers, often under difficult conditions, with her three children in tow. Penkovsky passed film cassettes concealed in a box of chocolates for the children. He seemed frenetic and driven; the CIA worried that he was meeting too often with Mrs. Chisholm. When the CIA finally deployed a trained officer to Moscow at the end of June 1962 to work on the Penkovsky case, the officer's work was short-lived. Penkovsky was last seen by the CIA at a U.S. embassy reception on September 5, 1962, and then disappeared.[26]

He fell under suspicion by the KGB, which had put Mrs.

Chisholm under surveillance. They had drilled a pinhole in the ceiling of his apartment study and put a camera there to monitor him. Another KGB camera in a nearby building photographed him in his apartment. A search discovered the Minox camera, as well as methods for encrypting messages, and a radio receiver he had been given for clandestine communications from the West. Penkovsky was arrested in September or October 1962. He was tried publicly and convicted of espionage, then executed on May 16, 1963.[27]

At almost the same time that Penkovsky was talking to the American and British officers in the hotel rooms, two more Soviet officers volunteered to become spies for the United States, both outside the Soviet Union. In 1961, Dmitri Polyakov, a Soviet military intelligence officer assigned to the United Nations, offered his cooperation in New York and became a source whom the FBI gave the code name TOPHAT. Then, in 1962, Alexei Kulak, a KGB scientific and technical officer, volunteered in New York to the FBI in exchange for cash. He became the FBI's source FEDORA. Both TOPHAT and FEDORA were important and valuable assets for the CIA and the FBI at different times in the 1960s and 1970s, but they were largely handled beyond the Soviet borders. In the back alleys of the world, it was possible for the CIA to recruit agents and spies, and to exploit volunteers, but not yet in the very center of the Soviet Union, on the streets of Moscow.

After the loss of Penkovsky, the CIA entered a long, unproductive period in Moscow. A major cause for this was the overwhelming influence of James Angleton, the counterintelligence chief at headquarters. He threw the CIA into a state of high paranoia and operational paralysis. A tall, thin, quirky man, gentle to friends and inscrutable to others, Angleton cut a distinctive figure in owlish eyeglasses, dark suits, and wide-brimmed hats. He lorded over his own autonomous office, keeping his files locked and separate from the rest of the CIA, sitting at a desk piled with dossiers and shrouded in blue haze from chain-smoking. He enjoyed two hobbies, growing orchids and twisting elaborate flies for trout fishing. Over twenty years as the CIA's chief of counterintelligence, from 1954 to 1974, Angleton created an extraordinary mystique about himself and his work. Secretive, suspicious, and tenacious, he became obsessed with the belief the KGB had successfully manipulated the CIA in a vast "master plan" of deception. He often spoke of a "wilderness of mirrors," a phrase he borrowed from T. S. Eliot's 1920 poem "Gerontion," to describe the layers of duplicity and distrust that he believed were being used by the KGB to mislead the West. In 1966, Angleton wrote that an "integrated and purposeful Socialist Bloc" had sought to spread false stories of "splits, evolution, power struggles, economic disasters [and] good and bad Communism" to a confused West. Once this program of strategic deception had succeeded, the Soviet Union would pick off the Western democracies, one by one. Only the counterintelligence experts, he said, could stave off disaster. Angleton's suspicions permeated the culture and fabric of the CIA's Soviet operations division during the 1960s, with disastrous results. Two directors of the CIA, Allen Dulles and Helms, let Angleton have his way. Angleton felt that no one and no information from the Soviet KGB could be trusted. If no one could be trusted, there could be no spies.[28]

Counterintelligence is essential for any spy agency to prevent penetration from the same espionage methods it uses against others. In the Cold War, that required a combination of outward vigilance, watching every move of the KGB and deceiving it when possible, and inward skepticism, ensuring the CIA was not swallowing any deceptions or double agents. Ideally, counterintelligence went hand in hand with collecting intelligence, yet there has always been a natural tension between them. A case officer might have painstakingly recruited an agent to produce a fresh stream of "positive intelligence," the fruits of spying, only to find a counterintelligence officer raising questions about whether the source could be trusted. The CIA needed both, but Angleton's counterintelligence juggernaut became overpowering in the 1960s; everything was labeled suspicious or compromised.

Angleton's adult life was forged in the world of deception. After graduating from Yale, he became an elite counterintelligence officer based in London for the wartime Office of Strategic Services, the OSS. There he witnessed the astonishing British deception operation against the Nazis known as Double Cross. The British identified German agents and turned them against the enemy, effectively neutralizing Nazi intelligence collection. After running agents in Italy, Angleton returned to headquarters to become the CIA's chief counterintelligence officer. He believed a massive KGB "strategic deception" was being played out against the United States. His friendship with Kim Philby might have played a role. In the 1950s, the British MI6 officer had been a confidant of Angleton's. Then, in 1963, Philby was revealed to have been a KGB spy, and he fled to Moscow. The CIA had long suspected Philby, but the confirmation might have been taken by Angleton as more evidence the KGB was on the march—everywhere.

The strongest influence on Angleton, however, was Anatoly Golitsyn, a mid-level KGB officer who defected in 1961. Golitsyn spun a vast web of theories and conjecture that reinforced Angleton's suspicions of a KGB "master plan" to deceive the West. At the CIA, others called it Angleton's "monster plot." Golitsyn said that every defector and volunteer to come after him would be part of the master plan. Certainly, the KGB did attempt deceptions, but Angleton pumped fear to new heights. In 1964, he initiated a hunt for a mole inside the CIA to find what Golitsyn asserted were at least five and perhaps as many as thirty agency officers or contractors who were Soviet penetrations. None were ever found, but several careers were ruined. Among those who came under suspicion was the first Moscow station chief and the Soviet division chief; both were later cleared. When another KGB officer, Yuri Nosenko, defected in 1964, he was incarcerated and interrogated by the CIA for more than three years because of doubts raised about his bona fides by Angleton and Golitsyn.

Over time, Angleton's suspicions seeped into the CIA's Soviet division. The poisonous distrust and second-guessing became serious obstacles to espionage operations inside the Soviet Union. Neither potential agents nor positive intelligence could get past him. The Moscow station was small, only four or five case officers, and they were exceedingly cautious, spending a great deal of time preparing dead drop sites—just in case there would be a spy. One case officer spent two years in the Moscow station without ever meeting a real agent. Robert M. Gates, who entered the CIA as a Soviet specialist in 1968 and later rose to become CIA director, recalled that "thanks to the excessive zeal of Angleton and his counterintelligence staff, during this period we had very few Soviet agents inside the USSR worthy of the name."[29]

A younger generation of CIA case officers—who joined the agency in the 1950s and chafed under the restrictions created by Angleton—wanted to lead the agency out of lethargy and timidity. Burton Gerber was among them. A lanky, curious boy, he grew up in the prosperous small town of Upper Arlington, Ohio, during World War II. Each morning, he delivered the *Ohio State*

*Journal*, a morning paper in Columbus, on his bicycle. While his mother made breakfast at 5:15 a.m., he folded each of the hundred papers and tucked them in a sack for his route. He often read the front-page stories from the war. He was thirteen years old in 1946, infused with a spirit of patriotism, and he often wondered what life was like in those distant lands he read about on the front page. He was determined to see for himself. He went to Michigan State University in East Lansing on a scholarship and earned a degree in international relations. He considered joining the foreign service, but in the late spring of 1955, the final quarter of his senior year, he agreed to an interview with a CIA campus recruiter. The CIA in those days was not discussed, nor was much known about it. The recruiter could not tell Gerber anything about the job, but would he be interested? Gerber said yes, took the application back to his fraternity house, filled it out, and mailed it in. Before year's end, Gerber had joined the CIA at twenty-two years old. After a brief, temporary stint in the army, he was trained by the CIA for espionage work and then sent to Frankfurt and Berlin.[30]

Berlin was a cauldron of espionage on the front lines of the Cold War. The Berlin Operations Base, known as BOB, sat in the middle of the largest concentration of Soviet troops anywhere in the world. The CIA sought to recruit Soviets as agents or defectors, but it was hard, painstaking work. Meanwhile, one of the biggest operations of the base was technical: a clandestine 1,476-foot-long underground tunnel into the Soviet sector in East Berlin used to place wiretaps on Soviet and East German military communications cables. A huge volume of calls and Teletype messages was intercepted; 443,000 conversations, 368,000 of them Soviet, were transcribed by the United States and Britain. The wiretaps worked from May 1955 until uncovered in April 1956.[31]

Gerber had been taught the traditional methods of handling human espionage agents—finding and filling dead drops, handling letters with secret writing, sending and receiving signals, and making surveillance detection runs. In Berlin during the 1950s, the common method for espionage was to coax sources from the East to come to a safe house in West Berlin for debriefing, as Kisevalter had done with Popov. It depended on the source's having freedom to move from East to West, which was possible until the Berlin Wall went up in 1961. A whole new set of obstacles then confronted the intelligence officers: how to run agents at a distance. The CIA still had little experience in the closed societies of the Soviet bloc. The agency's thinking at headquarters was dominated by veterans of the Office of Strategic Services, the World War II intelligence agency, who had carried out daring paramilitary exploits during the war but believed that impersonal methods, such as dead drops, were safest.

A dead drop is a method of exchanging messages and intelligence in a secret location, known to the agent and the handler, who leave materials and pick them up from the concealed spot but never see each other. To the new generation of officers who joined the CIA after the war, the dead drop seemed to be the epitome of caution. They were restless and impatient and began to innovate and experiment with new methods. The Berlin base became a laboratory for running spies on the other side of the Iron Curtain. Instead of just inviting agents to a safe house, the officers created more imaginative techniques for espionage to penetrate forbidden zones.

Fortuitously, Angleton's suspicions did not extend to Eastern Europe. He didn't seem to care or pay much attention, although the Soviet satellite states were setting up secret police organizations modeled on the KGB and its predecessors.[32] The back alleys of Berlin, Warsaw, Prague, Budapest, Sofia, and other cities of Eastern Europe became a proving ground for younger CIA case officers. They invented new ways to conduct espionage in "denied areas," as the CIA called them. The methods were important, but even more significant was the mind-set. Gerber had been inspired to do the most important job of the day, which was to fight communism and the Soviet Union. He and his classmates, on their first tours abroad, did not want to sit in their chairs. They were not intimidated by the Iron Curtain. They had chosen espionage as a career and disdained passivity. Gerber always disliked the term "denied areas." Denied to whom? Not to him, nor to his classmates.

Not to Haviland Smith, either. When he arrived at the Berlin base in 1960, he was full of ideas and became a pioneer in the new thinking that he had first developed in Prague.

A graduate of Dartmouth, Smith served in the Army Security Agency as a Morse code and Russian-language intercept officer from 1951 to 1954 and was later in the graduate program in Russian studies at the University of London, where he did a few odd jobs for the CIA. Smith had a very high language aptitude and spoke French, Russian, and German. He joined the CIA in 1956 and was selected for a tour in Czechoslovakia. While he was deep in language training, headquarters suddenly asked him to take over as Prague station chief in 1958. His predecessor wasn't particularly active and left abruptly. When Smith arrived in March, he had functioning Czech-language ability but little preparation for the kinds of clandestine operations he wanted to undertake. He hadn't been trained in the tradecraft of espionage—how to mail secret letters, select and load dead drops, detect and deal with surveillance, or conduct an agent meeting—in a hostile, surveillance-heavy environment. Smith would have to figure it out for himself.[33]

Smith discovered there were dozens of sophisticated radios in the Prague station, and his army intercept experience proved useful. He found the radio frequency used by the Czech security service in their surveillance vehicles monitoring the U.S. embassy and was able to break their voice codes. If Smith had to put down a dead drop or mail a letter, he turned on the radio first, then ran a tape recorder to capture the broadcasts. He put down the drop or message, then went back and checked the tape. If he was under surveillance while filling the drop, he aborted the operation. If there was no evidence of surveillance, he signaled the agent to pick it up. "Prague was a perfect place for the kinds of operations we were contemplating," he recalled. "A beautiful old baroque city, it was untouched by war. It was full of narrow, old streets, arcades, and alleys." Through trial and error, Smith found that most of the time he was under surveillance. Once, he thought he was free but discovered he was being watched by twenty-seven different vehicles. He was shocked and became convinced that whatever espionage he could carry out would have to be done under surveillance. He just could never assume he was free. This was an important early lesson for working in "denied areas."

Smith began to experiment. He sought to establish regular, observable patterns of behavior that would lull the surveillance teams into complacency. He became a slow, careful driver with the purpose of convincing the Czech surveillance that whenever he went out, on foot or in a car, they already knew what he was up to and left him alone. He went to get a haircut at 10:00 a.m. every other Tuesday, then returned directly to the office, driving slowly. After six months, he realized that no surveillance was on him for the haircut ride, so long as he wasn't away more than forty-five minutes. Smith always drove his babysitter home each evening, a forty-minute ride. After a while, the surveillance tired of that, too. Smith had created two opportunities for operational activity—a gap—and he might be able to squeeze in the time for a mailing, a dead drop, or something else. In those rigid, careful routines, Smith discovered a behavior of the secret police that had not been realized before. They could be lazy, orthodox, and conventional. The illusionist might deceive them.

Even with this knowledge, however, Smith was restless. The

patterns might create a gap, but they were still too rigid. He wanted more flexibility, to be able to carry out a headquarters instruction on the shortest possible notice even when under surveillance. This led him to push the concept of the gap even harder. He found that it was possible, walking or driving the back alleys, to create momentary visual blackouts. He could disappear for a very brief period in a way that would seem normal to the watchers and, if done properly, would allow him enough time to make a brush contact, mail a letter, or put down a dead drop while completely out of sight. The idea was simple: he turned corners. When he was being followed on foot, two brisk right turns around a block would string out the surveillance to the point where he would be completely out of sight from the moment he turned the second corner until the lead watcher caught up and came around the same corner—maybe only fifteen to thirty seconds. That was enough.

Smith also perfected the concept of a brush pass, in which the agent appears at just the right moment in the gap. The agent brushes by the case officer, delivering or accepting a package, then escapes. The secret police would never see the agent on the other end of the brush pass if it worked right; the agent would be gone in a flash. Much depended on finding the right location, with jutting corners to block the line of sight of surveillance and a fast escape path for the agent.

Smith was sent to Berlin next. It was a different kind of city, more spread out, but he still operated in the gap and under surveillance. His ideas suggested a real change was possible from the old days: the ability to run espionage operations in the pressure-cooker environment of closed zones. At the suggestion of headquarters, Smith began to train others in Berlin on his new methods, building in everything he'd learned about working "in the gap." For years that followed, moving "through the gap" became a watchword and a trusted method for CIA case officers.

In 1963, Smith returned to the United States and set up a course for officers heading to Eastern Europe and the Soviet Union that incorporated the new tradecraft. But he found there was still caution and timidity in the CIA leadership. Smith was asked to train a Czech intelligence source in the United States. The agent absolutely refused to use dead drops because the incriminating secret messages and film would be out of his hands—and could potentially be discovered by the Czech secret police. When Smith showed him the brush pass method, the agent readily agreed to use it, because he would put his material directly into the hands of the CIA. At headquarters, a request was made to Helms for permission to use the technique operationally in Prague. Without even asking questions about it, Helms refused, saying he had "sores all over his ass" from the Penkovsky case and was not getting involved in "that sort of thing" again, Smith recalled. The Czech agent went to Prague without permission to use the brush pass, and a year went by. Smith hammered away at headquarters, seeking approval. A steady stream of valuable agents was beginning to show up in Eastern Europe, and Smith felt the dead drop routines were completely inadequate.

In 1965, Helms agreed to an experiment. He sent his deputy, Thomas Karamessines, to a demonstration of the brush pass. Smith set it up in the lobby of the grand old Mayflower Hotel in downtown Washington. In the demonstration, the brush pass was carried out so deftly that Karamessines missed it. The key had been sleight of hand: a case officer dramatically shook out a raincoat with his left hand just as he handed off a package to Smith with his right. Karamessines saw the raincoat but not the package. Smith had learned this technique from a professional magician. The next day, Helms approved the use of the brush pass in Prague. The Czech agent subsequently passed to the CIA hundreds of rolls of film. The brush pass, with modifications, was later expanded into all of Eastern Europe and the Soviet Union.

The younger generation adapted as they went along. David Forden, a case officer who had been tutored by Smith, went to Warsaw and invented a technique using a slowly moving car to slip around corners, in the gap, and exchange packages with agents. It was a sort of brush pass using the car. "I submitted a proposal for what I thought was a valuable tradecraft tool to meet people in areas which were heavy in surveillance against American spies," Forden recalled. "I got a response from the front office of the division, 'Risky. Dangerous. Won't work.' To which I replied, 'Look, all this is risky and dangerous. But it will work.'" Forden later became the case officer for one of the CIA's most productive and significant agents, Ryszard Kuklinski, a Polish army colonel who provided critical intelligence on the Warsaw Pact.[34]

Gerber experimented with an even more radical idea than the brush pass—meeting with an agent personally. The brush pass was a very swift transaction while under surveillance. Gerber's ambition was to bring off a real meeting with the agent, away from surveillance. Headquarters was aghast, but Gerber thought he could make it work during his next assignment, to Sofia, Bulgaria. The personal meetings wouldn't be long, and Gerber thought they could be managed with care. A written message passed in a dead drop was limited to what was on the page, but in person Gerber could look in the eyes of the agent, ask a question, absorb the body language and the mood. He also concluded that being a case officer and a station chief meant taking calculated risks. Espionage required going out on a limb. Gerber's enthusiasm for meeting agents in person never dimmed.

In the first years of the Cold War, the dearth of human source intelligence from inside the Soviet Union forced the United States to turn instead to technology, an American strength. First with the U-2 spy plane in the 1950s, and then with satellites known as Corona, Gambit, and Hexagon, launched in the 1960s and 1970s, overhead photography and signals intelligence opened vast new spying vistas. The most advanced satellite system, Hexagon, was capable of photographing 80 to 90 percent of the built-up areas of the Soviet Union twice a year, and a single Hexagon swath covered an area 345 by 8,055 miles. For American decision makers, the satellites were a godsend for tracking strategic weapons and a bulwark against surprise.[35]

But how to steal secrets inside the vaults and the minds of people—the secrets that a satellite could not see? The CIA groped for effective techniques to spot, recruit, and run agents against the Soviet target. At one point, an internal CIA study proposed looking for outliers, misfits, and the psychologically troubled among Soviet diplomats.[36] Another theory was that a new generation of spoiled younger people, the Soviet "golden youth," would be more likely to become agents or defect.[37] A third idea offered by a CIA psychologist was to pursue those who had marriage difficulties or who felt frustrated in their work, personally insulted or blocked in some way.[38]

Gerber, back at headquarters by 1971, never believed in a single formula. Rather, he emphasized pragmatism: find out who has the secrets and build bridges to them. "What works, works," he often said. But Gerber also knew that the CIA, burdened by the legacy of suspicion, was not particularly welcoming to volunteers in Moscow. Those Russians who dared show up at the embassy would usually be asked a few questions and shown the door. Rarely was there an effort to find out if they were genuine. Angleton's influence cast a long shadow.

With a small staff and acting entirely on his own hunch, Gerber began a systematic study, pulling the files of every person who had volunteered information in Moscow going back a decade and a half, and in Eastern Europe a decade. He yanked the dossiers and cable traffic, scrutinizing every scrap. Taken together, the files seemed to shout that Angleton was wrong to have such blanket suspicions. It appeared to Gerber that the CIA had been routinely turning away genuine volunteers, throwing away what might be valuable intelligence. He concluded that it would be far more productive to check out those who offered their services, rather than assume all were part of some KGB deception plot. He felt the CIA ought to be smart enough in Moscow to sift the genuine sources from the fake ones. Also, he noticed a pattern. Those volunteers whom the KGB used as dangles—a trap— were usually already known to the intended recipients, perhaps someone they might have met once or twice before. That's how the KGB worked; to snare someone, they set out bait that would be recognized, to sugarcoat the trap. In the files, Gerber found there were also patterns for the kinds of people the KGB would *not* use in a trap. They had never offered up a serving KGB staff officer; they just didn't trust their own to go off in a relationship with an American case officer. They also didn't use someone who was a stranger to the recipient. Gerber's conclusion: don't be afraid to accept something from a person you've never seen before; it is probably not dangerous. It might be useless but probably not dangerous. However, Gerber thought, if a Soviet acquaintance seems eager to thrust an envelope into your hands, be careful; it may well be a deception.[39]

These conclusions came to be known at the CIA as the Gerber rules and marked a turning point. They upended the Angleton thinking. *Not every volunteer was a dangle.* Gerber wrote a report on his conclusions in May 1971. Helms had finally had enough of Angleton's influence and appointed a new Soviet division chief to clean house. The new chief was David Blee, a veteran of the OSS who had been dropped behind enemy lines in World War II and later joined the CIA at its founding in 1947. Blee, who came across as mild and austere, an old-school intelligence officer who was station chief in South Africa, Pakistan, and India, and later chief of the Near East division, had never had any experience with the Soviet Union, and that is just what Helms needed, someone who was not part of the Angleton fog of suspicion. Blee put out the word: the time had come to get serious about opening the mail inside the Soviet Union. Angleton was forced to retire in December 1974, but even before he left headquarters, a new era was dawning. The more aggressive approach began to pay off.[40]

That January, the CIA had recruited a Soviet diplomat then serving in Bogotá, Colombia. Alexander Ogorodnik was the son of a high-ranking Soviet naval officer, thirty-eight years old, tall, and attractive, with an athletic build and dark hair. Ogorodnik was serving as an economics officer in Bogotá. He had plenty of problems. He was under pressure by the KGB to be an informer, a role he did not want but was afraid to refuse. He was married but had a Colombian mistress. He had purchased a car, which was unusual for a Soviet diplomat, and he seemed to enjoy the high life around town. He also needed money.

A CIA officer made a pitch to Ogorodnik in a Turkish bath in a large downtown hotel in Bogotá. Ogorodnik didn't hesitate and said yes. He told the officer he loathed the KGB and wanted to change the Soviet system. But his motivation was also personal. He wanted to be paid handsomely. He agreed to let the CIA keep most of his salary in escrow, but he used some of it to purchase emerald jewelry for his mother and modest luxuries for himself, such as contact lenses, which were unobtainable at the time in the Soviet Union.[41]

With gusto, Ogorodnik plunged into spy training in Bogotá. Normally, according to a former high-ranking CIA official, such operational training would take months of study and years to perfect, but Ogorodnik mastered it all in a matter of weeks. He learned how to photograph documents, at first with a 35 mm camera and later with a new CIA miniature camera, known as the T-50. The tiny camera was concealed inside a large fountain pen. The film in the T-50 was not very light sensitive. The camera needed strong light on the documents and to be held very steady.

One day, Ogorodnik had a surprising announcement for his CIA handlers. The Soviet embassy had received a top secret policy paper on China that could be read only in a closed room inside the KGB offices. Twice, Ogorodnik tried to take the fountain pen into the room, but he could not escape the watchful gaze of the guard. Finally, he appeared at the hotel room door and declared to his CIA tutor, "I think I've got it." The CIA man rushed the camera to a waiting courier, who carried it by hand on a plane to headquarters at Langley, Virginia. The camera had captured all but two of the fifty pages.[42]

Ogorodnik was transferred back to Moscow in 1974, putting him in an even better position to become an agent for the United States. He told the CIA he had just one request: a suicide pill, in case he was caught. The CIA was reluctant, and Ogorodnik flew home to Moscow without the pill. But he did carry a book; concealed inside was a schedule and instructions for communications with the CIA.

The CIA was finding its way out of the wilderness of mirrors. Ogorodnik was the first agent of this new period, but he would not be the last.

# 2

# MOSCOW STATION

**M**arti Peterson led a stressful double life in Moscow. At the U.S. embassy, she worked in a busy staff job, five days a week, eight hours a day. The embassy employed dozens of Soviet workers, and Peterson was side by side with eight of them, all women, potential KGB informants. Peterson did her work well, showed up on time, and after hours went out with other single men and women from the embassy staff. Everything in her apartment—clothes, purses, shoes, shopping bags, letters from home, music, and books—was that of a young American embassy worker. But at midday, she would often slip away, saying she was going to lunch, and spend an hour in the CIA's Moscow station typing up a report or preparing an operation. At night and on weekends, she checked and photographed rendezvous sites, delivered and retrieved agent packages, handled electronic gear to communicate with spies, and kept a constant watch for any sign that the KGB might know what she was doing. Her life was an exhausting split screen: she maintained the routines of a normal embassy staffer by day while carrying a full load for the CIA the rest of the time. The two roles had to be separate, the first convincing, the second invisible.

Peterson was the first woman to serve as a case officer in the Moscow station. She had been handpicked by the station chief, Robert Fulton, who calculated that the KGB would overlook a woman, because they used only men in such roles. Fulton, then forty-nine years old, had devoted his career to the shadow war against communism. He served in the Korean War as a military intelligence officer and joined the CIA in 1955. His assignments later included espionage operations in Finland, Denmark, Vietnam, Thailand, and the Soviet Union. Spying was his life. He was a pillar of support for Peterson, waiting patiently in the station during the lunch hour for her to show up from her cover job, always attentive, and coaching her on her tradecraft. He had a sparkle in his eye and never took himself too seriously.

When she got to Moscow in 1975, Peterson was thirty years old and was just emerging from her own private hell of grief and uncertainty. In her twenties, she had accompanied her husband, John Peterson, to Laos, where he was running CIA paramilitary operations during the Vietnam War. On October 19, 1972, John was killed when his helicopter was shot down. The loss crushed her, and for a while she felt adrift, pained by the antiwar protests in the United States. Eventually, she decided to follow in John's footsteps and joined the CIA in 1973. She was the daughter of a Connecticut businessman with a liberal arts education, a product of the Cold War years, with strong memories of air raid drills in school. She was motivated more by a can-do spirit than by any ideology. When a friend suggested she go into clandestine operations, she seized the chance. Peterson was attractive and single, and Fulton had guessed correctly: on her arrival in Moscow, the KGB failed to detect she was an intelligence officer.[1]

The Moscow station was a cramped box of a room on the seventh floor of the embassy, the only place Peterson could be herself. Outside, she had to live her cover, and the rules were strict; she could not even share a cup of coffee in the cafeteria with the other CIA people, nor socialize with them, because there were

Soviet employees all around who might inform the KGB. Once safely inside the station, she could relax, unwind, and talk openly. She took the CIA's training courses before leaving the United States, practicing such things as how to put down a message for an agent, using a beanbag tossed from a moving car at the Hecht's department store parking garage in northern Virginia. Her beanbags hit the target, but real operations were far more difficult and stressful. Her first weeks in Moscow were spent learning the streets, driving her boxy Zhiguli car all over the city, often accompanied by a female friend.

A small CIA-built radio receiver allowed case officers to monitor KGB surveillance broadcasts while on the street. Peterson heard nothing. The men in the station envied her ability to move around unfettered. Peterson realized that some suspected she just didn't see the surveillance. She was determined to prove herself but at the same time suffered her own insecurities. Could it be that she didn't see the KGB was watching her from the window of an apartment building, or maybe it was the policeman up in the "bird's nest" on the boulevard intersection? It would have been much easier to just give in and say yes, that she was under surveillance, than to keep trying to prove there was none. But she saw none, and that's what she told them. Peterson often used John's Nikon SLR camera with a wide-angle lens to photograph sites for possible dead drops or clandestine meetings. No one on the street ever asked her what she was doing.[2]

When Peterson arrived at the Moscow station, the Ogorodnik operation was already in full swing. The spy had been given a code name, CKTRIGON. The CK was a digraph that indicated the Soviet division. When Ogorodnik left Bogotá and returned to Moscow, he drew an assignment in the Soviet Foreign Ministry. It wasn't at a high level, but it gave him direct access to secret cables arriving from and going out to Soviet embassies around the world. For the CIA, that was just perfect. After a delay,

Ogorodnik provided a steady stream of secret documents from the Foreign Ministry. He mastered the T-50, and his photographs were always in focus and proper alignment. He followed procedures agreed on in Bogotá and made signals to the CIA by parking his car between 7:00 and 7:15 p.m. in front of his mother's apartment building.

Once, when Ogorodnik signaled he was ready to deliver a package, Fulton went to collect it himself. Calmly, he put his dog, Goliath, in the car and set off for a forest on a wooded hill overlooking the city near Moscow State University. As Fulton drove there, he saw the KGB surveillance team lazily tailing him. He often walked his dog in the woods, so they did not suspect anything unusual. When Fulton opened his car door, the dog suddenly bounded into the forest of birches and pines, Fulton chasing him. The dog urinated on a tree, precisely where the package had been left. Fulton quickly snatched it up and stuffed it into his coat pocket before the KGB could see what was happening. He took it home but did not open it, suspecting the KGB might have a video camera in his apartment. The next morning, it was opened in the station. It contained ten rolls of film and a note.[3]

In 1976, fresh signs of difficulty cropped up. Ogorodnik inexplicably missed signals in February and March. Then, in April, Peterson was assigned to fill a dead drop, her first operational act in Moscow. The package was to be placed at the foot of a light pole on a cold and snowy evening. Carefully constructed by the CIA technical operations officers, the package looked like a crushed cigarette pack, but inside were a miniature camera, rolls of film, and a message. Peterson deftly laid down the package as she simultaneously pretended to pause to blow her nose and adjust her boot. Cold and anxious, she walked on for an hour, following the plan agreed to earlier in the Moscow station, then returned to the site to see if the package had been retrieved.

It was still there. Ogorodnik had not come. She picked it up and headed home, uncertain and worried.

When Peterson went on another foray on June 21, she was carrying the most important package the CIA had ever prepared for Ogorodnik: the suicide pill he requested. Concealed inside a large hollowed-out log created by the CIA was a handsome black fountain pen, with a cyanide fluid capsule inside, and another pen, identical on the outside, with the T-50 miniature camera inside. The cyanide cartridge in the pen was fragile and could easily be crushed by biting down on it. Peterson had cradled the hollowed-out log under her arm, set it down near a lamppost in a wooded area, and left the spot. Then Ogorodnik arrived, picked it up, and left behind what looked like a crumpled milk carton smeared with mustard plaster—to resemble vomit and deter anyone from picking it up. An hour and a half later, Peterson returned to the lamppost, scooped up the milk carton, slipped it quickly into a plastic bag in her purse, and walked to a nearby bus shelter. She was elated. The next step was to put a thin red line with lipstick on the bus shelter, to signal Ogorodnik that she had recovered his package. But in her excitement, she pressed too hard, the lipstick smashed in her fist, and left a red blob. She felt a rush of adrenaline from the successful exchange, but a hollow sensation, too. While walking, Peterson had a lot of time to think about Ogorodnik. She had never met him in person. He had to feel terribly alone. She wondered if he feared arrest. Would he find the courage to use the suicide pill? Would he mistakenly think the end was near and commit suicide prematurely?[4]

Later in 1976, in a moment of panic, when he thought he was under suspicion, Ogorodnik threw out his pen with the cyanide capsule. He asked for another. Peterson prepared to deliver it again at the same site, in a hollowed-out log. But this time, an hour before he was supposed to pick it up in the forest, Peterson saw Ogorodnik drive by in his car, just as she approached the park. She knew it was his car by the license plate, but what really unnerved her was the sight of a woman with a ponytail on the passenger side. Who was she? Peterson found a remote spot and hid in the woods, tense and motionless. At the proper hour, Ogorodnik came by, alone, carrying a briefcase, and picked up the log. "Ponytail" was nowhere to be seen.

When work got stressful in the long, dark winter months, Peterson sought release in cross-country skiing in the forests outside the city. The Moscow station had selected a dead drop site for Ogorodnik in the forest. He had signaled that he was ready to drop a package on Saturday, January 29, 1977, at 9:00 a.m. The site was near a boulder. Peterson had seen a sketch of the location.

On the morning of the drop, a blizzard covered Moscow. Peterson drove out to the country, seeing almost no one, parked her car, and slipped through the forest on her skis. The boulder, as big as a Volkswagen, was buried in snow. She had hoped to see Ogorodnik's footprints, but the snow was as pristine as white sugar icing. No trace of anyone. Peterson hunted for the package but couldn't find it. She was certain it must be there; perhaps Ogorodnik left it on the wrong side of the rock. She started digging—and found nothing. Growing frantic, she uncovered and sifted through every bit of snow around the boulder.

There was no package. Peterson went home, worried and exhausted.

Earlier in January, Fulton, the station chief, was filling up his car at a gas station used by diplomats and other foreigners in Moscow. It was a small pavilion, with pumps out front and a Russian sign, "No Smoking." Fulton was just getting back into his car at 6:00 p.m., and at least five vehicles were waiting behind him. People were standing around, talking.

As Fulton opened the car door, a man walked up to him. The man spoke in English. "Are you American? I would like to talk to you."

Fulton had not noticed the man until he actually spoke. Fulton said it would be difficult to talk right there and asked him what he wanted.

"Oh, it would be *difficult*?" the man said, his words stilted, as if he had expected that was what Fulton would say.

Switching to Russian, the man said, "Excuse me," leaned slightly into the car, and put a folded piece of paper on the seat. Fulton realized that the man had been holding the note in his palm and seemed to have given some thought to what he was doing.

The exchange lasted no more than fifteen seconds. The man walked away from the gas station and turned down a side street. Fulton headed back to the Moscow station and saw no one following him.[5]

Once safely in the station, Fulton examined the note. It was written in Russian on both sides of a single sheet of white paper, folded up within a second sheet that was blank. Fulton sent a cable to CIA headquarters, describing the man as in his late fifties or early sixties, about five feet six inches, 175 pounds, dressed "as an average Soviet, wearing dark overcoat and fur hat." Fulton reported that his car was the only one with license plates indicating he was an American in the gas station at that time. In the abbreviated style of such cables, Fulton added that the man was "obviously waiting for American to show up." The man "appeared in no way to be nervous and obviously had approach well thought out."

In the note, the man said he wanted to "discuss matters" on a "strictly confidential" basis with an "appropriate American official." The note said nothing about who he was or what he wanted to talk about, but he sketched out a detailed plan for the next step, suggesting either meeting at a Metro stop—the underground subway—or in a car.[6]

Fulton was apprehensive. It was not unusual for Soviet citizens to give notes to Americans, and many American diplomats who left car windows open a crack in the summer found messages slipped through them. But Fulton had learned to be careful. The KGB often attempted to lure CIA officers with dangles. Sometimes, the trap was so crude it could easily be dismissed, but others were harder to detect. The KGB had a long history of skillful deceptions. They would lure a CIA officer to a meeting, then the officer would be ambushed, declared persona non grata, and expelled.

Every move of the Moscow station was coordinated with headquarters. Fulton told headquarters that the note from the man at the gas station conveyed a "carefully thought out" plan for a meeting but provided few details. The note "is conspiratorial, which might suggest some intel background," he wrote. Fulton said he was "very much aware" the approach could be a KGB dangle, and he would like to have a better idea of what the man wanted. Fulton said he would signal to the man that he was interested in the "car" option but not hold a personal meeting just yet. If the man was a dangle, Fulton did not want to put his foot into a trap.

But Fulton was also intrigued. The note had a ring of authenticity to it. Fulton thought if he took the first step, perhaps the man would come back with more information. He drove his car to the spot the man had mentioned, but he didn't see the man anywhere. Later, CIA headquarters said they did not want to pursue the contact, fearing it was a trap, and instructed Fulton to do nothing more.[7]

On February 3, the man appeared again. This time, he approached Fulton's car on a street very close to the embassy at 7:00 p.m., after dark. Fulton happened at that moment to be sitting in his car with the engine running. There was a Soviet militia post nearby, but the car was obscured by a high snowbank along the street. The man's face appeared at the driver's side window, and he tapped on it. When Fulton rolled down the window, the man dropped a note into the car. He then turned and left. No one was following him.

The note again proposed a signal and a meeting. The man said the signal should be delivered on the next evening, by parking the car on a nearby street. Fulton sent a cable to headquarters, saying the man's motives were "still not clear," so he did not respond.

Two weeks later, on February 17, Fulton left the embassy around 6:45 p.m. and, as he approached his car, noticed the man leave a phone booth that was nestled in the shadows of an apartment building, about thirty feet away. Fulton was climbing into the car when the man approached him.

"What do you want?" Fulton asked.

The man said he wanted to give Fulton another note. He tossed a folded letter into the car, turned on his heel, and quickly left. Fulton saw no one around, got in his car, and calmly drove home. He saw no one following him.

When he opened the letter, Fulton found four handwritten pages. He sent a rough translation to headquarters the next morning. The man wrote that he realized why his repeated requests were being ignored. "My activities may have brought suspicion," he said, adding that he understood full well the CIA was fearful of being trapped by the KGB. But, the man added, if he had wanted to do that, he could have done so already. This was not his intent or his method. "I'm an engineer and not a specialist in secret matters," he said, promising to provide more information about himself to dispel the mistrust but urging the CIA to handle his next message very carefully. "I work in a closed enterprise," he said, which meant a secret Soviet facility, probably related to defense or military work. In order to pass notes, the man wrote, he had been waiting for hours at more than one location to find just the right moment, a time-consuming and stressful vigil. He implored the CIA to make it easier and to show up for his next note on the following Friday.

Fulton asked CIA headquarters for permission to go ahead. He was impressed by the man's tenacity. He told headquarters that the risk wasn't great to park his car on the street and wait for the man to thrust an envelope through the window. The man "has essentially already done this twice," he said, and the KGB could have ambushed them earlier if they had wanted to.

Fulton realized there would be doubts at headquarters. They might well ask, wasn't it rather unlikely that a Russian man in Moscow, without any help at all, would have singled out the CIA's station chief to deliver a note? At the time of the first note in January, the United States had just expelled a KGB officer at the United Nations—could this be the setup for retaliation? Still, something about the man led Fulton to think he was genuine. Fulton told headquarters he believed the man had chosen him by coincidence at the diplomatic gas station and probably memorized the car's license number, and thus it was "not unusual" that he would continue to seek him out. Fulton said he would "under no circumstances" proceed to other sites that could be a trap.[8]

Headquarters was wary and told Fulton not to give the man a signal.

Just a few months later, in May 1977, the man approached Fulton for the fourth time. He had been hiding in a phone booth near Fulton's car and was carrying a package. Fulton saw KGB guards nearby, so he did not take the package.

The man banged on Fulton's car to get his attention.

Fulton ignored him, as headquarters instructed.[9]

———

By the summer, Fulton's tour was over. The new chief of the Moscow station was Gardner "Gus" Hathaway, who brought a different style. He had grown up in southern Virginia and never lost his slight accent, with its gentle rolling *r*'s, or his gentleman's manners, which combined with a powerful sense of mission. Hathaway, fifty-three years old, served in Berlin for the CIA in the late 1950s and later in Latin America and had a hard-charging way about him, a zeal for operations.

All through the spring and early summer of 1977, the Moscow station struggled with setbacks in the Ogorodnik case. A hollow log was left for Ogorodnik in February, but he did not show up. He emplaced a dead drop on schedule in April, but when the station's technical officers opened it, they concluded it was put together by someone else. His photography, usually perfect, seemed careless.

Hathaway wanted to recontact Ogorodnik and get the operation back on track. The CIA sent the agent a message by a coded shortwave radio broadcast, instructing him to leave a signal with a small red mark on a "Children Crossing" traffic sign if he was ready for another dead drop.

Early on the morning of July 15, 1977, Peterson drove by the sign, and the mark was there, but something didn't look right. It was bold, cherry red, as if it had been deliberately stenciled. A real agent doesn't have time to *stencil* a signal like that. She went to the station and told the others what she had seen. The signal was there, yes, but it seemed odd. Peterson suggested that someone else place the next drop. She had a knot in her stomach. The stenciled mark should have made Hathaway more cautious, but it didn't. He was eager to keep going.

That day, Peterson worked her usual day hours at her cover job. At 6:00 p.m., she went to the station and reviewed the operations plan at the small conference table in Hathaway's office. Then she went home, changed into comfortable clothes, a summer blouse and platform sandals. She pulled back her hair to conceal the blond streaks. She would never look like a Russian, but she wanted to blend in as much as possible. She attached a tiny CIA radio receiver that detected KGB transmissions to her bra with Velcro. She connected the neck loop antenna and then inserted a very small wireless earpiece, entirely concealed by her hair.

By car, she went on a long, winding surveillance detection run around town, designed to flush out any KGB monitors. She parked her car, entered the subway, changed at three stations, and exited at the sports stadium just as a crowd was leaving a soccer game. She slipped into the crowd, finally arriving at the site for the dead drop, located in a small stone tower on a railroad bridge spanning the Moscow River.

She walked up forty stairs to a point on the bridge where she had left packages for Ogorodnik before. In her bag was a piece of crumbly black asphalt that had a hidden compartment inside holding messages and a miniature camera for Ogorodnik. At 10:15 p.m., barely dusk in Moscow during the summer, Peterson left the chunk of black asphalt in a narrow square window in the stone tower of the bridge, pushing it exactly one arm's length from the edge. She began to descend the steps when she saw three men in white shirts rushing toward her. She had nowhere to escape and wasn't about to jump into the river. Grabbed by the men, she felt a jolt of anger that it was the KGB. A van pulled up, and more men clambered out. Peterson kicked one of them hard, but they restrained her. A KGB officer began to take flash pictures. Then, groping her, they discovered the radio receiver but didn't know how to peel apart the Velcro. Next, they produced the black asphalt chunk they found in the tower. Peterson insisted, loudly, that she was an American citizen, they should call the embassy, they could not detain her. "Let me go!" she shouted. One of the KGB men said, "Please keep your voice down." Peterson kept repeating the embassy phone number. Finally, they got the radio receiver off the bra and found the neck loop. However, they never discovered the small wireless earpiece.

Peterson was taken to KGB headquarters, the Lubyanka, and interrogated. She had a sinking feeling when they brought out the asphalt chunk, removed the four reverse-threaded screws, took off the lid to the hidden cavity, and emptied it in front of her, a technician pulling out each item as the interrogator watched. There was a message for Ogorodnik imprinted in tiny letters on 35 mm film, contact lenses and fluid, rolls of tightly wound rubles, and emerald jewelry. When the big black fountain pen was pulled out, the chief interrogator sharply instructed the technician to put it down and not touch it. His tone suggested that he was aware of the cyanide capsule the CIA had given to Ogorodnik. In fact, Peterson knew this pen concealed a camera, not the cyanide capsule, but she realized very quickly, by the interrogator's manner, that Ogorodnik had been caught.

She was released later that night, the usual procedure in espionage arrests. The embassy's consular affairs officer came to get her. His eyes were wide with disbelief; he thought she had been a bureaucrat, not a case officer on the streets. The consular affairs officer drove her to the embassy, and Peterson went immediately to the Moscow station, knowing that shortly she would be declared persona non grata in the Soviet Union. Over the next few hours, well past midnight, sitting in the middle of the station, she recounted the events, sometimes with profanity, as her colleagues listened, and one of them took notes for a cable back to headquarters. The cable was sent out at 3:30 a.m. Moscow time.

Sad, exhausted, and uncertain about how Ogorodnik had been discovered, Peterson had little sleep before she flew out of Moscow the next day, Saturday, July 16.

At headquarters, it was a crushing blow. Ogorodnik was a prized agent, the first to show the Angleton years had finally been left behind. He had been lost, and no one knew why. James Olson, a case officer, recalled the scene at headquarters soon after word reached the Soviet desk. "The entire USSR desk, from the lowest clerk to the crusty old chief, were all crying," Olson remembered. "It was because we lost TRIGON. We knew TRIGON was gone."[10]

Peterson later learned that Ogorodnik had been arrested at his apartment. He was stripped to his underwear. Knowing the KGB would be eager to learn every detail of his work with the CIA, he offered to write a confession. They handed him his pen, and he bit down on the barrel with the cyanide capsule inside. He died on the spot, before the KGB could learn any more.[11]

## 3

# A MAN CALLED SPHERE

**O**n the long trip home, Marti Peterson struggled with the unanswered questions. She didn't know why the case had fallen apart. Her surveillance detection run had been long and thorough, and she had seen no signs of the KGB, yet they were lying in wait at the bridge. Even after they grabbed her, they still didn't know she was CIA; she had eluded them for two years. So how did they figure out the precise time and place for the dead drop? Was there a slipup? Was there surveillance she didn't see? A communications leak? Did Ogorodnik make a mistake? Or something worse?[1]

Peterson left Moscow quickly in the clothes she was wearing the night of the ambush. In Washington, she bought a new dress. On Monday, July 18, less than seventy-two hours after the debacle in Moscow, she walked up the steps to the main entrance of CIA headquarters at Langley. In her new identification photograph taken that morning, she is smiling, a bit hesitantly, her eyes clear and bright. The debriefings revived the same questions she had asked herself about Ogorodnik's missed meetings, the deteriorating quality of his photographs, the inexplicable events in the forest, and the woman with the ponytail. Then, in a corridor at headquarters, she saw Fulton, her mentor, for the first time since he had left the Moscow station. They embraced and fought back tears, no words to speak the sorrow they felt.

On the seventh floor of CIA headquarters, Peterson entered the large office suite of Admiral Stansfield Turner, the new director of central intelligence, who after four months in the job was still finding his way. Turner had a very forceful public presence, but in private he was cordial and reserved. He sat down at the head of a long conference table, dismissed the CIA officer who had brought Peterson, and motioned to her to take a chair at his right. After she recounted everything that had happened, Turner asked her to accompany him to meet President Jimmy Carter at his regular briefing the next day. There would only be nine or ten minutes to tell her story.

On Tuesday, they entered the Oval Office. On the coffee table in front of Carter, Peterson placed a replica of the black asphalt chunk used to hold the secret messages for Ogorodnik and the CIA's site sketches, to help illustrate what happened. The president was engrossed by her account. At one point, the national security adviser, Zbigniew Brzezinski, spoke up, filling in details, such as the name of the agent, Ogorodnik, and the name of the Moscow railroad bridge where she had been ambushed. Brzezinski, whose father had been a Polish aristocrat and diplomat in the anticommunist Polish government before World War II, devoted his career as a professor to chronicling the decline of Soviet communism. He knew perhaps better than anyone in the room how valuable and unusual this spy had been. "I greatly admire your courage," Brzezinski told Peterson as she was leaving. Ten minutes had stretched to more than twenty. Peterson left the Oval Office alone and had to ask a White House secretary how to find her way out to the street. Later that day, Turner sent her a breezy, handwritten thank-you note. "You are the only person who has stood face-to-face with the KGB and the President of the United States all within three days," he said. "I admire and congratulate you."

But privately, Turner was brooding about her expulsion. The events in Moscow meant something was wrong.

Stansfield Turner grew up in Highland Park, Illinois, an affluent small town on the lakeshore north of Chicago with stately homes and tree-lined streets. His father, Oliver, was a self-made businessman who filled the house with books. His mother drilled into him values of honesty and integrity. Turner became an Eagle Scout and president of his high school class, went on to Amherst College, and, after a lobbying campaign by his father, won admission to the U.S. Naval Academy. When he graduated in June 1946, Turner stood at twenty-fifth in a class of 841. He was at the top of the class in aptitude for service—qualities of leadership, integrity, reliability, and other traits of a superior officer. But Turner chafed at the academy's courses, heavily oriented toward engineering, seamanship, and science. His interests ran far beyond. Rather than plunge immediately into a navy career, Turner won a prestigious Rhodes Scholarship to Oxford University, where he studied politics, philosophy, and economics.[2]

On returning to the navy, Turner went to sea on destroyers but was impatient with the minutiae of shipboard life. He wanted to think big and be at the center of change. In the 1950s, he was selected by a new chief of naval operations, Arleigh Burke, to put together a group of junior officers to tell Burke what was wrong with the navy and how to fix it, an assignment Turner found exhilarating. Then Turner was selected to work with the whiz kids under Robert McNamara in the 1960s, when systems analysis was all the rage. When Admiral Elmo Zumwalt became the new chief of naval operations in 1970, he put Turner in charge of new initiatives in his first sixty days. Through it all, Turner became convinced the military was hidebound and desperately needed new thinking. He once used systems analysis to study naval minesweeping and showed how it could be done better and faster from a helicopter than from a ship. Yet Turner's zeal for change often ran headlong into inertia, especially in the Vietnam War years, when military morale and discipline were sapped by defeat and a loss of support at home. Appointed commander of the Naval War College in 1972, Turner seized the opportunity to overhaul the curriculum, making it more rigorous and demanding. Through all his assignments, he preached the virtues of discipline and accountability.

Turner's class at the U.S. Naval Academy included a somewhat shy and skinny fellow from a backwater peanut farm in Georgia, Jimmy Carter, who also applied for a Rhodes Scholarship but did not get it. Carter stood at fifty-ninth in the class. Carter and Turner did not know each other then. Carter went on to become a nuclear submariner, farmer, and governor of Georgia. In 1973, Turner invited Carter to speak at the war college and was impressed. The following year, in October 1974, they met again at Carter's offices in Atlanta. Carter fired rapid questions at Turner for half an hour about the state of the U.S. military and the navy. When it was over, Carter said, "By the way, the day after tomorrow, I am announcing that I'm going to run for president of the United States."

Carter triumphed in the 1976 presidential campaign by emphasizing trust to a nation battered by the Vietnam War and the Watergate scandal. He projected a fresh, moralistic approach to government—"I'll never tell a lie"—and a break with the sordid scandals in Washington. Among them, in Carter's view, were the disclosures, starting in late 1974, of illegal CIA surveillance of American citizens, including antiwar activists. Three separate investigations of the CIA followed over the next sixteen months, revealing more unsavory operations. When Carter took office in January 1977, the CIA was still reeling from these probes.[3] The agency had three directors in four years. The outgoing director, George H. W. Bush, a Republican appointed by President Ford, was affable and well liked at the CIA, and he wanted to remain, but Carter demanded a clean break. Carter at first chose Theodore Sorensen, the Kennedy speechwriter and a Democratic lawyer, to lead the CIA, but Sorensen withdrew when it was disclosed he had once been a conscientious objector and opposition to the nomination mounted in Congress.

At the time, Turner had become a four-star admiral and was serving as commander in chief of Allied forces in southern Europe. When Turner first got the call to come to Washington, he hoped he was being considered for a military appointment as chief of naval operations or vice-chief. At the White House, Carter greeted Turner warmly in his private office, then asked him to head the CIA.[4] Turner was not ready for this and protested that he might be better in a military position. But Turner quickly grasped that Carter had made up his mind. In fact, it was Turner's military career and reputation for discipline and integrity that appealed to the new president, who had promised to turn a new leaf at the CIA. Turner took the CIA job, but "I walked out in a real daze."[5]

In the early months in office, Turner and Carter were both fascinated by stunning advances in technology, such as the revolutionary KH-11 satellite that transmitted electronic images directly to the ground, rather than using the cumbersome previous method, in which film canisters were ejected from a satellite and captured by airplanes on descent. The KH-11 images could be seen in real time instead of days or weeks later. By coincidence, the first images were received at the CIA just hours before Carter was inaugurated president. The next day, Carter was shown the photographs in the White House Situation Room. "It was a marvelous system," Turner later recalled, "much like a TV in space that sent back pictures almost instantly."[6] Turner saw the technical side of intelligence collection as the wave of the future. He wanted intelligence that could be delivered when it was needed.

As CIA director, Turner took home draft National Intelligence Estimates on weekends and marked them up with red pencil. The estimates are the highest product of "finished" intelligence that the CIA provides to decision makers in government, reflecting the results of espionage as well as analysis, and they are usually created and polished by dozens of officials before being disseminated. It was unheard of for a director to take them home and personally edit them. Separately, Turner displayed an independent streak in his thinking about the world and a fondness for analysis of it. He strongly questioned the U.S. military's gloomy estimates of the expanding Soviet military threat. This deeply irritated the Pentagon, but Turner insisted that aspects of American strength were far superior and should be taken into account. He wanted a genuine balance sheet, not just a catalog of the latest Soviet threats.[7]

However, Turner was singularly unprepared for the risky world of running spies. Espionage meant persuading people to betray their country and to steal secrets. Unlike most other agencies in the U.S. government, the CIA's purpose was to violate the laws of other countries. In the clandestine service, the people who engaged in this practice believed they served a noble cause. Turner never understood them, and they saw him as distant and aloof. Robert Gates, who served for a while as Turner's executive assistant, recalled that "the cultural and philosophical gap between Turner and the clandestine service was simply too wide to be bridged."[8] Turner said he wanted the CIA to have a higher ethical standard and efficient structure, like a corporation. But people in the clandestine service were put off by his preaching and moralism. Their work was often dirty and ruthless. They also resented how one of Turner's coterie of assistants, Robert "Rusty" Williams, went poking into private lives, asking about affairs and divorces, which were common in the high-stress world of operations.[9] Also, in 1977 Turner eliminated hundreds of positions in the clandestine service. The cuts were overdue—the directorate was overstaffed from the Vietnam War—but Turner was brusque and maladroit in carrying them out. Many old-timers were offended, and resentments ran deep.[10] "He was never quite convinced about human intelligence," recalled a CIA official who worked closely with Turner. "Sometimes it was good, and sometimes it was bad. He thought we got more out of technical intelligence, it was more reliable."

Within weeks of his meeting with Marti Peterson in the Oval Office, Turner's suspicions deepened that something was wrong with the Moscow station.

On the evening of August 26, 1977, Dick Combs, a political officer, was working late in the U.S. embassy in Moscow, writing a report. His office was on the same floor—the seventh—as the CIA station. A marine guard burst into the office and asked Combs, "Do you smell smoke?" Combs had been puffing on a pipe and did not, aside from his own. But he soon realized a fire was spreading across the eighth floor, just above him. It started after hours when a transformer ignited in the economics section. The embassy had been a firetrap for years. A recent refurbishment used paneling that was highly flammable, and the marine guards were unable to stop the flames with fire extinguishers. The Moscow fire department did not arrive immediately, and the first firemen on the scene seemed poorly trained, with outdated equipment and leaky hoses. The ambassador, Malcolm

Toon, rushed to the building from a diplomatic dinner, still in black tie, and was on the street below, while the deputy chief of mission, Jack Matlock, hustled to the ninth floor. Matlock loved books and tried to save his library as the fire worsened. Later, more experienced firemen arrived, some of them KGB officers, certainly aware that the CIA's Moscow station was in the building, hoping to scoop up sensitive documents or enter classified areas. At one point when it looked as if the entire building might be consumed in fire, the ambassador gave orders to find the CIA station chief, Hathaway, and order him to leave. A staffer found Hathaway guarding the station on the seventh floor, dressed in a London Fog raincoat, his face smudged with soot, blocking the way for any KGB "firemen" who might try to break in. He refused to budge, despite the ambassador's order.[11]

How did the fire start? At headquarters, the CIA knew that the Soviets routinely bombarded the U.S. embassy in Moscow with microwave signals. Turner brought this up constantly, saying he was worried about the "beams" at the embassy. Separately, after the fire, Turner wondered if the KGB could have deliberately caused the spark that started it, if not using the "beams," then some other way. What was going on in Moscow? First, the loss of Ogorodnik. Now a mysterious fire and KGB "firemen."

Still more trouble followed. In September, the Moscow station lost another agent, Anatoly Filatov, a colonel in Soviet military intelligence who had begun working for the CIA while stationed in Algiers in earlier years. Filatov was swapping a package with a CIA case officer, a "car toss," or quick exchange as two vehicles pulled alongside each other. The KGB was lying in wait. They arrested Filatov, and the CIA case officer and his wife were expelled.[12]

Turner was shaken. Was the KGB listening to their communications? Had they penetrated the Moscow station? Was there a mole somewhere? When a system wasn't working, Turner felt, the correct response was to fix it. Now he wanted to do the same at the CIA. He took an extraordinary step. He ordered a freeze on CIA operations in Moscow—a total stand-down. The Moscow station was told not to run any agents, not to carry out any operational acts.

The stand-down was unlike anything the Soviet division had experienced before. Turner insisted it would continue until the division could *guarantee* there would be no further compromises. This left many officers in the clandestine service bewildered. Did Turner not grasp the basics of espionage operations? The case officers and their agents were never free from risk. They could *never* guarantee there would be no more compromises.[13]

In Moscow, Hathaway was furious; Turner's action seemed incomprehensible. It ran against everything Hathaway stood for—against his sense of mission and desire for aggressive espionage operations. Instead of running agents, Hathaway's case officers were forced to sit on their hands. Hathaway kept them busy as best he could, looking for new dead drop sites and making maps, preparing for the day they could resume running spies.[14]

Meanwhile, the station began to lose intelligence sources, and one of them was the valuable volunteer from the early 1960s, Alexei Kulak, the KGB scientific and technical officer codenamed FEDORA by the FBI. A war hero in the Soviet Union who joined the KGB and was assigned to New York, Kulak walked into the FBI field office in New York in March 1962 and volunteered to work for the United States for cash. He was overweight, a heavy drinker who loved big meals. Kulak served two tours in the United States and in those years was considered an authentic source by the FBI, but by the mid-1970s they began to lose confidence in him and suspected he was controlled by the KGB.[15] In 1976, Kulak was preparing to return to Moscow, probably never to return to the United States. Hathaway, then getting ready to take the reins as chief of the Moscow station, went to New York

City to personally recruit Kulak for the CIA. The meeting, in a hotel room, was filled with tension, as an FBI man berated Kulak and Hathaway struggled to win his confidence. Hathaway won out, and Kulak agreed to work for the CIA once he returned to Moscow. He left the United States equipped with dead drop and signal sites. His CIA crypt was CKKAYO.

In early July 1977, he filled a dead drop in Moscow for the first time, and the contents were startling. Kulak provided a handwritten list of Soviet officials in the United States who were attempting to steal scientific and technical secrets. Even more promising, he said in the fall he would provide "lists of all Soviet officials and scientists worldwide involved in the collection of U.S. scientific and technical information," as well as five- and ten-year plans of the KGB's scientific and technical directorate. This would be a gold mine, a KGB blueprint ten years into the future on one of the biggest issues of the day, Soviet theft of Western technology.

Right on schedule in the autumn, Kulak signaled for the dead drop. But at this point, Turner's stand-down was in effect, and the Moscow station did not respond. Kulak signaled a second time. The station did nothing. Hathaway was forced to watch as a valuable source was frittered away. The Kulak operation withered.[16]

The man who had first approached Fulton at the gas station was standing on a street corner near a market in Moscow on December 10, 1977, looking at the license plates on every car, searching for the prefix D-04 that signified an American diplomat's vehicle.

More than a year earlier, he had heard an astonishing news report while listening to a Voice of America broadcast on a short-wave radio in his apartment. He learned that a Soviet air force pilot, Victor Belenko, flew his MiG-25 interceptor from a Soviet air base in the Far East to a civilian airport in Japan and defected. It was a daring escape from the Soviet Union, and Belenko was granted asylum in the United States. As a defector, Belenko provided the Americans surprising new details about the feared and mysterious Soviet interceptor, designed to chase and shoot down the high-flying SR-71 "Blackbird" U.S. reconnaissance jet. In Japan, Belenko's plane was disassembled by a U.S. and Japanese team, which yielded still more secrets, especially regarding the interceptor's radar and avionics.[17]

The Russian man on the street corner carried a letter in his pocket. Since January, he had been trying to contact the CIA by spotting cars used by the Americans. Starting with his approach to Fulton at the gas station, he had made four approaches, but all were ignored or rebuffed. Then he went on a long work trip out of town and lost track of his quarry. Now he was searching again for the Americans.

At the market, he spotted a car with the plates. An embassy employee got out of the car. The Russian man quickly walked up to him, handed him the letter, and pleaded that it be delivered to the responsible U.S. official.

The embassy employee who received the letter at the market was the majordomo of Spaso House, a portly man who managed the U.S. ambassador's residence in Moscow. When he brought the letter to the CIA's Moscow station, Hathaway opened it and found two typewritten pages of intelligence about radars for Soviet military aircraft.

In the letter, the man described how, after Belenko's defection, orders came down to modify the radar in the MiG-25. He then wrote something that seized Hathaway's attention. The man said he had access to development of a "look-down, shoot-down" radar system. He also said he could provide schematics for a radar that was becoming the basic unit for interceptors like the ultrafast MiG-25.

Again, he provided some scenarios for a possible contact and said he would be waiting for it on January 9, 1978, in the New Year.

He wanted "to do what Belenko did," he wrote. But he still did not say who he was.

The next morning, Hathaway went to visit a friend who was a defense attaché in the embassy.

"What the hell is look-down, shoot-down radar?" Hathaway asked, getting right to the point.

The friend replied, "Are you kidding? That's one of the most important damn things in the world!"[18]

Such a radar would allow Soviet aircraft at a higher altitude to spot low-flying planes or missiles against the contours of the earth. At the time, it was believed the Soviet warplanes lacked the capability; the MiG-25 flown by Belenko did not have it. Moreover, Soviet ground-based radars also couldn't see targets at low altitude, and the United States had spent years preparing to exploit this vulnerability, either with low-altitude bombers or with advanced cruise missiles to fly under the Soviet radars.

Hathaway was frustrated by the stand-down and by Turner's fears. "What the hell is wrong with headquarters?" he asked. "They have lost their mind! What are we going to do, sit on our ass?"

While he had a healthy respect for the KGB, Hathaway knew they weren't perfect, and he felt confident the CIA could run agents in Moscow. "You have to understand, everyone in the station, to a man, knew exactly, we can operate against these people," he said. Hathaway felt Turner wasn't getting good advice. He insisted that Turner send his close aide, Williams, to Moscow. Once he arrived, Hathaway took him out on a surveillance detection run, to see the KGB's methods firsthand—methods that were sloppy, even if the surveillance was pervasive. Hathaway and Williams listened to the KGB radio transmissions with the small CIA scanners. "We hit a red light, and we could hear *pomidor! Tomato!* They were dumb enough to yell 'red light,'" Hathaway recalled. He sent Williams back to Langley with a plea: let the Moscow station come back to life. Williams seemed to get the point. But Turner was unmoved, and there was no change in the stand-down.

After delivering the note in December 1977 about "look-down, shoot-down" radar, the man at the gas station was given a CIA code name, CKSPHERE.

Hathaway pressed headquarters to examine the information CKSPHERE had provided. From the notes earlier in the year and in December, Hathaway saw the man was an engineer at a top secret military research laboratory.

In an internal memo on December 29, headquarters responded with an evaluation. At this point, it was critical to decide: Did the engineer have anything really important to offer? The headquarters evaluation was equivocal:

> The subject matter of Source's reporting, airborne radio
> location stations, i.e. radars, is extremely important.
> When he talks about a radar that "can work against the
> background of the earth," he is talking about a "look-
> down, shoot-down" radar. We know that the Soviets do not
> have a particularly effective look-down, shoot-down radar
> and that they are working very hard to solve this problem.
> An effective look-down, shoot-down would pose a serious
> threat to both the B-52 bomber and the cruise missile
> and information on Soviet state-of-the-art in this field is
> responsive to very high priority intelligence requirements.
> His offer to provide schematics and sketches of current
> systems would be of considerable assistance to the analysts.

But the evaluation concluded,

The information provided by CKSPHERE is of intelligence
value but its possession by the U.S. Government does not
do grave damage to the USSR.[19]

Hathaway was stunned. How could headquarters miss the
obvious fact that the engineer's information would indeed do
grave damage to the Soviet Union? On January 3, 1978, just six
days before the planned meeting, Hathaway sent his own argument to headquarters:

If CKSPHERE's information on the current state of Soviet
look-down, shoot-down radar is accurate, the development
of an effective LDSD radar must be a very high priority
Soviet goal in view of the cruise missile threat. Should the
Soviets develop an effective LDSD radar, would detailed
information on it be considered in the category of "grave
damage to the USSR"? Would detailed information on
it enable the US to counter its effectiveness? In other
words, assuming CKSPHERE is who he says he is, and is in a
position to monitor Soviet attempts to develop an effective
radar, would it be worth the risk of a PNG?[20]

The last line about a "PNG" referred to the risk of a case officer's being expelled or declared persona non grata, as had happened to Peterson.

Hathaway believed the information from CKSPHERE was far
too valuable for a KGB dangle. They wouldn't waste military
secrets that way. In preparation for a meeting on January 9,
Hathaway's team sent a detailed scenario to headquarters, seeking approval to meet CKSPHERE. They proposed a face-to-face
walk, to ask the engineer who he was, what he wanted, and

whether he had more information to provide. In particular, the station wanted to ask him about a weapons system mentioned in the December note. The engineer had indicated he could obtain schematics for a Soviet radar package code-named AMETIST or "amethyst," that he had described as becoming the basic unit for interceptor aircraft like the MiG-25. They would also press him for more about look-down, shoot-down radar. Depending on how long that might take, they would set up a schedule for future meetings, with four possible sites designated at thirty-day intervals. The engineer would be encouraged to stuff envelopes through the window of a car, as he had done before.[21]

Hathaway was eager to resume espionage operations, to get back in the spying business. He was following the Gerber rules, which meant check out a volunteer, don't dismiss him out of hand.

The plan went all the way to Turner on January 3, 1978, stamped "SECRET" and "WARNING NOTICE— SENSITIVE INTELLIGENCE SOURCES AND METH- ODS INVOLVED."

In a summary memo describing the plan, Turner was told that CKSPHERE was "a middle-aged Soviet engineer who has made five approaches to Moscow Station since January, 1977." The summary memo recalled that the Moscow station did not follow up on these approaches because the man "did nothing" in the first four attempts to establish who he was and out of concern that it was a KGB provocation. Also, there was a desire to avoid an incident while the Carter administration was just settling in. But the summary memo noted that CKSPHERE had been more forthcoming in his last note, passed at the market on Decem- ber 10, 1977.

Was the intelligence really that good? The summary memo, like the earlier headquarters evaluation, was not overly enthu- siastic. The MiG-25 radar update "does not do serious harm to the Soviet government," it said, although look-down, shoot-down radar is "of high priority intelligence interest."

Under a section titled "Risks," the memo advised caution. Turner was told,

> We have no proof that CKSPHERE is a provocation, but his approach to us has many of the earmarks of previous cases that we found to be under KGB control. Even if he was bona fide in the beginning, his several attempts to contact us could have brought him under discreet coverage by the KGB. At best, we view CKSPHERE's bona fides and potential as unproven—in contrast to existing sources in Moscow whom we have not been able to contact during the operational standdown.

Turner was given two choices: Option B was go ahead and meet the engineer on January 9. But the summary memo concluded, "We recommend Option A—do nothing." The reason? It was too risky. If the operation went bad, the memo said, it could lead to a third expulsion, prolong the stand-down, or even lead to closure of the Moscow station. Rather than contact the engineer, Turner was advised, "Our primary obligation and objective should be to resume secure and productive contact with the proven sources in Moscow."

Turner agreed—the decision was Option A.

"Do nothing."[22]

# 4

# "FINALLY I HAVE REACHED YOU"

The engineer still did not give up. On February 16, 1978, more than a year after the first approach at the gas station, Hathaway drove out of the embassy compound onto a side street. He slowed at a dark intersection. Suddenly there was a tap-tap on the window. His wife, Karin, sitting beside him, strained to see and rolled down the car window. The engineer was standing outside, leaned close, and shoved an envelope through. "Give to the ambassador," he said urgently in Russian. The envelope fell onto Karin's lap. The engineer turned quickly and disappeared. Hathaway made a U-turn, drove straight back to the embassy, and took the envelope up to the station.

The envelope contained a new letter from the engineer. He wrote that he felt caught in a vicious circle: "I'm afraid for security reasons to put down on paper much about myself, and, without this information, for security reasons you are afraid to contact me, fearing a provocation." He then scribbled out his home phone number, except for the last two digits. At a given hour in the coming weeks, he promised to stand on a street at a bus stop, holding a plywood board. Written on it would be the last two digits.

Not taking any chances, the Moscow station sent a case officer on foot to look for the numbers, and also sent Hathaway's wife, Karin. She drove their car by the bus stop, spotted the man, and noted the two numbers.[1]

Hathaway again pushed headquarters for permission to respond. The stand-down was still in effect, but Hathaway wanted approval to carry out a simple operational act—to make a contact. As it happened, just as the engineer made his last overture to Hathaway, the Pentagon sent a memo to the CIA expressing great interest in any intelligence about Soviet aircraft electronics and weapons control systems.

That tipped the balance. Headquarters relented and gave the green light to the station for a contact with the engineer.

Hathaway decided they would call him from a public phone on the street, but he knew it was risky; if a CIA officer was spotted by the KGB using a public phone, it might be traced. All the pay phone booths were numbered, and KGB surveillance could easily ask for an immediate trace of the call. On February 26, a case officer from the Moscow station went on a long surveillance detection run to avoid the KGB and then called the engineer's home phone number from a phone booth. The man's wife answered, so the case officer hung up. Two days later, the case officer tried again, with the same outcome.[2]

On the evening of March 1, darkness had fallen when the engineer approached Hathaway and his wife as they were getting into their car on Bolshoi Devyatinsky Pereulok, a tree-lined lane bordering the embassy compound. Hathaway was unlocking the car door on the driver's side when he saw the engineer coming, recognized him, and extended his left hand. The engineer quickly placed a packet of taped paper into his hand. In Russian, the engineer said, "Pozhaluista," or "Here you go," and Hathaway responded, "Spasibo," or "Thank you." Hathaway noticed a pedestrian about twenty yards behind the engineer but did not think the handoff was visible in the dark. The engineer did not break stride as he passed and then slipped away down another side street. Hathaway went back up to the station—telling the guard at the gate he had "forgotten something"—and opened the packet.

Inside, he found eleven handwritten pages, in Russian, on both sides of six large sheets of paper. As before, they were folded inside two other pieces of paper to form a three-by-four-inch package, sealed with white paper tape and light brown glue. There were a few words in English on the outside saying please pass to the responsible person at the American embassy.

The note was the breakthrough they had been waiting for.

The engineer revealed his identity. He wrote,

Since on 21 Feb 78, you did not call me either from 1100 to 1300, nor later, and since on that same evening auto D-04-661 . . . was parked by house number five on Bolshoi Devyatinsky Pereulok, I assumed (although this seems improbable), that the missing numbers of my phone, shown on the board by house number 32, were not observed from a passing car and could not be written down. To eliminate any doubt, I am submitting basic information about myself. I, Tolkachev, Adolf Georgievich, was born in 1927 in the city of Aktyubinsk (Kazakhskaya SSR). Since 1929, I have lived in Moscow. In 1948, I completed the optical-mechanical tekhnikum (radar department) and in 1954, the Kharkovskiy Politechnicheskiy Institute (radio-technical department). Since 1954, I have worked at the NIIR (p.o. box A-1427). At present I work in a combined laboratory in the position of leading designer. (In the laboratory there exists the following hierarchy of positions: lab assistant, engineer, senior engineer, leading engineer, leading designer, chief of the laboratory.) My work phone: 254-8580. Work day is from 0800 to 1700. Lunch from 1145 to 1230.

My family: wife (Kuzmina, Natalia Ivanovna), 12-year-
old son (Tolkachev, Oleg).[3]

Just to be sure, Adolf Tolkachev wrote down his home phone
number again, 255-4415. He gave his home address, 1 Ploshchad
Vosstaniya, apartment No. 57, ninth floor, a distinctive high-rise
tower near the embassy, where he had lived since 1955. The building had multiple entrances, so he added, "Entry in the middle of
the building from the side of the square."

Tolkachev also volunteered instructions for how to call him
without being detected. If a man phoned, he should identify
himself as Nikolai. If a woman, as Katya. Tolkachev said he had
spent "hours and hours roaming the streets" in search of U.S.
diplomatic cars and, even when he found one, often did not leave
a note right away out of fear of being detected. He said he was
now desperate for a positive response to his prolonged effort, and
if he did not get one this time, he would give up.[4]

In the note, Tolkachev provided precious new intelligence, far
superior to what could be gained by other means. He reproduced
quotations from top secret documents and offered more details
about look-down, shoot-down radar. The note included an
extremely important piece of identifying information: the post-
box number of the institute where Tolkachev worked, A-1427.

The CIA now confirmed that Tolkachev was a designer at one
of the two research institutes for Soviet military radars, especially
those deployed on fighter aircraft. He worked at the Scientific
Research Institute for Radio Engineering, known by its Russian
acronym, NIIR. It was about a twenty-minute walk from his
apartment.

The time had come to give him a positive response. At last, the
Moscow station was revving up again.

———

The case officer who had made the phone call from the pay phone was John Guilsher. A handsome man, forty-seven years old, with dark eyebrows and graying hair swept straight back, he was quiet and reserved. He loved the outdoors and once aspired to be a forest ranger, but Russia took him in a different direction.

Guilsher's parents and grandparents had seen their families and fortunes destroyed by the upheavals of the last century in Russia—war, revolution, and exile. Guilsher's parents, George and Nina, grew up in Petrograd, children of the nobility in the twilight years of the imperial court. They had known each other from childhood. George attended the Imperial Lycée and worked in the tsar's Ministry of Finance. He later fought against the Bolsheviks after they seized power, serving in one of the White armies that were supplied by the Americans and the British. A brother also served with the Whites and was killed early in the conflict. George was the only member of the immediate family to survive the war. He fled with the defeated White soldiers to Constantinople, landed in New York City in 1923, and was reunited with Nina, who had suffered her own harrowing escape after five years of impoverished, desperate existence in revolutionary Petrograd. They were married in 1927 in New York, where George became a production manager for the equipment manufacturer Ingersoll Rand.

They had three children; John was their second son. He grew up on 122nd Street in New York City in the years before World War II, then the family moved to Sea Cliff, Long Island, after the war. They escaped the summer heat at an aunt's house in Cornwall, Connecticut. Although they came from well-off families in Russia, they arrived penniless in America, and the early years were lean. When John and his brother were very young, their sister recalled, they were often seen wearing clean and crisp little boy sailor suits, suggesting a certain prosperity. In truth, they each had only one, and their mother washed and ironed them every night. Russian was spoken at home, and their father was often deep in conversation with friends about literature and politics in the Old World. He kept a diary in which he tracked all the historical events of Russia, including specific decrees, birth dates of famous writers and other notable people, and also the saints of the day. He collected Russian stamps and took his sons to museums. John Guilsher had never been to Russia, but Russia was all around him.[5]

In 1945, when John was fifteen years old, his father suddenly died of a heart attack. While supporting his mother with summer jobs, including one shoveling out coal furnaces, Guilsher went to the University of Connecticut on a scholarship and studied forestry. His brother had settled far away in Alaska, and John visited him there, enthralled by the big sky and open spaces. When the Korean War broke out, John joined the army but spent his tour on loan to the National Security Agency. In 1955, at the end of his military service, he joined the CIA and was sent to London, where he worked on the Berlin tunnel recordings.

Before his departure to London, he had met and fallen in love with a beautiful young woman, Catherine, known as Kissa, who was also a scion of Russian nobility. Her father had fled the Bolsheviks and settled in Belgrade, where Kissa was born. The family was uprooted again by the upheaval of World War II and fled to the United States. By her teenage years, Kissa had felt the wrath of both communists and Nazis and was eager for a better life. She met John one summer evening in Washington, where she was studying at George Washington University. They were engaged for two years while he served in London and she finished her degree. They married in London in 1957. John was already starting a career in the CIA, but on their honeymoon he wistfully broached the possibility of giving up intelligence and following his dreams to work in forestry in Alaska. Kissa protested, emphatically. Guilsher spent the rest of his career in the CIA.

John spoke Russian with a very slight accent that suggested he was from the Baltics, but his language skills were superb and proved to be extremely valuable in those early years of the Cold War. In the 1950s and early 1960s, he participated in two of the CIA's most significant operations against the Soviet Union: the Berlin tunnel and Penkovsky.

When Hathaway was assigned to become chief of station in Moscow in 1977, he handpicked Guilsher to join him. They had never served together, but Hathaway knew of Guilsher's language skills. One day, Kissa and their children were summering at the family home in Connecticut when John called with the news: they were bound for Moscow. She was delighted, despite the hardships. They were going back to the land of their forebears, not as children of the nobility, but to carry out espionage against the Soviet Union. They were unsentimental about it; the Russia of their ancestors had been destroyed by the Bolsheviks. John had been working against the Soviet target for twenty-two years from various posts outside the country. But this job would be different. Previously, he had been a language officer, unraveling the spoken and written word. Now, for the first time, he would be a case officer, running agents on the street, inside the Soviet Union. And Kissa would be helping him.[6]

They arrived in Moscow on July 16, 1977. An embassy officer was sent out to meet them at Sheremetyevo International Airport. After they cleared passport control and collected their dog from the veterinary station, the embassy officer confided some shocking news: Marti Peterson had been caught placing a dead drop, and she was leaving Moscow at that very moment from the same airport. John immediately grasped the consequences: Ogorodnik was compromised and would probably pay with his life.

A few weeks later came the Moscow embassy fire, then the second agent was caught, followed by Turner's order of a stand-down. Guilsher found the mood grim in the Moscow station. The quarters were cramped, and there was construction all around to repair the fire damage.

Guilsher also was a target of close surveillance by the KGB— more so than most. His apartment was bugged. When John and Kissa wanted to talk about anything sensitive, they wrote notes to each other, but carefully, on wood or metal, so as not to leave an impression on the page underneath that could be read later by the KGB. John repeatedly insisted to Kissa that they live a "low key" and mundane life in Moscow, repeating their routines over and over again so the KGB wouldn't notice anything out of the ordinary—drawing on the 1950s lessons of Haviland Smith. Kissa chafed at the restrictions; she was as outgoing and person-able as John was reserved.

The KGB surveillance could be surprisingly unsophisticated. John and Kissa more than once went to a closet to reach for an overcoat, only to find it was missing, apparently taken by the sur-veillance people to implant a microphone. The coat would myste-riously reappear later. One summer evening, the family decided to meet some friends at a restaurant outside Moscow and dis-cussed the trip over a phone line, knowing the KGB was prob-ably listening in. As they drove, the Guilshers counted no fewer than three surveillance cars in front and behind. Then they got a little lost. One of the KGB surveillance cars pulled off to a side road unexpectedly. The Guilshers didn't know where they were going, so they just followed. The KGB surveillance took them right to the restaurant.

At the same time, the KGB could also be quite sophisticated. In 1978, inspectors uncovered an antenna in the chimney of the embassy building. The purpose of the antenna was never dis-covered. Typewriters were examined that year, but the technician did not find any bugs. In fact, the Soviets had begun in 1976 implanting hidden listening devices in IBM Selectric typewriters sent by the State Department to the Moscow embassy and Leningrad consulate for use by diplomats. The bugs, which contained an integrated circuit, would send a burst transmission with data from the keystrokes on the typewriter. Ultimately, sixteen typewriters were bugged and remained undetected for eight years, although none were located in the CIA's Moscow station.[7]

On the street, Guilsher learned to spot surveillance. The large Soviet-made Volga sedan used by the KGB had a V-8 engine with a distinct growl compared with the four-cylinder engine in other cars. John also discovered the smaller surveillance cars, the Zhigulis, often displayed a telltale, small triangle of dirt on the grille, apparently where the brushes at the KGB car wash didn't reach.

Back when he was preparing for the Moscow assignment at CIA headquarters, Guilsher had seen the first note handed to Fulton by the Russian man at the gas station. He thought it sounded sincere and not typical of provocateurs or dangles. Later, working in the Moscow station in late 1977 and early 1978, Guilsher translated the notes given to Hathaway by the engineer. Guilsher thought it was unlikely that any of the man's notes had fallen into the hands of the KGB. The man was careful to deliver them only when Hathaway was obscured by trees or a high snowbank.

Now they knew his name was Adolf Tolkachev. But what did he really want? Guilsher would find out. He was chosen to be Tolkachev's first CIA case officer.

On March 5, 1978, four days after Tolkachev had given the package to Hathaway, John and Kissa Guilsher went to the Bolshoi Theatre for a ballet performance of *Anna Karenina*, choreographed by the famed ballerina Maya Plisetskaya. They dressed up for the occasion and sat in a box for diplomats. Kissa knew John had something to do that night, and when they sat down, she was surprised to discover that sitting next to her in the box was a Soviet woman who worked in the embassy, dispatching maids, drivers, and helpers. Her name was Galina, a slight, thin woman with dark hair whom Kissa knew well and believed to be working for the KGB.[8]

John had told Kissa that at intermission he would go make a phone call. He would be free from surveillance for a few minutes, he thought, and he had already staked out the phone booth. As soon as the lights went up, he excused himself.

When John got up, Galina saw him, and she started to rise out of her seat, too. Kissa had to think fast. "Where are you going?" she asked. Galina said she was going to the ladies' room. Kissa then tried to talk her out of it. There would be big crowds during intermission, she said. "Who wants to mingle with them?" It worked; Galina agreed it would be better to wait a few minutes.

The delay was just enough time for John to reach the pay phone and call Tolkachev.

Guilsher decided to follow Tolkachev's instructions and introduce himself as Nikolai. He needed to reassure Tolkachev that the proper people had received all the materials that Tolkachev had provided and that the United States was interested in learning more. But it had to be done in a way that could not be detected if someone was listening to the call.[9]

Standing at the phone booth, Guilsher made the call at about 10:00 p.m.

Tolkachev: Allo.

Guilsher: Hello, this is Nikolai.

Tolkachev: (*Slight pause.*) Yes, hello.

Guilsher: Finally I have reached you. I have received all your

letters, thank you. They were very interesting. I will want
to recontact you again later.

Tolkachev: You should be aware that on the 9th I'm going on
temporary assignment to Ryazan, on Saturdays it might be
difficult to reach me, it is best to call on Sunday like this.

*(A pause. Tolkachev was apparently ready to say something else
but did not.)*

Guilsher: See you soon. Goodbye.

Tolkachev: Goodbye.[10]

Guilsher went back to his seat in the theater and sat down.
Kissa looked at him: *You okay?*

Yes, he nodded as the curtain went up and the lights dimmed.

Hathaway had bridled at the stand-down. He felt Turner's
order to stop operations in Moscow was wrongheaded and costly.
Certainly, the tantalizing first contact with Tolkachev suggested
they should resume full espionage operations. In March, a crisis erupted involving Alexei Kulak, the overweight KGB officer
who had been abandoned because of the stand-down. A message
from headquarters informed Hathaway that Kulak, then living
in Moscow, might face arrest and could be exposed as a spy for
the United States. Hathaway felt a special obligation to Kulak,
whom he had personally recruited in a New York hotel room.
The problem, headquarters reported, was that a new book, just
published by the author Edward Jay Epstein, contained enough
details to pinpoint Kulak as an American agent. If the KGB followed up on details in the book and arrested him, Kulak would
certainly face charges of treason, punishable by death. Headquarters decided that Kulak must be contacted and warned of
the breach. A high-risk operation was hastily put together to
spirit Kulak out of the Soviet Union, if necessary. Despite his
misgivings about Moscow operations, and despite the stand-
down, Turner approved the mission to warn Kulak.[11]

To carry it out, Hathaway would have to evade KGB surveillance at all costs. Once a week, Hathaway's secretary had set a familiar pattern of going ice-skating with her husband. Hathaway put on a disguise to look like his secretary, complete with a mask, and left the compound posing as her, with her ice skates in his lap and her husband driving. The militiamen at the gate didn't notice. Once the car was far enough away from the gate, he ripped off the mask and, filled with anxiety, leaped out of the car. He didn't know what to expect. When he saw all was quiet, he began a long, winding surveillance detection run for several hours on a cold Moscow night. His plan was to offer Kulak an escape from the Soviet Union, known as exfiltration. Hathaway carried a camera in order to get a recent photograph of Kulak for a new passport. In fact, the Moscow station had never before carried out an exfiltration. Such operations required months of planning, and Hathaway had only days.

After hours of walking the Moscow streets to make sure he was free from surveillance, Hathaway climbed the steps of Kulak's building, planning to knock on the door. But a *dezhurnaya*, a female attendant, was sitting there, and she stopped Hathaway. He turned around and left, forced to abort the operation. The next night, he made another attempt and called Kulak on a pay phone from the street. Kulak immediately recognized Hathaway's distinctive southern Virginia drawl. Hathaway delivered the news about the breach, and Kulak responded quietly, without hesitation or a sense of fear. He thanked Hathaway for the effort but said he would be fine and did not want to be smuggled out of the country. There was nothing more Hathaway could do. Hathaway and the CIA had lost Kulak as an intelligence source.[12]

Despite the setback, Hathaway was eager to move ahead with Tolkachev. On March 21, 1978, he sent a cable to headquarters suggesting they move at "full speed." At the start, he proposed to "pull together a basic commo package which we can first put down black," meaning by a case officer who was not under KGB surveillance. Then the CIA would telephone Tolkachev and tell him where to pick it up. The package would give Tolkachev a basic means to send messages back and forth to the CIA, allowing them to probe deeper into what he knew and what he might be able to give them. Inside the package, Hathaway proposed to include an operations note, known as an ops note, providing Tolkachev instructions on what to do next. Hathaway felt a personal meeting was the fastest way to get answers, and he very much wanted a personal meeting. But it was also the riskiest way.[13] More than one uncertainty hung over the plan. The station did not yet know much about their agent, what he wanted, or what he could do.[14]

In a reflective cable to headquarters, Hathaway wrote of Tolkachev,

> Obviously, his demands or preconditions will have bearing on our choices in how to handle operation. Does he wish to exchange info for money? One time or indefinitely and continuously? Is exfiltration a demand? Non-negotiable? By when? In sum, without first knowing just what he has in view, it will be difficult to make detailed or long-run plans for him. Our impression, however, is that despite his "Belenko" remark, he is thinking about passing info over a period of time, wants a camera to maximize his productivity, and is eager to establish ongoing long-term relationship. Thus, while we must be prepared to be flexible until we learn just what CKSPHERE's terms are, we feel our best bet for now is to proceed with plans for

straightforward ongoing communication with motivated agent whose needs can be reasonably and effectively satisfied. At the same time, we would try to learn early on what CKSPHERE's needs are, and make necessary adjustments of plans to satisfy them.[15]

In the same message, Hathaway also raised the question of whether to issue a CIA miniature camera to Tolkachev at this early stage in an operation. A camera could make it easier for him to copy documents, but there were serious dangers if caught. A spy camera could easily incriminate him. "When do we give him one, and what kind do we give him?" Hathaway asked headquarters. "Obviously, the sooner we give CKSPHERE a photo capability, and thereby the means to deliver bulk intel, the sooner we can resolve the bona fides question"—a reference to the CIA's need for Tolkachev to prove his credentials.

But headquarters remained reluctant. Hathaway was instructed to use "as simple an approach as possible." For now, there would be no document camera nor a personal meeting.

A cable from headquarters on March 24 acknowledged that the intelligence Tolkachev had provided so far "goes beyond what the Soviets would pass to us if this were a controlled case," or a dangle. That was good news; at least Tolkachev's information had passed the first hurdle. The CIA's usual approach to testing the bona fides of an unknown source would be to check any *new* information and look for that which could be confirmed by what was already known from other sources. However, Tolkachev's notes contained intelligence so new that it could not be verified. It might be a windfall, but it might be a trap; the question could not be easily resolved.[16]

Hathaway had no choice but to take it slowly, one step at a time. He and Guilsher put together a new plan. The main purpose would be to clear up the uncertainty about the agent's true identity and access and secondarily to see what more he could obtain in "positive intelligence," the agency's jargon for the fruits of spying. Hathaway and Guilsher wrote that they hoped to set up the communications with Tolkachev "in such a way as to minimize risk to us" but at the same time "we wish to reduce risk to CKSPHERE to the bare minimum consistent with our own protection." They added, "Unfortunately, here we confront a tradeoff: what is safest for us may be most risky for him, and vice versa. What we are looking for, then, is optimum balance of protection to both ourselves and agent."[17]

Still, headquarters was stubbornly doubtful. An internal review at Langley on April 13 again was cautious, warning that even if Tolkachev's initial approach the year before had been genuine, he might have been noticed by the KGB during his attempts to contact the CIA. He could be carrying out a KGB deception operation, designed to fool the Americans. The review concluded there was only a 50 percent chance that the Tolkachev operation was valid. Such a conclusion was a big red flag for the CIA leadership that made it even harder for Hathaway to proceed.

Turner, the CIA director, was briefed on May 7. Two days later, in Moscow, Guilsher called Tolkachev and told him to wait for two or three more weeks and that after that he'd be needed for about an hour on the appointed day. Tolkachev said he had no plans for vacation.

He would wait.

Then, in May 1978, headquarters began to see things in a more favorable light. One of Tolkachev's handwritten notes was passed to the CIA's Office of Technical Service for analysis by handwriting experts. The experts observed, "The writer is intelligent, purposeful, and generally self-confident. He is self-disciplined but not overly rigid. He has well above average intelligence and has a good organizing ability. He is observant and conscientious and pays meticulous attention to details. He is quite self-assured and may plow ahead at times in a way which is not discreet or subtle. All in all, he is a reasonable, well-adjusted individual and appears intellectually and psychologically equipped to become a useful, versatile asset."[18]

On May 17, headquarters sent a cable to the Moscow station that contained a far more positive evaluation of the Tolkachev material. The CIA's analysts found nothing to contradict what Tolkachev had passed them so far. The evaluation concluded that "many of the details in the reports agree with data from other sources and available technical analysis" and "there do not appear to be any other data which conflict with details in the reports." So, the cable went on, headquarters was feeling "a strong temptation" to accept the new information Tolkachev had provided, not the least because it tended to confirm their own previous speculation about Soviet fighter developments. But at the same time, doubts at headquarters lingered. The cable reported, "Since the data would have a major impact on our assessments of air defense capabilities, we are resisting, at least until bona fides are established, the temptations to accept in toto the contents of the reports."[19]

It was progress—but still not a green light for the kind of operation Hathaway wanted to carry out. He was impatient. Nearly a year and a half had already gone by since Tolkachev's first approach at the gas station, and they still did not have a working relationship with him.

With Guilsher and others in the station, Hathaway began planning what they would give the agent in their first package. If there was to be a list of intelligence questions, how should they be phrased so they would not appear too blunt? Where to put down the package so it could easily be retrieved by Tolkachev but not discovered by the KGB? What should Tolkachev do in response?

The Moscow station planned to use a dead drop, the classic impersonal exchange. Inside the package would be instructions for preparing three letters in "secret writing" to the CIA. On one side of the letter—the "cover" side—the CIA had penned what would appear to be a letter from an excited Western tourist, in a flowery and feminine handwriting. "Dear Gramps," it began. "Zounds! I can't really believe it. But here I am in Russia! Thank you, thank you—a million times thank you for convincing Mikey and me to include Russia on our itinerary. It is absolutely fantastic." But on the reverse or "secret" side, Tolkachev was told, he could use concealed writing, answering the CIA's questions and providing more intelligence. The secret writing was imprinted by use of a specially treated carbon paper that the CIA provided to Tolkachev. After writing on the secret side of the "Dear Gramps" letter, Tolkachev was told to fold it up and put it in the regular mail in Moscow, to an overseas address that looked innocuous but was in fact controlled by the CIA. If all went according to plan, the secret writing would be invisible if the KGB opened the letter, but it could be deciphered by the CIA when the letter was received.

Hathaway also insisted on giving Tolkachev a onetime pad. This is a chart of numbers, randomly keyed to letters, that would allow Tolkachev to encrypt his secret writing. It could only be decrypted by someone with the same pad; the CIA would have the other one. It would be used once and discarded.[20]

On June 1, 1978, headquarters approved Hathaway's plan. The dead drop would contain the secret-writing instructions, intelligence questions, and an ops note. This was to be the CIA's first real communication with Tolkachev, and drafts were sent back and forth between the station and headquarters, revised and polished for weeks. The ops note began,

Finally, the moment has come when we can share our thoughts and plans with you, and to take the first steps in arranging what we hope will be a long and mutually beneficial relationship. First of all, we are very thankful that you contacted us and wish to apologize for having taken so long to respond in a more definitive manner to your numerous and well thought out attempts to establish this contact. We were very glad that you, displaying great sensitivity, understood what was required to convince us of your sincerity. We deeply respect your courage and decisiveness in transmitting to us the necessary information about yourself and your work, and your excellent sample of valuable and interesting materials. All this has allowed us to begin working on a plan for future continuous communications with you.[21]

On August 24, 1978, Tolkachev's materials were secreted in an oversized, dirty mitten like that used by construction workers around Moscow. At 9:15 that evening, Guilsher went out in his car and drove around for a bit, parked it, and took the mitten with him, riding the Metro until he was in Tolkachev's neighborhood. He stashed the mitten behind a telephone booth on a lane just off Krasnaya Presnya, a square with a large Metro station close to Tolkachev's building.

Then Guilsher, from the phone booth, called Tolkachev at home.

Tolkachev: Allo.
Guilsher: Adolf?
Tolkachev: Yes.
Guilsher: This is Nikolai. Do you have a free half hour to leave the house?
Tolkachev: Yes.
Guilsher: Then depart your building, go towards the rear of

the building, pass a Metro on your right and another on
your left, and follow the main road—

Tolkachev: Oh, you mean Krasnaya Presnya?

Guilsher: Yes, proceed to the street called Trekhgornaya.

Tolkachev: You know, I have lived here a long time but I
don't know all the streets here.

Guilsher: It will be the second street, possibly the third, to the
left. Once you turn left into Trekhgornaya you will notice
a phone booth on your right. I have left a package in . . . a
glove for you behind this booth.

Tolkachev: Good, I will go at once.

Guilsher: I hope to hear from you soon, goodbye.[22]

Guilsher then left the site in the direction he expected Tolkachev to approach from. He saw a figure that matched previous descriptions of Tolkachev walking toward the phone booth.
Guilsher slipped away. In his cable recounting the conversation,
he said he "got the impression" that Tolkachev "was alone when
he openly spoke about how to get to the site." In previous calls,
Tolkachev had been much more circumspect.

Guilsher also noted that Tolkachev sounded like a "layman"
and "definitely not" a member of the KGB. Tolkachev followed
instructions to signal the CIA that he had received the construction mitten.

In September, the "Dear Gramps" letters arrived successfully
from Tolkachev. All three showed signs of having been opened by
the KGB, but the secret writing had gone undetected. The letters
squelched any doubts at headquarters. Each carried encrypted
material, largely technical in nature, responding to the CIA's
questions with information that was consistent both with earlier
intelligence and with Tolkachev's claims of access to top secret
documents. The letters included intelligence on a new Soviet
airborne radar and guidance system, the results of performance

tests of new Soviet aircraft radar systems, and the status of work on weapons-aiming equipment for various Soviet aircraft.[23]

The secret writing and onetime pad had been executed perfectly. The CIA realized that they were dealing with an organized, precise person who followed instructions, a genuine volunteer with great potential.

Tolkachev also sent them a tantalizing hint: he had a ninety-one-page notebook crammed full of information he wanted to deliver.

With the arrival of the secret-writing letters, the CIA had successfully carried out a clandestine exchange with the agent, but it was cumbersome, and they still lacked a long-term plan for communications. Hathaway was eager to press ahead. He wanted to end the stand-down once and for all. He proposed to headquarters that they carry out a personal meeting, a method that would allow the CIA to examine more deeply what the agent could do and what he wanted.

In a cable to headquarters, Hathaway and Guilsher proposed repeating the August routine with the construction mitten: calling Tolkachev, but this time meeting him by the telephone booth. They would ask him to bring the notebook. Guilsher would conduct a walking meeting with Tolkachev and stroll toward the Moscow River. A big advantage was that the area was dark and fairly deserted at night.[24] On November 4, headquarters came around to Hathaway's suggestion of a personal meeting, "the primary purpose of which is to find out just who CKSPHERE is, what precisely he wants, and to negotiate the terms, means and general parameters of our continued cooperation." Turner approved the plan on November 21. This effectively marked the end of the stand-down, more than a year after it began.

The hope was that a meeting would lead to a long-term channel for keeping in touch with Tolkachev, but Hathaway still faced difficulties. Guilsher was being subjected to increased sur-

veillance, and he might not be available for the personal meeting. The Moscow station also wanted to provide more detailed
questions for Tolkachev, and headquarters agreed. Much would
depend on how Tolkachev answered the questions, which probed
his living and job situations, family, privacy at home and work,
vacation plans, hobbies, security, health, whether he owned a
camera and a radio, access to classified documents, description of
his office desk, what equipment he worked on, names of supervi-
sors, and what journals he had access to.

Finally, they were almost ready. A last step was to inform the
U.S. ambassador, Malcolm Toon. The ambassador didn't like the
idea. If the meeting blew up, it could be embarrassing.

But Hathaway persuaded him it was necessary.

# 5

# "A DISSIDENT AT HEART"

On New Year's Day 1979, Moscow was locked in the grip of a frigid cold wave. Windows frosted over, cars would not start, and the streets were nearly deserted. John Guilsher noticed that KGB surveillance had almost completely disappeared, perhaps because of the holiday and the numbing cold. He decided this would be the day. From their apartment, John and Kissa drove their daughter Anya to a birthday party at the U.S. embassy compound. When it was over, about 5:30 p.m., with the city already shrouded in darkness, they headed home. Not far from the apartment, they stopped the car. John silently got out from behind the wheel and disappeared down a narrow lane. As he left the car, he was dressed in a plain overcoat and fur hat, looking like a Russian pensioner, unremarkable in the night. Kissa drove home.

Guilsher boarded a bus and then got off at a Metro stop close to Tolkachev's apartment, the same location where they had placed the construction mitten in August. He examined the broad, open area and saw no one watching him. His radio earpiece, set to monitor any transmissions from the KGB, was quiet. Guilsher went to a phone booth and placed a call to Tolkachev. Guilsher introduced himself as "Nikolai" and asked Tolkachev to come "at once" and bring "the materials." Fifteen minutes later, Tolkachev appeared.

He was neatly dressed, somewhat shorter than Guilsher, with a long oval face, slightly jutting jaw, a rugged appearance, and a few gold or silver teeth. Calm and disciplined, Tolkachev did not look around nervously. He kept to the subject they were discussing and answered questions clearly.

When Guilsher asked if he brought the notebook, Tolkachev slipped it out of his coat. Normally, Guilsher carried a briefcase, but he left it at home, thinking that on a holiday it would look out of place. Guilsher tucked the notebook under his belt and felt the sting of icy air on his midriff.

Then he asked Tolkachev the question that had nagged at them all: What was his motive for taking such a big risk? Tolkachev replied, hesitantly, that it was a complex question, one that would require a lot of time to discuss.

Guilsher prodded him again. Why?

Tolkachev responded only that he was "a dissident at heart."

Then Tolkachev had a question for Guilsher. He wanted to know how much the United States had paid Belenko, the MiG-25 pilot who defected to Japan in 1976. Guilsher had anticipated the question. He said he didn't know how much Belenko had been paid but offered Tolkachev 1,000 rubles a month for his cooperation. Tolkachev asked Guilsher for 10,000 rubles for his work so far. Guilsher said it would be no problem and gave Tolkachev 1,000 rubles. It was a ridiculously small sum, perhaps three times the monthly salary of a mid-career Soviet academic, while the intelligence Tolkachev had already provided was worth tens of millions of dollars to the United States. Guilsher gave Tolkachev some additional questions to answer next time they met.[1]

Guilsher cautioned Tolkachev that money had often been the

undoing of agents. He recalled the 1977 arrests of two agents in Moscow, which had been written about in the newspapers, saying it was because of money. This was stretching the truth—they were arrested for other reasons—but Guilsher thought it might give Tolkachev second thoughts. Besides, Guilsher said, there was not much to buy in Moscow, which was plagued by shortages. Tolkachev acknowledged the risk, saying he would be careful and sensible. He told Guilsher his family did not really need more money. He could explain any cash as part of an inheritance from his mother, who had died recently. Guilsher got the distinct impression that Tolkachev wanted money as a sign of respect, to show that his efforts were valued.

The streets were empty as they walked, two men in overcoats, speaking quietly, enveloped in Russia's winter darkness. Their words were terse and to the point. Guilsher, who had never before been a case officer on the street, wanted to get it right. He asked Tolkachev if he had a private office where he could use a camera to photograph documents. No, Tolkachev said, but if he had a camera that was relatively quiet, he could probably linger at the office at the end of the workday, perhaps for twenty or thirty minutes until the doors were locked, and photograph documents. Guilsher was impressed with the answer; it showed Tolkachev knew his limits and how not to raise suspicions. Tolkachev said a camera would relieve him from writing up so much by hand. Guilsher promised to deliver a camera soon.

Tolkachev said he had absolutely no privacy in his apartment. The family telephone was in the kitchen, and his wife or son often answered. There were only two other rooms. He confessed he had spent hours waiting by the phone for "Nikolai" to call. When he needed to work in private on the ninety-one-page notebook, he had retreated to the Lenin Library, the largest public library in Moscow, hunching over the notebook for hours, alone.

For forty minutes, they walked and talked in the biting cold. Guilsher sensed it was time to part. They shook hands, and Tolkachev disappeared into the night.

Guilsher took the bus toward home, the notebook still tucked into his belt. He uttered not a word about the meeting to Kissa and went to bed with the notebook under his mattress. The next day, he carried it to the station. The first thing he did was send a cable to headquarters that the meeting had come off without surveillance and that he had given Tolkachev 1,000 rubles and additional questions. Guilsher wrote, "There were no untoward incidents. CKSPHERE handed over 91 pages of what I think will be invaluable intelligence."[2]

Then, in a longer cable, Guilsher described the meeting. Guilsher said he was "highly impressed by the coolness and professional behavior" of Tolkachev. "On a day when the average Soviet was somewhat inebriated, he appeared to be absolutely sober," Guilsher wrote. Tolkachev had allowed Guilsher to steer the direction of their conversation and appeared to accept him "as an expert in whose hands he placed his future safety."

As case officer, Guilsher's entire focus was on the operational details, such as communications, meetings, and planning. The "positive intelligence," the information about Soviet military radars and other matters contained in Tolkachev's ninety-one-page handwritten notebook, was rushed directly to headquarters, where it was translated and carefully analyzed.

Immediately, headquarters had reservations about the money, unsettled by the prospect of Guilsher delivering wads of cash. What Guilsher had told Tolkachev was certainly true: a trail of money had often led agents to be careless and cause their own downfalls. Guilsher reassured headquarters on January 22 that Tolkachev was "keenly aware" of the dangers and agreed to warn him again at their next meeting. During the walk, Guilsher said, he raised with Tolkachev the possibility of a hard-currency escrow account in his name in the West. This would be safer, but

Tolkachev brushed it off, saying he would never have any use for it. Guilsher urged headquarters not to renege on the 10,000 rubles he had promised. They still had to earn Tolkachev's trust. "At this point, we feel it is essential to live up to our arrangement and pass him the requested sums," he wrote to headquarters. By delivering the money promptly, he added, "we hope to instill in him a complete trust in us and, once he is confident we will live up to our part of the bargain, we can begin to probe delicately to try to resolve this ticklish topic." Guilsher suggested they wait six months before bringing it up again.

The first meeting touched off a flurry of activity. Now, at last, the Moscow station was back in the espionage business. Every action of human intelligence collection—putting down a dead drop, such as the construction mitten with secret writing hidden inside, or making a call from a phone, or writing an operations note to an agent, or preparing sites for meetings and signals—demanded intense preparation by the station and frequent cables back and forth to headquarters. Running a spy was undertaken with the concentration and attention to detail of a moon shot: neither the station nor headquarters wanted to leave anything to chance; not even the smallest nut or bolt could be out of place. Photographs and maps were prepared of each site; surveillance detection runs plotted; scenarios scripted and rehearsed; and the question was asked again and again: *What could go wrong?*

Guilsher had to speak up for the agent in the back-and-forth with headquarters; become a friend and confessor to the agent; serve as the agent's adviser and protector; provide equipment, training, money, and feedback; become the trusted face of the CIA and the United States to someone who had never set foot in America—and all of this with a man he hardly knew. Every case officer worked with the realization that no agent was ever completely knowable. They behaved in unpredictable ways, often beyond the control of their handlers.

Guilsher's next move was to write a personal letter for a package they would deliver to Tolkachev in February. He drafted the letter in a way that he hoped would be unambiguous, praising Tolkachev as "reliable and calm," expressing confidence that "you will always act sensibly," that "it will be possible to count on you to observe the instructions" in the communications plan, and that "you will calmly fulfill the role that you have chosen."

Then Guilsher shifted tone to that of coach, saying that Tolkachev must strive to "not attract attention in any way." He explained, "One has to look and behave like the average person on the street; in the office, not to show too much interest in the work of others, not to request materials from the first department which are not connected with your work and not to work late too often, i.e., stay in the office by yourself." The First Department was the repository in Soviet research institutes for top secret documents and also a security office for keeping watch on workers and controlling clearances for access to the secret materials. Further, Guilsher instructed, "In your private life it is important to establish a pattern of life that will cover our contacts and will not arouse suspicion at home. Mainly, it is necessary to act calmly and not to rush."

Guilsher appealed to Tolkachev to "share with me, at any time, any thoughts which you cannot discuss with your wife and friends." He urged the spy to speak up if there was anything that worried him. He closed the letter, "I shake your hand, Nikolai."[3]

On February 17, 1979, Guilsher went on a surveillance detection run and, free from the KGB, laid down a package for Tolkachev to pick up. Once again, the package was hidden in the dirty construction mitten. This time it contained one miniature camera, known as a Molly, a light meter, film, camera instructions, an operations note, the personal letter from Guilsher, an evaluation note from CIA headquarters, further questions or "requirements" from the CIA, a communications plan, and 5,000 rubles, or half what Tolkachev had requested for his work so far.

The evaluation was upbeat but not specific, saying the secret-writing letters had been prepared with "fine technique" and the information "very well received." The ninety-one-page January notebook showed "painstaking effort and dedication," and the CIA was "very impressed," but the evaluation stopped short of details, except for one.

Tolkachev was given a very specific request: to obtain any information he could about a radar known as the RP-23. This would be "of utmost value."

In March, a cable from the Moscow station to headquarters noted that Tolkachev was now "fully operational." But the CIA's agent and his case officer were still finding their way.

Guilsher had instructed Tolkachev on the procedure for confirming an impromptu meeting. Under the plan, the CIA provided Tolkachev with a set of quick meeting sites, locations that were close to his apartment building. Each was given a Russian code name, such as NINOCHKA. The plan was that Guilsher would call Tolkachev's home phone and ask for "Ninochka," signaling a desire to meet at that site. If he could come on short notice, Tolkachev would say the caller must have a wrong number and hang up—then go out the door.

However, when Guilsher made the first phone call one day in February, asking for "Ninochka," Tolkachev made an error. "Is this Nikolai calling?" he said.

That wasn't the right answer. Guilsher hung up.[4]

Guilsher tried again on the evening of April 4, asked for "Valery," and this time it worked. Tolkachev was out the door quickly. They met for fifteen minutes at site VALERY and traded packages. Tolkachev gave Guilsher five cassettes of exposed eighty-frame film from the Molly miniature camera, fifty-six

pages of handwritten materials, including a long letter to the
CIA, and four sketches.[5]

Seven days later, headquarters sent Hathaway and Guilsher a
hint that Tolkachev's material was impressive. "You will be interested to know," the cable said, "that the material from the January package" had been formally distributed "in a document over
100 pages in length" and "initial reaction from the Air Force is
highly enthusiastic, and the material is clearly having a significant impact." In fact, the January notebook had contained a rich
harvest of secrets. Tolkachev had included a detailed description
of the sensitive work in which he was involved, as well as exact
formulas, diagrams, drawings, and specifications of weapons
and electronic systems. He copied by hand top secret documents
authorizing the construction of new types of aircraft not yet
known in the West, such as the Sukhoi Su-27 advanced fighter.
He had carefully drawn various diagrams on oversized graph
paper. Every document was neatly recorded, every word legible. The notebook contained vital details about aircraft design,
speed, radio frequencies, weapons, avionics, radars—a look at
blueprints still on the drawing boards, and a glimpse of planes
that would not be flying for a decade.[6]

Guilsher's two meetings with Tolkachev had been productive,
but the men had not engaged in the kind of free-flowing conversation that would reveal Tolkachev's motives or thinking in
any depth. Guilsher was hungry for more. In the long letter Tolkachev handed to him on April 4, there were tantalizing hints
that Tolkachev was a strong and unwavering personality, a person who took the long view. In the letter, Tolkachev laid out a
plan to spy for the United States for twelve years in seven stages.
He described what materials he would provide and when. It was

an extraordinary blueprint and a declaration of his seriousness. Tolkachev said his goal was to damage the Soviet Union to the maximum extent possible. "I have selected a course which does not permit me to move backwards and I have no intention of veering from this course," he wrote. "Since I have tasked myself with passing the maximum amount of information, I do not intend to stop halfway."[7]

Another clue to his personality, Guilsher saw, was Tolkachev's stubborn and determined effort to contact an American, which he now revealed in some detail to the CIA in his long letter. "The idea to pass a note by a car or in a car did not come at once," he wrote. "At first I tried to find out if it was possible to establish communications at exhibits in which the USA participated. This turned out to be difficult since the exhibits are relatively rare and there are always many people present." Then he went on solitary walks around central Moscow. He had spotted a car with the license plate D-04-526, the "04" indicating it was driven by Americans. This led him to decide to make contact by sliding a note through an open car window or talking to the driver. "At first," Tolkachev recalled, "I naively thought that it is only necessary to select a convenient moment, to come up to the car, to request a conversation, and that I will be welcomed with open arms." He added, "I started to search for a place where one could approach a car. Thus started my purposeful walks along the streets of Moscow and along Devyatinsky Lane that lasted many days and many hours." This was the small street along the edge of the embassy compound where he had approached Hathaway.

Tolkachev had memorized a few sentences in English, just in case he encountered an American. Finally, he saw the car with the D-04-526 license plate at the gas station on Krasina Ulitsa, a street just blocks from his apartment building, on that cold evening in January 1977. "The moment was suitable," he recalled, "deserted, at that moment there were no Soviet and no socialist bloc cars at the gas station." He approached Fulton and repeated the English phrases he had memorized, including the question he asked Fulton, "Are you American? I would like to talk to you." On hearing Fulton's rebuff, "I passed a note and quickly departed."

After dropping the note, Tolkachev recalled, he expected events to unfold rapidly, but nothing happened for months. He kept trying, over and over again, but was getting nowhere. The more Guilsher learned of Tolkachev's story, the more he could sense this was a driven man. What propelled him was not yet entirely clear, but Tolkachev was not a casual walk-in. He was dogged and resolute.

Tolkachev also displayed an engineer's exactitude. In his letter to the CIA, he wrote a precise account of how secret documents were handled at his institute. He drew hand sketches to illustrate it. Secret documents were kept in the First Departments, in two separate buildings—Tolkachev called them buildings one and two, located "on sketch four." He described how an employee could receive a secret document at any time during the working day and keep it all day. The document would have to be returned by 5:00 p.m. "As a result," he added, "it is possible to leave the institute for one and a half or two hours during the course of the day with a secret document. This must of course be done illegally, for example under an overcoat, raincoat, or suit jacket. Naturally only documents of small size can be taken out in this manner." It was prohibited to bring a briefcase into the building, and shopping bags were checked at random, but often. A separate, classified library held the top secret scientific studies and dissertations, Tolkachev wrote. "I can make use of all the materials in the secret library." Thus, both the First Department and the library held classified materials.

Tolkachev had identified a gaping hole in the security cordon.

He could simply walk out of the institute with the documents in his coat pocket.

Guilsher had twice used dead drops to communicate with the spy, but now he learned that Tolkachev's patience was running thin. Tolkachev said it was getting hard to explain at home why he had to run out after each phone call. Tolkachev appealed to Guilsher, saying that "psychologically" it would be better for him if they just accepted the risk and met each other periodically in person, not fooling around by stashing a dirty construction mitten behind a phone booth, where it might be found by a stranger. This was another sign of Tolkachev's unflinching personality. If he was going to risk his life in espionage, he wanted to know and meet the person for whom he was putting himself in such danger. The impersonal dead drop gave him no chance for such contact.

Then Tolkachev made one more request. He asked the CIA for a lethal cyanide pill, to commit suicide in case he was discovered. This was known at the CIA as an L-pill. The *L* stood for "lethal." The L-pill had been issued to Ogorodnik two years earlier, and he used it to commit suicide soon after his arrest. Guilsher realized that winning CIA headquarters' approval for supplying one to Tolkachev was going to be very difficult. There were always fears at headquarters that an agent would panic and take the suicide pill unnecessarily or that it would be discovered and betray the spy. On May 1, headquarters cabled, "As we have on previous occasions, we would like to stall on this question." The cable suggested it would be best for Guilsher to deflect the request in person at the next meeting with Tolkachev.[8] Guilsher wrote back on May 4 that he agreed, and "every effort will be made to stall on this question."[9] On May 7, headquarters offered Guilsher "talking points" to discourage Tolkachev:

A. The mental burden of having this
   item on his person at all times.
B. The problem of concealment.
C. The risk of premature use of the item through
   misjudgment of an actual situation.
D. The possession of this item closes all
   options available in case of apprehension by
   authorities, even for extraneous reasons.[10]

Guilsher now had a sketchy impression of Tolkachev: someone who was committed to espionage, had access to secret documents, with the organized and precise mind-set of an engineer.
But Tolkachev's requests and desires would test the outer bounds
of espionage in Moscow. The CIA felt that the personal meetings
that Tolkachev wanted were the riskiest method of all; just being
seen with a foreigner on the street could spell trouble if spotted
by a trained KGB surveillance team. Tolkachev's demands for
more money were unsettling. His "special request," the L-pill,
carried the risk of a fatal misjudgment.

Still, Guilsher concluded that Tolkachev was a solid, straightforward person, someone they could work with.

# 6

# SIX FIGURES

In his long April letter to the CIA, Tolkachev wrote disdain-fully of Soviet ideology and public life. He said that politics, literature, and philosophy had been "enmeshed for a long time in such an impassable, hypocritical demagoguery" and "ideological empty talk" that he tried to ignore them. Tolkachev said he hadn't been to a theater in a long time. Although he enjoyed classics, contemporary Soviet plays were "full of ideological gibberish." It was a common attitude. On the street, the party's grand declarations were etched into the concrete facades of Metro stations and factory gates, giant banners of self-congratulations. But to most Soviet citizens of the late 1970s, the promises of a bright communist future were long forgotten. These were the years of stagnation. The Soviet Union devoted such enormous resources to the arms race that its economy sputtered out only the most shoddy goods for consumers. Shortages were frequent and annoying. People waited in lines for hours to get shoes or a winter coat. Tolkachev's high-rise apartment building at 1 Ploshchad Vosstaniya, one of Moscow's seven distinctive, spired towers, had been constructed in 1955 with four high-ceilinged food shops at the street level, one on each corner for meat, fish, dairy, and bread. Modeled on an elegant turn-of-the-century Russian gastronome in Moscow, the four shops were resplendent with red-and-white inlaid marble, floor-to-ceiling windows, luminescent chandeliers, and mighty central columns. The goods had never been bountiful, but in the years after the shops were built it was possible to just walk in and find smoked fish and sausage. By 1979, the stores were in decay, the shelves nearly empty. Theoretically, the Soviet state provided for almost everything—medical care, schooling, transportation, work. But the system was rotting from within. The shortages forced many people to deal in a vast shadow economy, struggling to survive through friends and connections, always on the lookout for a tin of meat, some good tea, or a delivery of shoes.[1]

Tolkachev's work at the institute offered him some privileges that buffered the misery and drudgery. Once a week, he was entitled to purchase a *zakaz*, a modest food ration distributed at the office, perhaps a can of instant coffee, or scarce tea, and maybe even a smoked sausage. But he was not part of the pampered elite. He did not belong to the Communist Party, kept to himself, and had become something of an ascetic. He did not own a car, nor a country house, or dacha, when he first volunteered to the CIA. He was at the mercy of the shadow economy for such things as medicine and clothing. On weekends or after work, he and his wife would search for goods in stores and markets. In a small crawl space in his apartment he hoarded building materials—boards, plywood, and pipes for small projects. He enjoyed working with his hands; he repaired his own radio and television. For relaxation, he much preferred camping trips, alone with his family in the rugged wilderness of forests and lakes, over a free pass offered by the institute to a crowded, state-run resort at Sochi on the Black Sea.

When it came to things he wanted, Tolkachev's primary focus

was his son, Oleg, who was fourteen years old in 1979. Tolkachev did everything he could for him. Surrounded by empty shelves in stores, young people in the Soviet Union had developed a hunger for consumer goods. They were influenced by what they learned and heard about the West. They prized rock music and were desperate for a pair of denim jeans. The Soviet central planning system had totally neglected denim jeans and later only came up with cheap imitations. But they could be found in the shadow economy, from street hustlers, or from overseas travelers. Oleg possessed a creative and artistic bent, and he sought out Western rock music.

Tolkachev didn't lack money. He earned 250 rubles a month, plus a 40 percent security bonus, or about 350 rubles. His wife's salary doubled this. At the time, the average Soviet pay was some 120 rubles a month.[2] But money could not buy goods that did not exist. The Russian language has a verb meaning "to get," which was used more commonly at the time than "to buy." What you could get often depended not on money but on connections or on the chance that a scarce thing became available unexpectedly. For a while, there was no tea, and then it would suddenly appear. This was the world that Tolkachev knew, a party-state that congratulated itself on its greatness but that had, over decades, become a dystopia.

When Guilsher read over Tolkachev's April letter, one section stood out. Tolkachev expressed irritation at the CIA's proposals for paying him. Guilsher's offer of 1,000 rubles a month was "distressing," hardly enough, Tolkachev wrote. He wanted much more as a sign of the "significance and the importance of my work and my labor." He promised Guilsher that he would not be reckless. He lamented, "To the present day, I have not felt adequate valuation of my lonely efforts to break down the wall of mistrust, and also the significance of the information reported by me in 1978." Guilsher knew it was true. But he also knew the CIA was right to be cautious. They could lose the spy by rewarding him with cash while his neighbors were stuck in a daily life of shadows and shortages. Even Hathaway, the station chief, had doubts. "What the hell is he going to do with all that money?" Hathaway often asked Guilsher. "Put it up in his attic and sit there with his feet in it?"[3]

Tolkachev, however, was stubborn. He at first asked for 10,000 rubles, and later 40,000 to 50,000 rubles, for the secrets he had already provided.[4] He insisted that in the future he be paid handsomely—in dollars. He demanded at least the same dollar amount as the pilot Belenko had received when he flew the Soviet MiG-25 to Japan in 1976. Tolkachev said he heard on a Voice of America broadcast that it was "six figures."

He, too, wanted six figures.

On May 1, 1979, headquarters sent a cable to Guilsher and Hathaway outlining a new plan for paying Tolkachev a six-figure salary. "We are prepared in principle to offer him a total of $300,000," the cable reported. But because it would be impossible for Tolkachev to store that much cash in Moscow, headquarters proposed putting the money in an interest-bearing account in the West, in either Tolkachev's name or someone else's name, or perhaps opening the account with $100,000 and paying him $50,000 a year for the next four years. The cable raised another possibility. "Since money is obviously not the only motivation, i.e., his comments about needing a 'pat on the back,' we wonder if some other form of commendation is not in order," the cable said. "We have in mind perhaps a medal, membership in our organization, and/or a certificate of appreciation ... Would any of these 'rewards' be psychologically effective to our cause?"[5] When Guilsher drafted the ops note he would give Tolkachev at their next meeting, set for June, he made sure to include a "well done" pat on the back. But over the next few weeks, the uncertainty deepened at headquarters about giving Tolkachev so much money. On May 18, Turner, the director of central intelligence, who had harbored such deep skepticism about human sources, approved giving Tolkachev $100,000 for his cooperation to date and "as a symbol of our good faith" while spreading payments over five years instead of four. Turner's decision, relayed to Moscow in a cable from headquarters, added a condition: "assuming his production continues."[6]

Guilsher felt all the hand-wringing at headquarters was senseless. Tolkachev had not been a reluctant spy. He had proposed a seven-stage plan for espionage over a dozen years and seemed hell-bent on carrying it out. On May 22, Guilsher shot back to headquarters that the offer "does not dovetail" with Tolkachev's desires. Linking the pay to his continuing production was foolish, he said, "since CKSPHERE's principal motivation is not money." He added that Tolkachev preferred an open-ended arrangement, while the headquarters plan would end after five years. Guilsher suggested that Tolkachev be offered the $100,000 and then $40,000 a year—without conditions.[7] Guilsher hammered away at the financial details, doing everything possible to deepen Tolkachev's trust, on the one hand, and deal with the concerns of headquarters, on the other. Guilsher wrote to Tolkachev in the ops note for their next meeting that the CIA would pay him $300,000, but the agency was worried about how to deliver it and where to put all the money. Guilsher proposed the CIA would open a savings account for Tolkachev in the West, pay him 8.75 percent interest a year, allow him to make withdrawals, and show him the passbook every time they met. Guilsher also suggested compensation by "some sort of valuables" besides money.[8]

In late May 1979, a handful of American intelligence experts, mostly specialists on Soviet weapons systems, gathered for a seminar in Washington in a high-security conference room. The attendees came from the air force, the navy, the CIA, and the Defense Intelligence Agency. They had each read the hundred-page secret report circulated in April describing the materials in Tolkachev's handwritten notebook passed to Guilsher on that freezing-cold New Year's Day.

The time had come to address the hard question: Was Tolkachev's information genuine? The purpose of the seminar was to scrub his material for any signs of disinformation. Two and a half years had passed since Tolkachev's first approach at the Moscow gas station, yet the intelligence agencies and the military still harbored skepticism. If Tolkachev was under the control of the KGB, if his documents were fabricated in order to send the United States off in the wrong direction, it would be calamitous to take the bait. The danger was certainly real; the KGB had a long history of skillfully using deception, disinformation, and misdirection. The United States had used the same methods against the Soviet Union.[9] At the same time, the United States was eager for insight and intelligence about Soviet military plans and intentions. If Tolkachev's access was real and his documents genuine, the payoff could be handsome: blueprints and research files from the most advanced laboratories in the Soviet military-industrial complex. The United States enjoyed an advantage over the Soviet Union in weapons technology, but there was always a fear of surprise by the other side. The spy could provide early warning about Soviet weapons development years in the future.

After the seminar was over, a brief summary was cabled by headquarters to Guilsher and Hathaway in Moscow. The summary reported that Tolkachev's documents, notes, and drawings offered a revealing glimpse into the long-closed world of Soviet military planning. "All participants reported that they were impressed with the product, to the extent that all checkable information is considered logical," the summary reported. "There is no factual statement that can be refuted. You will be pleased to know that CKSPHERE's product provided the frame to pull together all the bits and pieces of apparent extraneous information collected heretofore so that a complete picture can now be made of Soviet advancement in this particular field. It is estimated that the product has saved us five years of R&D time."[10] The specific field of Soviet "advancement" referred to here is not known precisely but was probably avionics and radars, including "look-down, shoot-down," as this was Tolkachev's area.

At that moment, the Defense Department's annual total budget for research and development, testing, and engineering was more than $12 billion, most of it for the air force and the navy to confront the Soviet threat with new and modernized weapons. By saving five years of spending, Tolkachev, in his first major delivery to Guilsher, had passed documents worth, at least, millions of dollars to the United States, and likely much more. The experts at the seminar were enthusiastic enough to draw up more questions to be passed to Tolkachev at the next meeting.[11] Hathaway recalled that when Tolkachev's materials arrived at headquarters, "People went wild. The military said, good God, where did you get that? Let's have more of it!"

In Moscow, Guilsher was getting ready for the upcoming rendezvous in June. "As you well understand," Guilsher wrote to Tolkachev, "your information is of critical interest to us and the small group of officials, at the highest levels, who are aware of your work, has asked me to extend their highest appreciation for your work, their highest esteem for you personally and an assurance that your product is of the highest value." Guilsher knew that Tolkachev was taking huge risks and reassured him that "your information, due to its very sensitive nature, is receiving very limited distribution under the highest classification and is only seen by the specialists who have the need to see it."[12]

The hundred-page summary of Tolkachev's intelligence had been printed in only seven copies, kept under tight security. The names of those who saw the intelligence were recorded on a registry known as a "bigot list" stored with the reports and requirements staff of the CIA's Soviet division. When it was translated and distributed, the Tolkachev material was often blended with other intelligence from other sources from the Soviet Union, so if there was a leak, Tolkachev could not be fingered as the source.[13] When sending cables from Moscow, the station routinely encrypted them, but in the case of Tolkachev extra precautions were taken. Any identifying information such as names, ages, locations, or physical characteristics in the cables was double encrypted. For example, a mention of Oleg would be changed to Alex before the cable was fully scrambled for transmission to headquarters. At Langley, the cable was unscrambled and the proper names or words put back in. That way, if the KGB had managed to intercept the cable, they still would not have a name or clue leading them to the agent's identity. Only a handful of people at headquarters knew the true identity of CKSPHERE.[14]

On June 6, Guilsher met Tolkachev face-to-face for the third time. When Guilsher spotted him, Tolkachev was wearing a dark tan raincoat with a yellow-and-brown-plaid shirt. After they exchanged paroles—a phrase known only to each of them, such as "Boris sends regards"—Tolkachev gave Guilsher twenty-nine pages of handwritten notes and ten exposed film cassettes from the Molly miniature camera.

When they talked, Guilsher asked about Tolkachev's health, recalling that he mentioned in his April letter that he suffered from leg pains, mostly in his shins, diagnosed as thrombophlebitis. Tolkachev replied there had been a misunderstanding; it was his wife who had the ailment. She had been treated at the local clinic with compresses and some ointment, but Tolkachev wanted to know if the CIA could come up with something more effective. It was just another small glimpse of the world of shadows and shortages in which Tolkachev lived every day. Guilsher gave Tolkachev some advice he'd been sent from headquarters about treatments.[15]

Guilsher then gave Tolkachev the ops note he had written, a list of questions or "requirements" from U.S. experts, a schedule for future meetings, and a Pentax ME single-lens-reflex 35 mm camera and lens for copying documents, with a clamp to fasten it steady to a chair or table. Guilsher went out of his way to explain the details about money: the CIA would maintain a dollar savings account, with interest, and give Tolkachev a "six-figure" salary, as he had requested. Guilsher pointed out that it was better to be paid in dollars than in rubles; the dollars were safe, compared with rubles, which could be lost in periodic currency confiscations and devaluations in the Soviet Union. Tolkachev's reaction was noncommittal. Guilsher observed that Tolkachev always kept his cool. On this day, he was absolutely unreadable.

Tolkachev mentioned to Guilsher, almost as an afterthought, that he didn't know what to do with all the money anyway.

Guilsher handed him another 5,000 rubles. They were together only fifteen minutes.[16]

On June 18, 1979, President Jimmy Carter signed the SALT II strategic arms treaty with the Soviet general secretary, Leonid Brezhnev, at the conclusion of a three-day summit in Vienna. Carter had come into office brimming with idealism about nuclear arms control, but by 1979 all he could manage was a treaty that barely slowed the arms race. During the negotiations for SALT II, the Soviets repeatedly expressed alarm about a new weapon being developed by the United States, the strategic cruise missile, a pilotless projectile carrying a miniature nuclear warhead that could fly high over hostile territory, then swoop down to fifty feet above ground level and steer toward its target with a sophisticated, terrain-sensitive guidance system. The Soviet Union did not have effective radars at low altitude, a gap in air defenses it had simply been unable to close. This vulnerability was one of the most important subjects in Tolkachev's reporting. In a White House meeting during the President Ford years, Undersecretary of Defense William Clements had once informed the president, "Our cruise missile projects drive them up the wall because their defense will not protect them from our cruise missiles, and they know it. Cruise missiles cause them plenty of pain and agony."[17] By the third year of Carter's presidency, the American cruise missile was fast becoming a reality. On July 17, a month after Carter signed the treaty with Brezhnev, a Tomahawk cruise missile successfully flew its first free-flight test by General Dynamics, which was locked in a competition with Boeing to build the new weapons system. The cruise missile didn't fly as fast as an intercontinental ballistic missile, but it was sneaky and nearly unstoppable. Secret tests by the U.S. military, completed in September 1978, showed that current Soviet air defenses were ineffective against it.

Still, there was one nagging uncertainty: What were the Soviets going to do about it?[18]

———

Tolkachev's notes and film from the June 6 meeting with Guilsher were sent back to headquarters. The notes were translated, and by June 25 the details were on the desk of George T. Kalaris, chief of the Soviet division. Kalaris was a tall man with a commanding presence who had spent most of his career in the clandestine service as an operations officer, working in Greece, Indonesia, Laos, the Philippines, and Brazil. He had won special admiration for acquiring a warhead and operational manual for a Soviet SA-2 anti-aircraft missile in Indochina. He knew the perils—and stress—of espionage operations. Later, he had been brought in to clean up the counterintelligence staff after Angleton's reign of paranoia. Then, in 1976, Kalaris was put in charge of the Soviet division. Direct in manner and conversation, he inspired confidence in those who worked with him.[19]

The moment he got the notes from Tolkachev, Kalaris realized they were something extraordinary. Despite all the Soviet complaints about the U.S. cruise missile, Tolkachev reported that Moscow's defense planners and weapons designers had "just started to study the problem" of how to respond.

*Just started?* This would give the United States breathing room and confidence that the weapons system could be effective for years to come. Immediately, Kalaris wrote a note to Turner, the CIA director, and the two deputy directors, describing Guilsher's meeting in Moscow, the handoff of notes, and the ten exposed film cassettes. "CKSPHERE's information continues to receive the highest evaluation," he wrote. In addition to the intelligence on the cruise missile, Tolkachev's notes contained information on a new surface-to-air missile system and confirmed CIA reports that the Soviets were building a new identification system for military units. "All of this will impact upcoming national estimates," Kalaris said, referring to the CIA's most important finished intelligence reports for policy makers in government.[20]

On the document routing sheet, Kalaris asked that his note

be kept out of the regular filing system; the fewer people to see it, the better. He asked that it be hand carried to Turner and the two deputy directors. One of them scribbled a single word on the routing sheet.

"Fabulous."

# 7

# SPY CAMERA

Tolkachev had access to extremely sensitive and secret documents, but it wasn't going to be worth much to the CIA if he could not copy them. At first, he memorized what he saw and wrote the texts by hand into a notebook, but that was not practical for larger quantities over the dozen years he envisioned spying. His ability to copy documents without being detected was the linchpin to everything he and the CIA wanted to accomplish.

The first camera the CIA had given him for copying materials was the miniature Molly, but it was not the CIA's best equipment. Headquarters informed the Moscow station on July 4, 1979, that the ten cassettes passed by Tolkachev to Guilsher were "basically unreadable," except for a handful of legible pages. The reason was poor focus and movement while Tolkachev was holding the tiny camera. This was a frustrating setback, not only for the loss of eight hundred frames of documents, but for the larger doubts it raised about the Tolkachev operation.

Tolkachev could not simply step into a back room at his institute and make photocopies. The Soviet authorities had long feared copiers. At its most basic, the machine helped spread information, and strict control of information was central to the Communist Party's grip on power. In most offices, photocopy machines were kept under lock and key.

"A copying machine is located in a special room and operated by four or five employees," Tolkachev wrote to the CIA of the situation at his workplace. "Entry to the copying room is not allowed to persons not working there." Secret documents would have to be submitted for copying by the First Department, while any worker could send in unclassified documents. But he added, "Before an unclassified document can be submitted to the copying department, an order must be filled out. This form must include a certification by the First Department concerning the classification of the document, i.e., a certification that the document is not classified. In these documents there can be no word or phrase revealing the nature of the enterprise or institute. For example, the First Department would not allow the following sentence: 'The radar station has several work modes.' The sentence would have to be changed to the following form: 'Item 4003 has several work modes.'"[1]

From Tolkachev's note, it was obvious that photocopies were not an option. The CIA would have to rely on cameras and film.

When spying for the CIA and the British in the early 1960s, Penkovsky had relied on the commercially available Minox Model III camera, which was also widely used by the KGB and other intelligence services. The camera was 3.2 inches long, 1.1 inches wide, and only 0.6 inches deep, small enough to fit in the palm of a man's hand with a four-element lens that could focus closely. The Minox was excellent for photographing documents, letters, pages of books, and envelopes but could not be easily used without others noticing. The shutter was noisy; it required two hands and proper lighting—not the best for covert photography.[2]

Penkovsky's arrest was due in part to a lack of sophisticated technology for espionage. After-action reports underscored the absence of effective gear for the operation, particularly in agent communications. "There simply were no suitable devices on Agency shelves for this type of operation," recalled Robert Wallace and H. Keith Melton in an authoritative history of CIA spy craft. "For instance, as late as 1962 the CIA had yet to develop a small, reliable document copy camera for agents."[3] But technology exploded in the years that followed. By 1970, the CIA's experts had begun working on an extremely small and quiet camera. The requirements were almost unimaginable: it had to be able to work effectively *inside* a KGB office without being detected. That became an urgent need when the CIA recruited Ogorodnik in Colombia in 1973. Under tight security, the agency hired a precision optical contractor to build a tiny camera, designated T-100, just one-sixth the size of the Minox, with a small, cylindrical shape that could be concealed in such everyday items as pens, cigarette lighters, or key fobs. The camera was "a jewel of watchmaking mechanical precision and optical miniaturization," wrote Wallace and Melton. The lens was made up of eight minuscule ground-glass elements, exactingly stacked one on top of the other to achieve clarity in photographing a standard letter-sized document. The film, lens, and shutter were housed in a single aluminum casing. As each picture was taken, the film automatically advanced to the next frame, up to a hundred. The assembly was closer to watchmaking than any commercial manufacturing process; each one was fabricated individually, under a large magnifying glass. The supply was very limited. When the British intelligence service asked if they could borrow the blueprints to open a second supply line, the CIA agreed—but the camera was so complex the British could not replicate it.

The camera's small size forced designers to use an extremely thin film. The answer was found in retired stocks of an Eastman Kodak film once made for spy satellites, sliced and wound into the miniature enclosure. After some technical problems with loading the film, the CIA developed a second-generation camera, the T-50, which had fifty exposures. With this camera, the agent would not have to fuss with changing film; he would just use the device and return it. For Ogorodnik, a luxury fountain pen was selected as the concealment, with the camera tucked inside. To photograph a document, Ogorodnik was trained to position his elbows on the table, hands together, and aim the pen down toward the document. Eleven inches from the page was the perfect distance. The camera was called the Tropel, after the Rochester, New York, company that made it for the CIA, and the camera worked splendidly in the mid-1970s for Ogorodnik.[4]

When Tolkachev began spying in early 1979, the CIA was reluctant to give him the elegant little Tropel. Tolkachev was a new agent, untrained and untested. Instead, they gave him the Molly. It was about the size of a matchbox, based on the Minox, built by a contractor to the CIA's specifications, and named after the contractor's daughter. The one given to Tolkachev bore the serial number 018 and came with a separate light meter. The film was wound into special cassettes, each about eighty exposures, packaged in boxes.[5]

By April, Tolkachev reported to the CIA he was having trouble with the Molly. He realized it was dated. "Having familiarized myself with the camera, I was somewhat disappointed, possibly this is tied in with my having more optimistic notions concerning the development of technology in this field," he wrote to the CIA.

In response, headquarters decided to give Tolkachev the 35 mm camera, the Pentax, and the clamp, which Guilsher passed to Tolkachev on June 6. The Pentax wasn't obviously spy equipment; it was in use all over the world and probably would not look entirely out of place if found in the apartment of a Soviet engineer. With the Pentax and the clamp, there was a good chance that Tolkachev's photography would not suffer from blurs or shake. As tradecraft, it dated back to at least World War II, when a spy for Germany had used a Leica 35 mm camera, held in place with a makeshift clamp, to photograph documents.[6]

The CIA pondered whether to also give Tolkachev the sophisticated Tropel cameras. In the end, headquarters decided to offer him two Tropels but with the caution that they were only for "testing" at home; he should not risk taking them to the office. In Moscow, Guilsher juggled these demands and uncertainties. He approved the plan to give Tolkachev the Tropel cameras but insisted that headquarters send to Moscow written instructions for using them, in Russian. The camera came in different sorts of concealments—a pen, a key fob, and a lipstick. It was important to make sure Tolkachev agreed in advance on the concealment and that it not look out of place with other things in his coat pocket. Tolkachev had told them he normally carried a pen and keys.

Everything had to be just right. The Tropel camera could be a death warrant if discovered by the KGB. It had no purpose other than espionage.

Two of the miniature Tropel cameras were in the package Guilsher handed to Tolkachev when they met again on October 15, 1979. One camera was red and the other black so that Tolkachev and the CIA could keep track. Each was preloaded with 120 frames of film and concealed in a pen, for "testing" at home.

When they met, Guilsher sensed that Tolkachev was irritated about something else. More than four months had passed since they had seen each other. Tolkachev complained that his request for a suicide pill, made in the spring, had been ignored for half a year. Tolkachev pressed Guilsher, saying he wanted it soon. Tolkachev described to Guilsher an incident in which the driver of a Moscow trolley bus had slammed on the brakes to avoid an accident, causing passengers to fall and seriously injuring some of them. He reminded Guilsher that he regularly took the bus and the streetcar with secret documents in his coat. What if that happened to him? Tolkachev promised he would carry the suicide pill with him only when he had secret documents on his person. The rest of the time, he would hide it at home. He promised it would be only a last resort. He did not want to face the ordeal of interrogation and trial. If caught, he wanted to take his own life.[7]

Tolkachev said he didn't want to waste precious moments talking about finances, but he had written out a reply to the CIA in an ops note. Guilsher put the note in his pocket.

The next morning, back in the Moscow station, Guilsher opened Tolkachev's note. After a few pages, he reached item No. 7, "Concerning Finances," and saw trouble. "The last financial proposals passed to me in June did not enthuse me," Tolkachev wrote. "These proposals sharply deviate from my desires, communicated in one of the notes.

"When I wrote about the remuneration of Belenko, like about the sum with six digits, I was inaccurate, since I had in mind not a figure with six digits, but a number with six zeros.

"According to the information available to me, his sum was equal to six million dollars."

Guilsher had read and translated all of Tolkachev's handwritten notes since his first days in the Moscow station. He had met with Tolkachev four times and felt he understood him. Yet there were moments when he was floored.

Tolkachev wanted *millions of dollars*?

He read on.

"Sometimes it appears to me that, in the matter of finances, a definite tactic is employed against me," Tolkachev complained.

"I understand the gradual approach in the question of finances, which you are carrying out with me. However, in order that your tactics in this matter not create stoppages or delays in the passage of information, and *would not bring about irreversible negative consequences*, I would like you to take into consideration the following factors when examining my financial position." Tolkachev wrote with a strong hand and underlined the words about negative consequences.

"My basic goal in working with you," Tolkachev went on, "consists of passing you the maximum amount of information in the shortest time.

"I do not limit myself to the passage of information on documents that have direct bearing on my work, but I actively seek out new important documents and try to receive access to them, in order to make photocopies.

"As you are aware, I started working with you voluntarily. In order to establish contact, from the moment the first note was passed until the first meeting, exactly two years was required. During these two years, I trained myself to accept the idea of the possible consequences of my actions. Today, just as before, I understood that the end may come at any moment, but it does not frighten me and I will work to the end. *However, I will not always work only on a voluntary basis.*"

Again, Guilsher saw the heavy underline.

"If I see that some game is being played with me or that I am being pressured, then I will cease my cooperation, besides I understand perfectly that I will only be able to end my cooperation by committing suicide." Tolkachev was ratcheting up the pressure with a threat to quit, but he was vaguely suggesting that if he did quit, he would face so many uncertainties—such as arrest by the KGB—that he would have no choice but to commit suicide on his own.

"I wrote about my approach to finances sincerely and openly.

I hope that you will answer me in the same spirit. I will not be discouraged by any answer from you.

"I suppose," Tolkachev said, "that several million dollars is not too fantastic a price for such information."[8]

In the weeks that followed, the CIA wrestled with Tolkachev's demand for millions of dollars. They wondered if he was bluffing. Guilsher sensed that they had reached a delicate moment. The response to Tolkachev had to impress him but could not be the sums he demanded. The CIA had never paid an agent on that scale.

On November 16, Guilsher and Hathaway sent a message to headquarters, pondering how to respond to Tolkachev. Perhaps they should challenge why he had escalated his demands from hundreds of thousands of dollars to millions? Or just act surprised? In the end, they thought it best not to antagonize Tolkachev but rather to chalk it up to "complete misunderstanding" and try to work it out.[9]

The CIA knew that Tolkachev was right. Several million dollars was not too fantastic a price for the espionage he was carrying out, looting the crown jewels of Soviet military research. But they just could not pay him that much, primarily because they feared he would flaunt it and jeopardize his own security.

On December 12, Kalaris, the division chief, wrote to Turner about the need to resolve the "six zeros" problem. His memo offered a revealing glimpse of how important the Tolkachev operation had become.

"As you are aware," Kalaris told the director, "I have been involved in this operation since the beginning. We have never had another case like it in SE Division."

Kalaris said the division was trying to follow operational rules they had developed from running earlier spies, but Tolkachev stood out as unique. In the earlier operations, such as Popov, Penkovsky, and Polyakov, the agents volunteered and largely functioned outside the Soviet Union. Tolkachev, however, was spying right in the heart of Moscow. Kalaris also reminded Turner of Tolkachev's stubborn drive to establish contact with the CIA and described Tolkachev as "a mature, low-profile man," compared with more youthful and exuberant agents they had dealt with.

"We still are not certain what motivated SPHERE to seek us out and work for us," Kalaris said. "Our best reading at this time is that he is inspired by vengeance. Up to this point and for the foreseeable future, the Division intends to treat this case with extreme caution because the chances of being 'taken for a ride' are high." But he also wrote, Tolkachev "has produced some extremely high quality intelligence which is already impacting on our Air Force; and he has promised more for the future."

The stakes were high, but Kalaris noted that the disagreements over money were creating "serious doubts about us in SPHERE's mind." Kalaris recommended that the CIA make a payment so generous that Tolkachev's doubts would be erased: 300,000 rubles, or about $92,000, at the December meeting. "I think it is important to demonstrate to him that we are not always going to nickel and dime him," Kalaris wrote.

He added that while the money should be delivered as proof of good faith, Tolkachev would have to be warned again about "the high risks he will be running by the mere possession of such a large amount." Still, "meeting his specific monetary request for the first time in toto will provide a good foundation to talk about the future."

Then Kalaris moved, gingerly, to the more difficult question.

"SPHERE has asked for ten million dollars, more or less, over the next ten years," he wrote. "We have not agreed to that and I propose that we do not agree to any such amount at this time."

Instead, Kalaris proposed to leave things somewhat vague. The CIA could point to the 300,000 rubles and tell Tolkachev "we will commit ourselves to pay him properly in the future, but the size of the payment will depend on our evaluation of the product." He added, "I think we should add that if he produces what he has promised, our estimate is that the material will be valued in the seven figures area. I would say no more than that.

"Having talked about a seven figure amount allows us to raise once again the idea of an escrow account for security reasons," Kalaris said. "If he balks, as I think he will to the suggestion of an escrow account, we can ask him to think about the possibility of leaving the USSR with our help."

This was a brand-new wrinkle. Kalaris informed Turner that the CIA would not have to actually commit itself to exfiltration—smuggling the agent out of the country—they could just gently suggest it. Although Kalaris didn't say so, the CIA had never before carried out a successful exfiltration from Moscow. Kalaris said he didn't know if Tolkachev had thought of leaving or would be interested. But there was another benefit of talking about it. It might help dissuade Tolkachev from the suicide pill. "We want him to live and enjoy the fruits of his labor," Kalaris wrote. "If he insists again that he wants the pill and will not accept no as an answer, we can agree in principle. We can delay delivery by almost a year by asking for his recommendations for appropriate concealment devices, etc."[10]

Charles Battaglia, an assistant who was close to Turner, was in the office when Tolkachev's demands for a big payment came up for discussion with the director. In Turner's mind, human agents were fallible and unpredictable, and this one was asking for millions of dollars. "I will never forget the look on Turner's face," Battaglia recalled. "He gulped." And then gave a green light.[11]

On December 15, headquarters sent word to the Moscow station that "we have received the go-ahead from the director" to give Tolkachev 300,000 rubles at the next meeting as "proof of our good faith and the value we place on the information he has provided." Headquarters cautioned that Tolkachev "cannot realistically expect us to commit ourselves to a specific dollar amount for his future product, although if he produces what he has promised us, it may be valued totally in the area of seven figures.

"We fully intend to pay him properly in the future but we will decide the size of each payment," the cable said, "based on the value of the information to us."[12]

In fact, the "value" of Tolkachev's intelligence to the U.S. military and intelligence agencies was soaring, already considered to be worth hundreds of millions of dollars. But CIA headquarters did not want to reveal this to Tolkachev. They needed to find a way to impress him, to show that his espionage was prized, while not forking over millions of dollars. The plan was to deliver a very impressive brick of rubles. Three hundred thousand would seem large enough to a Soviet engineer whose monthly salary was 350 rubles. (The value was much less, however, than the $300,000 approved for Tolkachev at headquarters seven months earlier.) Guilsher, who would deliver the cash, was instructed to ask again about paying Tolkachev in precious stones or valuables or with deposits in an escrow account in the West. Guilsher was also instructed to suggest the CIA would work out a plan for Tolkachev to escape the Soviet Union, a promise of exfiltration some time in the future, not immediately.

On the sticky question of the suicide pill, Guilsher was told to keep stalling and attempt to discourage Tolkachev. This was the demand that Tolkachev felt strongest about yet headquarters was most reluctant to meet. "You may tell CKSPHERE that we are seriously considering his request," headquarters told Guilsher, "but still feel he would be making a mistake in having this item in his possession."

# 8

# WINDFALLS AND HAZARDS

In subfreezing cold, walking for twenty minutes in a vacant lot by some old garages, Guilsher met Tolkachev for the fifth time on December 27, 1979. Tolkachev was in a good mood and seemed glad to see Guilsher again. He had threatened to stop spying for the CIA in his October letter, but Guilsher realized right away that Tolkachev had done just the opposite. He was working with more energy and determination than ever. As they strolled, Tolkachev slipped a package to Guilsher. Inside were five electronic components from a Soviet radar and a line diagram with each. Tolkachev told Guilsher they were left over from "the time when I worked on experiments finalizing the RP-23 complex." This was the radar the CIA had described as being "of utmost value" earlier in the year. The electronic components were an intelligence windfall that would help the United States determine how Soviet radars and avionics worked—and build countermeasures to blind them.

Tolkachev also gave Guilsher eighty-one rolls of exposed 35 mm film, carrying hundreds of pages of secret documents. The Pentax camera had jammed and wouldn't advance the film, so he returned it to Guilsher, asking for two replacements. As they walked, Guilsher handed Tolkachev a package with four miniature Tropel spy cameras for the months ahead, color coded: blue, gold, silver, and green. Tolkachev returned to Guilsher the red and black Tropels he'd been given in October for "testing," with exposed film inside.

Guilsher, who had taken a briefcase with him, handed Tolkachev the big brick of cash, 150,000 rubles. The CIA had obtained the bills from a banker in Switzerland so they could not be traced to the United States. It was only half the amount that Kalaris had suggested, but the impact was immediate. Tolkachev was pleased by the money and said it was in line with the value of his work—not the paltry 5,000 rubles he'd been given at meetings earlier that year. Tolkachev said that he didn't really need the money and would probably just stash it away somewhere.

Then he confessed to Guilsher that his demand for millions of dollars was "not realistic" and not meant to be taken literally.

Guilsher again raised the possibility of an escrow account in the West. This time, Tolkachev didn't reject it out of hand.

Very carefully, Guilsher brought up a possible exfiltration. Tolkachev brushed it off. He said he would never even consider it.

Tolkachev brought some worrisome news. The procedures for handling secret documents in his office had tightened. Previously, he could check out classified reports from the First Department by signing for them on a permission sheet that remained on file with the department. At lunchtime, he could conceal the documents in his coat, leave the building, photograph them at home when he was alone, return to the institute after lunch, and put the documents back. At the main gate, where he showed his building pass, they would rarely check whether he was carrying anything.

Now, Tolkachev said, in order to check out documents from

the First Department, he was required to leave his building pass with the clerks in that department. Without the pass, he could not leave the building at lunch nor photograph secret documents at home. The only documents he might be able to take home were less sensitive technical journals. Tolkachev boasted to Guilsher he had beat the system—he pulled a "ruse"—on December 24 and slipped some top secret documents out of the building. He photographed them in his apartment. But he was facing a big setback; his usual habit of just walking out with documents in his coat pocket was not going to be possible.

Tolkachev sternly reminded Guilsher of his still-unfulfilled demand for the suicide pill. He felt he was in more danger. He had been signing out documents that were clearly not related to his current work. If questions about a leak were raised, his signatures were all over the permission sheet. He implored Guilsher to get the suicide pill—no more delays.

Before parting, Guilsher surprised Tolkachev. As a gift for the holidays, Guilsher brought him two books by dissidents that were unavailable in Moscow, including one by Alexander Solzhenitsyn, who had been exiled from the Soviet Union in 1974. Despite all that had happened that year, Guilsher reported, Tolkachev "was delighted."[1]

As they parted, Guilsher walked away from the vacant lot, and Tolkachev abruptly came running back in his direction. Guilsher was startled and feared that he was about to be ambushed. But Tolkachev caught up to him and explained that he had written an ops note and forgotten to give it to him. He handed the note to Guilsher and slipped away into the night.[2]

Back in the station, Guilsher read the ops note. Tolkachev insisted that the suicide pill was becoming "more essential for me." He told Guilsher that he felt increasingly vulnerable to "unforeseen circumstances," perhaps even a leak from the United States. Then he explained that every time he took a document from the First Department, he signed the permission sheet, with his last name and signature. It was on file if the KGB ever decided to investigate. He wrote,

> The number of documents drawn by me greatly exceeds
> my productive needs. For example, I will never be able
> to explain why I needed the technical descriptions of
> the AVM RLS RP-23, N-003, N-006, N-005 . . . This is
> also hard to explain because our laboratory has stopped
> overseeing the RLS RP-23, N-003, N-006 in September,
> 1978, and our laboratory was never even involved in
> issuing the documentation for the RLS N-005 or its serial
> introduction. The listed considerations induce me, already
> for the third time, to turn to you with the request that I be
> passed the means of self-destruction at once.[3]

Behind the codes and numbers in Tolkachev's note lay an astounding intelligence take. He had provided the United States with blueprints for several of the most modern radars then being developed and installed on Soviet interceptors and fighter planes. In December, the Defense Department told the CIA in a memorandum that as a result of Tolkachev's trove of documents the air force had completely reversed its direction on a $70 million electronics package for one of the latest U.S. fighters.[4]

But Guilsher could see a larger crisis looming. Tolkachev had signed out so many documents he had left a road map of his own treachery. That permission sheet could wreck the whole operation. And now Tolkachev's easy method of copying documents at home at lunchtime was imperiled by the new restrictions, requiring him to turn in his building pass.

---

For two and a half years, Gus Hathaway had fought hard to keep the lights on in the Moscow station. He pushed back against Turner and the stand-down. He insisted that Tolkachev was genuine. He brought Guilsher to Moscow. He stood guard against KGB intruders during the embassy fire. He suffered through the loss of Ogorodnik and Kulak but knew that losing an agent was a constant risk in the battle against the KGB. Hathaway eventually got the Moscow station back into spy operations, and even with setbacks the CIA had come a long way since the paralysis of the 1960s, when there hadn't been an agent in Moscow worth talking about.

Hathaway was preparing to end his tour and return to headquarters to become chief of the Soviet division, but his last weeks in the Moscow station were filled with anxiety. In late December 1979, the Soviet Union invaded Afghanistan, setting off a new period of tension with the West. The decade of détente was over. The SALT II Treaty was shelved in the Senate, a new European arms race got under way, and the United States threatened to boycott the upcoming Moscow Olympics.[5]

For the Moscow station, the Afghan invasion meant trouble. Hathaway warned headquarters on January 9, 1980, that the KGB would intensify surveillance on the streets. Having come so far with Tolkachev, he was determined not to lose him and vowed to step up security measures in the "deteriorating political situation." He said the CIA station would monitor, electronically, "all known and suspect surveillance frequencies" on days when they were planning to meet Tolkachev. They would also pay special attention to the surveillance around the embassy and keep watch on Tolkachev's apartment windows for signs of activity.[6]

Tolkachev's words to Guilsher and his letter in late December—describing the new security procedures at his institute, warning of his vulnerability for having signed out so many documents, and his "ruse" to steal more—worried headquarters. "Chilling," observed one headquarters cable.[7]

The new security restrictions preventing Tolkachev from taking documents home to photograph might prompt him to take an even bigger risk, the CIA feared, such as sneaking the tiny Tropel cameras into his office. Already, Hathaway and Guilsher realized, Tolkachev was ignoring their plea to be careful. They needed to do something that would strengthen his confidence and their sway. On January 8, they wrote to headquarters, insisting it was time to give Tolkachev the L-pill that he so often demanded. They hoped it would reassure Tolkachev the CIA was paying attention to his needs.

Tolkachev's appeal for the suicide pill the previous month made "valid points and draws logical conclusions," they told headquarters. Tolkachev was right to feel vulnerable, they added. His security situation was worsening because of his own tendency to overproduce, to take out documents without a justifiable cover, and to carry them home. Guilsher and Hathaway told headquarters, "CKSPHERE is not heeding our requests to proceed slowly and is charging ahead, following his desire to pass the maximum amount of materials in the shortest period of time." They were not surprised by his willingness to commit suicide for a cause, they wrote. "He is apparently following course of action inculcated in every Russian citizen from childhood, i.e., it is glorious, courageous, and manly to make the ultimate sacrifice for the Motherland. There is no immoral connotation to making courageous and glorious decision to end one's life while fighting for the cause. CKSPHERE's cause is to do the greatest damage to the Soviet authorities that he possibly can." Guilsher and Hathaway recalled that Tolkachev "calmly and logically" promised that "he has the control and willpower" to refrain from using the L-pill until the very last moment. They reminded headquarters that if compromised, Tolkachev would certainly face KGB interrogation, trial, and execution. "We must reexamine his request" for a suicide pill, they wrote.[8]

The question was taken to Turner, the CIA director, on January 17, 1980, in a memorandum carried by hand to his seventh-floor office. It was signed by Warren E. Frank, who was acting chief of the Soviet division until Hathaway arrived. In his memo, Frank predicted that Tolkachev "will probably continue to press hard" for the suicide pill, and he offered an excerpt of Tolkachev's note in December saying the suicide pill was becoming "more essential for me."

The Moscow station had made a strong appeal for the L-pill, but it was watered down by Frank before reaching Turner. Frank proposed that Guilsher "make another effort" to persuade Tolkachev "of the inadvisability of having an L-pill." Guilsher had already done this. Frank laid out four "talking points" that Guilsher could use in talking with the restive agent. Guilsher had already received similar talking points from headquarters eight months earlier. However, in this list, a new point was included: "The Director of our organization has very strong, personal reservations, on both moral and operational grounds, against the issuance of this capability."

The Moscow station wanted a clear and straightforward decision to give Tolkachev what he demanded. Instead, headquarters responded with fog and caution. Frank proposed giving the spy a vague promise the CIA would deliver the L-pill later. This was another way to stall. Even if Turner approved the L-pill in February, Frank suggested, "we will still easily be able to defer the issuance of the pill until winter of this year, based on the summer hiatus as well as manufacturing and concealment delays." Frank's memo asked for Turner's approval for what was essentially a compromise—a vague promise to provide the pill some-day, but only if Tolkachev "continues to feel it is necessary."

Turner was unhappy with all of it. As Frank had writ-ten, Turner opposed the L-pill on both moral and operational grounds, and on the memo he scribbled the operational reasons. "We are concerned (in part from experience) that availability of L-pills can encourage an agent to take risks that are not pru-dent." He also wrote, "The KGB is well aware of our distribu-tion of L-pills to an agent and would doubtless be thorough in searching."

At the bottom of the memo, the division had typewritten "APPROVED" with a space for Turner's signature. On Janu-ary 24, Turner wrote "Not" in front of "APPROVED" and said Guilsher should keep stalling and attempt once again to dissuade Tolkachev.

"Do not make commitment on this exchange.

"Stan."[9]



Guilsher and Hathaway were sorely disappointed. Guilsher felt he understood Tolkachev's thinking and feared an angry reac-tion. He archly reminded headquarters that "talking points" had already been covered with Tolkachev and further discussions along those lines "will only alienate him." Moreover, he said, if Tolkachev were told the request was still pending, it could "lead to loss of this valuable asset."

"Do we want to risk this?" he asked plaintively.

Guilsher also reminded headquarters that Tolkachev had warned them in October not to play games with him and had threatened to quit. At the time, Tolkachev had written, "I under-stand perfectly that I will only be able to end my cooperation by committing suicide." Guilsher pointed out that he wouldn't need the CIA's suicide pill to take his own life. It was a very tough message to headquarters, suggesting the operation could collapse and they might forever lose Tolkachev, both the man and the espionage operation, because of Turner's refusal to approve the suicide pill. Guilsher offered one last-ditch idea. In the next meeting, he said, he could tell Tolkachev that he should write a "personal letter" to the head of the CIA, appealing for the L-pill.

That would at least keep the "special request" alive.[10]

Beyond the suicide pill, Guilsher and Hathaway faced a troubling dilemma in January 1980. Tolkachev was producing extremely valuable intelligence but taking too many risks. To improve his security, they might have to slow down his spying. That trade-off would be hard enough, but there was another factor: any effort to slow down Tolkachev would collide with his personal desire to damage the Soviet Union as much as possible. They might not be able to slow him down.

The Moscow station and headquarters wrestled with this knotty problem day after day. The library permission sheet was the biggest danger. If it was ever examined closely by the authorities, they would immediately spot the excessive number and scope of the documents Tolkachev signed out. On January 12, headquarters told Guilsher and Hathaway "we certainly share your deep concern" about it. "Unfortunately, the damage has been done, as the log sheets in the First Department are there for the checking." Headquarters suggested Tolkachev invent a cover story, "however thin," for why he needed all the extra documents he had checked out.[11]

But the problem ran deeper than covering past actions. Tolkachev was taking more and more risks, including his daring "ruse" to spirit documents out of the institute in December. On

January 16, headquarters acknowledged, "Clearly we have to try to improve his security, slow him down."[12] Headquarters suggested they withhold a replacement 35 mm Pentax camera from Tolkachev so that he could not take any more documents home to photograph. This could alleviate some of the security concerns: he wouldn't be carrying top secret papers out of the institute. But it would also mean a loss of productivity. Tolkachev had already delivered to the CIA thousands of pages of valuable intelligence using the Pentax camera. Tolkachev, his enthusiasm undiminished, raised the prospect in his December note of a "quick delivery" of documents in January. Headquarters threw cold water on that idea, telling the Moscow station, "At all costs we must avoid any hurried, possibly suspicious act like a 'quick delivery.'"[13]

Guilsher's instinct was that withholding the Pentax camera would be a mistake. He and Hathaway were "convinced," he wrote to headquarters, "all our urging will go unheeded," because "nothing will deter" Tolkachev "from his goal of doing maximum damage in shortest time." In a flurry of messages, headquarters expressed concern that Tolkachev was heading toward disaster.[14] Guilsher replied that they must brake Tolkachev softly, "without damaging his motivation, offending him, or having him lose faith in us."

Aside from Tolkachev's immediate security risks, Guilsher had a nagging worry about a longer-term danger. As Tolkachev turned over more and more documents, additional military and intelligence experts in the United States would see them. Over time, the design of U.S. weapons would change, battle tactics would be revised, and countermeasures would be created, all based on what Tolkachev had provided. Guilsher wrote to headquarters, "It is not inconceivable word will eventually trickle back to Soviets that we are in possession of certain types of information. Investigation of possible leaks at Soviet end could quickly point finger at CKSPHERE."[15] The first thing the Soviets would look at was the permission sheet with all Tolkachev's signatures on it.

Guilsher felt squeezed and impatient. Headquarters wanted to reject Tolkachev's demands for the L-pill. Headquarters wanted to reject Tolkachev's request for the 35 mm camera. Headquarters wanted to slow down the agent who, if anything, was racing ahead.

The CIA's miniature Tropel camera, while an ingenious feat of engineering, was not foolproof. In January, headquarters reported to the Moscow station that film from the black Tropel, which Tolkachev exposed in the fall—one of the two for "testing"—was unreadable. All the frames were underexposed, and precious intelligence was lost.[16] The Tropel cameras required a minimum of thirty-five to fifty foot-candles to get a clear photograph.[17] Tolkachev told them he had taken special care in using the Tropels. He had fashioned a knitting needle on a small chain, hanging from his wrist, to help him judge the exact distance for good focus, and CIA analysts spotted the shadow of the knitting needle in his pictures. At home, where he could control the lighting, Tolkachev was still having difficulties. He said there was an ample thirty-five to fifty foot-candles for the first eighty frames he had shot, and somewhat less for the other forty frames, yet the exposures from the black Tropel were unreadable. The CIA's technical experts had been working on an experimental, improved version with a wider lens opening that would work better in low light. But this was still being built, not in Tolkachev's hands.

On January 28, the Moscow station asked headquarters to send two Pentax 35 mm camera bodies and a clean lens—without delay. This time, headquarters said yes.

———

The Moscow station held a going-away party for Hathaway in January, but he didn't like such festivities and excused himself to go to the industrial-sized paper shredder in the hall just outside the station. It was more than a paper shredder: it was a monster that turned documents to dust and could destroy them fast, just in case they ever had to get rid of everything suddenly. There, Hathaway stood in his final hours in Moscow, feeding documents into the rumbling, vibrating machine.

His successor was an old friend, Burton Gerber, who had been among those ambitious officers who joined the CIA in the 1950s and pursued a more aggressive approach to espionage. Gerber subsequently served in Tehran, Sofia, and Belgrade and developed the "Gerber rules" for vetting potential agents. Given the shifting rotations and promotions, Gerber wasn't sure if he would ever be in line for the coveted Moscow post. When the offer came, he eagerly accepted it—chief of the most important station in the world.

Gerber arrived in Moscow the third week of January 1980. He was a demanding boss, a no-frills and no-nonsense workaholic, known for pushing people hard and letting them know when something wasn't up to his standards. But he was also considerate of the hardships endured by officers and their families—long hours, disappearances, and constant tension about surveillance and secrecy. Gerber knew by heart all the names of the wives and children of his case officers and asked about them, even as he drove his officers to work harder and longer. His lifelong hobby was the study of wolves, and he kept a picture of a wolf in his office. He also put up a photograph of Rem Krasilnikov, the chief of counterintelligence for the KGB. Gerber wanted to remind himself that Krasilnikov's presence was always out there, his men lurking on the streets. Gerber would have to defeat them.

Instead of the sleek IBM Selectric typewriters used by some others in the station, Gerber brought an old manual typewriter—

and he typed fast on it. He believed that case officers should
know their city and know their targets. One officer in the station
recalled that Gerber would occasionally buy propaganda picture
cards of leading Communist Party members, then mischievously
come up to case officers in the station and hold up a card. "Say
you are on the street and you see this guy," he would ask a case
officer. "Who is it?"

Guilsher had been meeting Tolkachev for a year and acutely felt
the burdens of keeping him safe and the operation alive. Getting ready for the next rendezvous, he drafted a very long ops
note that he knew Tolkachev would read after they had parted.
The letter allowed Guilsher to say more than was possible during
a short encounter. Guilsher warned Tolkachev that the invasion
of Afghanistan could prompt the KGB to tighten surveillance
on the streets, and they might have to use dead drops to communicate, even though Tolkachev disliked dead drops. Guilsher
reassured Tolkachev that the CIA would understand if he could
not provide as many top secret documents as before, at least for
a while. "Please do not feel badly about this situation, work quietly, and don't remove from the first department those materials
which are not connected to your work," he wrote.

At the same time, Guilsher's letter conveyed an entirely
different and unmistakable message: the United States was
hungry—absolutely starving—for more of Tolkachev's valuable
intelligence. Guilsher sketched out a wide array of secrets that
Tolkachev might purloin. "We were very glad to receive from
you electronic components," Guilsher said, asking Tolkachev
for more, such as pieces of metal from airplanes and technical
devices. The "alloys from which they build airplanes present a
great interest," he wrote. "We will be very grateful." He added,

"I remind you that we wish very much to receive telephone and other handbooks of the institutes, ministries and other institutions with which your institute works." Guilsher said the CIA wanted to know about individuals and "who goes abroad, if you know this." The CIA wanted to know what Soviet engineers had learned about American technology—"please give details" about which "data, materials and information" were making their way to the Soviet defense industry institutes. The CIA wanted Tolkachev to concentrate on more about future weapons systems, including the nascent Soviet effort to build an airborne warning and control system plane and a vertical takeoff and landing fighter, both then on the drawing boards. The CIA wanted to know about "further new developments of systems in phases one through five" of research and development. "I remind you that we are interested in everything you know about civil defense, in your institute and also in the country in general. Let's say, are there signs that more attention is now paid to civil defense?"[18] The wish list went on and on. The CIA wanted to know everything possible about what was contained in the secret library in the institute, including how materials could be taken out, how the permission sheet worked, and how long the documents could be kept out. The CIA wanted to know what levels of secret documents were kept there, whether they concerned future or present weapons systems, and whether the library contained information on aviation and radars, materials that airplanes were built from, design of airplanes and rockets, lasers, directed-energy research, aerosols, alloys and special metals, air strike tactics, electro-optics, tactics of forward air control and close air support, and command-and-control systems. The CIA wondered if Tolkachev could take a light meter reading in the secret library and maybe photograph several samples of the kinds of documents "which you can logically remove for your work."[19]

Guilsher also was puzzling over a new idea for obtaining

the secret documents. Under the new security procedure, Tolkachev was required to turn in his building pass while checking
out secret documents from the First Department. This meant he
could not leave the institute and smuggle the papers out of the
building, because he would not have a pass to come and go. But
Tolkachev had come up with an idea: What if the CIA could
fabricate a replica of his building pass? He could leave one pass
with the First Department when he checked out documents and
show the replica at the building entrance. Guilsher again wondered, what could go wrong? Would it look odd if Tolkachev
had left his building pass at the First Department at the time of
signing out documents but was seen holding up an identical pass
on leaving or entering the building a few minutes later? Could
he get caught that way? Still, the idea of a fake building pass was
appealing to the CIA. If successful, it would be a splendid act of
deception in service of their most valuable agent.[20]

In the letter, Guilsher gave Tolkachev a fresh schedule for
meetings over the next twelve months and new instructions for
how to signal readiness for a meeting after a long pause. The
instructions reflected the case officer's attention to detail. On the
first day of any month, Tolkachev should make a mark at a certain site "with that yellow wax pencil which I gave you—such a
mark will be more dependable than chalk which can wash out
or be erased. I remind you that the signal is a horizontal mark
10 cm. long at waist height."

On the evening of February 11, 1980, Guilsher set off on a long
surveillance detection run. He arrived twenty minutes early at
the site for his sixth meeting with Tolkachev, a spot near Leningradsky Prospekt, a major thoroughfare that heads northwest
out of the center of the metropolis. Guilsher circled around the

site, casing it carefully. After Tolkachev showed up, they talked as they walked, crisply running down their agenda. Guilsher gave Tolkachev the two Pentax 35 mm cameras. In exchange, Tolkachev passed back the four Tropel cameras, blue, gold, silver, and green, which he had used to photograph documents. Tolkachev also handed Guilsher a nine-page ops note.

Tolkachev said that from now on, to confirm a meeting date, he would turn on the kitchen light in his apartment between noon and 2:00 p.m. The light was clearly visible from the street. They agreed to meet again in May. Guilsher warned Tolkachev of increased KGB surveillance.

Tolkachev then asked about the suicide pill. Guilsher told him, reluctantly, that the "special request" had been turned down by headquarters.

Tolkachev was shattered. He mumbled that this would be a major psychological blow to him. Guilsher saw that Tolkachev, who up to that point had stood erect and alert, suddenly changed. He looked crushed and spiritless.

Guilsher immediately shifted gears. He urged Tolkachev to write a letter to the "highest level" in the United States, requesting a reconsideration.

Guilsher then told Tolkachev that his tour was ending and he would be leaving Moscow in late summer. They parted after only twenty minutes. Guilsher walked away in the darkness, the Tropel spy cameras and letter in his pocket, brooding at the image of Tolkachev crumpling before his eyes.[21]

The next morning, Guilsher arrived early in the Moscow station, and Gerber was waiting for him. Guilsher described how Tolkachev had nearly collapsed at the rejection of his request for a suicide pill. The reaction was even more severe than he had expected. In a cable to headquarters, Guilsher and Gerber reported that the agent "has suffered a major psychological blow that will adversely affect the future of operation if we do not reverse decision." But there was little more they could do until Tolkachev wrote his appeal letter. They told headquarters the setback was made worse by Guilsher's request that Tolkachev "limit his production and lie low" and by Guilsher's impending departure. Guilsher was the only face Tolkachev had known from the CIA for more than a year.

Guilsher opened Tolkachev's ops note. It was businesslike and well organized, with precise details about his use of the color-coded Tropels to photograph documents. Tolkachev numbered everything; for example, "Document RE10 was photographed with the gold camera." He also reminded the CIA that he was way out on a limb because of the long list of documents he'd taken out of the First Department. If there was a leak from the United States, he wrote, "then my situation will become hopeless." Guilsher certainly agreed.

In the note, Tolkachev returned to the contentious topic of money, but he was apologetic. He said there had been misunderstandings, "my mistake." He acknowledged creating confusion when he "started talking about a six digit figure when I had in mind six zeros." Tolkachev explained that he was certain Belenko had received $6 million and that had influenced his thinking, but he had never demanded a specific sum. He said he would let the CIA decide how much to pay him, based on the value of his espionage. His expectations for a large paycheck were still high. He asked the CIA to put his money in hard currency in an escrow account, as long as he could withdraw it at any time.[22]

Guilsher expressed sympathy with Tolkachev on the money question in a note to headquarters. "We can easily imagine the difficult position CKS finds himself in when negotiating due reward for his efforts," Guilsher wrote. "He obviously fears he will be taken advantage of (large government vs. one helpless individual) when he has committed treason and already passed invaluable materials to us." Guilsher added that Tolkachev was still talking "in terms of millions."

That spring, the air force reported that Tolkachev's material had dovetailed with other intelligence on Soviet weapons systems, and much of the Tolkachev material was quite damaging to Moscow. The air force said Tolkachev had provided a wealth of science and technology information, and his primary value was providing a detailed picture of new Soviet weapons systems that would not be available from other sources for many years, if ever. In March, Guilsher and Gerber raised the question with headquarters of what Tolkachev was really worth. In a cable, they pointed out that previous evaluations from the military had been glowing. The evaluations had praised Tolkachev's materials as the "first information" about some weapons, as the "only information," "first hard information," and declared, "Time saved on research and development of U.S. countermeasures to these systems has been reduced by minimum of 18 months, for one system as much as five years." Another called Tolkachev's intelligence a "gold mine" and "one hundred and eighty degree change in seventy million dollar project."

Guilsher and Gerber inquired if the intelligence community could put a dollar value on it all:

> For instance, how much can we expect to save on R and D? Have we discovered vulnerabilities in our systems that we can now correct? Can we develop new countermeasures against Soviet systems? Do we have true

picture of Soviet capabilities in field? Has CKS provided information on systems for which we had no data before?[23]

The answer to all the questions was that Tolkachev had provided intelligence that was, as headquarters put it, "essentially invaluable." Headquarters added, "We suspect CKSPHERE himself, fully aware of the extraordinary value of his materials, realizes we cannot pay him the exact amount the production is worth, even if we could calculate it."[24]

Next, headquarters sent the Moscow station an internal CIA evaluation of Tolkachev's materials. The internal evaluation declared, "The timeliness of these reports is especially significant in terms of savings to the intelligence community. With other systems such detail and understanding are not obtained until years after deployment. The definitive data in these reports will save many years of analysis and debate in the intelligence community."[25]

Although the 150,000 rubles that Guilsher had given Tolkachev in December 1979 quieted his anxiety, the CIA had never really settled on how much to pay him over the long haul. Tolkachev was waiting for their decision. In March 1980, Gerber wrote to Hathaway, now the Soviet division chief, saying that before the next meeting with Tolkachev they would have to "make some realistic plans for future" and "decide on commitments we will live up to."[26] The Moscow station suggested a total compensation package of $3.2 million. It was still a tiny fraction of the value of Tolkachev's intelligence to the U.S. government, but much more than he had been given so far.

Hathaway knew well how troublesome the question had become; he had wrestled with it himself as station chief. In early April, Hathaway responded, "The problem is basically one of not so much how much his information is worth, rather how much can he handle, and frankly how much can we reasonably pay him. I say reasonably since, if we took the total value of his information, we would frankly be talking about astronomical figures. I do not mean to be cruel, but we are not a business and we can compensate him reasonably without paying the maximum."

Hathaway also wanted to slow down Tolkachev. "We here are obliged to do everything to slow him down," he wrote. "A reasonable sum will, I think, help slow him down, whereas large (indeed justified) sums may egg him on even more." While the CIA would build up Tolkachev's account, "we do think your final figure of 3,200,000 is high."

Soon after writing this, Hathaway told Gerber he would go to the CIA director with a plan to pay Tolkachev $200,000 for his work through 1979, $300,000 for 1980, $400,000 for 1981, and half a million dollars for every year thereafter. It would be, he said, "the highest salary ever paid to any single individual in the history of this organization."[27]

Once again, Turner put on the brakes. On May 10, 1980, he approved a pared-down package: $200,000 for 1979 and $300,000 for every year after. Hathaway told Gerber and Guilsher that he was sure they would be disappointed. "I share your disappointment," he said. But "it is an enormous amount of money." He expressed confidence that Guilsher could "use his persuasive talents and his special relationship with CKSPHERE to get this across."[28]

Another factor crowding in on Guilsher was exfiltration. Tolkachev had earlier said he would never consider leaving the Soviet Union. But in his February ops note, he suddenly expressed interest in the idea. "I never thought about the possibility of exiting the USSR," he said, but "if a realistic possibility exists for exfiltrating me and my family, then, no matter what the inherent risk connected with it, I would like to take advantage of this possibility. My family does not know about my activity."

Tolkachev asked for more details—how long would they have to prepare?[29] Guilsher felt this new interest in exfiltration was a signal that Tolkachev was growing pessimistic about his future in Moscow.[30] Perhaps if the CIA gave a positive nod to exfiltration, Guilsher thought, it would ease Tolkachev's demands for millions of dollars. At headquarters in May 1980, Turner approved giving Tolkachev "the commitment to exfiltrate him, his wife and his son if and when circumstances dictate, with resettlement in the West."[31]

Guilsher began to draft the ops note he would give Tolkachev at their next meeting. He knew that Tolkachev had been shattered by the decision on the L-pill. Now he had to talk Tolkachev through more unpleasant news. Guilsher had "absolutely no doubt" that Tolkachev would be "highly shocked and unhappy" with the pay package.[32] Guilsher tried to break the news gently. "The evaluation of your materials is very high and it has been decided to grant you the highest salary that our organization has ever paid," Guilsher wrote, laying out the sums that Turner had approved. There were a lot of zeros, but not millions. Guilsher wanted to "cushion" the blow by promising exfiltration, but that was also problematic. By merely discussing it, they would raise Tolkachev's expectations for departure. The CIA did not want to exfiltrate Tolkachev unless there was an emergency. They wanted a productive, deeply embedded agent like Tolkachev to remain in place as long as possible. Guilsher didn't promise anything swift. He reminded Tolkachev that he would have to tell his family about exfiltration, and if they were to hesitate, "problems may arise." He outlined for Tolkachev what the CIA would do for him in terms of resettlement in the United States.

The Tolkachev operation was now growing quite complex— the issues of exfiltration, money, photography, security, and the suicide pill were all interlocked. The Moscow station and headquarters chewed over each of them in detail, with cables back and forth, but every move had the potential for error and to upset Tolkachev, as happened with the suicide pill. The CIA had attempted to manage Tolkachev through carefully calibrated offers of money and exfiltration, but looming over it all was the reality that Tolkachev did not always listen to his handlers. He had an unshakable determination to steal as many secrets as he could. He did not want to be slowed down.

Tensions between the Soviet Union and the West deepened considerably in the spring of 1980. The United States boycotted the Moscow Summer Olympics in response to the invasion of Afghanistan, sharply offending the Soviet leadership. When the dissident physicist Andrei Sakharov spoke out against the invasion, he was detained and exiled to Gorky.[33] The Olympics were scheduled to open in July, and for weeks beforehand the streets were crawling with extra militiamen, many of them brought to Moscow from the provinces. All this made John Guilsher's next move even more risky and intricate.

On the evening of May 12, Guilsher put on a disguise. It was his first experience with the procedure known as identity transfer, a trick that played on a KGB weakness. Although the KGB scrutinized all Americans in Moscow, they could not surveil them all, so they ignored many who were considered ordinary workers, not involved in intelligence. A CIA officer could disguise himself as one of the embassy workers the KGB had ignored and slip out of the compound without attracting attention. The trick worked. Guilsher escaped the compound without the KGB's spotting him. He was hoping to make an impromptu call to Tolkachev followed by a meeting on the street. But when Guilsher called, he heard a voice that was not Tolkachev's and aborted the attempt.[34]

The next attempt to avoid the KGB was an elaborate ruse.

Guilsher notified the Soviet authorities that he planned a short trip abroad. He flew out of Moscow as planned, but then he abruptly returned, earlier than he had notified them. He hoped to meet Tolkachev before the KGB realized he was back. But when Guilsher got to passport control on his premature return, he noticed special attention was being paid to him, and he decided not to go ahead with the meeting.

Two missed meetings and blanket surveillance on the streets did not deter Gerber. He wrote a cable to Hathaway after Guilsher's second attempt failed on May 21. Although "not optimistic" about a natural break in surveillance, Gerber said it was essential for Guilsher to meet with Tolkachev once more. Guilsher was due to end his Moscow tour that summer. With the delicate issues of money and exfiltration, Gerber cabled, "we prefer have CKSPHERE discuss these critical matters with familiar face rather with total stranger in fall." Although Gerber believed that the station's case officers should be interchangeable in operations, Guilsher was the only case officer he could send now, the only one known to Tolkachev.[35]

The two failed attempts to meet with Tolkachev in May led to an important new dimension in the operation. The CIA's prowess with technology was growing, and it dreamed of using electronics to evade the KGB and carry out espionage unfettered. Through the 1960s, communications with agents in hostile areas were largely carried out with a small number of proven techniques, like secret writing, microdots, radio broadcasts, and dead drops. But starting with the 1970s, thanks to the revolution in microelectronics, technology began to transform the way case officers communicated with their agents, and the CIA attempted to maintain a cutting edge. An example of this was the first in a family of small electronic devices known as the SRAC, for short-range agent communications. An early version of the device, called Buster, had been given to Dmitri Polyakov, the general in

Soviet military intelligence, the GRU, who volunteered in New York in 1961 and was code-named TOPHAT by the FBI. Later, he was run by the CIA in Rangoon and New Delhi and now was back in Moscow, where he rose to become commander of the GRU training academy. The new device, it was hoped, would make it easier for Polyakov to communicate with the CIA and avoid the KGB. The device was a handheld communications system, which consisted of two portable base stations—each about the size of a shoe box—and one agent unit that could be concealed in a coat pocket. With a tiny keyboard one and a half inches square, the agent would first convert a text message into a cipher code, then peck the code into the tiny keypad. Once the data were loaded—Buster could hold fifteen hundred characters—the agent would go somewhere within a thousand feet of the base station and press a send button. The base station could be moved around, placed in an apartment window, or a car; the agent would have to be told approximately where. In essence, Buster was a primitive text messaging system. Its advantage was safety: the agent could communicate without actually meeting a case officer on the street. However, there were problems with using such equipment in the field. Buster was clearly spy equipment and would fatally compromise an agent if caught with it.

Hathaway, now division chief, was a technology enthusiast, eager to deploy new gadgets to frustrate KGB surveillance. Ideally, Buster could ease the risk of personal meetings with an agent in parks and on dark street corners. "Think of how we'll save this poor bastard from the danger of going out and meeting somebody from the agency," Hathaway said, a reference not only to Tolkachev but to any CIA agent who could make good use of the gadget.

Over time, Buster underwent major improvements. The next model was called Discus. It was also handheld but much easier for the agent and the case officer to use. The Discus eliminated the need for the bulky base station and could transmit to a case officer holding a second small unit several hundred meters away. Most significantly, Buster had required the agent to encrypt his message by converting it to cipher code, painstakingly by hand, before typing into the device, while Discus used automatic encryption. The keyboard was larger, and it could transmit significantly more data. Moreover, Discus had a verification system so the agent knew the message had been received. The Discus was way ahead of its time; there were no consumer handheld devices available then, nothing remotely like the BlackBerry or the iPhone.[36]

In June, Hathaway urged the station to consider giving a Discus unit to Tolkachev. He said Tolkachev could use the device to signal the CIA when he was available for a meeting and perhaps "select important portions of documents and transmit them to us." He speculated that Tolkachev could use Discus to alert the Moscow station about where to pick up film and other materials in a dead drop. Hathaway expressed confidence the Discus would "enhance security and production of this operation." The Discus beckoned as a kind of invulnerable magic carpet that would soar over the heads of the KGB. While the traditional method of dead drops usually took a day or longer to signal, emplace, and collect, the electronic communicator could transmit urgent intelligence almost instantly.[37]

Gerber, however, thought the Discus was ill-suited for Tolkachev. He had experimented with the device and knew that operating it was far more complicated than just pressing a button. He tested the Discus in a Moscow vegetable market while looking over cucumbers and tomatoes as his wife, Rosalie, held the second unit in another section of the market. For an exchange, the Discus required both sender and receiver to be static. Gerber tried to send a signal. He immediately realized that an agent would have to be looking down into his pocket until the red verification light flashed, or else he would not know the message went through. The red light flashed only after a pause. Was peering into one's pocket, watching for the light to flash, the kind of body language that would give away an agent? Was it worth the risk? Moreover, Gerber surmised that the agent would have to give some kind of warning to the CIA that he was about to transmit on Discus. That signal was another operational act. Also, sites had to be selected and tested in advance for Discus transmissions; the radio waves tended to bounce around, and not all locations were suitable. What's more, the testing also put the signal in the air, briefly, where the KGB might notice, and it required case officers to be exposed. Was it worth the risk?

Gerber doubted that Discus could ease the security dangers for Tolkachev and thought it might bring new ones. "Do not think now is the time to discuss topic with him," Gerber responded to Hathaway. He added, the "value of CKSPHERE production is in voluminous reproduction of entire detailed documents, not just in few tidbits" that could be transmitted by Discus. Gerber insisted that they continue personal meetings for the large amount of material Tolkachev was delivering. Gerber wanted a sure, steady process. He said that giving Tolkachev a Discus might spur him to speed up and take risks. He also pointed out that Tolkachev's own preference was for meetings, not dead drops. Tolkachev "has strong psychological need for direct personal contact."[38]

On June 11, Gerber sent a second strong cable to Hathaway, saying he had raised using the Discus with the case officers at the Moscow station. "We conclude that in this operation we have more to lose than to gain," he wrote. The device wasn't very useful in sending or receiving complex messages, such as those concerning "requirements," or what secret materials Tolkachev might gather. Moreover, the Discus would bring Tolkachev and CIA case officers into frequent and close proximity to each other on the street, which the KGB might notice as a pattern. To evade the KGB, different sites would have to be selected for every transmission. It just wasn't worth it. Gerber thought to himself that perhaps Turner would like to eliminate human intelligence and just rely on technology, but it could not be done.

They needed to look the agent in the eye, and Tolkachev needed to shake the hand of a case officer he could trust.[39]

# 9

# THE BILLION DOLLAR SPY

On June 17, 1980, Guilsher put on a disguise once again and headed out to the street. The KGB watchers didn't see him; the disguise worked exactly as intended. After a surveillance detection run, he met Tolkachev at 10:55 p.m. for their seventh rendezvous. The sky was luminescent. In good spirits, Tolkachev told Guilsher he had not encountered any difficulties. He was relieved they could meet before his summer vacation because he had been very busy. He had good news: in February, the tightened security arrangements had suddenly been abandoned. Once again, it was no longer necessary to deposit the building pass when checking out documents. The reason was a bureaucratic logjam: the clerks in the department, mostly women, were swamped with all the building passes coming in and could not get out for lunchtime, a break when they usually searched for food and goods. So the director of the institute went back to the old rules: documents could be taken in the morning and brought back in the late afternoon.[1]

Ever zealous, Tolkachev took advantage when the gap in the cordon opened up. From February to June, he brought thousands of pages of secret documents home to photograph with the Pentax. He told Guilsher that he had 179 rolls of film in his briefcase. But Guilsher didn't seem to be carrying anything to take it away.

Guilsher said he had a plastic bag, which he pulled out of his pocket.

Tolkachev shook his head. The film just wouldn't fit. Tolkachev handed Guilsher his personal briefcase, laden with the 35 mm cassettes. Take the whole thing, he insisted.

Guilsher handed Tolkachev the CIA's new, improved Tropel cameras, saying the agency was hopeful they would make it possible to photograph documents in low light, perhaps in his office. But right away, Tolkachev waved him off. He told Guilsher that it was just not possible to use the miniature Tropel cameras at work. There wasn't enough time either at the start of office hours or at closing, when other people would not be around. He gave the older Tropels back to Guilsher and didn't want the new ones.[2] He seemed to have hit his stride with the Pentax 35 mm camera. Guilsher told headquarters that the Pentax "permits voluminous photography," far more than using the Tropels.[3] The Pentax had become Tolkachev's most fearsome weapon in his effort to inflict damage on the Soviet Union.

Guilsher briefly sketched out the CIA's latest offer to compensate Tolkachev. He emphasized that the proposed salary was higher than that of the president of the United States. He reminded Tolkachev that the CIA would have to bear the considerable expense of his resettlement in America if they went ahead with exfiltration. Tolkachev was stone-faced and showed no sign of reaction. Guilsher had seen that face before.

It was a bittersweet moment for Guilsher, whose family history had played out on these magical Russian summer evenings. His entire career had been devoted to the Soviet target, listening to tapes from the Berlin tunnel and debriefing defectors and agents. His gift had been his language skills. Now, with Tolkachev, as a case officer on the street, he had run one of the deepest penetrations of the Soviet Union ever accomplished.

As the moment came to say farewell, Guilsher knew he might never see Tolkachev again. They had met each other eighteen months earlier on a frigid Moscow street corner. They had only minutes remaining, and both men, reserved and stoic, struggled to find words.[4]

Tolkachev asked if Guilsher would return to Moscow. Guilsher said there was a limit to good things. It was unlikely he would ever come back. Tolkachev commented that he was reading the dissident books Guilsher had brought him as gifts, slowly, when the conditions were right. They shook hands and exchanged a final farewell. Tolkachev seemed nervous and eager to end the meeting. Guilsher told headquarters the next day the "main reason appeared to be desire to get home at a reasonable hour."

It was nearly midnight.

The intelligence "take" from Guilsher's meeting with Tolkachev was massive; the film carried about sixty-four hundred pages of secret documents. Hathaway sent a summary of the latest intelligence to Turner, the CIA director, marked "SECRET/SENSITIVE," which reported,

> CKSPHERE was met on 17 June 1980 at which time
>      he delivered 179 rolls of 35 mm film of sensitive
>      documentary information on Soviet airborne radars
>      and armament control systems. Specifically, the
>      material includes:
> —The first documentation on the technical design
>      characteristics of the new Soviet AWACS (it was
>      CKSPHERE who first alerted us to the existence of

this system and enabled us to locate it in overhead
photography).

—extensive documentation on a new modification of the
MiG-25, the first Soviet aircraft to be equipped with
look-down/shoot-down radar; this aircraft, used in
conjunction with the AWACS, will effectively extend
the Soviet air defense perimeter against NATO aircraft
and air-launched cruise missiles.

—documentation on several new models of airborne
missile systems and technical characteristics of other
Soviet fighter and fighter/bomber aircraft to be
deployed between now and 1990.

Hathaway's memo added, "This volume of documentary
intelligence is double the totality of what CKSPHERE has delivered
in the past 18 months of our relationship."[5]

Along with the documents, Tolkachev gave Guilsher a melan-
choly ops note. He said the permission sheet he had signed to get
secret documents was at this point several times longer than that
of other workers. "As long as the KGB has no suspicion of a leak
of information on Soviet radar systems for interceptor aircraft,
then my work at NIIR and my 'permission' card may possibly
lay quietly. But if a suspicious signal is received from America,"
he added, "my card will undoubtedly be the first one the KGB
will pay attention to." He went on, "I assume that before asking
me why I took out such a large quantity of documents, the KGB
will search my apartment. Things I can hide in the apartment
from members of my family I can never hide from the KGB."
He was referring to a hiding place for spy gear he had created in
his apartment.

Then he ramped up his demand for exfiltration. "Today, I am
turning to you with specific request that my family and I be exfiltrated from the USSR. This is how matters stand." Guilsher's
fears had come true; since the CIA had suggested exfiltration,

Tolkachev's hopes for it were soaring. However, Guilsher knew that Tolkachev had said nothing about revealing this momentous step to his family, so perhaps there was still time.

Tolkachev said he was "under a growing threat," and with his signatures on the permission sheet "my future can be considered to be doomed." He wanted planning for exfiltration to begin "as soon as possible." He added, "I understand perfectly well that for you, the exfiltration of my family and me is tantamount to the death of an agent who provides good quality information. Unfortunately, this loss is unavoidable. It is just a question of time. Therefore, your sincere answer on whether you will attempt the exfiltration or will let fate decide this question is very important to me."

Tolkachev's ops note was tinged with sadness, suggesting that he felt his end was near. Referring to the next scheduled meeting, in the autumn, he said, "if it takes place and I am still functioning," and "if I am not discovered by then."[6]

Along with the ops note, Tolkachev enclosed a note titled "To Leadership of the Center," his appeal for the suicide pill.

He pointed out that "my relationship with you developed neither simply nor quickly," recalling the long delays before the CIA would meet with him and the disagreements over his compensation, and for "almost a year and a half" he had been seeking the suicide pill from the CIA "but always with negative results."

Tolkachev added that since he began working as a spy, several years had passed. "During this time, despite the fact that there have been many distressing moments for me, I have never deviated from the outlined plan. I am reminding you of all this so that you understand that I have sufficiently strong nerves. I have enough patience and self-control to put off use of the means of suicide until the last minute. I insist that means of suicide be passed to me in the near future because my security situation must be considered precarious."[7]

Besides, Tolkachev reminded the CIA, the reason he checked

out so many documents was to answer *their* questions. He then spelled out details of the "traces" that remained of his espionage and said suicide was a way to keep the KGB from uncovering those traces. "Suicide, without any question marks, can protect the work I have begun, that is, can keep secret the volume of my activity and the methods by which I was able to carry out this activity."

Guilsher was in the final weeks at the Moscow station and, with Gerber, wrote a lengthy cable to headquarters taking stock of the operation. They could afford to take a breather, because Tolkachev would be out of touch in the summer months, on vacation. The cable they sent on June 24 described Tolkachev as under "tremendous pressure and strain" in a "bleak" security situation. They outlined the various ways things could unravel. They said "leaks at our end pose serious threat" and could lead to an investigation "that would quickly uncover him." Or, a routine check of document sign-out records would also expose him. An "alert First Department clerk" might notice the large number of records he had signed out. And "accidental discovery" of Tolkachev's carrying out the documents under his coat—or even a recognition of the pattern in which he went home each day at lunch after checking out documents—"could blow" the operation, they warned. On top of all these "serious factors" affecting Tolkachev's security, "there are undoubtedly others as well."

"We reluctantly conclude there is little we can do," they told headquarters. "We are dealing with driven man who dedicated to inflict most damage possible on Soviet regime. He will continue to produce, be it from First Department or secret library, and will probably not heed our urgings to slow down."

In view of the security situation, "can we realistically expect operation to last several more years?" they asked. They did not think so. They added, "It appears CKS is coming close to fulfilling production plan he proposed to us and we accepted." Thus, they said, it was "critically important" to have a "clear-cut picture of where we stand" on Tolkachev's work so far and what espionage he could carry out in the future. With Tolkachev's pressing for exfiltration, Guilsher asked headquarters what the impact would be if Tolkachev were no longer in Moscow. Would it be a huge loss? Guilsher warned headquarters directly: the "operation cannot continue indefinitely."

"Gloomy" was how Guilsher described Tolkachev's letter seeking the suicide pill. "If uncovered," he warned, Tolkachev "will have unpleasant dealings with security organs and will then certainly be shot. As death in case of compromise is inevitable, CKS should be given choice of using 'special request' and avoiding agony of facing authorities." Having the suicide pill available "in case of need" would give Tolkachev "much needed psychological and moral support." Guilsher cautioned headquarters yet again that "additional delays and rejections of 'special request' will alienate CKS at critical state of operation and could lead to serious handling problems or even end of production."[8]

At headquarters, Hathaway was sympathetic. Unlike the last time Turner was asked to approve the suicide pill—when the request was watered down by the acting chief of the division—this time Hathaway didn't mince words. He wrote a strong memo that echoed the thinking of his chief of station and case officer. Providing Tolkachev with the L-pill would be "a significant psychological boost to him," Hathaway said, describing Tolkachev as "a mature, sensible and cautious individual" who needed an escape hatch in case he was arrested by the KGB.[9]

In July, Hathaway responded to earlier questions from the Moscow station about the value of Tolkachev's intelligence. He said that even if Tolkachev departed the Soviet Union, "the value of his product would not diminish for at least 8–10 years." Why? The weapons systems that Tolkachev had already betrayed to the United States were either just becoming operational or on the drawing boards, and they could not be easily replaced. On the other hand, if Tolkachev continued spying in Moscow, the yield could be even greater, as new weapons systems came across his desk year after year.

Tolkachev's amazing haul of documents, blueprints, and diagrams was made available in its raw, untranslated form to very few people in Washington. One of them was a special assistant in the air force who had used the intelligence to "terminate or reorient" research and development programs of the U.S. military. Tolkachev was providing a road map to the United States for compromising and defeating two critical Soviet weapons systems: the radars on the ground that defended it from attack, and the radars on warplanes that gave it capacity to attack others. This was an incomparable advantage in the Cold War competition. Hathaway had asked the U.S. Air Force to estimate what Tolkachev's intelligence was worth, in a broad way. Could they put a dollar amount on how much they had saved in research and development costs? The answer was "somewhere in the neighborhood of $2 billion," Hathaway reported to Gerber. That was before they even looked at the 179 rolls of film delivered to Guilsher in the briefcase.[10]

Tolkachev was the billion dollar spy.

# 10

# FLIGHT OF UTOPIA

On the day in July 1979 that he arrived in Moscow as a new case officer, David Rolph took the elevator in the U.S. embassy to the ninth floor, walked past the marine guards, through the chancery, then down a back stairs to the seventh floor. There, at the landing, the door on the right opened to the embassy political section. On the left, an unmarked door had a cipher lock. Rolph punched in the code. After the first door, he saw a second one that looked like a bank vault. It had a combination lock but was open during the day when people were inside. He walked down a short hallway, past the small alcove on the left with the paper shredder. Turning to the right, he grabbed the lever on another door and opened it with the soft whoosh of an air lock. He entered a windowless rectangular box of a room, with a low ceiling, shielded in corrugated metal and isolated from the embassy walls to avoid eavesdropping or penetration. This was the Moscow station.

David Rolph was thirty-one years old and filled with anticipation. He was beginning his first tour for the CIA, and he yearned for an operation of his own, to get out on the streets and run an agent.

At one end of the station, the station chief worked from a cramped office with a desk, a safe, and a small conference table barely large enough for the case officers to squeeze around. The rest of the station was jammed with their desks, lined up along each side, typewriters, file cabinets protected by combination locks, and maps of Moscow on the walls. One large map was covered with colored, numbered dots to indicate meeting sites, signal sites, dead drop locations, and who was responsible for each. Music drifted from a cassette player. Clipboards held the latest cable traffic. Rolph was assigned the desk closest to the chief of station's office. Across the room sat Guilsher, who was running the Tolkachev operation. Guilsher always looked dignified and often wore a blazer and tie to work. "Guilsher always looked like a president," recalled one of his colleagues. By contrast, when they weren't working their daytime cover jobs, Rolph and the younger case officers often showed up in jeans. Rolph's first impression was that Guilsher was a bit stiff and formal, but any doubts were dispelled when he saw Guilsher at work. He was totally preoccupied with Tolkachev and often returned from their meetings with a detailed recollection of what Tolkachev had said, despite the distractions, tension, and exhaustion. When Guilsher spoke, Rolph listened intently. There was much to learn.

Rolph's own journey to the Moscow station had begun as a young boy on the front lines of the Cold War in Europe. When he was ten years old, he had tagged along with his father, Arthur, a lieutenant colonel who commanded a battalion of the Sixth Armored Cavalry responsible for border security in West Germany, where it met Czechoslovakia. Arthur took his son to see a frontier that bristled with hostility: watchtowers, dog patrols, killing zones, and machine gun nests. If a real war ever broke out in Europe, this was the place that would be overrun by invading Warsaw Pact tanks and troops. For Rolph, the border left a deep impression: the land beyond the fences looked mysterious, and he was intrigued and fearful. Later, when his family returned to the United States, Rolph studied Russian at the University of Kentucky and was planning to attend graduate school to study Russian history, but the Vietnam War loomed. By lottery number, he was facing the draft, so he enlisted. For his initial training, he selected language study in Russian. Later, he became an officer. More than once, he was shoulder to shoulder with men destined for Vietnam, but he did not go. The army sent him instead to West Berlin as an intelligence case officer.

He wore civilian clothes and worked from a small office in the Berlin Brigade, the garrison for occupation forces of the United States. His mission was to take lists of recent refugees who had come over from East Germany, Czechoslovakia, and Hungary and knock on their doors, seeking out tidbits of intelligence about the armies of the Soviet Union and the Warsaw Pact. It was hard work, often frustrating. "It was really collecting ash and trash," he recalled later. "We were trying to scrape together low-level fragments of tactical information. And when we found someone, and they were willing, then of course the big question was, would you go back for us? Do you want to visit your aunt and uncle in Prague? Would you be willing to drive by the base and take some pictures?" Occasionally, they came across a good source but not for long. The promising cases were quickly transferred to the CIA. The CIA base was in a building close by the Berlin Brigade. "All the routine cases they would say to us, 'Good job, keep it up!' Then a good one would float to the surface, and they would take it."

Even so, Rolph relished the intelligence work. He had a competitive instinct to crack open secrets in the "denied areas" of the East, those dark lands he saw beyond the wall. But he concluded that clandestine human intelligence gathering was a backwater in the army and would never make much of a career. He left the military after a few years and returned to the United States for graduate school at Indiana University to earn a doctorate in Russian history, hoping to become a professor. On closer inspection, this, too, seemed a dead end. The job market was thin. Out of pragmatic concerns for his family—a second child was on the way—he went to law school instead, thinking it would at least be lucrative. Rolph earned a law degree from Indiana University and began to practice law, but after a year as an attorney his heart wasn't in it. He felt the pull of those boyhood memories. When he heard a CIA recruiter was coming to a nearby town, he drove there for an interview and filled out the application. Nothing happened for a year; then suddenly he was offered a job. He reported to the CIA for training in 1977.

It was a time of widespread doubt about America's role in the world, but Rolph shared none of these doubts. He believed deeply in the battle against communism and the struggle to protect freedom, an outlook born not so much from ideology as from his own experience. He knew the Soviet Union in earlier decades maintained a vast system of penal colonies populated by tens of thousands of people who were incarcerated for their thoughts and nothing else. He knew well the ugly reality of the Berlin Wall, the dirty, plowed strip laden with watchtowers, mines, barbed wire, automatic weapons, electric-shock fences, feral dogs, and probing floodlights. The Cold War had to be fought, and Rolph wanted to be part of it.

During his initial training at the CIA, Rolph was asked if he had a preference for where to serve. The CIA was divided into geographic divisions. Many young trainees did not want to go to the Moscow station, because it was known as a difficult place to run spies. It was all "sticks and bricks," some said disdainfully: laying down dead drops and impersonal communications, not handling agents eye to eye. But Rolph repeated to anyone who would listen: he wanted the Soviet division.

Sometimes, the CIA sent young case officers to the Moscow

station who had never served abroad with the CIA; that way, the KGB would be less likely to spot them. But at the time, there was only one vacant slot in Moscow, working with a cover in the defense attaché's office. The CIA hesitated. Two years earlier, the slot was held by a CIA case officer who was ambushed and expelled. If a new man walked in, the KGB might immediately assume he was an intelligence officer. Despite the misgivings, Rolph got the job. He took the basic CIA training course and then more training for espionage operations in "denied areas," practicing how to dodge the relentless surveillance of the KGB.

At the time, he learned the Moscow station was carrying out one of the most extraordinary technical operations yet attempted against the Soviet Union. High-resolution imagery from a spy satellite showed that workers were digging a trench and laying a communications line along a country road between the Krasnaya Pakhra Nuclear Weapons Research Institute, located at Troitsk, twenty-two miles southwest of Moscow, and the Defense Ministry in the capital. The CIA planned to put a silent wiretap on the line, an electronic collar that would scoop up the secrets and record them, without being detected. The wiretap would be placed in a manhole along the road where the cable was buried. Rolph was assigned to the nascent project while still in training. An exact mock-up of the manhole had been built near Washington, D.C., by a CIA contractor for training. Step one was to pry off the heavy manhole lid. Rolph was instructed how to use a crowbar and hook to remove it. Once he was inside, a case officer's patience and skill would be sorely tested. Trainees had exercised in blindfolds to see if they could enter the manhole and carry out the operation by feel alone.

Rolph was thrilled to be selected for the mission. In training one day, he hoisted the heavy manhole cover using the crowbar and hook. Then suddenly he dropped it. The manhole cover smashed down on his thumb. Rolph felt a jolt of pain. He turned to his supervisor and tried to seem unperturbed.

The supervisor took one glance at his thumb, which was limp, and sent him to the hospital. It was broken.

A few days later, wearing a cast, Rolph returned to headquarters. He volunteered to resume the training on the manhole as soon as the cast came off, in a few weeks. But his superiors waved him off, saying there wasn't time; they didn't want to delay his arrival in Moscow. Rolph felt angry at himself and sheepish about the accident, but he didn't linger over it. He had been selected for Moscow duty and was proud to be going. He felt like an astronaut chosen for an Apollo mission. Soon, with his cast off and his training complete, he walked into the Moscow station.

Rolph arrived as the days of timidity in Moscow—the days when there hadn't been an agent worth the name—were over. The station, once frozen by Turner's stand-down order, was now buzzing with activity. Tolkachev was producing huge volumes of secret documents, and the manhole wiretap was about to be emplaced and connected. Then, just as Rolph found his desk in the station, yet another audacious operation got under way, and he would be part of it.[1]

That summer, Victor Sheymov took advantage of the warm evenings to stroll with his wife, Olga, on the broad avenues of Moscow. Sheymov was thirty-three years old, one of the youngest majors in the KGB. He held an extremely sensitive job in the directorate responsible for the agency's encrypted communications with its stations—each known as a *rezidentura*—around the world. Sheymov worked in "the Tower," a building at KGB headquarters that housed the Eighth Chief Directorate, located behind the Lubyanka, a foreboding prerevolutionary stone structure that had come to symbolize the power of the KGB and its Soviet predecessors. Before coming to the KGB, Sheymov worked on missile guidance systems. His father was a military engineer and his mother a doctor. His reputation was that of a young electronics whiz: he had recently been dispatched to China to solve an eavesdropping case that no one else could crack, and he did. But privately, Sheymov was seething.[2]

It was hard to say when the disenchantment set in. He had been promoted so rapidly that he had never acquired the blithe passivity of the older generation. He was young enough to be offended when things weren't right. Early in his days at the KGB, he had been assigned to a secret unit that prepared briefings and analysis for the Politburo. The briefings were altered to meet specific orders and were full of deceptions and fabrications. Sheymov was appalled. He saw a chasm between the reports to the bosses and the reality on the streets. One day, he went to the KGB library and asked the woman at the desk if he could read a history of the Communist Party. He saw himself as a scientist, an engineer, someone who respected facts. Maybe he could find answers to his questions in such a book. Everyone who had a college education had to take a course on the history of the party; what could be more loyal than a curiosity about the history of the party? The librarian asked him for his identification card, perhaps intending to report him to superiors. He could see it on her face: Why would anybody be reading such a thing? Sheymov played it cool, pretended to be interested in another book, and walked out as soon as he could.

Then a friend in the KGB named Valentin died suddenly and mysteriously. Valentin had been youthful and healthy, a cross-country skier. His father was a member of the Central Committee. But Valentin was a nonconformist type, telling Sheymov that he despised his father and the party hierarchy. He had called them a "disgusting gang" in the presence of his father. After the death, Sheymov discovered that his friend was probably murdered by thugs from the KGB. At Valentin's funeral, he stood over the casket and silently vowed to exact revenge.

In the months that followed, Sheymov pondered what to do. He was more and more disillusioned. It was fashionable among younger people at the time to be cynical about the system, to affect Western dress and culture, and to make wicked jokes about Brezhnev and the aging, dysfunctional party leadership. But most people just talked in private; they did not act on their thoughts. In 1979, Sheymov decided to act. He started to plan for an escape. He was determined to strike a blow at the system, a damaging blow. Olga was frightened—their daughter, Yelena, had just turned four years old—but she vowed to stick by him.

At first, Sheymov hatched a plan to contact an American intelligence officer. Sheymov had never been to the United States and harbored no illusions. He knew from reading secret cables that the United States was the enemy, and his logic was simple: the enemy of my enemy is my friend. He wanted to take his revenge by going to America.

He knew it would be risky. He possessed a top secret security clearance. If discovered, he would be immediately arrested and probably executed. Yet Sheymov was streetwise about Moscow, an intelligence officer trained to move about without being detected. He devoted hours to searching for a car with the license plates of an American diplomat. But Sheymov could not find a car with D-04 plates. He then decided to write a note, in case he encountered an American intelligence officer. "Hello," it began, "I am a KGB officer with access to highly sensitive information." He hinted that his dissatisfaction with the system demanded "action" and proposed a meeting at a tobacco kiosk near a Moscow Metro station. But Sheymov could not find anyone to give the note to. One night, he confessed to Olga that four of his ideas for contacting the Americans had all come to nothing. He had even concocted a reason to visit the Foreign Ministry for a meeting, thinking he might find the car of an American diplomat there. He planned to bump into the American car with his own, creating a small fender-bender incident at which he could leap out and give the driver his note. At one point, Sheymov spotted an American car, but when he tried to scrape it, the driver pulled away just in time. The note was in Sheymov's palm that day but never delivered.

Finally, Sheymov came up with a far more ambitious plan.

In October 1979, he was on a business trip to straighten out embassy communications in Warsaw. He had brought his father's thick eyeglasses and stopped at an optician, asking if he could get them repaired. That was a nice little cover story. The eyeglasses had another purpose. One afternoon, he went to see a movie with some KGB colleagues. He excused himself just as the film was starting and caught a taxi to the American embassy. His plan was to walk up to the door of the embassy wearing the glasses as a disguise, but he had made one mistake. It turned out that his father's eyeglasses were so thick he couldn't see a thing. Nearly blind but undaunted, he stumbled toward the marine guard and said, "I need to speak to the representative of American intelligence." The guard looked at him and replied, "I am the representative of American intelligence." Sheymov responded with a backup line he had memorized: "Then I need to speak to duty diplomat."

Soon, Sheymov was face-to-face with the Americans, took off the glasses, and told them he wanted political asylum in the United States. He wrote on a piece of paper, "KGB." They escorted him to a windowless room. The conversation was stilted: the Americans spoke Polish but not Russian; Sheymov had just fragments of English. They photocopied his passport and asked him a few questions, such as who was the KGB chief in Warsaw. Sheymov's answers satisfied them he was indeed a KGB officer.

"What's your line of work?" one of the Americans asked.

"Cipher communications," Sheymov said. The Americans looked at each other with surprise.

"Are you a cipher clerk?" one of them asked.

"No, I am responsible for the security of the KGB cipher communications abroad," he replied.

The Americans were dumbstruck. A man with the keys to the kingdom, the ultrasecret codes to Soviet communications, was volunteering to defect. They asked if he wanted to be whisked out of Warsaw immediately. No, Sheymov replied—he wanted to bring his wife and daughter to the United States. He told the Americans he would soon be returning to Moscow. They told him he was crazy, but he insisted. On a sheet of paper, he wrote his proposal for a rendezvous, early in 1980, and he handed it to one of them.

The CIA then set up a plan to communicate with Sheymov in Moscow. He gave them an address that was not his own. He was told to expect a letter by regular mail. If anyone opened it, the letter would appear to be from an old friend, someone with an innocuous name, say Smirnov, recalling a training exercise years before. When he got the letter, they said, he should wet it down and invisible writing would appear on the other side with instructions for how to signal he was ready to meet the CIA.

As they walked out, one of the Americans asked Sheymov if he had ever heard of Halloween. No, he said, what's that? The American explained it was a holiday, taking place that very evening.

"You've pulled one hell of a trick-or-treat," he said.

"I'm sorry?" Sheymov replied.

"Oh, never mind. You'll find out." They put him in a car and dropped him at the movie house ten minutes before the film was to end.

When the Moscow station got word of the Sheymov case, Hathaway was finishing his tour. He had to make a decision:

Who would handle the new agent? He could not give the case to Guilsher, who was busy running Tolkachev. His other senior case officer, James Olson, would be valuable but was deeply involved in the sensitive manhole operation. There were a few other possibilities, all skilled case officers but without polished Russian-language skills. Hathaway gave the case to David Rolph, the new arrival, who spoke Russian well and was eager to show what he could do.

A code word for Sheymov was sent from headquarters to the Moscow station: CKUTOPIA.

The code name suggested sky-high expectations, yet much about Sheymov was entirely unknown. Did he really serve as a master of KGB overseas communications? How could they check? How could they get a peek at the kind of intelligence he would produce? What did he want? The Gerber rules, fashioned nine years earlier, still mattered.

Sheymov wanted exfiltration, with his family. There were files in the station with the code word CKGO, containing scenarios for getting an agent out of the country, but the Moscow station had no experience; it had never been done from the Soviet Union. A KGB man with such top secret clearances couldn't just go to the airport and fly away. Travel abroad was tightly controlled for all Soviet citizens. Moreover, Sheymov might have been subject to KGB counterintelligence surveillance in Moscow. If there were any suspicions, he would be arrested.

Rolph made a rather unconventional suggestion to Hathaway. He said they should give Sheymov a pair of new Tropel cameras in one of the first meetings. They could ask Sheymov to photograph the most sensitive documents on his desk and then return the cameras. When they developed the film, they would see whether he had the access that he claimed and whether it was worth it to take him and his family out. Immediately, headquarters objected to giving the cameras to a completely unknown and untested agent. What if he was a dangle? What if he delivered the precious technology right into the hands of the KGB? And what if he got caught with the cameras? But Hathaway liked the idea and backed up Rolph. At one point, he wrote a stern cable to headquarters saying that he, Rolph, and all the other case officers in the station thought it was a good idea to give Tropel cameras to the new agent. *Could they all be wrong?* Headquarters relented. The Tropels would be shipped out soon.

As Gerber arrived in January to take over as chief, the Moscow station mailed the letter to Sheymov with the invisible writing. The signal, the letter explained, was to be made on a Sunday at a location that the CIA had given the code name BULOCHNAYA, or "bakery." Every Sunday, Rolph drove to church services, a route that took him past the site. He kept an eye on a concrete pillar at one corner of an apartment complex. Then, on a Sunday in late February, he spotted the black *V* drawn by hand. Everyone on the street was walking by as if it meant nothing. But it was the signal from Sheymov. They would meet soon.

Before every operation, a case officer planned and carried out a surveillance detection run. Rolph wanted to be absolutely certain he was free from KGB surveillance. With help from the other case officers and the technical operations team in the station, he worked up a plan. It was far more ambitious than usual and based on something Guilsher had once attempted unsuccessfully. Rolph went over it, minute by minute, with Gerber, who pressed him about every possible fault. *What happens if . . . ? What happens if . . . ?* Finally, the chief was satisfied.

Rolph bought a round-trip ticket on the Soviet airline, Aeroflot, from Moscow to Frankfurt, with a Friday departure and a return the following Thursday. He properly notified the Soviet administrative office, which provided services to diplomats, that he was coming back on Thursday, confident they would report it to the KGB. Then he packed his bag and caught the flight out. From Frankfurt, Rolph took a train to Vienna on Saturday. He was so filled with anxiety he could hardly sleep. On Monday, he went to the airport and, for cash, bought a one-way air ticket back to Moscow on the next Austrian Airlines flight. The KGB was expecting him to return on Thursday, on Aeroflot. Once he landed on Monday afternoon, he went through passport control, but he knew it would take them a while to report his arrival to the KGB. This was the "gap" he was trying to exploit, a simple lapse in bureaucracy that would give him a few hours. He was "black"—free from surveillance.

At the time he landed in Moscow, the wife of another case officer was bringing a small duffel bag to Rolph's wife, who was a teacher. As Rolph's wife finished her classes, she took the duffel bag and began her own surveillance detection run through the city by car. The bag held a light disguise for Rolph, an ops note, and CIA questions to be given to Sheymov.

From the airport, Rolph took a taxi toward the city. He abruptly got out at a busy Metro stop, Dinamo, about halfway into town. The stop was on one side of the broad Leningradsky Prospekt. Rolph walked, casually, around the Metro stop and then toward a building marked "Aeroflot" on the other side of the highway, all the while looking for possible surveillance. When he reached the building, his wife picked him up in the car. They began another long surveillance detection run. Finally, satisfied that he was completely free from surveillance and having put on the disguise, Rolph got out of the car. His wife sped off for a few hours to a planned dinner party with friends.

By 8:00 p.m., Rolph was walking near a statue of Aleksandr Griboyedov, a Russian playwright and diplomat who was killed by an angry mob in Tehran while serving as ambassador to Persia in 1829. The statue stood high on a pedestal near the Kirovskaya Metro station at Chistye Prudy, a broad, tree-lined park with a boulevard on each side in an old section of Moscow filled with narrow lanes and a maze of passageways.

Rolph was near the statue when he saw the man he was looking for, carrying a magazine, approaching from the Metro.

Rolph spoke first. "Victor Ivanovich?"

"Yes."

"Good evening. I am Misha." Rolph extended his hand.

Sheymov shook it, but he told himself it was important to establish that this man was really an American intelligence officer. He might be walking into a trap.

They started walking. Both were in their early thirties. Rolph saw that Sheymov's face was smooth, clean, boyish. He wore a military-style cap. Sheymov thought Rolph spoke Russian with an accent, although it didn't necessarily seem to be an American one. Sheymov noticed that Rolph didn't wear gloves—a Russian would.

Physically, Rolph was coiled, thinking that any second the klieg lights would come on, the KGB officers would spring from the bushes, and he and Sheymov would be ambushed.

Sheymov had taken a roundabout subway route to avoid surveillance, but he was also worried and tense. He knew more than Rolph did about how the KGB worked, that they used "floating" surveillance teams, which roamed the city and could appear randomly. He noted a nearby phone booth was empty; at least that was a good sign.

Both men had been trained to carry out operations with a basic principle: once it begins, don't think about it. Both knew that their business was to spend hours and hours planning, but in execution an operation would be brief and had to be flawless. The metaphor in Rolph's mind was of an actor stepping on the stage: once the curtain came up, you just did your best to perform. Sheymov believed the worst thing an intelligence professional could do would be to give in to fear. That meant losing control.

"You might be KGB," Sheymov said to Rolph.

"I can't be KGB, I speak Russian with an accent," Rolph protested.

"Okay, but they can speak Russian with an accent, too," Sheymov said.

The two men walked through the park, away from the Metro and the statue. Darkness enveloped them. They kept quizzing each other, both looking for any sign of trouble.

Sheymov repeated that he wanted to be exfiltrated with his family. Rolph responded that it was a tall order and might take twelve to eighteen months to prepare. He told Sheymov that he would have to provide some information first. Rolph thought they might meet again in a month or two, but Sheymov said, why wait? He would be ready in a week. Sheymov insisted that they meet in person. He did not want to communicate with the Americans by dead drop. He told Rolph that KGB counterintelligence had made a long list of people arrested for working with spies—caught in a dead drop, caught using a radio. *No one* had been caught in a personal meeting. Sheymov wanted to see his CIA case officer face-to-face. Rolph agreed.

They parted, and Rolph took a Metro a few stops toward the center of Moscow. His wife picked him up in the car, and they headed home. The next morning, everyone crowded around Gerber's conference table to hear what had happened.

Rolph thought he might have a month to prepare for the next meeting, but now he had only a week. He surmised that the KGB had figured out his trick of going abroad and returning home early, so he could not repeat it. The Moscow station created an elaborate plan for the next meeting. Rolph would be the primary case officer, but if he came under KGB surveillance, there would be a second and a third officer nearby on the streets, having completed their own surveillance detection runs, ready to slip into his place, just in case. They did a month's work in just a few days.

As it turned out, Rolph was clear. The meeting began without trouble. Rolph asked Sheymov some questions from headquarters about complex mathematics and cryptology, and Sheymov answered into Rolph's small tape recorder. They again discussed exfiltration. Sheymov wanted $1 million upon his arrival in the United States, immediate citizenship, and lifetime health benefits for his family. Rolph didn't make any promises. He asked Sheymov for mundane but essential details about his family: clothing sizes, medical histories, weights, and shoe sizes. And he needed recent photographs of everyone for the new identity documents they would get after exfiltration, on the other side.

At one of the first meetings, Rolph gave Sheymov the CIA's miniature Tropel cameras. Rolph said to him, "Photograph the most highly classified papers you have. Don't take chances with other people around. But you have to prove to us that you are who you say you are." Sheymov agreed. He returned the cameras with exposed film and was given a fresh supply.

Sheymov suggested the CIA fake the drowning of his family in a river so the KGB would not suspect they had defected. Rolph responded that the CIA and Sheymov had more important things to do—to ensure the actual exfiltration was a success. In fact, Rolph had given plenty of thought to what would happen once Sheymov and his family vanished. Inside the Moscow station, Rolph discussed how to make Sheymov "disappear without a trace." They would leave the apartment exactly as it was—a cup of tea unfinished on the table, the bed unmade, a newspaper open, their clothes still in the closets. They talked about whether the disappearance could be explained as a drowning, but Rolph and the other case officers didn't dwell on it. That was not something they could plan; it would just have to play out. The KGB would probably be much more inclined to blame an accident or crime, and it might be quite a while before they realized Sheymov had defected.

Rolph and Sheymov were walking down one of the narrow lanes in Moscow when they saw them, at the same moment. The nightmare scenario: two men in a playground sandbox. They could be anybody, but both intelligence officers instantly thought surveillance.

The narrow streets left them few escape routes, and if it were really the KGB, they would be boxed in at both ends of the street. As they got closer, Sheymov sensed they were not KGB but perhaps militiamen—crude, jumpy, capable of demanding papers, but not as threatening. Sheymov went over and asked one for a match. Then, after returning to Rolph, as they passed the two men, Sheymov berated Rolph as if they were having a family argument. His outburst carried them well past the men. Sheymov noticed they were in identical warm coats and reindeer-fur-lined hats. He and Rolph turned the corner onto the next street.

They looked at each other.

"Criminal surveillance," Sheymov said. "The militia."

"How did you know?"

"Just a hunch."

"Boy, that was a close call," said Rolph. "Do you still like personal meetings?"

"Sure, now where were we?"

The Tropel cameras Sheymov had used and returned to Rolph were carried by hand back to the United States. Meanwhile, the tape recording of Sheymov's answers in Russian about cryptology was translated in the station by Guilsher. When the film was developed, with more than a hundred pages of information, and the answers translated, an urgent message arrived at the Moscow station: Sheymov was for real. The intelligence was sensitive—the Soviets would never have used it for a dangle—and extremely important. The Soviet Union was installing new encrypted communications equipment around the world. Sheymov could unlock those messages. Rolph had told Sheymov that exfiltration might take twelve to eighteen months, but now there was a fresh urgency. The National Security Agency wanted him brought to the United States—fast.

Sheymov had given the Americans a tantalizing taste of his material, but he possessed much more. He knew the clock was ticking: the longer he was in Moscow, the greater the chance he would be discovered. Also, the size of what he wanted to deliver to the United States was too large to be transmitted in any dead drop or other means in Moscow. To damage the Soviet Union and save himself, he had no choice but to defect.

The CIA and the National Security Agency also realized the information Sheymov possessed would be immensely valuable as long as the Soviet Union did not know it was missing. Once discovered, the Soviets might change the codes. So they had to get Sheymov out without the KGB knowing he had gone to the United States, at least for as long as possible.

In the Moscow station, Rolph reached for the files marked CKGO. Not only did he get his first operation, but it was to be one of the most audacious ever attempted.

At their third meeting, Sheymov delivered photographs of his family that the CIA could use for preparing documents and the other information Rolph had asked for. The biggest hurdle for the exfiltration was Sheymov's young daughter. Two adults could remain silent for the forty-five minutes or so it would take to smuggle them across the border in a van, but a four-year-old girl? How to keep her quiet? Rolph secured from the CIA five samples of sedatives suitable for a small child. He was worried; he thought for sure Sheymov would refuse to take them. Rolph had a daughter about the same age, and he would never have given her any pills from the KGB, but to his surprise Sheymov agreed. Sheymov gave the CIA carefully hand-drawn charts on his daughter's breathing and pulse each time she took a tablet. They selected one sedative for the exfiltration.

The Moscow station had conducted five meetings with Sheymov over a period of about ten weeks. The pace was unprecedented.

Although he preferred personal meetings, Sheymov signaled at one point that he wanted to use a special kind of dead drop, known as a foot-timed drop, in which the package is left by the agent and picked up by the case officer in short order. Rolph saw the first signal, then waited for the second signal that the drop had been filled before he went out on an evening walk. He retrieved Sheymov's package intact and took it to the station the next morning. Among other things, he found an ops note from Sheymov tucked into a small glass bottle with a stopper, about two inches high. Rolph thought that Sheymov was being extremely careful, putting the note in the bottle to keep it dry. But actually, Sheymov had another purpose in mind. The label on the bottle said it held fifty tablets of extract of valerian, an herb for soothing nerves. He intended it as a signal to Rolph that all was going well and not to worry. No one in the station grasped the implication.

The final days had arrived. Sheymov was supposed to check a lamppost in Moscow for a signal from the CIA that all was ready to go. He and Olga rode a streetcar to the location, careful to be looking casual and not staring at each passing lamppost. But when they reached the stop, they realized all the lampposts had been ripped down for a construction project.

"What do we do now?" Olga asked him.

"We go," Sheymov said. "I think at this point it would be more dangerous for us to wait than to try." He sounded more confident than he felt.

The plan was to take a train to a secluded, forested point between Leningrad and the border with Finland, from which the CIA would whisk them out, hidden in a vehicle. The date was May 17, 1980. The operation was extremely sensitive. The White House knew about it but had instructed Gerber not to inform the U.S. ambassador at the time, Thomas Watson Jr. If the plan fell apart, all the blame would be laid on the CIA. But everyone in the station knew about it. The case officers had all contributed to the elaborate plan.

Rolph wanted to wait around the station that Saturday for word of what happened, but Gerber said it made no sense. He did not want to alert the KGB to any unusual activity. Gerber told the communicator on duty that he was expecting a message about an operation. If the operation was a success, the communicator should put a piece of paper with a large handwritten numeral 1 on the inner door to the station, the one that looked like a bank vault with a combination on it. If a failure, he said, write a 0.

Late on Saturday afternoon, Gerber went to the embassy building, ostensibly to pick out a film to watch at home that night. He briefly opened the outer door of the station and looked at the inner door.

A big 1 was taped to the door. Sheymov was out! The flight of CKUTOPIA was over. Moreover, Sheymov had left behind clues to throw off the KGB. For months, they thought he had been murdered along with his family, although they could not find proof.

Rolph's operation was brief but highly successful. A few months later, when Rolph was back in the United States, he met Sheymov again at a temporary safe house in northern Virginia. They embraced. Sheymov said to Rolph, "The whole time we

Adolf Tolkachev on a vacation at the Baltic Sea, early 1970s.
*Courtesy of a family friend*

A 1948 school photo. *Courtesy of a family friend*

Tolkachev in 1984. *Courtesy of a family friend*

The Moscow gas station where Tolkachev made his first approach to the CIA, January 12, 1977. *Courtesy of Valery Smychkov*

Robert Fulton, CIA Moscow station chief at the time. *Courtesy of the Robert M. Fulton Trust*

Fulton cabled headquarters about the Russian man who approached him at the gas station.

This building housed the U.S. embassy at the time of the Tolkachev operation. The CIA station was on the seventh floor in 1977. Tolkachev's high-rise apartment building can be seen on the left. *AP Photo/Tanya Makeyeva*

Gus Hathaway, Moscow station chief, with a Soviet militiaman at a guard shack in front of his apartment. The militiamen called out to KGB surveillance teams on the comings and goings of Americans. CIA case officers sometimes used "identity transfer" to evade them.
*Courtesy of Karin Hathaway*

Gus Hathaway in the Moscow station after the embassy fire in August 1977. During the fire, Hathaway blocked the KGB from entering the station. *Courtesy of Karin Hathaway*

Hathaway (in raincoat) on the street the morning after the fire. *Courtesy of Karin Hathaway*

Stansfield Turner, a Navy admiral who became CIA director in 1977, worried that something was wrong in the Moscow station and ordered a stand-down of all operations. *AP Photo/Bob Daugherty*

CIA headquarters, Langley, Virginia, 1979. *AP Photo*

CIA case officer Marti Peterson at KGB headquarters, July 15, 1977. She was detained after loading a dead drop for agent Alexander Ogorodnik. After his arrest, he committed suicide with an L-pill concealed by the CIA in a fountain pen. *Courtesy of H. Keith Melton and the Melton Archive*

On her return to CIA headquarters, Peterson briefed Turner and then President Carter. *Courtesy of Martha Peterson*

Alexander Ogorodnik, a Soviet diplomat, who became CIA agent TRIGON. *Courtesy of Martha Peterson*

John Guilsher, at home in Moscow. He was Tolkachev's first case officer. *Courtesy of Catherine Guilsher*

Guilsher at Moscow station.
*Courtesy of David Rolph*

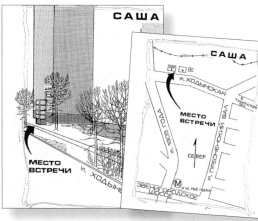

Guilsher and others in the station prepared maps and illustrations for Tolkachev showing where to meet—here, a location codenamed SASHA.

The first spy camera given Tolkachev to copy documents was a "Molly," above right, but the results were unsatisfactory. Later, the CIA gave him the ultratiny Tropel spy camera, concealed in a key fob, left. Below, a page from Tropel instructions. The Tropel was a wonder of optical engineering. Tolkachev once used it to photograph documents in a men's room stall. *Courtesy of H. Keith Melton and the Melton Archive*

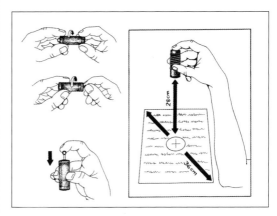

David Rolph, Tolkachev's second case officer. Before handling Tolkachev, Rolph managed the daring exfiltration of agent CKUTOPIA. *Courtesy of David Rolph*

The "V" signal on the pillar left by CKUTOPIA. Rolph spotted it one Sunday in early 1980, and the operation began soon after. *Courtesy of David Rolph*

The CIA attempted to replicate Tolkachev's building pass to facilitate removing secret documents from his institute. Despite much effort, the plan worked only briefly in the summer of 1982. Above, the inside of the building pass; below, the exterior, and CIA translation of a note from Tolkachev, who gave Rolph a piece of the pass to help replicate the paper and colors of the ink. *Courtesy of H. Keith Melton and the Melton Archive*

In the propusk B are colored strips of paper and a strip of material, cut out from the cover of my propusk.

Burton Gerber, Moscow station chief 1980–1982 and later Soviet division chief, with his wife, Rosalie. Gerber helped develop CIA rules for vetting new agents and later innovated with the use of "deep cover" case officers in Moscow. *Courtesy of Burton L. Gerber*

Robert Morris in his cover office. *Courtesy of Robert O. Morris*

Tolkachev's apartment building was home to the Soviet aviation and rocket elite. He lived on the ninth floor. To signal he was ready to meet the CIA, he opened a small window, called the *fortochka*, above the main window. *Courtesy of the author*

Tolkachev's most important spy gear was a Pentax ME 35 mm single-lens-reflex camera. He photographed thousands of pages of secret documents with the camera and a clamp provided by CIA. *Courtesy of Titrisol/Wikimedia Commons*

# WANTED BY THE FBI

**ESPIONAGE; INTERSTATE FLIGHT - PROBATION VIOLATION**

## EDWARD LEE HOWARD

FBI No. 720 744 CA2

Photograph taken 1983

Aliases: Patrick Brian, Patrick M. Brian, Patrick M. Bryan, Edward L. Houston, Roger H. Shannon

### DESCRIPTION

| | | | |
|---|---|---|---|
| Date of Birth: | October 27, 1951 | Hair: | brown |
| Place of Birth: | Alamogordo, New Mexico | Eyes: | brown |
| Height: | 5'11" | Complexion: | medium |
| Weight: | 165 to 180 pounds | Race: | white |
| Build: | medium | Nationality: | American |
| Occupations: | economic analyst, former U.S. Government employee | | |
| Remarks: | knowledgeable in the use of firearms | | |
| Scars and Marks: | 2-inch scar over right eye; scar on upper lip | | |
| Social Security Number Used: | 457-92-0226 | | |
| NCIC: | DO5407191911091419 | | |
| Fingerprint Classification: | 4 0 1 R 10 19 | | |
| | S 17 U IIO | | |

### CRIMINAL RECORD

HOWARD HAS BEEN CONVICTED OF ASSAULT WITH A DEADLY WEAPON.

### CAUTION

HOWARD SHOULD BE CONSIDERED ARMED AND DANGEROUS AND SHOULD BE APPROACHED WITH CAUTION INASMUCH AS HE HAS BEEN CONVICTED OF ASSAULT WITH A DEADLY WEAPON AND IS PRESENTLY ON SUPERVISED PROBATION.

A Federal warrant was issued on September 23, 1985, at Albuquerque, New Mexico, charging Howard with Espionage (Title 18, U.S. Code, Section 794 (c)). A Federal warrant was also issued on September 27, 1985, at Albuquerque, charging Howard with Unlawful Interstate Flight to Avoid Confinement - Probation Violation (Title 18, U.S. Code, Section 1073).

IF YOU HAVE ANY INFORMATION CONCERNING THIS PERSON, PLEASE CONTACT YOUR LOCAL FBI OFFICE.
TELEPHONE NUMBERS AND ADDRESSES OF ALL FBI OFFICES LISTED ON BACK.

William H. Webster
DIRECTOR
FEDERAL BUREAU OF INVESTIGATION
UNITED STATES DEPARTMENT OF JUSTICE
WASHINGTON, D. C. 20535
TELEPHONE: 202 324-3000

Entered NCIC
Wanted Flyer 574
October 4, 1985

The FBI's Wanted poster for Edward Lee Howard, 1985.

Howard in Moscow, 1995.
*AP Photo/Tanya Makeyeva*

FBI surveillance was under way but missed Howard when he escaped on September 21, 1985, in Santa Fe, New Mexico.

SECRET

Memorandum J.H. Geer to E.J. Sharp
Re: Administrative Inquiry into the Disappearance of Edward Lee Howard from Santa Fe, New Mexico, September 21, 1985

DETAILS: At the request of the Assistant Director, IMTD, Assistant Director Glover, Inspection Division, had an administrative inquiry conducted in order to establish how Edward Lee Howard disappeared from Santa Fe, New Mexico, on 9/21/85, while under FBI physical surveillance. This administrative inquiry was conducted and included interviews of personnel in Albuquerque, San Diego and Los Angeles as well as FBIHQ. A copy of this report is attached for your review. (original memo only)

A thorough review of this administrative summary has been conducted and it is IMTD's recommendation that administrative action be considered for _____ who was assigned to the lookout on 9/21/85, the date of Howard's disappearance.

_____ performance was less than adequate and is a critical element in the disappearance of Howard while under physical surveillance. It is noted that _____ after having been placed on notice that the Howards were to leave their residence, and knowing the approximate time that the babysitter was to arrive at the residence, failed to notice the departure of the Howards from their residence and also failed to notify the surveillance teams of the Howards' departure. _____ further failed to notify the surveillance teams of the babysitter's arrival _____ recorded an incoming call from Mrs. Howard wherein she stated that she was at Alfonso's Restaurant and, although he recorded this call _____ failed to notify the surveillance units of this call. _____ also failed to notice the return of Mrs. Howard to her residence.

_____ was further delinquent in his performance in that he failed to report problems he experienced with the surveillance monitoring equipment and he made entries into his surveillance log which he later admitted he could not sustain.

_____ responsible for the disappearance of Howard.

Above, Tolkachev leaving his car at the roadblock on June 9, 1985, moments before he was seized by KGB officers, below. *Courtesy of H. Keith Melton and the Melton Archive*

A painting of Tolkachev, by Kathy Krantz Fieramosca, hangs at CIA headquarters.
*Courtesy of the artist*

were meeting, I wasn't really sure whether you were actually CIA. The one thing that proved to me you were CIA and not KGB is when you gave me those medicines to test on my daughter. Because the KGB is heartless. They would have given me one pill and said, *do it*. I knew I was working with a humane organization when you gave me five medicines."

Now Rolph was ready for his next assignment, Adolf Tolkachev.

# 11

# GOING BLACK

Late in the afternoon of October 14, 1980, David Rolph walked out of the Moscow station and went home. An hour later, he returned to the embassy gate with his wife, dressed as if going to a dinner party. A Soviet militiaman, standing guard in a small shack outside the embassy, saw them enter. Rolph and his wife vanished into the building, navigating the narrow corridors to one of the apartments.

The door was already ajar. Rolph pushed it open.

They whispered not a word. The apartment belonged to the deputy technical operations officer in the Moscow station, an espionage jack-of-all-trades who helped case officers with equipment and concealments, from sophisticated radio scanners to fake logs. The Moscow station had two, the chief and his deputy. They had been highly trained by the CIA, similar to the case officers, but with different skills; they usually did not run agents on the street.

Three days out of four, the chief tech officer had no surveillance, and when he did have it, he tried to build the familiar patterns of activity that case officers believed the KGB would grow accustomed to. He stuck to very unremarkable routines, visiting stores and garages, foraging for supplies, repeating the same trips day after day. Sure enough, the KGB's interest waned. Yet the techs were an essential part of the station's espionage operations.

The deputy tech motioned wordlessly to Rolph after he entered the apartment. The men were approximately the same height and physique. In total silence, Rolph began to transform himself to look like his host. The deputy tech had long, messy hair. Rolph put on a wig with long, messy hair. The deputy had a full beard. Rolph put on a full beard. The deputy tech helped Rolph adjust and secure the disguise, then fitted him with the SRR-100, a radio scanner, antenna, and earpiece to monitor KGB transmissions on the street. The earpiece was made by the Swiss hearing aid company Phonak, and it was the most delicate part, disguised with a CIA-developed color-matched silicon to replicate the inner ear's contours and shadows.[1]

Rolph heard a voice boom from the doorway. It was the chief tech officer, who had just arrived and was deliberately speaking loudly, assuming they were being overheard by KGB listening devices. "Hey, are we going to go and check out that new machine shop?" the chief asked. The real deputy replied, aloud, "Great! Let's go."

But the real deputy did not leave the apartment. The man who left the apartment looking like him was David Rolph. The real deputy pulled up a chair and settled in for a long wait. Rolph's wife, in her dinner dress, also sat down and would remain there for the next six hours. They could not utter a word, because the KGB might be listening, and an elaborate deception was under way. The identity transfer had begun. Rolph was off to meet Tolkachev for the first time, if he could get free from surveillance on the streets.[2]

The point of the identity transfer was to break through the embassy perimeter and return without being spotted. Rolph knew the KGB was not interested in the two technical officers and usually paid little attention when they drove out of the compound in search of food, flowers, or car parts in an old beige-and-green Volkswagen van. On this night, the van pulled out of the embassy at dusk. The chief tech was at the wheel, Rolph in the passenger seat. The van windows were dirty. The militiamen just shrugged. It looked like the two supply guys on the prowl again.

Once on the street, the van took a slow, irregular course. The chief tech knew the city well, because he had less surveillance and was out driving often. Rolph scanned the street, looking for signs they were being followed. The chief tech also had a practiced eye for surveillance and kept a close watch on the rearview mirror. They searched for cars with the telltale triangle of dirt on the grille, left there by the KGB car wash. They looked for panel trucks idling for no reason. The KGB had many ways to confuse them, including a reclining seat to conceal one of the officers and a switch in unmarked cars that could turn off just one headlight so the same car would look different on a second sighting.

Rolph thought to himself that he had one advantage: he was the orchestra director. He was the only one who knew where he was going. Everything they might do was in reaction to him. Normal drivers would pay no attention to the VW van. At a stoplight, they would pull right up alongside or behind. Rolph was watching for something that a normal car wouldn't do. If there was a stoplight, why did the third car behind them pull in behind a bus? That was an indicator, and Rolph was collecting them, sifting, processing what he saw.

In departing the embassy in disguise, he was playing a game entirely based on deception; his goal was not to be noticed as he slipped out. But over the next few hours, he would gradually unfold a new approach. He would become more open and teasing. He would try to flush out the KGB. Ultimately, his mission was to "get black," to completely shake the surveillance. But getting black required a long, exhausting test of nerves, even before he would get his first chance to look Tolkachev in the eyes.

On a surveillance detection run, the case officer had to be as agile as a ballet dancer, as confounding as a magician, and as attentive as an air traffic flight controller. Rolph had drilled in the CIA training courses, and he knew from his early days in army intelligence how important it was to absorb the lessons of those drills, mastering a sense of time and distance, exploiting the optics of moving through the gap. Rolph also planned meticulously, avoiding the hot spots and hidden cameras on the Moscow streets. Once, he was in the middle of a four-hour-long surveillance detection run and thought he was black. All of a sudden official-looking Zhiguli and Volga cars were whipping around turns and speeding back and forth. Rolph cursed to himself, "I've just walked into a beehive." He later discovered he had happened upon an obscure KGB training academy in the middle of a practice session. The Moscow station kept track of the known hot spots with red pushpins on the city map so they could avoid them.

In his last review of the plan with Gerber, hours earlier in the Moscow station, Rolph went over the route, the contingencies—each turn, each cover stop. What Rolph remembered was how Gerber treated every operation as if it were his own. He thought of the smallest details: body language, gestures, appearances, and illusions. Rolph once thought he'd never find another chief of station like Gus Hathaway, the tireless operator. Then he worked for Gerber, an intense, precise choreographer of espionage.

The van stopped at a flower shop. Rolph remained in his seat. Buying flowers was a routine, their first cover stop, a pause to see if the surveillance cars or foot patrol teams would get careless and stumble over themselves. Rolph kept his disguise on, in case they were questioned, but did not go into the flower shop, knowing that the harsh white light could expose the imperfections. Better to remain veiled behind the dirty window in the van.

The first cover stop had an important function: the abort option. If there was surveillance, Rolph could always break off here and go home with minimal losses; the KGB would have no inkling that he was headed to a meeting with an agent. By experience, Rolph had learned it was always best to catch the KGB at the start of a run, when they were more easily detected. If you saw the same red car three times, that was a clue. But as time passed, detection became more difficult. If the KGB was suspicious, they could throw more cars and more teams into the hunt. This made Moscow different from other cities. Rolph had the advantage in knowing where he was going, but the KGB had limitless resources they could devote to the chase if they became suspicious. They could put a dozen cars on his tail, and he would not see the same one twice.

The first part of a surveillance detection run was always in a moving vehicle, for more control. In the VW van, Rolph and the chief tech enjoyed nearly 360-degree vision and plenty of agility. They could accelerate, forcing the KGB watchers to keep up and perhaps reveal themselves. Or they could make abrupt U-turns, perhaps coming face-to-face with the surveillance car, if it existed. The KGB always sent out teams of three and four cars, so the goal was to trip them up, maneuver so they would have to show their presence early. Time and distance could be leveraged to Rolph's advantage. It was a lesson that Haviland Smith and his peers had discovered in the 1960s.

After an hour and a half of driving, darkness had settled over the city, and Rolph began a mental countdown. His next move required a decision based on what he had seen and his instincts.

The rule of thumb was to advance to the next stage only if he was 95 percent certain he was black. The reason was simple: he had the upper hand in the car. On foot and alone, he would be much more vulnerable. Rolph had known case officers who could not cross this threshold. They would "feel" surveillance, even if they had not seen it, and turn back. They were never criticized for this; it might have been a good call. But the decision to go ahead, to take the risk of a meeting with an agent, was much harder. The agent's life was at risk. Rolph weighed what he had seen on the darkening streets. He was 95 percent sure he was free from surveillance. He looked to the chief tech, who agreed. While the van was still moving, Rolph quickly slipped off the disguise and put it into a small sack on the floor. He grabbed the shopping bag that had been prepared for Tolkachev and slipped into a woolen coat. The van stopped very briefly. Rolph slid out and walked briskly away. The chief tech went to look for a quiet place to hide the van and take a walk in the park.

Soon, Rolph reappeared on another broad avenue a few blocks away, and he walked directly into a crowd waiting for one of the electric trolley buses that prowled Moscow's major arteries. He boarded the trolley at the rear door. To an outsider, Rolph resembled just another tired worker going home, standing wearily, squeezed in tightly. But in reality he was watching every move around him. No one on the bus could see it, but the small radio device in his ear was wirelessly connected to a receiver, about the size of a thin cigarette pack, held in the pocket of a white cotton harness that wrapped around his chest. A necklace of wire served as antenna and also handled the connection to the earpiece. In earlier years, case officers had to rather clumsily plug in crystals that might pick up a KGB transmission, and it was hit or miss. But Rolph was wearing a new model that scanned multiple KGB bands automatically. It gave him a leg up on the KGB; he could listen to them as they talked to each other. The downside was that it was so sensitive that it picked up squelches, jibs, and jabs of a dozen or more surveillance teams that could be three-quarters of a mile away and may not be following him, or even know about him. The radio was a wonder of concealment and smarts, but it was a secondary tool; it could provide warning of surveillance but not prove Rolph was free from it. Confirming that he was free from surveillance was the single most critical factor in what he was about to do.

Rolph scanned the trolley passengers, taking careful note of those who boarded with him. Then he abruptly stepped toward the door and jumped off at the next stop, watching to see who followed. So far, nothing seemed out of place.

On foot, he began the final stage of the surveillance detection run. Rolph was physically fit, and his head was clear, but his year in Moscow had taught him that surveillance detection runs were grueling. The late autumn weather felt raw, moist, and heavy. After he spent hours walking in the open air, his lungs ached. His mouth grew dry, but there was nowhere he could safely stop. Every doorway or public space could be a trap, and Rolph knew that the KGB peered down at sidewalks and streets from telescopes mounted in windows above. They had thousands of people watching.

The radio scanner was quiet but for the usual patter and static. At a small theater, Rolph pivoted on his heel and pushed open the doors. This was his second cover stop. He checked out the play board and notices on the wall, without saying anything. He almost never came to this theater. He listened intently to the radio but heard nothing. His goal was to force the KGB men to do something out of character, to slip, so that he could spot them before they could call in reinforcements and blanket the streets. Rolph left the theater with tickets for a show he had no intention to attend. The real show was coming up soon. The theater had triggered no sign of surveillance.

The next cover stop would certainly send the KGB into fits, should they see him. Rolph avoided the Metro—there were monitoring cameras inside most stations—and walked toward an antiques store, far from his usual routines. He had been there once before, with his family, but he would never go to an antiques store alone at night during the week. The point was to ramp up his challenge to the KGB, forcing them to act.

Still nothing.

He walked into a nearby apartment building and started climbing the stairs. This would trigger a KGB ambush if they were following him. They could not allow him to disappear from sight in a multi-floor apartment building. In fact, Rolph had nowhere to go in the building and knew not a soul who lived there. He was just trying to provoke the KGB. At a landing on the stairs, he sat down and waited.

No one came running up the stairs.

Rolph turned around. For three and a half hours, the KGB had been nowhere in sight. Still, to make sure, he walked to a small park near the apartment building. The park was lined with benches. Tall apartment buildings loomed on all sides, leaving the benches in darkness. Rolph hoped that his presence in the park, so far from home or the embassy, would raise hackles, and if nearby, the KGB would leap out and grab him. Better to face them now than to take them to Tolkachev. He carried no passport, no identification, but he did not fear being caught. He could explain being in a park, and they would be no wiser. But he must not lead the KGB to Tolkachev. Rolph looked at his watch. He was twelve minutes from the meeting site.

Time to go. He was 100 percent sure. He rose from the bench.

Suddenly he was jolted by a squelch in his earpiece, then another, and a third. They were loud, clearly from the KGB's surveillance teams. Rolph didn't know why. Did they see him stand up? He stood frozen, rigid, tense. The squelch could sometimes be used as a signal, without words, from one KGB man to another. But the noise could also have been related to something else, on a street a half mile away. It could have been a ham-fisted operator who hit his button by mistake.

Rolph often repeated the words "when you're black, you're black." In his mind, it meant that when you are black, you can do anything, because nobody is watching you.

Nothing. No sign of anyone in the park. Rolph let his shoulders drop and took a deep breath.

When you're black, you're black.


Rolph circled the meeting site once on foot, still alert to any signs of surveillance. The site was designated OLGA, not far from the German embassy. He recalled the scare over those two men he'd seen in the playground sandbox on that first night with Sheymov, six months earlier. But he saw nothing. Rolph thought it was a good place for a meeting, with a few apartment buildings, some low-lying shabby garages, not many people on the street.

Then he spotted Tolkachev. Rolph had read the entire file and was briefed by Guilsher. He felt that he would recognize Tolkachev upon seeing him the first time and imagined a warm hello, face-to-face. But now Rolph was walking *behind* a man who was shuffling along. He looked as if he might be Tolkachev. Rolph had almost overtaken him. The man was stooped a bit. The plan was to exchange greetings, and if the response was correct, Rolph would know he was Tolkachev. Rolph was uncertain what to do. He might be looking at the wrong man, but there was no harm in using the greeting. If it was the wrong man, the Russian would probably just look quizzically at him and ask what the hell he was talking about.

From behind, Rolph said out loud, "Privet ot Kati!" Or, "Hello from Katya!"

The man turned around and said clearly, "Peredaite privet ot Borisa." Or, "Send regards from Boris."

That was the coded answer. Rolph smiled slightly, looked at Tolkachev, and extended his hand. Tolkachev shook it. He was wearing a black jacket and a brimmed cap and seemed even smaller than Rolph had anticipated, no more than five feet six inches tall. His face was chiseled, the nose aquiline, but Rolph noticed it was dented at the top. Rolph's watch said 9:00 p.m. It was Tolkachev's eighth meeting with the CIA.

Rolph knew that his most important goal at this moment was simply to build the kind of trust that Tolkachev had in Guilsher. He kept his first remarks light and reassuring, and he gave Tolkachev an ops note that he had painstakingly drafted in the Moscow station.[3] He noticed right away that Tolkachev did not respond emotionally. His face was impassive.

Then Rolph delivered some good news: Tolkachev's "special request" for the suicide pill had been approved by the CIA in response to his written appeal in June. Gerber had pushed headquarters. "What we must not do," Gerber insisted, "is allow this question to dominate the operation and we are frankly concerned that the longer the giving of the special request is delayed that is what we are going to face."[4] At the news, Tolkachev finally seemed to relax. Rolph said he would deliver the pill at their next meeting. The CIA could put it into a pen or something else that Tolkachev normally carried in his pocket. The Moscow station had been fretting over the choice of concealment. It had to be good enough so it could never be discovered but easy enough to carry in case of dire emergency. When Rolph asked about it, Tolkachev replied indifferently, saying he didn't have a preference. In the ops note, Rolph said of the suicide pill, "I can only hope that it will give you the peace of mind you desire."[5] In the note, Rolph also gave Tolkachev a list of questions to answer that would help in planning for exfiltration, such as clothing and shoe sizes, what medicines he and his family used, what cities or places they were permitted to visit, and when they would go on vacation.

Tolkachev was apologetic: in the summer months, it was harder for him to sneak documents out of the institute because he didn't wear an overcoat. He had photographed only twenty-five rolls of film since the last meeting with Guilsher in June. He passed them to Rolph, along with a nine-page note.

Tolkachev was still very worried about the library permission sheet, which carried his signature for so many top secret documents. He knew it would incriminate him, and he offered a new idea. Earlier, he suggested that the CIA fabricate his building pass in order to defeat the security procedures. Now he wondered, could the CIA also fabricate a copy of his library permission sheet, with just a few signatures? He could find a way to substitute the fake sheet for the real one. Tolkachev handed to Rolph some written diagrams and notes and a photograph to help the CIA make a copy of it.

The minutes were ticking away, but Tolkachev had more to say. He told Rolph he had purchased a car, a small, ocher-colored Zhiguli, the Soviet Everyman car modeled on the boxy Italian Fiat. Tolkachev wanted to use the car for future meetings. They might be able to talk for a longer stretch without being detected. Who would suspect two friends sitting in a car? Tolkachev told Rolph, briefly, that he was still unhappy with the money the CIA was giving him and promised to write about it later. He reminded the CIA of his patience, however, in the letter he handed to Rolph. "I only want to note, one more time," he wrote, that the "gradual and dragged out approach from your side to the questions of finances does not affect the general process of my cooperation with you."

Fifteen minutes had already passed, and Tolkachev had one more request. He handed Rolph a piece of paper. When Rolph looked down, he saw it was printed in English in block letters:

1. LED ZEPPELIN
2. PINK FLOYD
3. GENESIS
4. ALAN PARSONS PROJECT
5. EMERSON, LAKE AND PALMER
6. URIAH HEEP
7. THE WHO
8. THE BEATLES
9. THE YES
10. RICH WAKEMAN
11. NAZARETH
12. ALICE COOPER

Tolkachev wanted the CIA to obtain rock music albums for his son, Oleg. He had copied the names down by hand, although he apparently did not know them well. "My son, as many of his contemporaries in school, has a passion for Western music," Tolkachev wrote. "Besides, I too, in spite of my age, like to listen to this music." He said the records were only available on the black market, but "I do not want to use the black market, because you can always end up in an unpredictable situation." He added that the list was to indicate the "tastes of my son," but he wanted "the most popular musical groups in the West, including the USA."[6]

Rolph was nervous because of the squelch he had heard in the park before the meeting. He knew that he and Tolkachev had been together only briefly but decided to cut the meeting short. Tolkachev did not object. They shook hands and parted. Rolph walked away quickly. At this hour in the city, there were not many people on the streets. Rolph returned to the parked VW van, which was waiting for him at a rendezvous point. The chief tech had taken a small surveillance detection run of his own before arriving at the point, just to make sure the KGB was not waiting for them. Once in the van, Rolph gave a thumbs-up, wordlessly. The tech reached down to the floor and grabbed a bottle of beer for each of them, a small ritual at the end of every run. It was so cold the beers had nearly frozen. They snapped off the tops, and Rolph, his throat dry from hours on the street, savored the icy beer. Then he put on the beard and wig, and they drove back to the embassy. The last feint in the identity transfer deception was important: they had to close the loop, crossing back into the embassy, undetected. The guards didn't give them a second glance. The gate opened, and Rolph's run was over.

A little while later, the Soviet militiamen in the shack took note that David Rolph and his wife left the embassy dinner party for home.

# 12

# DEVICES AND DESIRES

**A**t last, Tolkachev would get his suicide pill. It arrived at the Moscow station by the regular secure delivery a few weeks after the October meeting in a package about the size of a cigar box. Rolph opened it. Nestled inside was the fountain pen with the L-pill, held in place by foam inserts, cut in the shape of a pistol.[1]

He gingerly examined the pen, then put it back and locked the box in a file drawer. Soon after, headquarters sent a cable with instructions, in Russian, on how to extract the fragile capsule from inside the pen and bite down on it.[2]

In the close-knit Moscow station, everyone shared everything. In Gerber's small office, they talked over plans for a surveillance detection run and new meeting sites they had cased the previous weekend. Sometimes they sketched on a chalkboard or rehearsed how they would handle a phone call in Russian with an agent. In advance of a major operation, wives would join them in the cramped station, sitting on the desks and floor, double-checking disguises and packages, examining maps and routes.

When Rolph told the others about Tolkachev's request for Western rock music for his son, they nodded knowingly. They'd seen it all over Moscow—young people yearning for consumer goods from the West: cassettes for tape recorders, magazines, nail polish and remover, Polaroid cameras, Scotch tape, T-shirts with English lettering, turtleneck sweaters, running shoes, and countless other things they could not find at home.[3] Tolkachev had also requested a catalog of Western stereo equipment. Why not give it to him? It seemed like such an inconsequential favor for an agent who was delivering massive volumes of intelligence. But Gerber was cold-eyed and not immediately swayed. What if Tolkachev, leading designer at a top secret Soviet military research institute, was seen by a neighbor carrying albums by Uriah Heep? Or what if the records were spotted in his apartment? Wouldn't that look suspicious?

Rolph wrote to headquarters that "sudden acquisition" of the records might raise eyebrows and demand "uncomfortable explanations." He added, "We know that records of the type he has requested are occasionally available in Moscow (on the black market) but the cost is generally high. If we knew his son already had a sizeable collection, adding a few more (cut by European companies) would probably do little harm. We would not, however, want to be his son's sole supplier." The stereo catalog might be easier to hide, he added, but "how his son might handle this 'windfall' is a big unknown." Would Tolkachev next ask them for a turntable and speakers? The tussle over the L-pill was still fresh in everyone's mind. The Moscow station did not want to reject such a simple request from Tolkachev, but they were worried about his security. They decided to pause, tell Tolkachev of their concern in December, and ask him how the records would be handled and stored. If Tolkachev could obtain a reel-to-reel tape player, they thought, the CIA might provide the music on tapes. That would be harder to trace.[4]

Day after day, with his Pentax camera clamped to the back of a chair, Tolkachev copied documents. The rolls of 35 mm film he gave to Rolph in October produced 920 frames containing 817 pages. Soon, headquarters was pressing Moscow for more at the behest of the "customers" of intelligence, primarily the air force, the navy, the National Security Agency, and the Defense Intelligence Agency. When he met Guilsher in 1979, Tolkachev had turned over five circuit boards from the RP-23 radar project and schematic drawings to go with them. The schematics were rushed to headquarters for translation and the electronics sent elsewhere for inspection and analysis.

Now, in the fall of 1980, headquarters wanted Rolph to ask Tolkachev for some additional circuit boards, or pieces of electronic equipment. The military customers were becoming insatiable, Rolph thought. He worried they were pushing so hard they might endanger Tolkachev's security. Rolph had always respected the logic in Tolkachev's method: removing documents, then returning them the same day. Nobody was the wiser once the papers were safely back in the files. But hardware was another story. If a piece of hardware was missing—because it could not be replaced—an internal investigation would most certainly result. This demand for electronics and spare parts could sink them.

Gerber resisted a suggestion from headquarters that they give Tolkachev a wish list of electronic parts. Just because Tolkachev had "passed a piece of equipment one time in the past does not shed any light on his continued access, his ability to remove such equipment safely or the degree of risk involved," he wrote. If they pressed Tolkachev for more spare parts, Gerber added, "he might consider that we are squeezing him and consequently become either more demanding or more difficult." Or, Gerber speculated, Tolkachev might get reckless and take chances to steal more circuit boards, endangering his security. "Armed with a list of specific material requirements, CKS is type of person who may manufacture transparent and dangerously insecure means to procure the items." Gerber suggested that they simply ask Tolkachev at the next meeting whether he could get his hands on any more electronics and added, "We believe it is of major importance to ensure that [Tolkachev] does nothing to harm his security."[5]

On Monday, December 8, 1980, at 8:25 p.m., Rolph went to see Tolkachev in a wooded park at the Moscow Zoo, located near Tolkachev's apartment building. Tolkachev often passed the zoo while walking to work. They had planned the meeting months earlier, and Rolph wanted to stick to the schedule, even though superpower hostility seemed to be ratcheting up again. On November 4, Ronald Reagan had been elected fortieth president of the United States. Then, in early December, there had been a scare over a possible Soviet invasion of Poland. In the end, Soviet troops didn't cross the border, but the Moscow station was braced for heavy KGB surveillance. Rolph was determined to go ahead with the meeting. "Just get it right on the street," Gerber told Rolph.

That night, the park seemed empty. Rolph intended to spend more time with Tolkachev than he had during the hurried meeting in October. Rolph carried with him a shopping bag, typical for any Russian on the street, with parcels wrapped to look like ordinary purchases of a Muscovite on the lookout for food and goods.

Tolkachev seemed relaxed. They strolled in the park like two old friends. Rolph was listening for surveillance on his SRR-100 radio but heard nothing; his eyes scanned the park for unwanted attention, but all was quiet. The park was so close to Tolkachev's apartment tower that Rolph could see it rise above the tree line.

Rolph reached into his shopping bag and gave Tolkachev the wrapped pen. Inside was the L-pill and the instructions. "This is what you wanted, the means for self-destruction," he said. He did not see the point of emphasizing once again that he hoped Tolkachev would never have to use it. Tolkachev looked pleased that at last he had the suicide pill in his pocket. Rolph asked him to examine the concealment at some later date and tell the CIA if he wanted something different from a fountain pen.

The CIA's technical division had worked for months to replicate the library permission sheet and the building pass for Tolkachev. Rolph gave Tolkachev the fakes, based on the drawings and photographs Tolkachev had provided in October. It was too dark to see them, but Rolph asked Tolkachev to examine them and report back later. The CIA had replicated the library permission sheet with just a few signatures. The fake building pass was not as urgent, but Rolph still hoped it might prove useful. He also remembered to bring batteries for Tolkachev's Pentax camera, small flat disks that were scarce in Moscow. Tolkachev was delighted. Rolph felt that his reaction said a lot about the man. Tolkachev was intent on photographing as much as possible, and the batteries would allow him to keep working without interruption.

Worried about Tolkachev's security, Rolph proposed some new procedures. On the day of a planned meeting, he said, Tolkachev must first signal he was ready by turning on the light in his kitchen between 12:15 and 1:00 p.m. The Moscow station would send someone out—maybe one of the wives—to check. The signal was code-named svet, or "light," and visible from the street. If the light was off, the CIA would not come to a meeting. Rolph also gave Tolkachev new plans for an "emergency call out" once a month, to be used for an impromptu meeting only if absolutely necessary. It was dangerous, but if Tolkachev had urgent developments or faced a real threat, it might be worth the risk. Rolph also suggested they set up a signal site at a market near the zoo. When Tolkachev's car was parked in a designated spot by the market at a preordained hour, it would indicate he was ready for a meeting.

For the first time, Rolph described to Tolkachev the capability of Discus, the CIA's agent communications device. He explained that the handheld units would allow them to send burst messages on the street while standing some distance away from each other, say several hundred meters apart. The device gave them a way to pass intelligence wordlessly and without actually meeting each other. Tolkachev brightened at the prospect of using it. Rolph said he would attempt to have Discus ready for the next meeting.

As they walked, Rolph asked Tolkachev whether he could get more circuit boards or electronic parts like those he gave to Guilsher a year earlier. Would it even be possible? Was it safe? Instead of brushing off the request, as Rolph assumed he might, Tolkachev said matter-of-factly that it was possible. He asked Rolph if the CIA could prepare a list. As it happened, Rolph already had one—sent from headquarters in the weeks before— and he gave it to Tolkachev. Rolph didn't ask him to look at it; they could barely see in the dark.

Rolph then spoke to Tolkachev about the CIA's worries over the rock music, approaching it gently, not wanting to trigger any anger or disappointment. If the albums were discovered, Rolph said, he was afraid they could get Tolkachev into trouble. How would he explain them? Are they available on the black market? Where do you plan to keep them? Will you have to hide them from friends and visitors to the apartment? Would your son's friends start asking uncomfortable questions?

Tolkachev grew animated, and his eyes flashed self-confidence. He told Rolph that he would have no difficulty explaining the presence of the albums in his apartment. They are all available on the black market in Moscow, he explained, but he was personally reluctant to go there. Tolkachev said he would accept the music on tape, if necessary, and told Rolph he already owned a Hitachi cassette player, about three years old, which he had purchased at a *komissiony magazin*, a store where people could sell their possessions on consignment, usually clothes but occasionally electronics.

Time was running out. Tolkachev gave Rolph a ten-page handwritten note, in which he proposed to finally settle the issue of his compensation.[6]

At the last minute, Rolph remembered there was an urgent question from headquarters. In August 1980, the United States had revealed the existence of "stealth" technology, making airplanes nearly invisible to radar. What did Tolkachev know about the Soviet response to the American "stealth" airplanes? And was there a Soviet stealth? Tolkachev said he had heard of the "invisible airplane" but didn't know the answer and didn't want to pass on information to Rolph about which he was uncertain.

They had been walking for twenty minutes. Rolph reached into his bag and pulled out two slender books in Russian as New Year's gifts from the CIA. One was a tract by Andrei Sakharov, the nuclear physicist turned dissident, whom Tolkachev admired. The other was a thin volume by Anatoly Fedoseyev, a prominent Soviet radar and electronics designer who had developed the vacuum tubes that were used in land-based radars that ringed the Soviet Union. Fedoseyev had received the highest state awards, including Hero of Socialist Labor and the Lenin Prize. He went to France in May 1971 as a ranking member of a Soviet delegation to the Paris Air Show, then defected to the United Kingdom. His disillusionment with the Soviet system had closely paralleled Tolkachev's—the shortages, the dysfunction, the failures of socialism. Fedoseyev described it in a book, titled *Trap*, that Rolph now handed to Tolkachev.

Sakharov had defected, ideologically, from the Soviet system.

Fedoseyev had defected physically. Tolkachev had defected, too, in his own way, landing hammer blows from within.

He thanked Rolph, but his voice trailed off. The hour was late. They shook hands, and he disappeared.[7]

At CIA headquarters, a turning point came in early 1981. Reagan entered office determined to ignite a sense of activism and renewed energy in the CIA, an instrument in his larger campaign to aggressively confront the Soviet Union. In a shift from the doubts of the Carter years, Reagan's approach to the world was unapologetically muscular and grounded in a belief in American exceptionalism, that the United States was the "last best hope of man on earth," as he often declared. Those who risked their lives for the United States around the globe—sailors, soldiers, aviators, and intelligence officers—carried a special mystique for Reagan; he believed, as the aviation pioneer General James Doolittle had suggested a generation before, that it was worthy to go to almost any length to protect freedom in the face of totalitarianism. To lead the CIA, Reagan chose William J. Casey, a New York lawyer and Republican stalwart who had served in the Office of Strategic Services in London during World War II and been chairman of the Securities and Exchange Commission in the Nixon years. Casey, who served as Reagan's 1980 campaign manager, was a rumpled, slightly stooped figure with wisps of white hair. His speech was often slurred and hard to decipher. But he was possessed of a rigid certainty about what he wanted to do. His appointment signaled a desire for espionage that was more daring and forward leaning. While Turner had sought to minimize risks, Casey relished taking them; while Turner had distrusted human sources, Casey demanded recruitment of more agents.[8] Casey also shared Reagan's enduring antipathy toward

Soviet communism, which dominated his thinking and drove his judgments.

On a cold morning in Washington, January 15, 1981, five days before Reagan was to take the oath, Turner, the outgoing CIA director, arrived at Blair House, the historic guest quarters across the street from the White House, where Reagan was staying. He was met by Reagan, the vice president elect, George H. W. Bush, who had been CIA director before Turner, and Casey. The occasion was Turner's final intelligence briefing, to share with the new president the nation's most closely guarded and sensitive intelligence secrets. As they sat in a private room, Turner outlined a covert action program in Afghanistan to support the fighters opposing the Soviet occupation. He described how U.S. Navy submarines had secretly tapped Soviet underwater communications cables. These were truly audacious operations. But the jewel of all jewels, he told Reagan, was a human source who worked in a Moscow military research institute. He not only provided hard documentation of Soviet radar and avionics capabilities in the present but also revealed research and development a decade into the future. His name was Adolf Tolkachev, and his intelligence was worth billions.[9]

Two months later, on March 10, 1981, the beat-up old beige-and-green Volkswagen van rattled out of the U.S. embassy compound in Moscow. Once again in disguise, Rolph slipped past the guards. His mission, to meet Tolkachev, was extremely delicate because he was carrying Discus, the CIA's electronic messaging device. Rolph did not want to get caught with it, nor did he want the KGB to ever lay their hands on one. For fifty minutes, he watched for possible surveillance from the van, zigzagging around town. Rolph heard some KGB transmissions on his radio, but they seemed unrelated to him. He then took off the disguise, stepped onto the street, and walked for an hour, listening carefully and watching. No signs of surveillance anywhere. At 9:05 p.m., he arrived at a meeting site, code-named ANNA, located in a park, and spotted Tolkachev, standing at a phone booth. He and Tolkachev began to walk and talk, choosing paths randomly through the park. A few people walking dogs and just strolling saw them but paid no attention.[10]

Rolph informed Tolkachev that the CIA had accepted his plan for the money. It was a deal—no questions asked. Tolkachev seemed satisfied and said no more about it.

Tolkachev reported that the CIA's replica of the library permission sheet was excellent. He had already replaced it, but the building pass was still not right. The color of the cover was off; it would not work. The cover and the inside page holding his photograph were made of different materials that the CIA had not adequately replicated. Nor did they properly reproduce the color of the swirls on the inside paper.

Rolph handed Tolkachev another parcel. Inside, he said, you'll find the *elektronniy pribor*, the electronic equipment, or the Discus. Be very careful, Rolph insisted, and read all the instructions before using it. Rolph repeated, "Read the instructions," and Tolkachev said he understood. Rolph also emphasized that Discus was for use when there was an urgent message that could not wait until their next meeting. He tried to keep the tone upbeat and confident: we want you to use it, he said, perhaps over the summer when we are not meeting regularly.[11]

Rolph did not reveal to Tolkachev that he and Gerber had serious doubts about whether Discus would be useful at all. In the Moscow station, one of the most basic principles of espionage was don't ever carry out operational acts without a solid justification. The Discus required operational acts, but for what? Tolkachev's great value was in the thousands of documents he copied, not short electronic bursts. As a practical matter, the CIA never had time to train Tolkachev or practice on the device with him.[12]

Gerber and Hathaway argued back and forth for months about Discus. Hathaway was a headstrong believer. The CIA's prized spy in Warsaw, Ryszard Kuklinski, was given an earlier version, called Iskra. Despite some malfunctions, Kuklinski used it to warn the CIA in January 1981 that plans were being drawn up for the Polish military in the event of martial law. In response, Hathaway sent a congratulatory note to the Warsaw station. "I hope this is the first of many, many more to come," he wrote. Later, after a second Kuklinski transmission, headquarters cabled to the Warsaw station that the spy "obviously likes his new toy."[13]

Hathaway felt that Tolkachev would like it too. The dream, to use technology for covert communications, was broadly shared among operational people at headquarters. They always attempted to push beyond where the KGB might be looking. In covert communications, that sometimes meant deploying an early version of technology, like the Discus; the thinking was that the most secret of all technologies is the one that the other person doesn't suspect exists.[14]

But Gerber responded that it was never that simple. Moscow case officers were under surveillance far more than in Warsaw. Why scramble a station officer for a message that might say, "Hello, all is fine"?

Despite the doubts, the Moscow station complied with Hathaway's request. The Discus was now in Tolkachev's hands. Rolph also gave him forty-two AA batteries.

Tolkachev handed over fifty-five rolls of 35 mm film that he had taken since their last meeting. He told Rolph that he might have only five to ten more rolls by June and didn't anticipate much production over the summer; with the warm weather, he could not wear the overcoat to hide the documents at lunchtime. He also planned a monthlong vacation.

Rolph knew that a lot of what Tolkachev planned to steal for the CIA had already been taken, well ahead of his own seven-stage, twelve-year schedule.[15] But just as Tolkachev reached this point, the appetite at headquarters was mushrooming. They seemed to want Tolkachev to produce fifty or a hundred rolls of film every time. Rolph was irritated at the demands but could see what was happening. Tolkachev's material was so valuable back at Langley that he was literally "paying the rent"—justifying the CIA's operational budget—and helping the agency satisfy the military customers. So headquarters was naturally inclined to push the envelope. They asked, *can he just check out a few more things?* Rolph felt that Tolkachev had single-handedly built a Brooklyn Bridge, and now headquarters wanted him to build a Golden Gate Bridge as well. Still, Rolph carried a letter that had been sent by headquarters, with a list of forty-five wide-ranging questions about Soviet weapons systems. He gave it to Tolkachev and asked for answers at their next meeting.

Tolkachev told Rolph that the concealment for the L-pill—the pen—was just fine and no changes were necessary.

Rolph noticed that Tolkachev's greeting had been warmer than before. When they met in the park, they grasped each other's arm, firmly. Tolkachev was talkative. All was well with his family and his work, he said. Rolph thought, he may be starting to trust me.

Headquarters had instructed Rolph to avoid talking about exfiltration. They wanted to keep Tolkachev in the Soviet Union as long as possible. But Tolkachev would not let go of the idea. In a speculative moment, he came up with a wild, dreamy plan and tried it out on Rolph, who could not quite believe what he was hearing. "Now, if you can have a special airplane that will fly in and pick me up, you could land it in a field someplace in the woods, and we would come running out of the woods, and get in the plane and take us out," Tolkachev said. It was totally unrealistic, Rolph thought. This was the Soviet Union, heavily armed. No American spy plane was going to successfully glide onto a field and carry Tolkachev away. But at least Tolkachev was talking to him and showing a human side.

Rolph reached into the bag and gave Tolkachev his last parcel, which contained seven cassettes with the recorded music he had requested. The CIA had bought the cassettes in Eastern Europe, so they could not be traced. Tolkachev was thrilled. They had been talking for only fifteen minutes, but to Rolph it had a slow-motion feel, as if they had been chatting for an hour. They agreed to meet again in the autumn, after Tolkachev's summer vacation. Tolkachev gave Rolph a seven-page ops note, handwritten.

Once again, Tolkachev slipped away into the darkness, and Rolph returned to the embassy as the shaggy-haired tech in the Volkswagen van passenger seat.

The next day, Rolph sent an account of the meeting to headquarters. He felt more than ever that he needed to emphasize how Tolkachev's eyes lit up when he talked about the music and why that was important for the operation. He wrote that it was "truly interesting and revealing" how Tolkachev changed from his usual unemotional demeanor when this came up. "All of his interest in music is always explained in terms of his son's affinity for it," Rolph reported. "Although certainly not to the point of an obsession, his concern over seeing this request through to the end is near paramount. One gets the impression that as a father he has not always been able to provide everything he might like for his son and through this channel sees an opportunity to do something very special that he could never otherwise hope to obtain." If the CIA could help Tolkachev with this, Rolph said, there was a chance "our stock will rise proportionately in his eyes."

Tolkachev was so enthusiastic that he asked the CIA for "the English texts of each of the songs contained on the cassettes." Rolph acknowledged "this is a somewhat unusual request and certainly unorthodox" but said Tolkachev made it "in all seriousness" and there would be little additional risk to carrying it out.[16]

In his written ops note, Tolkachev apologized that he could not obtain any more circuit boards or electronic parts from radar equipment: none were available, and even if they were, the risks would be too high.

Rolph felt his duty was to explain Tolkachev to headquarters, to be an advocate, just as Guilsher had been. Faced with unceasing demands from headquarters for more production, Rolph wanted to impress upon them that Tolkachev was not a robot with a Pentax camera. He was a man who felt isolated and often needed to let off steam and feel rewarded. On April 2, 1981, Rolph sent an interpretive cable to headquarters. He wrote that Tolkachev displays "definite tones of frustration and discouragement when he discusses his personal requests." He added that, in Tolkachev's mind, if the CIA now trusts him with sophisticated technical gear like the miniature Tropel cameras and Discus, then "we should equally trust him and his sense of responsibility with the items which clearly mean something to him, that is his personal requests." Those items included the music cassettes and a pair of Western stereo headphones, which Tolkachev had also requested in his ops note. Headphones and music cassettes would not stand out; they could be seen in some Moscow apartments. "We have increasingly come to the conclusion that in addition to the 'get the system' motivation, CKS is motivated by certain material impulses and particularly wants to reward his son with some benefits," Rolph wrote.[17]

His message, in short: don't quibble over a pair of headphones for the billion dollar spy.

In June 1981, headquarters, ever dreaming that technology would provide the extra edge over the KGB, sent an entirely new communications device to the Moscow station. It was, supposedly, even better than the Discus and would finally give the CIA an invisible and secure channel for messages to and from agents. The messaging system would connect directly from a ground transmitter to an American satellite. The Discus was strictly terrestrial: it could work for a few hundred meters, from man to man. But the new system, although bulky, could send a message straight from curbside to satellite and directly to the United States. It was based on U.S. Marisat satellites that had been launched in 1976 for ship-to-shore communications. Headquarters sent a cable to the Moscow station, suggesting they give the advanced new device to Tolkachev.

The suggestion came just as new reports were arriving about a possible Soviet invasion of Poland. At headquarters, the CIA was seriously worried that a fresh crisis in Poland might lead to a dramatic break in U.S.-Soviet relations and perhaps an abrupt closure of the Moscow station. How would they maintain contact with Tolkachev? Headquarters insisted that the Moscow station think ahead and be prepared. Gerber believed a break in relations was far-fetched, but he could not ignore the insistent messages from Langley.

Gerber's doubts about the new device ran deep, just as they had with the Discus. The whole Tolkachev operation "has been geared for the long run," he insisted in a cable to Hathaway. A meeting schedule was already in place for the next fifteen months, more than sufficient in the event of tensions or surveillance.

Tolkachev was providing intelligence "of long range benefit to our govt and it's not day to day intelligence." Gerber added, firmly, "While we cannot predict there will not be an interruption in station ability to function here that will last longer than a year, there has been nothing we have seen which would indicate that an invasion of Poland would result in the breaking of diplomatic relations with the Soviet Union."[18]

Privately, Gerber was fuming. He had good personal contacts in Moscow and had been talking to a Polish diplomat. He felt confident the Soviets were not going to invade. But headquarters was pushing him to do something, so on June 24 the station prepared a contingency plan and a letter for Tolkachev, to be delivered only if events dictated. The plan was to give him the new communications device, just in case.

Two days later, headquarters proposed a major change. Enthusiastic about the new communications device, they suggested that Tolkachev return the Discus and use the satellite system for *all* communications, in between personal meetings, "whether or not station stays or goes."

In fact, Tolkachev had not used the Discus once since he first received it. He had not even marked a signal that he wanted to use it.[19] Gerber and Rolph quickly sent a protest back to headquarters. Again, they did not think the station was going to be kicked out of Moscow. They had "serious reservations" about using the new satellite device for all communications, starting with the fact that there had not yet been a single successful test of the machine from Moscow. Two attempts had failed. Besides, they pointed out, it wasn't simple to get the Discus back. They couldn't very well call the apartment and ask Tolkachev to just bring it to a meeting. Gerber and Rolph were annoyed. They said Tolkachev's silence was probably because he was following to the letter their instructions to use it only for emergencies. Tolkachev "is an intelligent and resourceful individual who appreciates the risk involved in frequent contact and unnecessary ops activity," they wrote. He just was being careful. Then, just as suddenly as it appeared, the promise of the new satellite message system vanished. It failed more tests. The Moscow station told headquarters "we are becoming less optimistic" that the machine was right for Tolkachev. Not least of the reasons was that it didn't seem to work.[20]

When headquarters developed the fifty-five rolls of film Tolkachev had given Rolph in the park, six were blank. It might have been a glitch; Rolph didn't want to bother Tolkachev about it but made a mental note to bring him a new Pentax camera body at the next meeting.[21] On the remainder of the film, the CIA found sparkling new gems from inside Soviet vaults. Seven rolls of film documented a top secret surface-to-air missile codenamed SHTORA, or "blind," as in a window shade—designed to be "not detectable by target aircraft" because of its "advanced and complex jam-proofing and secure operating procedures." Other rolls covered topics in computer logic for radar systems and provided the CIA with a set of logs of secret technical reports as they arrived at Tolkachev's institute in 1978, 1979, and 1980, which would allow the Americans to accurately judge the state of Soviet military high technology.[22]

The billion dollar spy had come through again.

CIA headquarters dispatched to the Moscow station a pair of German-made stereo headphones, catalogs for stereo systems, and albums by Alice Cooper, Nazareth, and Uriah Heep.

# 13

# TORMENTED BY THE PAST

**H**is family and friends called him Adik. His eyes were the color of ash, under a broad forehead and thick brown hair, with a crook in the bridge of his nose from a boyhood hockey accident. He stood about five feet six inches tall. Tolkachev seemed a quiet fellow to those who knew him. He liked tinkering with electronics and enjoyed building things with his hands, holding a soldering iron or wood plane, fixing a radio, or hammering together a cold frame. Tolkachev was so reserved that he never told his son what he did at work or took the boy to his office.

But inwardly, his mind was not at ease. He was haunted by a dark chapter of Soviet history, and he wanted revenge.[1]

Tolkachev was fifty-four years old in 1981. He suffered from high blood pressure and tried to pay attention to his health, jogging in the spring, summer, and fall and skiing in the winter. He drank alcohol only rarely. He was usually up before dawn, especially in the long winter, according to letters he wrote to the CIA. Every other day during the week, he got out of bed at 5:00 a.m. and went for a run outdoors, if it wasn't raining or biting cold. He usually took the main elevator down to the ground floor and pushed open the heavy door onto the tree-lined square, Ploshchad Vosstaniya, or Square of the Uprising, commemorating the revolts against the Russian tsar and later the Bolshevik Revolution. Day after day, he ran the same route: first across the square toward the broad boulevard known as the Garden Ring Road, then a right turn toward the U.S. embassy, past the guard shacks that stood in front of the embassy, then another right turn, down a small lane and the spot where, three years earlier, he had handed a letter to Hathaway, in the shadow of a small Russian Orthodox church.[2] Tolkachev knew these streets well; he had walked and run them tirelessly in earlier years, searching for cars with license plates indicating they belonged to American diplomats, hoping to drop a note through an open window.

In a letter to the CIA, Tolkachev described himself as a morning person. "You probably know," he wrote, "that people are sometimes divided into two different types of personalities: 'skylarks' and 'owls.' The first have no trouble getting up in the morning but start getting sleepy as evening approaches. The latter are just the opposite. I belong to the 'skylarks,' my wife and son to the 'owls.'"

After his jog, Tolkachev said, he usually woke his wife and son and made them breakfast. Natasha, who worked in the antenna department of the institute, was a heavyset woman, and she often left for work before Tolkachev, in order to catch the bus. Tolkachev liked to walk to work, through the backstreets.

Their son was growing fast and stood five inches taller than his father. Oleg had not been a rebellious teenager, but his interests ran more toward his mother's side—arts, culture, music, and design—than toward his father's penchant for electronics and engineering. Oleg attended a special school that emphasized English instruction. He was already reading Kipling and Asimov and was consumed with Western rock music. Adik liked his son's music, even if he had only a very weak understanding of

English. He was personally fond of jazz, which had been some-what subversive in Soviet times.

Adik tried to bridge the age gap with his teenage son. They went skiing together in the winter, and in the summer months the family often roughed it on camping trips around the Soviet Union. Once they went to the Baltic Sea, and another year to Lake Valdai. Because he held a security clearance, Tolkachev could not get permission to travel abroad. "I always go with my wife and son," Tolkachev wrote to the CIA of his vacations. "We usually rest in wooded areas on rivers or lakes in a primitive manner, i.e., in camping tent, we cook on a campfire, etc. This year we also plan to go camping with a tent and backpacks." He added, "I consider that I have the normal attachment to the family that exists in mankind."

Tolkachev's imposing apartment building featured a twenty-two-story central tower with a spire, flanked by two eighteen-floor wings. Those who lived there included Mikhail Gromov, who set a world record flying over the North Pole; Georgi Lobov, a decorated World War II and Korean War fighter ace; and Sergei Anokhin, renowned for his pioneering aviation feats, such as putting a MiG-15 into a supersonic dive. Valentin Glushko, the principal designer of Soviet rocket engines, also lived there, as did Vasily Mishin, who led the Soviet effort, ultimately unsuccessful, to build a lunar rocket. They were the Soviet aviation and missile elite.[3] But Tolkachev was a loner. He had once socialized with workers at his laboratory, he told the CIA, but now, "possibly because of age, all these friendly conversations started to tire me and I have practically ceased such activities." He wrote, "During the past 10–15 years the number of my personal friends has sharply decreased. They are not out of commission . . . but my contacts with them have become very rare and accidental."

Tolkachev's apartment was quite comfortable, with two rooms, a small kitchen, a bath, and a toilet. Above the kitchen door was the crawl space, or *entresol*, which ran thirteen feet long and about three feet high. In this space, he stored his camping tent, sleeping bags, and building materials, as well as his spy equipment from the CIA. His wife, slightly shorter than Adik, was not agile or tall enough to reach it, and his son had no reason to. Tolkachev kept his tools in the *entresol*: a gauge for checking current, a soldering iron, and wire. For wood projects, he had stowed away his drill, plane, and saw. There were three other storage areas in the apartment, all of which he had built.

Adik was thirty years old when he married, late for a young Russian man of his generation. His wife was then twenty-two years old. Tolkachev wrote to the CIA, "I apparently belong to those who love once."[4]

Adik and Natasha lived and worked in the closed cocoon of the military-industrial complex, a sprawling archipelago of ministries, institutes, factories, and testing ranges. Tolkachev had the highest-level access to state secrets. Their public behavior was governed by survival in the Soviet party-state system, which dictated conformity. By day, they played by the rules. By night, their private feelings were vastly different. Their thinking was forged in a profound moment of sorrow and loss in Natasha's childhood, during Stalin's purges of 1937, a loss that propelled Adik into the world of espionage.

Natasha's father, Ivan Kuzmin, was editor in chief of the newspaper *Lyogkaya Industriya*, or light industry. He put a splash of happiness on page 1 of the paper for New Year's Day 1937, a photograph that might have come from any family, including his own: an outsized image of a beaming mother, arms hoisting high a toddler with an enormous smile and grasping a doll in one hand. A festive New Year's tree stood behind them.

The photograph radiates confidence in the future, but it is a posed and artificial buoyancy. The child's arm is outstretched, beckoning like Lenin. It is accompanied by flowery commentary which declared that the Soviet Union was being "directed by the life-giving force of socialism, the Bolshevik Party, and Stalin's genius."[5] The newspaper was the daily chronicle of the textile industry, crammed with material from factory workers, directors, and occasionally Communist Party officials. Much of it was simply letters from worker-correspondents, each known as a *rabkor*, who wrote short bits and pieces about mills and factories, ideas for improved efficiency, and the use of technology and equipment. The front page often featured a large photograph of a young weaver and her success story—how she started her career at a mill, gained experience and skills, and one day suggested and introduced a method that enormously boosted efficiency. The paper printed a mixture of genuine commentary by workers and party exhortations at a time when the Soviet centrally planned economy was in a breakneck phase of industrialization. A headline declared, "It is important to achieve a decisive breakthrough in the implementation of the plan!" When a high-ranking party official or minister gave a speech, the paper often published the transcript on page 1. Page 2 carried daily tables of production—how much cotton, flax, hemp, jute, wool, silk, leather, and other materials were produced where. The third page was almost fully devoted to the ideas and suggestions of workers about how to increase production, and the newspaper was expanding its horizons to cover all aspects of light industry.

Kuzmin, then thirty-six years old, never signed articles. He appears to have been more like a moderator among competing voices, selecting the *rabkor* reports and perhaps writing the unsigned front-page editorials. A member of the Communist Party, he had been editor for four years. The paper, created in 1932 in a merger of other publications for textile workers, carried reports and correspondence from all kinds of people: weavers, engineers, and factory directors. But it was still a mouthpiece of the party-state.

In January 1937, readers could not miss the darkening clouds. The newspaper's front page carried exhaustive coverage of the second of three Moscow show trials. Stalin was brutally snuffing out his rivals one by one, a harbinger of the coming Great Terror. In the first trial, in August 1936, sixteen defendants, including the Bolshevik revolutionaries Lev Kamenev and Grigory Zinoviev, were accused of disloyalty and conspiring with Stalin's exiled rival, Leon Trotsky. All of the defendants were sentenced to death and shot. The second trial focused on seventeen defendants who were considered lesser leaders of the plot. Thirteen of them were later executed and the rest sent to labor camps. Kuzmin's newspaper published all the materials of the second trial, including full transcripts of the interrogations and reactions from readers. "Destroy the villains!" one reader wrote. "Shoot the fascist hirelings, despicable traitors! This is the unanimous demand of the working people of the USSR!" declared another. When the defendants were convicted on January 30, the newspaper published the text of the verdict. On February 1, the newspaper declared that Soviet workers "greeted the verdict of the Trotsky gang with deep satisfaction."[6]

The truth was far different. "Fear by night, and a feverish effort by day to pretend enthusiasm for a system of lies, was the permanent condition of the Soviet citizen," wrote the historian Robert Conquest.[7] "The terror of 1936–8 was an almost uniquely devastating blow inflicted by a government on its own population, and the charges against the millions of victims were almost without exception entirely false. Stalin personally ordered, inspired and organized the operation."[8]

On May 1, 1937, the Politburo members who were standing next to Stalin on the reviewing stand for traditional May Day celebrations in Red Square seemed to be unusually nervous, moving uneasily from one foot to the next. The reason for their anxiety: one of them was suddenly missing. Yan Rudzutak, a former full member of the Politburo, had disappeared, arrested at a supper party after a theater performance. The secret police detained everyone at the party, too. Three months later, four of the women were still in prison in their bedraggled evening dresses. After Rudzutak's arrest, the next echelon of Moscow's administrative and party elite began to vanish. "An atmosphere of fear hung over the Party and Government offices," Conquest wrote. People disappeared on their way to their jobs in the morning. "Every day, another Central Committee member or Vice Chairman of a People's Commissariat or one of their more important underlings was disappearing."[9]

After slicing through the party elite, the purges expanded later in the summer and into the autumn of 1937, wave after wave of suspicion, denunciation, arrest, and execution. One of the largest was the "kulak" operation, referring to the more prosperous farmers who had been forced off their land during Stalin's disastrous forced collectivization of agriculture, more than 1.8 million of them sent to prison camps. Now nearing the end of the standard eight-year term, the kulaks were soon to return; Stalin feared a wave of disgruntled and embittered people coming home. The hammer fell with a secret police order, No. 00447, in July 1937, which set the pattern for the mass killings of the following two years. The document ordered arrests by quota— thousands and thousands at a time—in specific categories, such as "*kulaks*, criminals and other anti-Soviet elements." The categories were so broad as to apply to almost anyone. People were arrested and executed for the slightest indiscretion, so they became extremely guarded in what they said in public; a single stray comment could be reported and lead to arrest, the charges entirely arbitrary. Tens of thousands of people were swept up suddenly, for no reason, from all walks of life.[10] The NKVD, forerunner to the KGB, divided all suspected "enemies" of the state into two categories: those who were shot, and those who were sent away to the camps for ten years. This was the biggest of the mass campaigns and accounted for half of all arrests and more than half of all executions—376,202 persons killed—in the two-year period.[11] The administrative class was sacked, arrested, and executed. In 1937, government ministers—known as commissars—for foreign trade, internal trade, heavy industry, education, justice, sea and river transport, and light industry were all removed and arrested.[12] There was so much paranoia that anyone who visited or knew someone who lived abroad could be suspect as an enemy of the people. Denunciations were often made recklessly and maliciously and could quickly lead to death. "Today, a man only talks freely with his wife—at night, with the blankets pulled over his head," said the writer Isaac Babel, who himself was arrested in the spring of 1939, charged with anti-Soviet activity and espionage, and shot in 1940.[13]

In 1937, Ivan Kuzmin, the newspaper editor, and his wife, Sofia Efimovna Bamdas, lived at 14 Staropimenovsky Pereulok, a small lane in the heart of Moscow. Their apartment was located half an hour's walk from the Kremlin. Sofia was also a Communist Party member and worked as head of the planning department in the Ministry of the Timber Industry. She was born in 1903 into a bourgeois Jewish family in Kremenchug, a town on the Dnieper River, in the Ukraine, once part of the Jewish Pale of Settlement.[14] The town was known for timber and grain exports. Her father, Efim, had fled to Europe and was prospering as a businessman in Denmark. Efim had two daughters, Sofia and Esfir, both of whom lived in Moscow.

Sofia went to visit her father in 1937, and that was the beginning of the end. He was a capitalist and a foreigner, more than enough to generate suspicion. On September 17, the secret police came to apartment 35. They arrested Sofia, then thirty-four years old. The charge was that she belonged to a subversive Trotskyist organization in the timber industry.[15]

When she was taken away and the door closed, she left behind a daughter, her only child, who was two years old.

Six days later, the secret police came for Ivan. He had refused to denounce Sofia. He was not at home; they found him at the apartment of a friend. He was taken to Moscow's notorious Butyrskaya Prison and charged with participation in an anti-Soviet terrorist organization.[16]

Sofia and Ivan never saw each other again. Her visit to her father in Denmark had prompted someone to denounce her. It is not known who, or what was said, but considering that her father was in private business and lived outside the Soviet Union, that was probably sufficient. Her trial was held on December 10, 1937, and she was convicted of subversion. She was executed immediately. The shootings usually took place at night.

In a frenzy of terror, vast numbers of people were sentenced each day, sometimes several hundred, and shot. According to Conquest, two days after Sofia was executed, on December 12, 1937, Stalin and his premier, Vyacheslav Molotov, approved 3,167 death sentences—and then went to watch a movie. Not all the executions were approved at such a high level; on a day in October, the secret police chief, Nikolai Yezhov, and another official considered 551 names and sentenced every one of them to be shot.[17]

Ivan had been arrested for "participation in an anti-Soviet terrorist organization" and convicted for "sabotage" and refusing to inform on others. He steadfastly refused to turn in anyone or to plead guilty. In March 1939, he was sentenced to ten years in the prison camps, with credit for nearly two years already served in jail. He was a son of peasants and was sent to a labor camp in the coalfields of Vorkuta, twelve hundred miles from Moscow and a hundred miles north of the Arctic Circle. He was held incommunicado—no letters allowed.

Their toddler daughter was sent to a state orphanage. So many people had been declared "enemies of the people" in those years that the orphanages were overflowing.[18] The daughter was fortunate in one respect: her parents had retained a nanny, whose name was Dunya. Out of compassion and perhaps fear, Dunya moved with the little girl from institution to institution as she grew up in the years after the arrests and the execution of her mother.[19]

In 1947, Ivan was released from the prison camp, but he did not return to Moscow right away. Still fearing arrest, he moved from city to city. Only after Stalin died in 1953 did he feel it was safe to come home and was reunited with his daughter, then eighteen years old. They were together only a few years. On March 23, 1955, Ivan Kuzmin was rehabilitated for "failure to prove a charge." But he did not live long after that. On December 10, 1956, he died of a brain disease in Moscow.[20]

The daughter of Sofia and Ivan, who suffered a childhood without parents because of Stalin's purges, married Adolf Tolkachev the year after her father died. Natalia Ivanovna Kuzmina was brimming with strong emotions. She managed to stay out of trouble, but those who worked with her knew of her feelings. She read the banned writer Boris Pasternak and the poet Osip Mandelstam. When Alexander Solzhenitsyn's novel *One Day in the Life of Ivan Denisovich* was published in 1962 in *Novy Mir*, a literary journal, she was the first in the family to devour it. Later, when possession of Solzhenitsyn's unpublished works was more dangerous, she was unafraid to pass around copies in samizdat. In 1968, after the Soviet invasion of Czechoslovakia, there was a rush in Soviet workplaces to pass resolutions supporting the action. She was the only person in her group to vote no. She was, in the words of a supervisor, "unable to be insincere."[21]

Her long ordeal and her deep antipathy to the Soviet party-state became Tolkachev's, too.

Adik was fourteen years old the night that German bombers attacked Moscow, July 21, 1941. The city in those years was a tinderbox, largely constructed out of wood, and the German planes dropped 104 tons of high explosive and forty-six thousand incendiary bombs, killing 130 persons, the first in a wave of aerial bombings that would go on until the following April. The Soviet capital was defended by over six hundred large searchlights and eight hundred anti-aircraft guns but only primitive radars.[22]

The bombings showed how the Soviet Union desperately needed improved radar, and the emerging technology of radar became the central focus of young Tolkachev's career.

Adolf Georgievich Tolkachev was born on January 6, 1927, in what was then the Soviet Socialist Kazakh Republic, now Kazakhstan. His family moved to Moscow when he was two years old. Little is known about his parents or his brother, who had only a tenth-grade education and worked as an electrical mechanic on the railroads. Adik went to a vocational school, the equivalent of a high school, where he studied electronics, finishing in 1948. He then went to the Kharkov Polytechnic Institute in the Ukraine, completing his studies in 1954 in the radio-technical department, chiefly about radar. In those days, students had no choice where they would work. Under an assignment system in the centrally planned economy known as *raspredelenie*, they were directed to jobs.[23]

Tolkachev was assigned to a military research facility, the Scientific Research Institute for Radio Engineering, known by its Russian acronym, NIIR. It was later given an additional name, Phazotron Scientific Design Association, or simply Phazotron. The institute was made up of two dozen structures crowded into a ten-acre compound near the Belarussky train station in Moscow, about two miles from the Kremlin. Along the eastern side of the compound, on a narrow lane, Electrichesky Pereulok, stood a long row of aging brick buildings, the exteriors decorated with baroque flourishes from the Russian architecture of the late 1880s. It was in these buildings that the institute had been founded in 1917 to fabricate instruments for aviation, including a simple but reliable device to measure wind speed. After that, the enterprise, known as Avia-Pribor, made watches, thermal instruments, and gramophones—and then radar.[24] While the bombs were still being dropped by German airplanes in January 1942, the buildings at Electrichesky Pereulok were given a new name, Factory No. 339, and became the first manufacturing facility for radar in the Soviet Union. In the 1950s, the facility expanded into research and development of military radars, which grew in sophistication from simple sighting devices to complex aviation and weapons guidance systems.

It was the only place Tolkachev had ever worked. Phazotron's radars for Soviet warplanes were named ORYOL, SMERCH, and SAPFIR. As in many other areas of technology, the Soviet Union struggled to catch up to the West. In the early 1970s, Soviet airborne radars could not spot moving objects close to the ground, meaning they could fail to detect a terrain-hugging bomber or cruise missile. This vulnerability became a major design challenge for Phazotron; the engineers were pressed to build radars that could "look down" from above and identify low-flying objects moving against the background of the earth. The United States was planning to use low-flying, penetrating bombers to attack the Soviet Union in the event of any war.[25]

At first, Phazotron produced an airborne radar known as the RP-23, or Sapfir-23, which provided limited look-down capability for MiG fighters. Then the institute was ordered to develop a more sophisticated model to be deployed on the MiG-31, a planned supersonic interceptor. But the task proved too difficult for Tolkachev's institute to complete. By one account, the institute made lavish claims for a new radar that it simply could not bring to fruition. Despite a wealth of experience, Phazotron was unable to solve the problem of tracking and destroying a low-flying object against the ground clutter of earth, nor had it been able to track multiple targets at once. Phazotron was forced in 1971 to transfer the plans to a competing institute, the Scientific Research Institute of Instrument Engineering, or NIIP. After years of work, the competing institute and several others solved most of the problems in a new radar, called ZASLON. Weighing a half ton, it was twice as heavy as the largest airborne U.S. radar, but it worked—and carried the first-ever Soviet airborne computer. The ZASLON was flight-tested for the first time in 1976 and by 1978 had been shown to track ten targets at once. The first MiG-31 aircraft carrying the ZASLON radar were entering service in the Soviet air defense forces in the autumn of 1981.[26]

By that time, Tolkachev had already delivered to the CIA hundreds of pages of blueprints and design specifications of Sapfir-23 and five circuit boards. He gave them plans and drawings of the ZASLON, too.

The painful history of the Kuzmin family was passed down to Natasha—and to Adik—in her father's last years. Ivan told his daughter the unvarnished truth: the terror of the arrests, the finality of the verdicts, the sudden destruction of their family. She learned that Ivan was punished because he stoutly refused to denounce his wife, Sofia.

In 1957, the year after Ivan's death, when Adik and Natasha married, the threat of Stalin's mass repressions had passed, but strong memories lingered, and the full scope was only beginning to reveal itself. Khrushchev devoted a speech to Stalin's excesses at the Twentieth Party Congress on February 25, 1956, blaming Stalin for the unwarranted arrest and execution of party officials during the purges, for the surprise attack on the Soviet Union by Hitler, and for other blunders, although not for the true scope of the repressions or the forced collectivization and famine, calamities for which Khrushchev shared responsibility. Nonetheless, Khrushchev had opened the door; he denounced the "cult of personality" that had allowed Stalin to amass such raw power. The speech heralded a period of liberalization known as the thaw, after the title of Ilya Ehrenburg's 1954 novel. Breaking with years of forced adherence to the dictates of socialist realism, some freethinking writers and artists dared push the boundaries of what was permissible, and hopes ran high that a different country might emerge from the Great Terror and the ravages of war. The Soviet launch of the Sputnik satellite in October 1957 fueled the optimism, especially among young people. Lyudmila Alexeyeva, a historian and human rights champion, recalled that in the years that followed Khrushchev's speech, "Young men and women began to lose their fear of sharing views, knowledge, beliefs, questions. Every night, we gathered in cramped apartments to recite poetry, read 'unofficial' prose, and swap stories that, taken together, yielded a realistic picture of what was going on in our country. That was the time of our awakening." The awakening undoubtedly swayed Adik and Natasha, too.[27]

Tolkachev told the CIA that "in my youth" politics had played "a significant role" but he had lost interest and then become scornful of what he called the "impassable, hypocritical demagoguery" of the Soviet party-state. He did not elaborate on this change, but by the mid-1960s, as the thaw was ending and with Khrushchev deposed, Tolkachev seems to have been thinking about how to express his unhappiness.

In May 1965, his son, Oleg, was born. Tolkachev said he did not act at the time because he did not want to endanger his family. "I waited for my son to grow up," he wrote to the CIA of his decision to remain quiet, saying he realized that "in case of a flap my family would face a severe ordeal."

Then, in the years that followed, the mid-1970s, Tolkachev found inspiration in Andrei Sakharov and Alexander Solzhenitsyn, voices of conscience who each waged a titanic struggle against Soviet totalitarianism. Sakharov, like Tolkachev, had a top secret security clearance, yet he possessed the courage to dissent. Tolkachev did not know him personally but knew what Sakharov stood for.

In the early months of 1968, Andrei Sakharov had worked alone, late into the evening at his gabled, two-story house nestled in the trees at Arzamas-16, the nuclear weapons laboratory, located in the city of Sarov, 230 miles east of Moscow. Sakharov was the principal designer of the Soviet thermonuclear bomb. A pillar of the scientific establishment who entered the Academy of Sciences in his thirties, he had profound doubts about the moral and ecological consequences of his work, and he played a role in persuading Khrushchev to sign a limited nuclear test ban treaty with the United States in 1963. Now his conscience was calling him again and would take him well beyond the closed world of Arzamas-16, where he had thrived and been recognized as a brilliant physicist.

Each night, from 7:00 until midnight, alone in the house in the woods, Sakharov worked on an essay about the future of mankind. It became his first significant act of dissent against the

Soviet system. Finished in April, the essay was titled "Reflections on Progress, Peaceful Coexistence, and Intellectual Freedom." Sakharov's mind ranged far and wide, warning that the planet was threatened by thermonuclear war, hunger, ecological catastrophe, and despotism, but he also offered idealistic and utopian ideas to save the world, suggesting that socialism and capitalism could live together—he called it "convergence"—and the superpowers should not be trying to destroy each other. He wrote candidly of Stalin's crimes. He insisted on a complete de-Stalinization of the country, the end of censorship, release of political prisoners, freedom of opinion, and democratization. The document was startling, visionary, and potentially explosive. Sakharov rewrote and polished his essay and at one point showed it to Yuli Khariton, the scientific director of the laboratory and a founder of the Soviet nuclear weapons program. The two of them were alone on Khariton's private train. "Well, what did you think?" Sakharov asked Khariton. "It's awful," Khariton replied. "The style?" Sakharov asked. Khariton grimaced. "No, not the style, it's the content that's awful!" But Sakharov had already begun circulating the essay in carbon copies, told Khariton he believed everything he had written, and could not withdraw it. In July, the manifesto was published abroad, first in a Dutch newspaper and then in the *New York Times* on July 22. The essay also circulated widely in samizdat, hand-to-hand copies, inside the Soviet Union. Sakharov was then suspended—effectively fired—from his job at the nuclear weapons laboratory.[28]

Only weeks later, on August 20–21, 1968, Soviet tanks and Warsaw Pact troops crushed the reform movement known as the Prague Spring in Czechoslovakia. Sakharov had been excited by the democratic experiment; the Soviet crackdown shattered his optimism. "The hopes inspired by the Prague Spring collapsed," he said. For many, the prospect of any liberalization inside the Soviet Union vanished. The thaw was over.

Among those who read Sakharov's "Reflections" in samizdat was Solzhenitsyn, whose trenchant, penetrating novels had depicted the dark corners of Soviet totalitarianism. His novel *One Day in the Life of Ivan Denisovich*, about the life of a man in the gulag, had been published in Russian during the thaw, but Solzhenitsyn's more recent works, *Cancer Ward* and *The First Circle*, were banned, and he was increasingly a thorn in the side of the Soviet authorities. The week after the Prague Spring was crushed, Solzhenitsyn and Sakharov met for the first time. Sakharov had come from deep within the establishment and Solzhenitsyn from without, the scientist in coat and tie and the writer dressed casually in old clothes. They sat in the living room of a mutual friend, curtains drawn to hide from the KGB. Solzhenitsyn was charmed by Sakharov's "tall figure, his look of absolute candor, his warm, gentle smile, his bright glance, his pleasantly throaty voice, the thick blurring of his *r*'s." Sakharov, too, vividly remembered Solzhenitsyn: "With his lively blue eyes and ruddy beard, his tongue-twistingly fast speech delivered in an unexpected treble, and his deliberate, precise gestures, he seemed an animated concentration of purposeful energy." Both men, each brilliant in his own way, became beacons of inspiration for Tolkachev.[29]

In the early 1970s, Sakharov plunged more deeply into the struggle for human rights, taking up individual cases of persecution and forming a committee on human rights with two young physicists. He began broadening his personal contacts with Westerners, a move that infuriated Soviet officials who had, until then, treated him with restraint.[30] In June 1973, Sakharov gave an interview to Olle Stenholm, a Scandinavian radio and television correspondent, and his remarks were published on July 4 in a Swedish newspaper. Sakharov was scathingly critical of the Soviet party-state for its monopoly on power—in politics, economics, and ideology—and most of all "the lack of freedom."

The interview made headlines around the world. The party-state took off the gloves. A sustained and ugly press campaign was waged against Sakharov. Forty academicians signed a letter saying Sakharov's actions "discredit the good name of Soviet science." Solzhenitsyn, who had won the Nobel Prize in Literature but was unable to receive it in person, urged Sakharov to keep a low profile; the regime was on the offensive against him and the broader human rights movement.[31] But Sakharov could not remain silent. The KGB warned him not to meet with foreign journalists, but days later he responded by inviting foreign correspondents to his apartment for a press conference at which he repeated his views on democratization and human rights.[32] Meanwhile, Solzhenitsyn's exposé of the Soviet prison camps, *The Gulag Archipelago*, was being readied for publication in the West. Sakharov and Solzhenitsyn had ignited a fire, and the KGB began to speak of them in the same breath. Yuri Andropov, the KGB chief, in September 1973 recommended taking "more radical measures to terminate the hostile acts of Solzhenitsyn and Sakharov."[33] In January 1974, Solzhenitsyn was arrested and deported from the Soviet Union. In 1975, Sakharov received the Nobel Peace Prize but was prohibited from leaving the country to receive it.

These events left a deep and lasting impression on Tolkachev. When he later recounted his disenchantment to explain his actions to the CIA, he identified 1974 and 1975 as a turning point. After years of waiting, he decided to act. "I can only say that a significant role in this was played by Solzhenitsyn and Sakharov, even though I don't know them and have only read Solzhenitsyn's works that appeared in *Novy Mir*," he wrote in a letter to the CIA.

"Some inner worm started to torment me," he said. "Something had to be done."

Tolkachev's expression of dissent began modestly, by writing

short protest leaflets. He told the CIA he briefly considered sending the leaflets in the mail. "But later," he added, "having thought
it out properly, I understood that this was a useless undertaking.
To establish contact with the dissident circles that have contact
with the foreign journalists seemed senseless to me due to the
nature of my work." He had a top secret clearance. "Because of
the slightest suspicion, I will be totally isolated or liquidated for
safety."

Tolkachev decided that he would have to find other ways
to damage the system. In September 1976, he heard the news
of Belenko's defection to Japan with the MiG-25. When the
Soviet authorities ordered Phazotron to redesign the radar for
the MiG-25, Tolkachev had a dawning realization: his greatest
weapon against the Soviet Union was not some dissident pam-
phlets but right in his desk drawer, the top secret blueprints and
reports that were the most closely held secrets of Soviet military
research. He could seriously injure the system by betrayal—
turning these vital plans over to the "main adversary," the United
States.

Tolkachev told the CIA he had never even considered selling
secrets, say, to China. "And how about America, maybe it has
bewitched me and I am madly in love with it?" he wrote. "I have
never seen your country with my own eyes, and to love it unseen,
I do not have enough fantasy nor romanticism. However, based
on some facts, I got the impression, that I would prefer to live in
America. It is for this very reason that I decided to offer you my
collaboration."[34]

Tolkachev was usually at his desk at Phazotron by 8:00 a.m., but
he did a lot of his best thinking outside the office. He often had
an inspiration at home or sitting alone in the early evening in the

Lenin Library. He jotted down notes, then took them to work and copied them into a special classified notebook, which was turned over to the typing pool.

His desk at the institute was in a large room on the fifth floor with twenty-four other persons. Fluorescent lights hung from a high ceiling. In front of him, two women sat, facing away. On his desk, he had two phone lines, one for internal calls, extension 159, and a city line; paper for taking notes; a notebook with a list of problems that needed to be solved; scrap notebooks for rough sketches; and reference works on radar. A file drawer held a set of papers about work schedules and copies of official notes he had sent to other institutes. Another drawer held electronic assemblies and parts needed for final checks of equipment he had worked on.

With secret documents tucked inside his coat, Tolkachev's walk home at lunchtime was easy and pleasant. The city's streets in 1981 were broad, but traffic was light. He often left the institute and cut through a neighborhood of boxy apartment buildings latticed with interior courtyards and small parks. He turned onto Novopresnensky Pereulok, a small lane, passing a kindergarten and a playground. Then he took Volkov Pereulok, a quiet backstreet that ran next to the Moscow Zoo, and his high-rise apartment loomed just beyond. It took him only twenty minutes to get home. The apartment was empty at lunchtime. He took out the Pentax camera, clamped it to the back of a chair, positioned a lamp nearby, and made copies of documents.

One day in 1981, Tolkachev was careless. When finished, he usually stowed the camera and clamp in the *entresol*, where they would be well hidden. But he hastily left them in a desk drawer. They were discovered by Natasha, and she immediately guessed what Adik was doing. She confronted him when they were alone.

Her concern was not the damage to the Soviet state. She hated the system even more than Adik did. Her lament was more personal. She did not want the family to get hurt in the way that her parents had suffered. She did not want to bring the wrath of the KGB upon them.

Tolkachev confessed to her. She demanded that he stop his spying, to spare the family any difficulty, and he promised to quit. But he did not.[35]

# 14

# "EVERYTHING IS DANGEROUS"

**D**avid Rolph had not seen Adolf Tolkachev for eight months. Tolkachev was not using the kitchen light, the SVET signal they had agreed upon to show that he was ready on the planned dates for a meeting. His kitchen window had been dark. On November 10, 1981, the next meeting date, Rolph went to the selected site, a park not far from Tolkachev's apartment building, and was relieved to find him waiting by the fountain. Rolph walked briskly down a flight of stone steps and greeted him warmly in the chill air. Tolkachev, his face brightening, said he had bought a car and motioned to Rolph that they should go take a look at it.

A moving car was a risky place to meet an agent; Rolph would have no control of where they were going. A parked car wasn't great, either. It could attract the attention of a curious onlooker or militiaman. There were also the *druzhinniki* to worry about, a government-organized neighborhood watch that wasn't always vigilant but whose members, wearing red armbands, might knock on the car window and demand identification. Still, there was no point in discouraging Tolkachev. He had a childlike excitement in his voice. They walked toward the car, talking, catching up.[1]

When Rolph mentioned Tolkachev's silence over the last few months, saying the Moscow station had been watching the kitchen light, Tolkachev interrupted him. He hadn't wanted to meet in September. In October, he did want to meet and signaled on the proper date by parking his car near the market, as Rolph had suggested. The CIA gave him a map and instructions for the site, designated MASHINA, or "car": park opposite the market between 12:45 and 1:00 p.m., back into the parking space, rear tires against the curb, go shopping for fifteen minutes.[2] Tolkachev followed the instructions exactly, but Rolph didn't show. Tolkachev had assumed the reason was an incident he read about in the newspapers. In September, the KGB ambushed a Soviet citizen while meeting an American and accused the American of being a spy. Rolph knew of the arrest—the station had indeed lost an agent, and a case officer had been expelled—but he reassured Tolkachev that wasn't the problem. The real reason was that Rolph didn't think the MASHINA site would be operative until November. He simply hadn't checked it. He apologized for the confusion.[3]

They reached Tolkachev's compact Zhiguli, tucked in between other cars parked closely together. They climbed in, Tolkachev behind the wheel. Rolph was thinking to himself that this might not be a very smart move. But they had a lot of business to do. Tolkachev was relaxed, in good spirits, and he seemed to feel like talking. Before long, Rolph noticed the windows were fogging up. It was like this at the start of every meeting: Tolkachev was a bundle of anxiety but had no one to share it with other than his case officer. He needed a release.[4]

Tolkachev passed twenty-three rolls of film to Rolph, fewer than last time but potentially carrying hundreds of pages of secret documents. One of Tolkachev's Pentax camera bodies was not working properly, and he returned it. Rolph handed back a spare Pentax camera body; he remembered to bring it because of the six rolls of blank film in March. Rolph also presented Tolkachev with a new set of stereo headphones and music for his son and a package containing 32,400 rubles.

Rolph explained that he brought Tolkachev a new, secure communications device, known as an IOWL, or interim one-way link. The gear included a commercially purchased short-wave radio, a smaller electronics block called a demodulator, and onetime pads. When Tolkachev tuned in to certain shortwave frequencies at specific times with the demodulator attached, messages could be downloaded secretly. Tolkachev appeared intrigued. In one of his first letters to the CIA, he had proposed using a modified radio for transmitting secret messages.[5]

At first, everything seemed fine, but as they talked, Rolph realized it was not.

The institute had once again imposed strict procedures on checking out secret documents. As before, the new rules required that Tolkachev turn in his building pass. Tolkachev glumly informed Rolph this meant he could not take documents home to photograph, which he had done so successfully for two years. The CIA's attempts to replicate the building pass had, so far, not satisfied Tolkachev. The colors and the paper were not quite right.

Tolkachev said he tried, and failed, to make the Discus work over the summer. He handed the device and instructions back to Rolph. He didn't appear to be frustrated; he had experience with electronics and understood that things could malfunction. Rolph was far more skeptical. He thought the Discus device had yet to contribute a single ounce of positive intelligence.

After the missed signals, Tolkachev proposed a new way to indicate that he would be ready to meet. Instead of the kitchen light, the CIA should look above the main window in his apartment, at the small, hinged window used for ventilation, known as the *fortochka*. They were common in all Russian buildings. On a meeting day, the *fortochka* would be open for a short period at midday if Tolkachev was ready. Rolph asked twice: Are you sure it will be visible from the street, nine floors below? Tolkachev assured him the open *fortochka* appeared as a black square above the reflective glass of the main window.

Tolkachev had personal requests, too. He wanted the CIA to provide him with a pocket tape recorder, information about recent events in Poland, and *My Life* by Leon Trotsky, which was banned in the Soviet Union. After twenty minutes, Rolph climbed out of the car and said farewell.

Tolkachev drove off. It was his eleventh meeting with the CIA. He said nothing to Rolph about his wife's discovery of his spying or his promise to stop it.

The next morning, back in the station, Rolph opened the ops note Tolkachev had given him. Of the forty-five questions the CIA had posed in March, Tolkachev had offered answers to only eleven and was apologetic. He wrote that his access to information was not unlimited, and he felt "sorrow" that he could not respond to the "wide themes" the CIA had asked about. Tolkachev said he couldn't possibly answer technical questions about weapons systems "with which I am not directly connected."

Rolph suggested to headquarters that they needed to be more careful about the questions. He expressed worry they were trying to "overload" Tolkachev "in areas where he has no hope of meaningful response." After two years of "prolific production," Rolph said they ought to do better than eleven out of forty-five by tailoring the questions to topics Tolkachev might know about. But the demands did not slacken.

————

In the autumn of 1981, Gerber flew back to headquarters and met Casey, the new director of central intelligence. Gerber had devoted much of his career to espionage against the Soviet target, and he was the kind of operations officer that Casey admired. In a letter to Reagan after becoming director, Casey confided a feeling that "I get better intelligence judgments from the streetwise, on the ground" operations people than the "more academic" analysts at headquarters.[6] During their conversation, Gerber remarked the Soviets were a nuclear-armed superpower but an economic basket case. "This is a country that can't even make toasters," he said. "And while they can make missiles, they can't feed their population." Gerber was drawing on his own experiences in Moscow, but Casey waved him off. Casey said the Soviets were advancing in Latin America and Africa, and they had to be confronted everywhere.[7] Reagan campaigned in 1980 on a promise to stand up to the Soviet Union, and he was now turning the promise into action.

At the Ottawa summit in July 1981, President François Mitterrand of France told Reagan some startling news. The French intelligence service had been running a secret and highly productive agent inside the KGB, a forty-eight-year-old colonel, Vladimir Vetrov. The operation was still under way. Vetrov had turned over to the French four thousand pages of KGB documents about a global effort by the Soviet Union to steal high technology from the West, especially the United States. The KGB had a whole section, known as Line X, to carry out the heist. With Mitterrand's approval, the French brought the documents to the CIA. The papers, known as the "Farewell Dossier," showed in remarkable detail how the Soviet Union had hijacked Western advances in electronics and other technology to benefit its military machine. With Reagan's approval, Casey launched a covert program, in cooperation with American industry, to rig hardware and sell it to Soviet buyers, matching the KGB's shopping list, including

contrived computer chips and faulty turbines. At the top of the
Soviet list was oil and gas equipment to control a huge new gas
pipeline to Europe. When the pipeline technology could not be
purchased in the United States, the KGB bought it from a Canadian firm. With Reagan's approval, the CIA engineered it to go
haywire after a while, to reset pump speeds and valve settings to
create pressures far beyond those acceptable to the pipeline joints
and welds. The system exploded. The result was the most mon-
umental nonnuclear explosion and fire ever seen from satellites
in outer space. The Farewell Dossier was run right in Moscow.
It reinforced something the CIA had concluded while running
Tolkachev: it was possible to carry out penetrating spy operations
under the nose of the KGB.[8]

Tolkachev surprised the Moscow station by signaling on December 7, 1981, that he wanted to meet right away. Rolph went to
see him the next evening, at 9:05. Tolkachev was chagrined over
the new security restrictions at the institute and his inability to
produce more documents. He gave Rolph six rolls of 35 mm
film, far fewer than in the past. Tolkachev seemed distressed.
He implored the CIA to once again make an attempt to replicate
the building pass. Tolkachev offered to loan his building pass to
the CIA so they could make a copy, saying he would not need
it during the January holidays. Rolph resisted the temptation to
take it, thinking there was no way to return it by the end of the
month. Rolph reassured Tolkachev that the CIA was willing to
be patient and gave him four books by Soviet dissidents. They
were together only fifteen minutes.

It was the last time they would ever see each other.[9]

Tolkachev's six rolls of film developed beautifully and included
the material that had been lost in March. Also, the twenty-three

rolls of film he delivered in November carried a list of all the technical documents that had arrived in the secret library of the institute for the second half of 1980. This was valuable intelligence, showing the state of Soviet advanced technology, but not quite as revelatory as his earlier documents, which contained blueprints of specific weapons systems. A cable from headquarters pointed out, "The value of the recent acquisitions, while of considerable import, generally does not equal that of source's earlier detailed documentary reporting on the ESHELON, GORIZON or SHMEL systems, some of which project Soviet R&D activities off into the mid-1980s to mid-1990s." Tolkachev seemed to be running out of targets for his espionage.[10]

Nonetheless, to encourage him, the CIA broadcast a secret message to Tolkachev on the interim one-way shortwave link, telling him the December film had processed perfectly.

Tolkachev never got the message. He hadn't turned on the shortwave.[11]

Rolph held a cover job in the defense attaché's office at the U.S. embassy, with the formal rank of attaché, but the KGB knew he was an intelligence officer. Still, Rolph evaded them, handling two major operations, CKUTOPIA and CKSPHERE, using surveillance detection runs, out-of-country scenarios, identity transfer, the SRR-100 radio monitors, and a blend of planning, patience, stamina, and good luck. He had benefited greatly from the mentoring of Hathaway, Gerber, and Guilsher. Perhaps most important, Rolph had earned the confidence of Tolkachev. He became a welcome and familiar face, listening to the spy's concerns and fears and building a personal bond of trust.

In early 1982, the Moscow station launched a shift in tactics away from Rolph's traditional case officer function—working all angles, building trust with the agent—to something different. The new approach was conceived by Gerber, the station chief, when he first arrived in Moscow. It called for adding to the Moscow station a new capability, a few case officers who would be under "deep cover," totally invisible to the KGB. They would be "black" all the time, and therefore more secure. This would be accomplished by putting the deep cover officers in innocuous cover jobs, with day-to-day routines that would lead the KGB to pay them little attention.

Most of the CIA's case officers in Moscow were under some kind of official cover, usually as a diplomat in the embassy or as a defense attaché, but they also spent a great deal of time in the Moscow station, working on espionage operations. By contrast, the "deep cover" officers would keep a healthy distance from the Moscow station. They would not have desks or type up reports there, nor participate in the important and lively discussions in Gerber's office. Despite the high stakes and constant risks, they would be rookie CIA officers, on their first tour, who had never been seen by the KGB anywhere else in the world. To preserve their deep cover, they would come to the Moscow station very rarely, and then only briefly, through a secluded entrance. The station would communicate with them using impersonal means such as dead drops, water-soluble paper, and intermediaries. All the hassles would be outweighed by one big advantage: they could evade surveillance.

Deep cover operations in Moscow were begun only after lengthy preparations and bureaucratic wrangling in Washington. The CIA had to negotiate with other agencies, primarily the State Department, for "clean slots," jobs that had never been used for intelligence personnel before. The State Department and the CIA, as institutions, were often at odds. Diplomats had long resented the spies in their midst, and the State Department hated to give up precious overseas slots to the CIA. Only a few people, including the ambassador and the chief of station, would know who was under deep cover. Headquarters arranged for the first deep cover officer to go through foreign-service training so he would look just like a State Department employee. The first deep cover officer arrived in Moscow in the summer of 1981, and after a few months of preparation Gerber wanted to put the new arrangement into action. He sent the officer to meet Tolkachev on February 15, 1982.[12]

Tolkachev carried a recognition signal, a book with a white cover, in his left hand. He greeted the new officer without any hesitation. It was 9:05 p.m., and they climbed into the Zhiguli. The officer delivered to Tolkachev four replicas of the institute building pass made by the CIA for him to examine and also handed him the Discus device once again, reassuring Tolkachev that it had been checked out in the CIA's laboratories and this time it would work. The CIA package for Tolkachev included a charger for the shortwave radio, a schedule of Western broadcasts in Russian that could be received on the radio, the Trotsky autobiography, information about the crisis in Poland, a small portable cassette recorder, batteries, more "positive intelligence" questions from headquarters, and a note of effusive thanks. "Your courage is truly an example to us all," it said.[13]

Although meetings with deep cover officers were intended to be brief, Tolkachev didn't know that, and he wanted to talk—as he had so often done with Guilsher and Rolph. He complained the CIA had used a wrong exchange rate to calculate his ruble payments, and he was owed much more. He said he needed film for the Pentax; there was a shortage in Moscow stores, and they would sell him no more than five rolls at a time. He wanted the CIA to provide him with a hundred rolls.

Tolkachev also acknowledged he hadn't turned on the short-wave radio and demodulator to receive the CIA's secret messages. He was uncertain whether he could pick up the broadcasts, and he had no privacy at home in the evenings. He said his family still didn't know of his espionage.

Despite these setbacks, Tolkachev said he was determined not to quit. He handed the deep cover officer a schematic diagram and another circuit board—only the second time he had provided the CIA with a valuable piece of Soviet electronics.

Then he gave the deep cover officer thirteen rolls of film. Surprised, the CIA officer asked how he was able to do that if there were restrictions at the institute.

Tolkachev said he had a friend in the First Department who would occasionally slip documents to him on request.

Isn't that dangerous? the officer asked.

Tolkachev laughed.

"Everything is dangerous," he said.[14]

Three weeks later, on March 8, 1982, the Moscow station received a signal from Tolkachev, saying they should prepare for the very first transmission by Discus. As Gerber had anticipated, the station was forced to scramble. The station had already cased several locations, known as Electronic Letter Drop sites. One envisioned Tolkachev transmitting across the Moscow River, with a case officer receiving the signal a few hundred yards away at a train station. The Moscow station wanted enough distance so as not to arouse the KGB's suspicions.

While the station didn't know why Tolkachev was getting in touch, the CIA prepared a message anyway to send him in reply, saying the last rolls of film were perfect and they would pay him a lot more rubles.[15]

The first successful Discus message from Tolkachev wasn't earth-shattering. Tolkachev wrote that he was eager to provide feedback about the CIA's four replicas of his building pass—they were "too light"—and he wanted an unscheduled meeting in three days.[16] On March 16, the deep cover officer went out to meet Tolkachev. It was 9:00 p.m. in Moscow, and Tolkachev was in good spirits, but worry creased his face. The security restrictions at the institute had been ratcheted still tighter. Now it was impossible for him to get any documents from the office, nor could he get them from his friend in the First Department. He had no film to give the CIA.

Desperate, and unhappy with the CIA's four replicas of his pass, Tolkachev gave strips of colored paper from the inside pages and a strip cut from the cover of his building pass to the officer; take that back to the CIA, he said, and let them make the replica from this! The officer urged Tolkachev to be careful and not to take any risks. Tolkachev seemed restless but also more introspective than in the past. The case officer wrote afterward to headquarters that Tolkachev "admitted that he had been careless early on in his relationship with us and agreed not to attempt further document photography" until they could work out some of the problems. Tolkachev "really seemed to pause and think about the need for caution."[17]

The meeting was quick, just fifteen minutes. The next day, the Moscow station opened Tolkachev's ops note. He "reluctantly" presented a wish list of more personal favors: a Sony Walkman for his son and earphones with a loop across the head, as well as pencils of various hardness for Oleg's mechanical drawing. He also wanted some Polish blades for his safety razor, writing that "shaving with Soviet razor blades is an unpleasant" experience. He apologized for asking for such trivial things, noting, "Unfortunately our personal life consists of all types of small things which sometimes exert an influence on the general mood."[18]

Gerber knew what he was talking about. The Soviet Union could make missiles but not toasters—or safety razors.

On May 24, two case officers went out on the street separately for a meeting with Tolkachev, hoping that one of them could get free from surveillance. Both carried identical packages. One of them succeeded and met Tolkachev at a site near his apartment building at 9:35 p.m. The case officer delivered a bulky bundle: twenty packages of razor blades, forty rolls of Western film that the CIA had repackaged in Soviet boxes, a Sanyo M6600F tape recorder, a Sony Walkman, a headset, extra batteries, and twenty-six boxes of drawing pencils for Oleg. The bundle was so large that at the last minute the Moscow station had removed another twenty rolls of film. They needed space to wedge in 98,850 rubles.

The package also included a new replica of his building pass.[19]

Over the summer of 1982, Rolph finished his tour in Moscow and went off to another assignment. In late September, Gerber also departed for a new assignment at headquarters. His farewell included a small gift from his colleagues in the Moscow station: a trophy-sized numeral 1 with a metal sphere hanging off the front. It was a memento of the big 1 that had been left on the station door when Sheymov was exfiltrated. The sphere was a reference to Tolkachev, the agent known as CKSPHERE. It became a tradition from then onward that the Moscow station put a numeral 1 on the door if a major operation was completed successfully.

That summer, Bill Plunkert arrived in the Moscow station to run the Tolkachev operation. He had been an athlete at Boston College, playing varsity baseball and soccer, and still enjoyed tennis when he could find the time and a court. Plunkert had thrived in assignments when he could meet and recruit people; Moscow was his first taste of "denied area" operations. But as a Soviet specialist, he thought there was nothing better than "wrestling the bear in his own cave," as he put it. Plunkert was intending not to be Tolkachev's case officer but to coordinate all aspects of the operation from the station. Then, in his first months, the operation seemed to be sliding into serious trouble.

At the time, the Moscow station was sending deep cover officers out to meet Tolkachev—sometimes two or three at a time. But then five scheduled meetings passed without a successful rendezvous. Plunkert felt the tension grow slowly. A missed meeting or two had happened before, but not five.

By December, the station was fraught with anxiety. In all the previous meetings, the Moscow station had made strenuous efforts to see Tolkachev in a safe environment, as certain as they could be that there was no KGB surveillance. Case officers had aborted a scheduled meeting if they had the slightest inkling of surveillance. Now the stakes were higher than ever—and Plunkert began planning for a meeting with Tolkachev no matter what, even if everyone on the street had surveillance. They would have to make it work. The Moscow station was a tense place under any circumstances, a small cockpit of high achievers, but at this moment the pressure and stress brought them together. None of them wanted Tolkachev lost on their watch.

Plunkert took upon himself the job of meeting Tolkachev. He realized if they lost touch with the spy, it would be an enormous setback for the CIA. If he made a mistake on the street that led to Tolkachev's arrest and execution, it would haunt him the rest of his life.

From the files, Plunkert felt he knew Tolkachev well—a middle-aged man, with short, quick strides that made it seem as if his feet barely made contact with the ground. The others who had met Tolkachev told Plunkert not to worry: the agent was a real pro, he would take care of the meeting, just let him do it his way. Plunkert also read that Tolkachev had a remarkable ability to just melt away. He looked like Mr. Everyman.[20]

After using the Jack-in-the-Box and jumping from the car on the night of December 7, Plunkert spotted Tolkachev. The spy looked just as he had been described: nondescript in a fedora, a brown overcoat, brown gloves, black shoes, and a gray scarf tucked inside his overcoat. They met as snow blanketed the city. They exchanged a verbal password. "C'mon, let's walk," Tolkachev said.

Plunkert's immediate impression was that Tolkachev looked worn and tired. His voice sounded a bit tense. Plunkert also noticed that Tolkachev looked older than the photograph he had seen. Tolkachev mentioned that he had been bedridden, suffering severe bouts of high blood pressure. But this had not deterred him from checking out top secret documents from the library at his institute, then photographing them when alone at home with the Pentax. As they walked, Tolkachev spoke faster, describing new security procedures he faced. Tolkachev was undeterred, as determined as ever.

Plunkert spoke in Russian, explaining why they had missed the earlier meetings: they had spotted KGB surveillance.

Tolkachev abruptly stopped in his tracks and looked at Plunkert wide-eyed. "You have surveillance?"

"No, no!" Plunkert responded, he meant on previous evenings. Tolkachev was relieved. They walked.

Plunkert realized every word was important and asked if he could turn on a recorder. Tolkachev said yes. Plunkert switched on his concealed tape recorder so the voices could be replayed later at the Moscow station and headquarters. They traded packages—film, batteries, and books for the agent, sixteen rolls of exposed film for the case officer.[21]

As they were almost finished, they heard a crunching of boots on the snow. Tolkachev and Plunkert glanced anxiously at a tall, senior army officer in uniform walking toward them. They froze. He walked right past, and they exhaled.

After just twenty minutes, they parted. When Plunkert glanced back to make sure Tolkachev was all right, he had melted away.

Plunkert walked back to the wide Moscow boulevard known as the Garden Ring Road and boarded a bus. He sat in the very back, behind all the other passengers. He took off his Russian coat and eyeglasses, then reached into the sack, grabbed his American street clothes, and put them on. It all happened very fast, just before the bus stopped, and he jumped off. No one had seen him, but he was still apprehensive. What if the KGB was now out looking for him? Two militiamen stood by the door at the embassy, as always. When Plunkert saw another American return from walking his dog, he rushed in, close behind. He walked to the apartment of two colleagues and silently handed them the package from the spy, to be brought to the station in the morning. Plunkert couldn't speak; the apartments were probably bugged. But he signaled thumbs-up and accepted a whiskey in a water glass. He felt a surge of relief and exhilaration.

The CIA attempted repeatedly to replicate Tolkachev's building pass, down to the delicate indigo swirls on the paper. At last, Tolkachev said the most recent replica, given to him in May, was good enough. For several months in 1982, he used it to smuggle documents out. But suddenly, in August, the institute security procedures changed yet again. Now there was an entirely new pass for checking out documents.

The CIA forgery, so long in the making, was rendered useless.

"It is now extremely difficult, if not impossible, for CKSPHERE to take documents home," Plunkert reported. "There are special permission slips which CKSPHERE could use, but extensive use of these slips would surely cast suspicion upon him." Plunkert wrote that his "visceral" feeling was that Tolkachev "is concerned, due to conditions of work and health, that life is getting tougher and that perhaps his best days are behind him."

Plunkert's observations threw the CIA into a fresh round

of uncertainty. In a cable to headquarters, the Moscow station described a confluence of factors weighing on Tolkachev: the new security rules, his mental state, and the fact that he was thinking about copying documents with much riskier means, such as the concealed Tropel cameras. Headquarters responded by saying perhaps they should ask for a six-month time-out, to give Tolkachev a breather. The Moscow station agreed. The station said Tolkachev seemed concerned about his security when he talked with Plunkert. "If he sees danger signs—and we think he does—it is possible they are more ominous than he is ready to admit," the station told headquarters.[22]

The film Tolkachev passed to Plunkert on December 7 processed perfectly: another 499 pages of secret documents.

For a spy who had saved the United States billions of dollars, Tolkachev's personal requests remained modest. His son, Oleg, had entered an architect's training institute, and drafting equipment in the Soviet Union was poor. Could the CIA find a better-quality set in Eastern Europe or the West? Even the erasers in Moscow were shoddy, Tolkachev complained. They left greasy marks on the drawings. Could the CIA find four or five better-quality erasers? "Czech erasers have pretty good quality," Tolkachev wrote. "My son has been able to obtain half of such an eraser from acquaintances, and we are using it now, but it won't last him for long." He also wanted two or three large bricks of Chinese dry black drafting ink and three or four high-quality drawing pens.[23]

Tolkachev informed the CIA he would accept precious valuables in lieu of cash, which he had previously rejected. Soon after this message was received, Thomas Mills, head of the U.S.S.R. branch in the division, got a most unusual assignment. He and

his wife, Joby, were asked to go to New York and find some valuables for Tolkachev—with agency money. Joby, who had studied
art in New York City, was thrilled. They went to A La Vieille
Russie on Fifth Avenue, a jewelry and antiques store established
in 1851. In the elegant shop, the CIA official and his wife bought
a very small but pricey Fabergé pin and a heavy gold necklace.
They brought them back to headquarters for shipping off to the
Moscow station in the pouch. Mills was told that if any questions
arose, Tolkachev would explain that the jewelry had been left to
him by his mother.[24]

The worry about Tolkachev after Plunkert's meeting with him
led the Moscow station to think again about whether it might be
necessary to suddenly exfiltrate him from the Soviet Union. By
early 1983, the station had written up a detailed plan to remove
Tolkachev, his wife, and their son. The CIA had done it in Moscow only once before, with Sheymov, his wife, and their daughter, although exfiltration had been successful in other countries.
The CIA had even built special containers for smuggling people.
But there was no enthusiasm at headquarters for exfiltration
of Tolkachev. The Moscow station plan landed with a thud at
Langley. The station was getting ahead of itself, headquarters
advised. Exfiltration with the family would be a "soul-searching"
question for Tolkachev and had not even been discussed with
him for more than two years.[25]

Nevertheless, the station was undeterred, perhaps out of an
abundance of caution. Two plans were drawn up, one long-range
and the other for an emergency. The station composed a long,
personal questionnaire for Tolkachev, to be delivered at the next
meeting, asking for passport photographs and probing Tolkachev for clothing measurements, medical history, locations of
his friends and relatives, vacation procedures, and methods for
calling in sick at work. "Is your family aware of our relationship?" the CIA asked. "If not, how do you plan to tell them?"

They did not know that he had already promised his wife he would quit spying.[26]

"Deep cover" had become an essential method for CIA clandestine operations in Moscow. But the work of a deep cover officer was far different from what Guilsher and Rolph had experienced. They had been advisers and confessors to Tolkachev. In contrast, deep cover officers worked at a distance from the station and from the agent. It was lonely, stressful, and risky. Robert Morris thought the relentless pressures of the job and the isolation were more like being an undercover cop.

Morris arrived in Moscow carrying a briefcase, and his documents identified him as nothing more than a State Department bureaucrat, one of the unremarkable administrative workers needed at the embassy. He played that role to the hilt, but he had arrived for a different purpose. He became the second deep cover officer assigned to the Moscow station, hoping to fulfill his ambition to be at the forefront of the Cold War struggle against the Soviet Union.

Morris, son of a high school sports coach who'd grown up in the Shenandoah Valley of Virginia, attended an all-boys New England college prep school and went on to Georgetown University. Restless at the university after just one semester, he left the school and volunteered for the draft at the peak of the war in Vietnam. A gung ho soldier who thrived in three years of hard training, he rose to become a first lieutenant in the Special Forces, second-in-command of a Green Beret A team, one of the most elite military detachments in the world. He was assigned to serve in Vietnam in 1971, but the war began to ebb, and he did not go. During all the rigorous training—airborne, underwater, and jungle warfare—Morris got to know an intel sergeant who had emigrated from the Ukraine and shared fascinating stories of life in the Soviet Union. Morris was drawn to the mystery of it all and took Russian-language lessons. When he left the service in 1972, he returned to Georgetown University to study Russian—and play football.

Morris dreamed of adventure. After graduation and knocking about in business for a few years, he was recruited by the CIA. When he arrived at headquarters in October 1980, he had just turned thirty years old. His hair was fashionably combed across his forehead, and he wore aviator-style glasses that gave him a modish look. Morris completed his training in the top echelon of his class. He arrived in Moscow in early July 1982. After he spent months carrying out his job as a bureaucrat, the KGB swallowed the cover story and lost interest in Morris, and he was ready to begin espionage operations.

Before a meeting with Tolkachev, both Guilsher and Rolph had spent hours planning in the station. But as a deep cover officer, Morris was on his own. When he sketched out a surveillance detection run, he had to send it to the station by the cumbersome equivalent of an interoffice dead drop—usually writing it out on water-soluble paper and emplacing it discreetly, such as sticking it with a magnet on a fire extinguisher somewhere inside the embassy, to be picked up by another case officer, and the process reversed when the station sent him an answer. He experienced very little of the camaraderie of the Moscow station. He did not write letters to the agent. He did not prepare packages; he just delivered them.

When there was an operation to be carried out, Morris went to the station for a brief meeting, no more than ten or fifteen minutes, taking a secret entrance. He memorized his instructions, and when there was a package disguised as a brick or a log, he put it in his briefcase and carried it back to his cover job in an administrative office full of Soviet employees, where he would sit tight, never daring to take his eye off the briefcase until he could go home.

His role was to be the perfect courier. The KGB overlooked Morris for many months as he moved about Moscow, filling dead drops for the station's various operations. He had to watch every word and every action. It was like acting on a stage, constantly, for months and months on end—never forgetting a line. The spring of 1983 was exceptionally busy. One night, in an unprecedented feat, Morris placed two dead drops in a row, in distant locations, without the KGB's catching even a glimpse of him. But Morris felt isolated. He had no way to let his hair down. He had to live his cover as a bureaucrat, and that meant no discussion at home, either, even though his wife had participated in most of the nighttime runs. After months of clandestine activity in which he escaped KGB notice, Morris drew a far more sensitive assignment—to meet Tolkachev in person.[27]

On March 16, he set out on a long surveillance detection run by car, by bus, and then on foot. Because his cover was that of a State Department bureaucrat, Morris did not wear the radio scanner that had helped Rolph listen to KGB transmissions; it would be awfully hard to explain if he were caught. Without the radio, he would have to make a judgment call about surveillance on his own instincts and observations. Two hours later, free from surveillance, he reached the planned site, a streetcar stop. A dozen people were waiting. Morris was excited; the adrenaline was rushing through him. He met Tolkachev after dark and walked to Tolkachev's car, parked at a nearby apartment building. Inside the car, Morris felt tense, but Tolkachev was calm and behaved as if he had been doing this forever. They handed each other packages: Morris gave Tolkachev a note that brought up exfiltration, outlined how the operation would work, and included the questionnaire. Tolkachev handed over to Morris seventeen rolls of film and a very long ops note, forty-two pages. The materials included surprising new intelligence about a "target recognition system" being developed for the MiG-29 fighter.

Morris thought Tolkachev looked good, his morale seemed high, and Tolkachev smiled when Morris presented him with the architectural drawing materials for his son. Morris said the CIA wanted to get answers soon about exfiltration—in April, if possible. Although Tolkachev hesitated, he agreed to a meeting in early April. They said farewell to each other after only twelve minutes.

Once he got home, at 10:00 p.m., Morris left the rolls of film in his coat pocket. He did not want to take them out, in case the KGB had a concealed video camera in the apartment. Late that night, he slipped into a closet in his apartment, curled onto the floor, and, by flashlight, wrote out a memo by hand on water-soluble paper to the Moscow station describing the meeting and what he had seen. This was the work of a deep cover operative—hiding in the bottom of his closet.

Tolkachev's ops note revealed that he had been through three "crises" of high blood pressure and was feeling exhausted. "It has become more difficult for me to work intensively, I tire much easier," he said. While in the past he would often go to the Lenin Library after work and quietly spend a few hours there, he said, "I am not always able to do that now." He asked the CIA to find some ginseng root, which he had heard was a stimulant, and a Russian organic medicine.

The note also contained another list of personal requests, primarily books for himself and his son. He wanted materials about Western architecture, not only with photographs, but also with English text, to help Oleg with his language skills. Tolkachev asked the CIA to find "topical detective stories" for his son, saying they were being passed around in paperback by his friends whose parents bought them abroad. Tolkachev requested more books about the Soviet Union that were factual, not polemics.

His curiosity centered on the years of Lenin and the Bolshevik Revolution, and the Stalin period, when his wife's family had been so brutally repressed. "Generally, an objective interpretation of the history of the October Revolution and Russian life in the 20s and 30s would definitely interest me," he wrote. He told the CIA he had devoured Trotsky's memoir, *My Life*, but was less interested in some of the other, more propagandistic books about the early Soviet years. He added, "I am interested in the memoirs of famous world political and military figures, writers, actors, artists, architects, etc." He asked for books with all kinds of political views, progressive and reactionary, and also wanted "the most important speeches, appearances, declarations of western political leaders," which were often unavailable in the Soviet Union.

Tolkachev said his wish list included the following:

1. Bible (in Russian)
2. Booklet, published in Washington, "About Soviet Military Power" (preferably in Russian)
3. Reagan's speech in which he mentioned Lenin's 10 principles
4. Memoirs of Golda Meir
5. Hitler's book *Mein Kampf* (in Russian)
6. Solzhenitsyn's book *August 1914*[28]

At first, headquarters was glad to hear from Morris that Tolkachev seemed to be in good shape and immediately began gathering all the books he asked for. "Absolutely delighted to hear that CKSPHERE is his old self again, in good spirits and improved health and apparently 'rarin' to get on with his work for us," headquarters cabled to the Moscow station on March 22.[29]

But a closer look at Tolkachev's long ops note told a different story. The station sent back a message, within hours, saying

Tolkachev, "a driven man," was struggling with his health and was "pushing himself hard." The station was also puzzled about the rolls of film Tolkachev had brought Morris. If the security restrictions were so tight—and he had not reported any change—how was he able to shoot seventeen rolls of film?[30]

On April 1, headquarters reported the film had been developed and printed "with excellent results," including approximately 525 pages of secret documents. "We use the word approximately because there are multiple fold-out pages of diagrams," headquarters reported. "In any event, another good job by CKSPHERE."[31]

Tolkachev had promised to give the CIA an answer about exfiltration and signaled for another meeting on April 23. Morris went and found him at 8:55 p.m. This time, because a group of children were playing noisily near Tolkachev's parked car, he drove a few blocks away and parked in a quiet spot on a nearby street. Time was short, but Tolkachev was firm: exfiltration was out of the question. He gave the envelope with the exfiltration plan back to Morris. At the same time, Morris handed back to Tolkachev the sensitive materials he had provided at the March meeting on the MiG-29 target recognition system. This was a standard procedure, to return to Tolkachev any original written materials once the CIA had seen them.

Tolkachev handed over fourteen rolls of film, despite all his complaints of tight security. He told Morris he had "circumvented" the system: details would be found in his twelve-page ops note. "It is extremely difficult just to sit and not produce," he added. Morris was out of the car and on his way in fifteen minutes.[32]

It soon became clear to the Moscow station that Tolkachev was taking more risks than ever. In his note, Tolkachev explained that in the early morning doors to the laboratory were unlocked around 7:30 but actual work didn't get under way until about

8:00. For five minutes after the doors were unlocked, he said, no one was present. "This is what I took advantage of," he wrote. Even so, he had to bring the camera to work three times "since it was only on the third time that I was able to get five minutes when nobody was in the lab." Tolkachev also described a "ruse" in which he had told others that a secret document was being examined by a supervisor at midday, but in fact he took it home to photograph. "This ruse, of course, is very risky," he acknowledged, "and it's not possible to use it more than two or three times."

Tolkachev's note explained his change of heart about exfiltration. He and his wife had close friends who left for Israel and then for the United States, he said. They had written back that they were growing nostalgic for Moscow. Tolkachev quoted his own wife as saying, "How can people decide to leave to who-knows-where? As far as I am concerned, I know for sure that I would immediately begin to suffer from nostalgia. Not only could I not live in another country but I couldn't even live in another city in the Soviet Union."

Tolkachev added that his son might want to travel someday but not leave permanently.

"Therefore, the question about my leaving the Soviet Union with my family for all practical purposes is closed. Of course, I would never go alone."[33]

The Moscow station and headquarters debated for weeks how to respond to Tolkachev's letter. "We are deeply concerned," headquarters wrote on June 13 about the risks he was taking. "The ruses he told us about in his April note are frightening enough; additional ploys which he said he also used but fails to describe may be even more alarming." Headquarters admitted that they were caught in a bind, one that had been evident since the early days of the operation. "How can we get CKSPHERE to control his risk-taking propensities and at the same time satisfy both his imperative to produce and our desire for his product?" Headquarters was leery about giving Tolkachev the small Tropel cameras, recalling that when he had used them in 1979 and 1980, the prints did not come out well because of insufficient light and poor technique. The light level in his office was only twenty footcandles, headquarters pointed out—barely enough for copying documents. Instead of cameras, wouldn't it be better to ask Tolkachev just to take notes of what was most important?

Yet the CIA wanted it all. They wanted Tolkachev to be safe, but they wanted to pump out all the secrets they could. Headquarters passed along to the Moscow station a fresh list of topics to ask Tolkachev about. "The major systems of current interest to us," headquarters said, "are the Tu-22M, Tu-160, Yak-41, IFF systems, and major modifications to the SAPFIR radar. Our first priority is for technical specifications, proposed or actual, on the above systems or on any new electronic or weapons systems, including missiles. Other details on capabilities, function and employment are also valuable, but may be lengthy." This spoke volumes about the state of the Tolkachev operation after four years. The Tu-22M and the Tu-160, known by NATO as the Backfire and the Blackjack, respectively, were supersonic strategic bombers, neither of which was directly in Tolkachev's line of work. Nor was the Yak-41, a vertical takeoff and landing aircraft that was never produced. The IFF (identification friend or foe) and SAPFIR radars were definitely within Phazotron's field of research, but Tolkachev had already provided extensive material on the SAPFIR. Tolkachev was being pushed to grab secrets well beyond those that he would normally see at the office.[34]

The CIA wrestled with whether to give Tolkachev new miniature spy cameras for use at his office. The station pointed out that the small Tropel spy cameras had improved somewhat; the minimum light was now twenty-five foot-candles. Headquarters was worried that sooner or later another Phazotron worker would see—one time too many—that Tolkachev was hunched over, elbows on his desk, hands clasping something, and grow suspicious. Tolkachev would "have to do any photography in the presence of other people," headquarters cautioned. "This of course is an extremely risky endeavor, and would require tremendous discretion and caution by CKSPHERE, and is not likely to help his blood pressure, either."[35]

But headquarters gave in. The Tropel cameras would be sent to Moscow.[36]

# 15

# NOT CAUGHT ALIVE

In the morning on April 26, 1983, the head designer at the institute, Yuri Kirpichev, called Tolkachev into his office to discuss some routine problems. Kirpichev was Tolkachev's superior. As they were talking, the phone rang. Kirpichev picked it up and, after several minutes of silence, asked the caller, "For what purpose do you need this?"

Then he added, "Very well, I'll do it."

The phone call had come from Nikolai Balan, head of the "regime," the overarching security office at the institute. The regime, which reported to the KGB, controlled the First Department and secret library and the clearance process for all workers. Every ten years, each employee had to answer a lengthy questionnaire. The questionnaires were then sent to the KGB for review and decisions about who would get top secret clearance. Tolkachev had the highest-level access.

The regime also was responsible for guards and building passes. The regime existed in every secret Soviet enterprise.

After the call, Kirpichev summoned the leading engineer at the institute, who had worked on the target recognition system for the No. 19 radar that would go into the MiG-29 fighter.

As Tolkachev listened, terrified, Kirpichev described the call. "By the end of the day," he said, Balan wanted "a list of persons familiar with the recognition system or having access to information about the recognition system with the RLS No. 19."

This was the information that Tolkachev had passed to the CIA in March.

"For what is this needed?" asked the leading engineer, protesting that they had never been asked to compile such lists before.

Kirpichev said he had asked the same question of Balan, who "answered me with nothing that was intelligible."

Tolkachev went back to his office, his head spinning. He felt paralyzed. He turned the conversation over and over in his mind, wondering whether he had been discovered. His first worry was about the handwritten notes on the target recognition system he had given the CIA. The notes had been returned to him, but had the CIA slipped up? Had someone else seen them?[1]

Tolkachev tried to come to grips with what he heard. If Balan was demanding a list of employees, that suggested a very serious leak of information about the target recognition system. But what did they know about the source? Did the KGB have a suspect, or were they just fishing?[2]

He concluded that one possibility was that the KGB had no idea where the information had come from. Actually, there were dozens of potential sources: institutes in Moscow, including his own and several others, or aviation and electronics factories far away that built radars and parts for them, located in the cities of Kazan, Ryazan, and Khmelnitsky. In that case, it would take time to investigate.

Another possibility, more ominous and frightening, was that they were closing in on him. If so, Tolkachev figured they would need only one or two days. By nightfall, the security office would already have a list of employees with access to the material. By the next day, the list would be sent to the KGB.

If they had managed to intercept Tolkachev's papers given to the CIA—he had written the information by hand—then it would be a simple matter to compare the handwriting with his answers on the clearance questionnaire, also written out in hand. Anyone could do it in a few hours. His last clearance questionnaire was completed in 1980.

Tolkachev made some hurried decisions. He would destroy everything the CIA had given him that could be incriminating, and he would not, under any circumstances, fall into the hands of the KGB, at least not alive.

He told his supervisor he would not be coming to work the next day. He didn't say why.

The next morning, April 27, after his wife and son left the apartment, Tolkachev gathered up all the spy gear and materials hidden in the *entresol*: the Pentax cameras and clamp, the dead drop and signal instructions, the dissident books, the bricks of rubles, the Discus, the shortwave radio demodulator— everything, including the L-pill and the schedule of future meetings. He loaded it all into the Zhiguli and drove out of Moscow. There wasn't time to signal the CIA or ask for a meeting.

He crossed the outer Moscow ring road and drove into the country, heading north on the Rogachevskoye Shosse, or highway. Soon the metropolis of concrete and asphalt gave way to thick forests and open fields. He turned eastward off the highway onto a narrow road, then northeast onto another country road that, after five miles, took a slow, lazy curve, revealing a small, rural village, Doronino. Only six houses stood by the road. One of them was a summer house, or dacha, that Tolkachev and his wife had leased in 1981.

When they were younger, they traveled widely around the Soviet Union, backpacking and camping, but now that they had a car, the dacha made more sense. It was common for people in the city to acquire houses in half-abandoned villages and repair them. Property rights were highly questionable; buying or selling a property was strictly forbidden, but there were other means. Tolkachev made a deal that was something like a lease.³ The houses were not expensive, but they demanded time and effort to fix up. Tolkachev searched for scarce construction materials and repaired the house himself, which he enjoyed. The house was about fifty miles from the city.⁴

An old iron stove stood in the center of the house. Tolkachev pulled the spy gear out of the Zhiguli, fired up the stove, and burned everything—including the rubles the CIA had given him, the instructions, the books, the cameras, everything except for the meeting schedule and the suicide pill inside the fountain pen.

When the fire cooled, Tolkachev realized that some metal parts from the Discus had not burned. He gathered them up.

As he drove back toward Moscow, he tossed the metal parts out the window, into the roadside ditch. What remained of the CIA's most sophisticated agent communications device was scattered into the weeds.

Tolkachev returned home. He took the CIA meeting schedule and copied it, using codes, into a magazine he kept at home, *Nauka i Zhizn* (Science and Life), and then destroyed the original schedule, too.

On April 28, before going to work, Tolkachev took out the pen with the L-pill concealed inside and put it in his pocket so he could grab it quickly if needed. He thought to himself that the most likely place for his arrest would be Kirpichev's office. He figured he would be summoned, and as he opened the door, the KGB would pull his hands behind his back so he could not grab the pen.

For the next several days, as a precaution, Tolkachev removed the fragile capsule from the pen and held it under his tongue every time Kirpichev summoned him to the office.

The arrest never came.

Tolkachev didn't signal the CIA at the time, but he wrote a long, detailed account about what happened, to pass at their next meeting in the autumn. He wrote that if the KGB already had his handwritten notes on the MiG-29 target recognition system, "then no measures would help me." But he added, "If I successfully did away with my materials in time, then the KGB will not be able to find documentary evidence of my relationship with you." If the KGB was embarking on a broad search for the source of a leak, there was nothing in the house or at the dacha that would be compromising.

After some time passed with no arrest, Tolkachev concluded that the KGB investigation was not focused directly on him. His panic subsided. But just to be safe, he decided to carry the L-pill in his pocket whenever he went to see the CIA case officer and whenever carrying secret documents from work.

Tolkachev was the Moscow station's crown jewel of human source intelligence collection, but the station had another top secret asset, an espionage operation of a different kind. Not a human source, it was a machine and another tangible sign of how far CIA intelligence collection had come in Moscow since the years of paralysis in the 1960s.

The operation was code-named CKELBOW, and it ranks as one of the most ingenious and daring of the Cold War. The heart of it was the underground wiretap on the sensitive data line running from the nuclear weapons facility at Troitsk to the Defense Ministry in Moscow. The CIA and the National Security Agency placed a listening tap on the cable by sneaking into one of the manholes along the route. All the case officers in Moscow had trained on the manhole mock-up back in the United States;

David Rolph had broken his thumb in the effort. Once the operation got under way, James Olson was the first to climb into the manhole in August 1979 for a survey and to take photographs. Later, a technical operations officer went down, to test which of the lead-sheathed lines should be tapped. After that, another technical officer installed the actual wiretap. The CIA cleverly concealed the device so it could not be detected by routine maintenance workers. It began to suck out the data from the cable and transmit them to a recording device the CIA had buried between two trees, twelve feet away. Every once in a while, the Moscow station sent a case officer to swap out the recorder and collect the data, a mission undertaken with all the precautions of meeting a human spy. The recording device ran on its own power source and stored huge amounts of data until it was retrieved. To deter the curious, the CIA stuck a warning label on the recorder in Russian that said, "Danger: High Voltage," and the recorder was protected by its own tamper-sensing alarm to silently warn a CIA case officer, at a distance, if anything had disturbed it. The operation cost the United States some $20 million.[5]

For all the technical wizardry, CKELBOW still required tending by people. On a pleasant Saturday in June 1983, it was up to Bob Morris to get the machine safely out of the ground and back to the station. Morris and his wife began the mission by carrying a box of sodas out to their car for a picnic in the countryside. Inside the box was concealed a plain backpack, and inside the backpack, the replacement recorder, a collapsible shovel, and animal repellent. After a long surveillance detection run, they took a bus, then a trolley, and began to hike by foot. Morris hefted the heavy backpack on his shoulders, and they both donned a light disguise to look more like Russians just out for fresh air. They walked during the afternoon until they reached two rows of trees, a windbreak, and, beyond the trees, an expansive field. Twilight was settling in. While his wife, who was also on a contract with the CIA, served as lookout, Morris searched for the spot—a break in one tree line—where the recorder was located. He had never been to the location before but had studied satellite photographs. He found the recorder quickly and began to dig. His wife stood watch. Morris pulled the old recorder from the ground and was securing the new one when he suddenly saw his wife shudder, as if she were about to let out a scream.

She gasped, and Morris turned his head sharply. He saw that two wild kittens had leaped out of the bushes and startled her. They were only weeks old and playful. Morris and his wife tried to remain silent and not break out laughing.

Morris secured the new recorder in the hole, lodged in some animal repellent, connected the wires, and covered it. The animal repellent was to keep out rodents. The CIA experimented with using tiger feces, actually acquired in India, thinking that the scent of tigers might scare away any animal. It didn't work; the other animals didn't seem to care whether there was a tiger in the woods or not.

Morris put the old recorder into the backpack and cleaned up the site to cover their tracks, and they retraced their steps—bus, trolley, then, as they approached the parked car, they removed the disguises and changed back to their picnic clothes. Morris put the backpack and the old recorder into the soda box and closed it, and they drove home. He carried the soda box past the Soviet militiamen and up to his apartment. The next day, the old recorder was passed by others to the station.

Morris breathed a deep sigh of relief. Nothing quite readied him for the stress and strain of working deep cover in Moscow.

He had largely escaped notice by the KGB, but in the autumn of 1983 he began to come under more surveillance. The next scheduled meeting with Tolkachev was set for September 20, but Morris had to abort because of surveillance. The *fortochka* was open to signal for a meeting on October 4, but Tolkachev did not show up. He signaled for a meeting on October 21, but there was surveillance, and the CIA had to abort. Tolkachev signaled for a phone call as a precursor to a meeting on October 27, and a case officer went out and called his apartment three times but only reached his son and his wife. Again on November 3, the *fortochka* was open, but Tolkachev didn't show. Morris, still under deep cover, was growing frustrated. For each meeting, there was an alternate window of time, an hour later. Each time Tolkachev didn't show, Morris would leave, stay black for an hour, and return at the alternate time, but to no avail. Morris had gone through the long surveillance detection runs, his adrenaline was pumping, and then—nothing. There was no explanation. One missed meeting was understandable, but from September to November 1983 five attempts to meet Tolkachev had failed.

Finally, on the evening of November 16, Morris broke through. He met Tolkachev at the streetcar stop where they had first encountered each other. Both felt immensely relieved. As they walked toward Tolkachev's car, Morris asked about the missed meetings. Tolkachev explained that he had come twice but had not seen Morris. He said his wife had opened the *fortochka* on three of the dates when he didn't show up. It was useless to use the telephone anymore, he said; between his teenage son and his wife, the phone was constantly engaged, and in any case there was no privacy.

In the car, Tolkachev had no film and said security was still tight at work. It was all explained in his ops note, he said, but he would not attempt any document photography for a while.

The two were thrilled to reconnect. Morris gave Tolkachev a package from the Moscow station that included two Tropel cameras, hidden in key fobs, and a new light meter. In a note, the CIA told Tolkachev that the tiny cameras had been improved somewhat to twenty-five foot-candles of illumination. Morris didn't dwell on the packages; he wanted to know about Tolkachev's health and well-being. At the end of the meeting, Morris said, "I can't begin to tell you how happy I was to see you tonight." Tolkachev replied, "Yes, I feel exactly the same way."

It was Tolkachev's eighteenth meeting with the CIA.[6]

The station was upbeat, at first, in cables to headquarters. "Meeting went perfectly in all respects and CKSPHERE is fine," the station reported. "The conversation during the meeting was lively and good natured; CKSPHERE seemed to be in a good mood."

But the bad news came as soon as the ops note was translated. In the note, Tolkachev described in detail the scare of the spring—the investigation, burning everything in the dacha's iron stove, the poison pill under his tongue. The scare reignited all the old anxieties about Tolkachev. "It is painfully obvious," the station told headquarters, "that CKSPHERE considers himself to be in great danger and his security situation continues to deteriorate.

"We are certain you will be as stunned as we are after you read it."

Tolkachev reported to the CIA that by autumn he had concluded that the KGB was carrying out a broad investigation, not directed specifically at him. Yet he felt it was possible they were still pursuing someone. Tolkachev said he was in a "waiting position" and, at least for a while, could not bring the CIA any more material about the MiG-29 target recognition system. He reported that workers in the First Department had begun making unannounced spot checks in his laboratory to find out if secret documents were misplaced in any way. At the same time, all employees were asked to submit new photographs—a new building pass "is in the works."

In a tone that was apologetic, Tolkachev said, "I was forced to take maximum care" in the emergency, and he was still not certain what triggered the investigation. He said he could provide no more documents until the next year. Tolkachev expressed a willingness to copy out passages of secret documents by hand, but that would not be easy. He had previously done the writing in the quiet of the Lenin Library after work, but lately he was too tired to go there in the evenings and unable to explain to his family why he was late. With the spot checks by the First Department, he said, it was risky to copy secret information by hand into notebooks on his work desk.

Tolkachev also revealed he was suffering from a new health problem. His broken nose from a hockey accident as a youth had not bothered him for years, but now he could barely breathe through his nose, and "it is beginning to make me very uncomfortable." It ruined his sleep and left him tired during the day. He warned the CIA that he might have an operation on his nose that would change his appearance. But they could recognize him by a familiar practice. Going to a meeting with a case officer, he said, "I will always hold in my left hand" a light-colored book, usually white.[7]

The CIA was shocked by Tolkachev's account of the scare. Headquarters called it "a chilling account" and added in a cable to the Moscow station, "We share your profound dismay and can only imagine the agony with which CKSPHERE has lived since late April, 1983." But there wasn't much they could do now. The next scheduled meeting was five months away, in April 1984. The Moscow station said that perhaps they should instruct Tolkachev to bury his Tropel cameras. But Tolkachev no longer had any communications gear, so there was no easy way to get him a message, unless he called for, or agreed to, an unscheduled meeting before April.[8]

Had there been a leak? Headquarters insisted not. A check showed that the material on the target recognition system had not been disseminated inside the U.S. government until June, so it could not have caused the April investigation.[9] Two years earlier, in August 1981, the CIA had been alarmed about an article in *Aviation Week and Space Technology*, a magazine that enjoyed good sources in the U.S. government and among defense contractors. The article had taken note of "significant gain in technology" in Soviet military avionics. Quoting unidentified navy intelligence officials, the magazine described "long-range, look-down/shoot-down capability" in a new fighter. But it seemed quite unlikely that this article had triggered a sudden security investigation in Tolkachev's institute twenty months later.[10]

The Tolkachev letter was given to a headquarters officer, fluent in Russian, who had access to all the files and was asked to interpret the state of mind of the billion dollar spy. The officer was impressed with Tolkachev's sense of mission and wrote, "There is no doubt whatsoever that CKSPHERE suffered a shock after overhearing the conversations in the head designer's office, a severe shock in contemplating the imminent possibility of the KGB closing in, however, the shock seems to have sprung not so much from the presumed close brush with the termination of his life as with the termination of his life's project. Self-preservation per se does not appear to play any great role, in fact, in the very midst of his shock he comes up with the firm resolve 'to undertake all measures not to fall into the hands of the KGB alive.' " According to the headquarters officer, Tolkachev was concerned not with saving himself but with saving his espionage, "a very practical and stubborn determination to weather out the storm and last as long as possible in order to do as much damage as possible to the Soviet government."

Tolkachev "exhibits legendary resilience and strength," the officer observed, "despite the shocking nature of the events and actions that he's describing, his tone is quite positive and strong. He describes everything almost unemotionally, in a conversational style of narrative, as though talking about how he spent his vacation." The officer continued,

> He approaches everything objectively, particularly his
> weaknesses. Although he believes that his conclusions
> were logical and justifiable, he does admit that his

analysis of events was "undoubtedly hasty," and further intensifies his self-judgment by underlining the words. He impartially dissects his analysis and shows how he was influenced by his one real fear . . . into reaching a state of near-panic. However, despite the fear and feeling of panic, his subsequent actions were a result of cool deliberation.

Thus, CKSPHERE destroyed all his equipment and incriminating material not out of fear for his life, because that fear didn't exist, but as a deliberate attempt to deprive the KGB of even the slightest crumbs of satisfaction aside from those that would inevitably fall their way once he was discovered.

The officer added, "CKSPHERE shows complete disregard for the fear of death, but he unhesitatingly exhibits his one real fear: to be caught by the KGB unawares . . . An intense hatred of the KGB permeates the description of all of CKSPHERE's imaginary 'dealings' with it. To this end, although he is forced to exercise restraint and lie low at the moment, it seems that CKSPHERE has also resolved to go on and 'not to be caught alive.' "[11]

# 16

# SEEDS OF BETRAYAL

Thomas Mills was an experienced hand at clandestine operations. Balding and slender, known by many for his mild manner, Mills was chief of the CIA headquarters branch that handled espionage operations inside the Soviet Union. In addition to his other duties, he spent time getting to know young case officers in training, before they left for Moscow duty. They usually came in to the Soviet desk once a week or so to read the message traffic. Mills also participated in the training courses in surveillance and tradecraft for new generations of case officers.

One evening in late May 1984, Mills and his wife, Joby, were entertaining diplomats from Eastern Europe as guests at their home in Vienna, Virginia. Mills heard an unexpected knock at the door and excused himself.

At the door was Edward Lee Howard, his face flushed with anger. Howard was a trainee Mills had supervised on the Soviet desk in 1982 and 1983. Howard was preparing to go to Moscow, where he would become the next case officer to handle Tolkachev. But the CIA lost confidence in him, and he had been forced out of the agency.

Mills walked out to the driveway, and he saw that Howard's wife, Mary, was with him, holding their toddler. A neighbor of Mills's, who had been a trainee with Howard, was also there.

Howard stood five feet eleven inches, with brown eyes and wavy black hair. His mood was dark and agitated.

Mills could not invite Howard inside; it would disrupt the dinner. He told Howard it was not a good time to talk.

Howard was brimming with resentment. He begged Mills to help him, to listen to him, perhaps to reverse the CIA's decision. Mills again said he could not talk.

Howard shot back with profanity—the CIA had fucked him!

Mary fought back tears.

Mills went back inside, unsettled by the encounter. Howard had been a lousy trainee. Mills was glad he was not being sent to the Moscow station. The CIA wanted nothing more to do with Howard. The psychiatrists said there should be a clean break, no coddling, no hopes of return. Howard's appearance at the door was a bad sign.

Howard possessed some of the CIA's deepest secrets. He washed out of the agency, and that was difficult enough. Now he was becoming unhinged.[1]

Edward Lee Howard was an air force brat. His father was a sergeant, a technician on guided missile electronics, and his mother came from a Hispanic family with deep roots in western New Mexico. As a boy, Howard explored his grandfather's cattle ranch in Alamogordo while his father was serving abroad, and later he saw the world, moving with his parents every two or three years to a new military base. After graduating from the University of Texas with a business degree, he volunteered to serve in the Peace Corps in Colombia, although he wasn't particularly happy there.

Howard subsequently worked for the Agency for International Development, managing loan programs in Peru. He received a master's in business administration from American University in Washington and then became head of the Chicago office of an environmental consulting firm. In 1976, Howard married another Peace Corps volunteer, Mary Cedarleaf, whom he had met in Colombia. He was in a management position at his company, Ecology & Environment Inc., and bought a house in the Chicago suburbs.[2]

Everything was fine, except Howard was bored. He drank too much and quarreled with Mary about the drinking. He longed to go back overseas. In 1979, he filled out a job application for the Central Intelligence Agency. He was twenty-eight years old, had traveled the world, showed some language abilities, was of Hispanic descent, and worked in businesses. The CIA had broadened its recruiting beyond the Ivy League networks of the past, seeking to compete with private business for the best and brightest young people. Howard was put through a battery of exams and a security investigation. In December 1980, he was offered a position in the clandestine service. His interest was in economics, and he hoped to get a nice assignment in Europe—perhaps collecting economic intelligence in Switzerland.[3]

Howard reported for duty at CIA headquarters in January 1981 and passed a routine polygraph test. He acknowledged drinking and using cocaine and marijuana in Latin America, but this did not disqualify him. He was warned not to use drugs again or he would be dismissed. Soon, he was deeply enmeshed in the basic career trainee program and appeared to be headed for Europe and a first assignment in East Germany.

In February 1982, he was unexpectedly offered a position in Moscow. It is not known why, but the author David Wise suggests that another candidate had pulled out and Howard was a quick substitute.[4] By his own account, Howard "never had any interest" in going to the Soviet Union, but he accepted the new assignment, figuring it would be "a rung up the CIA career ladder for me."[5] He began studying Russian at Georgetown University and on Saturdays would go to CIA headquarters to read the message traffic.

Howard was on the Soviet desk from February 7, 1982, until April 30, 1983. He had access to the day-to-day operational cables from the Moscow station, in which Tolkachev was identified as CKSPHERE. It is not known whether Howard learned Tolkachev's true identity. But Howard was in the "pipeline" for Moscow, preparing to work with Tolkachev, so he might have read more deeply into the operation, including Tolkachev's 1978 letter to the CIA revealing his identity and profession.[6]

Mary also joined the CIA and went through the training courses. Her role in Moscow would be to support his operational forays, primarily as a lookout for surveillance. Both of them took the CIA's rigorous training in "denied areas" operations, learning how to detect and evade KGB surveillance. The course involved weeks of demanding exercises on the streets of Washington. FBI special agents posed as KGB surveillance teams, forcing the young case officers to sharpen their skills. Mills, who had gone through the exercises a generation earlier with his wife, sometimes participated in the training. He saw Howard in action one day and thought he was slow. Mills also noticed that Mary was shy and frightened. An exercise involving a simulated ambush by gun-wielding FBI officers reduced Mary to tears.

Howard's training also included preparations for crawling into the manhole and servicing CKELBOW, the underground cable tap outside Moscow. The training involved a ten-mile hike with a thirty-five-pound backpack, to simulate the experience of replacing the data recorder clandestinely. Usually, for training, the backpack was weighted with stones, but Howard cheated, stuffing cardboard into the backpack instead. The incident was known to the trainers but not reported to superiors at the time.

Howard and his wife were also taught the Jack-in-the-Box procedure for escaping surveillance and practiced jumping from a car at just the right moment. Howard's jump was rehearsed on a grassy strip near the Kennedy Center in Washington.[7]

By early 1983, Howard seemed to be on track for Moscow. To improve his cover as a budget officer in the U.S. embassy, he took a course sponsored by the State Department to train diplomats. He received a commission signed by President Reagan and Secretary of State George Shultz, dated March 11, 1983, confirming he was a new officer of the U.S. diplomatic service. That same month, his first child, a son, Lee, was born. The family's passports were sent away for multiple-entry diplomatic visas to the Soviet Union. They were scheduled to leave for Moscow in late June. For the CIA, Howard was to be a deep cover officer, a rookie selected in part because he was young and clean and would hopefully be overlooked by the KGB.[8]

Before leaving, Howard was required to take a routine lie detector test. After the test was conducted in April, he recalled, the examiner shook his hand and wished him well. But there were anomalies in the results that caught the attention of security officials. Howard was asked to take a second polygraph. The results indicated deception about some crime in his past. Howard admitted that once, when drunk, he had filched $40 from a cosmetic kit left on the seat next to him by an airline passenger. He was asked to take a third polygraph and was so nervous about it that he swallowed a tranquilizer beforehand, infuriating the examiner. Then he was asked to take a fourth lie detector test, on April 29. The tests repeatedly showed deception about some criminal act and in Howard's responses to questions about drug and alcohol abuse. Within days, the CIA decided not to send Howard to Moscow, and a panel of top agency officials was convened to decide his fate. The CIA could have sidelined him into a nonsensitive job, but instead the panel decided he should be immediately forced out. David Forden, who was chief of the division while Howard was in training, recalled that the panel, on which he served, made a quick decision. Describing Howard as a "loser," Forden added, "I said let's get rid of this guy. He was a bum."[9]

On May 3, at headquarters, Howard was told he would not be going to Moscow. He was presented with an ultimatum: resign from the CIA or be fired. The CIA did not explain why. His wife, Mary, then on maternity leave as a CIA employee, demanded to know why, and the CIA would not say. Howard told his wife "they were convinced I was lying."[10] He was correct. The CIA did not think they could trust a trainee who had just failed four consecutive polygraph tests with their most sensitive operations in the Soviet Union. The CIA director has the power to unilaterally remove the security clearances of an employee, effectively ending his or her employment. Howard signed the resignation paper. But before he could be escorted out of headquarters, he made a photocopy of his CIA access badge, bearing his photograph and a number, and copied some notes to take with him.[11]

The CIA said he would be kept on the payroll for six weeks and should visit the agency's senior psychiatrist, Bernard Malloy, and report for a physical examination.[12] The agency also prepared a résumé he could use for future employers, saying he had spent two and a half years as a "foreign service officer" at the State Department. It didn't mention the CIA.[13]

Howard was "dumbfounded." He later recalled, "I was disoriented by the way they had pulled the rug out from under me—and angered by the callous way they had fired me and thrown me out on the street."[14] He decided to return to New Mexico, and he managed to get a job with the Legislative Finance Committee of the state legislature as an economics analyst, estimating oil and gas revenues. Howard told people who asked that he was being prepared for an assignment in Moscow by the State Department but did not want to go with a baby, so he had quit.[15] He bought an adobe-style ranch house at 108 Verano Loop in Eldorado, south of Santa Fe, and prepared to "pick up the pieces and start a new life," Mary recalled.[16]

Howard had signed a secrecy oath and was expected to keep his secrets forever—even after being forced out of the CIA. The CIA could end his employment but had no power to carry out law enforcement inside the United States. If Howard became a security risk, that was a counterintelligence matter, under the purview of the FBI. At the time, the CIA did not inform the FBI that a trainee who had access to secret operational files had been forced out. The CIA's approach was to keep its troubles in the family. However, even if the CIA had alerted the FBI at this point, it is not clear the bureau would have taken any action.[17]

Howard was seething, gripped by a desire to exact revenge on the CIA. In the weeks after he was forced out, he walked into the consulate of the Soviet Union, located on Phelps Place NW, in the Kalorama neighborhood of Washington, and left a note on the desk of the receptionist. The note was signed "Alex." It also contained the photocopy of his CIA badge, mentioned that he had been headed to the Moscow station, and said he had information to sell for $60,000. Howard left instructions for meeting him at some later date at the U.S. Capitol, and he included a random number code. Howard told his wife, Mary, that it was safer to leave a note at the consulate than at the Soviet embassy, located on Sixteenth Street NW, because there were no FBI security cameras monitoring the consulate, as at the embassy.[18]

Howard set the meeting with the Soviets for an upstairs bathroom at the Capitol on October 20, 1983. From his training, he knew the FBI is prohibited from entering the Capitol; they could not spot him there. The Capitol also offered many areas thronged with tourists. Howard spent several hours sitting outside the Soviet consulate, in a park, pondering what to do, but eventually decided against going to the Capitol for the meeting. On coming home, he told Mary that he just could not do it.[19] Victor Cherkashin, the second-ranking KGB officer in Washington at the time, said the KGB had received Howard's letter but also decided not to go to the Capitol meeting, fearing that it might be an FBI setup.[20]

Howard began making strange phone calls to Moscow. Late at night, often drunk, he called a U.S. phone number he had learned at the CIA, a special tie-line to the Moscow embassy that allowed diplomats to make calls back and forth to the United States without going through decrepit Soviet landlines. The tie-line was not secure, probably monitored by the KGB, and intended for personal calls and official calls that were routine. One evening, when it was already morning the next day in Moscow, Howard called the embassy, and a marine guard answered the line. Howard began reeling off a series of numbers from a sheet of paper and then hung up.[21] Another time, he identified himself by name and asked to leave a message for the Moscow station chief that he was "not showing up for his physical." There was no reason for Howard to make the call about his physical; the station chief already knew he wasn't coming. The chief reported the call to headquarters, which summoned Howard and lectured him about the calls.

In fact, Howard was attempting to use the phone line to alert the KGB. "My call to the CIA station chief about the physical effectively revealed to the Soviets that my job was to have been a deep cover CIA officer," Howard later wrote, saying he "made that call deliberately and in anger."[22] Another time, Howard used the phone to call Moscow and ask for Raya, a tall, blond Russian woman who worked in the U.S. embassy, in charge of such things as getting visas for diplomats, housing, and hiring Soviet employees. She told embassy officials about the call and undoubtedly told the KGB, too. "The important thing was to let them know how he could be located," said one CIA official who reviewed the record. Howard "was being very cool, operationally."

In the fall of 1983, Howard wrote an open letter to the Soviet consulate in San Francisco. The letter appeared to be an ordinary one from a citizen, expressing concern about U.S.-Soviet relations. Howard signed his own name. He told Mary that he wrote it as a "tease," assuming that the CIA or the FBI would see it and become upset at his direct contact with the Soviets.[23]

Howard's drinking grew worse. He was drunk on February 26, 1984, when he confronted three strangers at a bar outside Santa Fe, New Mexico. Howard, who owned firearms and had a license to buy and sell guns, kept a Smith & Wesson .44 Magnum revolver under the seat of his Jeep. He provoked a confrontation with the strangers and at one point aimed the gun through the open window of their vehicle. When one of them pushed it away, the gun fired through the roof. They attacked Howard and seized the weapon. No one was injured by the gunfire, but Howard was beaten and spent a night in jail. He later pleaded guilty to three counts of assault with a deadly weapon and was fined $7,500, ordered to see a psychiatrist, and given five years' probation.[24]

His state of mind was clearly unsettled. He had come out to New Mexico optimistic about starting over, perhaps even running for political office, but Mary recalled that after the drunken brawl he gave up hope.

He "began talking about going to the Soviets."[25]

---

In May 1984, Burton Gerber, who had been Moscow chief of station from 1980 to 1982 and who had been at the forefront of a generation of officers who pushed for more aggressive methods to spy on the Soviet Union, was appointed chief of the Soviet division. Soon after, the Edward Lee Howard mess fell into his lap. Gerber had not hired Howard or fired him, but now he faced the question of what to do about him. The confrontation with Mills on the driveway was a bad sign. From reading the file and talking to people, Gerber learned that the agency's psychiatrist had insisted on cutting off all contact with Howard after he had been forced out. Gerber concluded that was a mistake. If Howard possessed sensitive information, then they should not give him the cold shoulder. When Howard applied for reimbursement for half of his psychiatric counseling bills, saying his troubles were caused by his time in the CIA, Gerber approved the payments.

In September 1984, two CIA officials flew to Santa Fe to check up on Howard. They were Mills, the Soviet branch chief, and Malloy, the agency psychiatrist. At a breakfast meeting in a local motel, Howard seemed to be on the rebound and getting his life back together again. He showed up well dressed, seeming optimistic about his future. The CIA officials told Howard that his counseling bills would be paid by the CIA.

During the conversation, Howard made a startling admission. He told the CIA officials he had stopped in the park outside the Soviet consulate and pondered what would happen if he went inside. Howard said he figured the Soviets were cheap, would not give him much money, and in the end he said he decided not to do it.[26]

He was lying. He had already done much more. Just days before the breakfast, Howard returned from a trip to Europe with his family. The CIA had inadvertently mailed Howard his family's diplomatic passports after he was forced out; he used them for the trip. Howard and his family visited Italy, Switzerland, Germany, and Austria.

One night in Milan, quite drunk, Howard disappeared from his family around midnight and returned at 4:00 a.m. He was stopped on the way home by a police officer who noticed he was drunk; Howard showed his diplomatic passport and was released.[27] During those hours, he probably made contact with the KGB. It is not known precisely what occurred, but Howard later boasted to a friend that Milan had been a "cover for action" to meet the Soviets and he had filled a dead drop there. Mary did not see anything unusual on the trip.[28]

Howard had only just begun.

In October 1984, he received a phone call at home from a man with a soft, pleasant voice and a slight accent. The man inquired about a manuscript that Howard was offering to sell, and by the way the question was asked, Howard realized he was referring to the letter he had left at the Soviet consulate in 1983. Howard replied that he had nothing to sell and not to call him again. But the man was persistent. He said he could make things very unpleasant for Howard or could make things very good for him. He said he might be willing to pay twice Howard's suggested price of $60,000. The caller told Howard to think about it, and he would call again at a later date.[29]

Cherkashin, the second-ranking KGB man in Washington, wrote in his memoir that he made the call, and Howard expressed "enthusiasm about the prospect of working for us." Cherkashin added, "I told him he'd have to travel to Vienna to meet his handler and that we'd contact him later to inform him when and how to go there. He agreed."[30]

After the call, Howard sent a postcard to the Soviet consulate in San Francisco, signed "Alex." It was intended to confirm plans for a January 1985 meeting in Vienna. He received a second call around a month later about the trip.[31]

Howard told Mary, "I'm going to get those bastards" at the CIA. "I'm gonna hurt them like they've never been hurt before."[32]

# 17

# VANQUISH

For Tolkachev, the security scare at his institute had been a jolt. A year later, he was still turning over in his mind what had happened. When he met a CIA case officer on the street the evening of April 19, 1984, Tolkachev passed a thirteen-page ops note, saying he was sorry for having panicked. "Today, sorting in my mind all the events that occurred in late April, 1983, I must admit that my actions were too hasty," he wrote. He apologized again "for having destroyed so much at that time" and "for not having passed any new information for a whole year."[1] Tolkachev gave the CIA officer twenty-six pages of notes and schematics on Soviet radars, which he had handwritten from memory, and returned two fully exposed Tropel cameras. He told the case officer that the security situation at the institute hadn't changed and was still very restrictive, although there had not been any surprise inspections since the previous autumn. He wasn't sure if this was an ominous sign or if the danger had passed. He wrote that it was possible the KGB knew of a leak but lacked enough details to track it down, or perhaps the KGB was just preparing lists of who knew what—so they could pounce when the time was right.[2]

The meeting was the first contact with the Moscow station since the previous autumn, when Tolkachev had revealed the scare. Out of touch for months, the CIA was worried about his frame of mind and in an ops note reassured Tolkachev that he had done the right thing. "You have reacted to a dangerous situation with great courage, realistic caution and admirable self-control," they wrote. "We understand your desire to leave nothing for the KGB and completely agree with your decision to destroy all evidence of your link to us."

Then, to "put your mind at ease" about security, the CIA gave Tolkachev a separate memo from headquarters that described how his materials were handled in the United States. The memo said that from the very start of the operation the CIA had established special procedures, including secure locations to store the files in the few agencies that received the intelligence, "and no other material except yours can be kept in these repositories. Neither the material itself, nor excerpts from it can be taken out of the repositories." Each person who read the material had to sign his name. "In this way we can always know who read which document and when." Also, the CIA told Tolkachev, only translations were distributed, not originals, and there were strict restrictions on who could even *talk* about the Tolkachev intelligence. The CIA insisted that the "target recognition system" that Tolkachev passed in March 1983 was not shown to experts in the U.S. government until well after the security scare at the institute, so there could not have been a leak from the United States.

The CIA's soothing words to Tolkachev were accurate as far as they went, describing the safeguards on distribution of his information to *outsiders*. But it did not even raise the idea of a betrayal from within.

In the ops note, the CIA advised Tolkachev that if more threats or investigations appeared, he should halt his work and lie low. "Despite the value of your information and the high esteem in which it is held by the most senior people in our government, your future welfare is a much more important concern to us," the CIA message said. If threatened, they added, "do not hesitate to destroy all materials and cease activity on our behalf for as long as is necessary."

But once again the CIA and the military "customers" also wanted Tolkachev to produce more material if he could. The case officer gave Tolkachev two more loaded Tropel cameras, each concealed in a key fob. The case officer also passed to Tolkachev another 120,000 rubles to replace some of what he had burned at the dacha. The Moscow station stashed some ginseng in the package and offered Tolkachev health advice, urging him to relax and cut down on salt in his diet. "We feel you are not only a colleague but a friend; as such, we ask you to please take care of yourself."[3]

Tolkachev had destroyed the Pentax 35 mm camera during the scare, leaving him only one method to photograph documents, using the two miniature Tropel cameras that Morris had given him the previous fall. He wrote in his ops note to the CIA that he had taken the chance and used them at work to copy documents that he could no longer smuggle out of the building because of the tight restrictions. However, his note was vague. He wrote that "from the point of view of security, it's more convenient for me to do the whole process standing up, not sitting down." It wasn't clear where he was standing up, or why. Tolkachev said he found it difficult to hold the tiny camera exactly twenty-eight centimeters from the page while standing. He said that he flattened the top of a knitting needle of precisely the right length, then attached the camera to it with a rubber band, effectively making a tripod. Tolkachev said he feared the needle was casting a shadow on the page, so he took time to photograph some pages twice. "Unfortunately," he said, "when I was photographing the second time, I was in such a hurry that I may have forgotten to unscrew the cap from the camera lens." In the future, he wrote, he wouldn't shoot every page twice because of time—"there's none to spare."[4]

He didn't say anything else about photography, and the CIA couldn't ask. He renewed his request for another Pentax 35 mm camera.

On April 27, headquarters reported that the results from the two Tropels that Tolkachev had given the case officer were "generally excellent" and one document was a "winner." The handwritten notes he made from memory were "very valuable and crammed with an extraordinary amount of minute detail."

"Our initial reaction after this preliminary reading is that CKSPHERE has almost completely recovered from his scare of the past year," headquarters concluded, "and is once again taking risks (i.e. photography in his lab) in his determination to inflict as much damage as possible on his system."

In his ops note, Tolkachev was more focused on his personal problems than in the past. He was still thinking of surgery to correct his broken nose. "You shouldn't be surprised if I come to one of the meetings with a straight nose," he wrote to the CIA.

He then revealed he had suffered another health crisis. "It's well known that health does not improve with age," he said, describing an attack of acute "chronic antacid gastritis" that hit him in March. "I had high fever, I was sick for two weeks and didn't go to work," he said. "After this crisis, the stomach pains continued for over a month. I was forced to go on a strict diet." A Soviet doctor had recommended rose hip and buckthorn oil, but the pharmacy shelves in Moscow were nearly empty; "it's practically impossible to get these oils even with a doctor's prescription." The medicine could be found on the black market, but Tolkachev didn't want to try it. "It would be great if you could obtain some rosehip and buckthorn oil for me," he said. Tolkachev also suffered from gum disease; his teeth hurt upon eating cold food, and he wanted a French medicine that also couldn't be found in Moscow, with instructions in Russian. He and his wife needed new eyeglasses too; Tolkachev provided the prescriptions. His son needed six to eight more bottles of India ink for his drafting equipment and a bottle of fluid to clean the equipment the CIA had provided him earlier.[5]

The CIA was reassured by all these requests. A cable from headquarters to the Moscow station observed that Tolkachev "has recovered his drive and is again determined to gather information for us according to a self-imposed timetable." Tolkachev "seems to be exhibiting again a compulsive urgency to get on with his self-appointed task," headquarters said. They began to assemble the items on Tolkachev's list, adding the German equivalent of Di-Gel and Maalox.[6]

In the summer of 1984, the CIA also changed Tolkachev's code name. Headquarters said it was a routine security procedure, because CKSPHERE had already been in use for six years.

His new code name was CKVANQUISH.

By autumn, Tolkachev seemed to have rebounded. On October 11, he met a case officer for twenty minutes, and the officer found him "more healthy and energetic" than in the spring. The case officer came bearing bulky packages for Tolkachev that included 168,750 rubles and much of his wish list. Tolkachev passed to the case officer two Tropel cameras with exposed film and twenty-two pages of handwritten material, including an ops note. He immediately asked about the Pentax camera and whether the case officer had brought it; he wanted it badly. But the CIA had decided not to give it to him, fearing he might take too many risks.

Tolkachev insisted that with the coming of winter, he could resume smuggling documents out of the institute, tucked inside his coat, despite the dangers. He told the case officer that the security situation appeared to be calm at his institute, with no new investigations. When the case officer said he was worried about the dangers, Tolkachev reminded him anew, "Everything we do is dangerous."

Then Tolkachev revealed why he was standing up when photographing documents with the Tropel cameras. He was taking the documents to a private men's toilet stall, locking the door, putting the documents on a narrow shelf under a tiny window, and photographing them with the miniature camera.[7]

In his ops note, Tolkachev pleaded with the CIA to bring the Pentax camera to their next meeting so he could be more productive, as he had in the past. Sure, he said, he could just make notes, that would be safe. But he added,

It's impossible to do a lot with such a method, while I've always strived, from the very beginning, to gather and to pass on the maximum information possible. And now, under conditions that are more difficult in comparison to the early period of my activity, my drive hasn't changed. I feel that I am already unable to lessen this drive, it is incited to some degree by the nature of my character. In this case, from my own experience I am once more convinced of the accuracy and truth of proverbs, such as, for example, "character cannot be broken."[8]

Tolkachev's photographs taken in the toilet were clear, except for a few frames where he failed to press the shutter down all the way. Headquarters said his note offered "the clearest picture we have yet had of a man 'driven' by the unchangeable nature of his character to disregard the risks he perceives in order to collect as much information as possible." But headquarters still balked at giving Tolkachev a Pentax to photograph documents. They decided on a compromise—give him more Tropel miniature cameras to use.[9]

Tolkachev's meeting in October—his twentieth with the CIA—was businesslike, but he was not as personally warm and forthcoming as he had been with John Guilsher and David Rolph. He didn't mention to the case officer that his son, Oleg, who had figured so prominently in his requests over the years, was married in Moscow on August 1, at nineteen years old, and moved out of the apartment to live with his new wife's parents.[10]

Tolkachev's notes gave headquarters a sense of renewed optimism about the operation. For the first time since 1982, he had answered the CIA's specific questions about Soviet weapons systems. The division's reports and requirements staff, which handled the incoming intelligence and outgoing questions for agents in the field, said Tolkachev's material "would seem to indicate that he has recovered from his security crisis."[11] The CIA also prepared an ops note for Tolkachev emphasizing how valuable his material had become and saying they didn't want him to take any unnecessary risks. "You should clearly understand," the ops note said, that "the information you provide to us, simply stated, is considered invaluable," prized not only by technical experts but by those making national security policy.

"To lose such information," the CIA said, "would be a severe blow to our government, gravely affecting our national posture both now and for many years to come."[12]

Tolkachev was five minutes late to his meeting with the CIA case officer on the night of January 18, 1985. The streets were piled with snow, temperatures plunged to fifteen degrees below zero, and he had trouble finding a place to park. When he arrived, they exchanged verbal paroles, a few pleasantries, and walked back to Tolkachev's car to stay warm and talk.

Tolkachev asked right away: Do you have the Pentax? The case officer said no, it was too risky. Tolkachev was disappointed but said he would abide by the decision, even though he yearned to return to the days of shooting dozens of rolls of film with the big camera, spreading documents out on the table in his apartment, the camera held by a clamp on the back of a chair, and with a good desk lamp to illuminate the pages.

In the toilet stall at the institute where he was photographing with the Tropel cameras, the window was painted over, in white. The light was soft on the best of days and worse when it was overcast outside. The small, solitary toilet was located in a building adjacent to his office, so he could easily carry secret documents there. There were no document control points in between, but just in case he usually arranged to make a cover stop at a friend's office to explain his presence in the building. In the toilet stall, he could lock the door and be alone. He told the case officer he had recently photographed a "very important document" using the small Tropel cameras. Tolkachev recited the title of the document from memory: "Overall Special Program of Scientific Research, Experimentation, and Practical Construction Work to Secure the Creation of Front Line and 'PVO' Fighters for the 1990s." The "PVO" meant air defense forces. The document would surely be another intelligence treasure for the CIA—Soviet military aviation plans well into the next decade. Still, Tolkachev said the photographs were made on an overcast day, and he sounded uncertain about his use of the miniature cameras in the dim light.[13]

He gave the Tropel cameras to the case officer, as well as handwritten notes, wrapped in a taped package. The case officer handed over several bundles to Tolkachev: five more miniature

Tropel cameras; another 100,000 rubles; a meeting schedule for the next three years; and instructions for new signal and meeting sites, including a location for the next meeting planned for June, code-named TRUBKA, or "pipe." The CIA's schedule and instructions were a clear indication that they planned to carry on with the operation for some time to come. The packages also included three books in Russian and an ops note telling Tolkachev how invaluable and important his material had been to the United States.

Tolkachev presented a long, personal wish list to the CIA. He needed a rear window defroster for his car. He continued to suffer from pain in his teeth and wanted more French medicine. He asked for albums and books on architecture for his son. He wanted soft-tipped French pens similar to those that had appeared the previous summer in Moscow; he gave a used pen to the case officer as a sample.

Tolkachev also was hungry for news published in the West. He wanted press clippings and Russian-language newspapers printed in the United States. He asked for information on arms control, important speeches by Western leaders, and press conferences of Soviet citizens—refugees and defectors—in the West. Tolkachev said his son regarded his English teachers as "very bad," and he asked the CIA to put together an extensive English-language training course, with cassette tapes, recording humorous stories and political speeches, all spoken by more than one person. He volunteered money from his escrow account to finance the work.

In the ops note for Tolkachev, the Moscow station reported that his account balance stood at $1,990,729.85.[14]

Time was short. The case officer's tape recorder was running. He asked Tolkachev about some current rumors: Had he heard anything concerning the health of the Soviet leader, Konstantin Chernenko?

No, nothing, Tolkachev said.

What about reports that red mailboxes on Moscow street corners were disappearing, and what did that mean?

Tolkachev said he didn't write many letters and hadn't noticed.

After twenty minutes, the case officer opened the car door and slipped away.

It was Tolkachev's twenty-first meeting with the CIA.

When the Moscow station opened Tolkachev's handwritten notes the next day, they found something odd. Pages he had numbered 1 to 10 were normal, then the material skipped to pages 34–35, then skipped again to 52–57. They did not know why.[15]

On balance, however, it seemed that Tolkachev was back on track. When the Moscow station sent a cable to headquarters describing the meeting, Gerber, the Soviet division chief, read it and wrote at the top of the page, "Great."

On January 31, headquarters sent a message to the Moscow station, saying "we remain optimistic" that Tolkachev's security crisis of 1983 "has abated." Headquarters added, "we are especially pleased" that the conditions for photography at the institute "are a lot better than they could have been," and "it is encouraging that he is not required to pass any document control points" on his way to the small toilet.[16]

Just a few days later, headquarters sent worrisome news. Tolkachev's latest film from the Tropel cameras turned out to be unreadable. The negatives were "extremely underexposed, caused by lack of sufficient light." The cameras were simply not working in the dim light. The valuable document Tolkachev painstakingly photographed in the toilet stall was lost. Also, there was another unexplained puzzle. The Tropel cameras used a screw-on cap at one end. "The end caps on two of the cameras were obviously switched," headquarters reported.[17] Was it a mistake made in haste or something else?

At CIA headquarters, an internal review of Tolkachev's

security situation, looking back over all the cables and notes of the last four years, was completed in February and sent to the Moscow station. It examined the system of building passes and library permission sign-out sheets for secret documents that Tolkachev had previously described. Although Tolkachev had been astoundingly successful at smuggling documents out of the institute and photographing them at home for several years, the review cautioned that the authorities "have established a series of interlocking restrictions and checkpoints" that would make it more difficult to smuggle documents out of the institute. The review added that "we are encouraged" by the news "that CKVAN-QUISH apparently can move freely within the institute grounds." It insisted that the CIA be vigilant and look for ways to lessen the danger to Tolkachev. Yet the review focused entirely on the risks to him by his own actions within the institute and said nothing about the dangers to him from elsewhere. The CIA mind-set was that security at its own headquarters was very tight, and it was unthinkable that a leak could come from Langley or the military "customers" who thrived on Tolkachev's intelligence.[18]

On March 4, the Moscow station put up a visual signal for Tolkachev, asking for a quick meeting. The station wanted to tell him that the last batch of film did not turn out and give him a new light meter and cameras with improved film for low light conditions. "We believe chances are very good that CKVANQUISH would be able to resume successful photography in the relatively secure conditions of the toilet," headquarters said.[19] But for some reason, Tolkachev did not respond.

The next week, the station saw a "ready" signal, although the officer wasn't sure, because it was not the same *fortochka* as before, but it was opened at the proper time.

Again, Tolkachev didn't show.

An alternative meeting date passed at the end of March, and he didn't show up again.[20]

# 18

# SELLING OUT

In January 1985, Edward Lee Howard flew to Vienna to meet with his Soviet contacts.[1] Howard told his wife, Mary, that the KGB wanted to check his bona fides and verify the information he was giving them. He was reimbursed by the KGB for his travel expenses, but he was told they would have to verify his material before he would be paid more. What exactly happened in Vienna is not known, but as Howard later described it to his wife, he was picked up in front of a movie theater and driven around for about half an hour to check for surveillance. He was impressed with the tradecraft. He was taken in through a back door to the Soviet embassy, where he talked with two officers who debriefed him—he identified them as Boris and Viktor—for three or four hours. They made him feel important, treated him with respect, poured drinks, and brought him caviar. One of the two men had flown in from Moscow. Howard said the Soviet officers were "still not totally convinced of his bona fides because they had been unable to verify some of his information." He said "he was to be paid a considerable amount of money" at a later meeting.[2]

From abroad, Howard sent a postcard to a friend that said, "I talked to my case officer."[3]

In April, Howard returned to Vienna, this time accompanied by Mary. She recalled that he paid for everything using traveler's checks, not his American Express credit card. They stayed at the four-star Hotel Beethoven for two days. Howard had filled out an application for employment with the United Nations agency in Vienna and written to them, saying he would be available for an interview on April 25, 1985. Once in the city, Howard's wife dropped him off at the UN office.[4] But that was just a cover story; Howard had earlier called the United Nations and canceled his interview.[5] He apparently met with the Soviet officers again at this time. Howard later wrote that he also went to Zurich, Switzerland, and "indulged a long-time fantasy of mine and spent $600 on a Rolex watch."[6]

Howard had much to offer the KGB. He knew of the presence of a spy for the United States deep in the Soviet military-industrial complex, and he knew of the presence of a wiretap on one of the Soviet Union's most sensitive underground communications lines. Howard was trained at the CIA for both operations. He knew much of the CIA's operational tradecraft and technology, such as the use of the tiny radios, disguises, surveillance detection runs, and the Jack-in-the-Box.

In 1984 and 1985, Howard confided to a friend, William Bosch, a former CIA case officer in Latin America who left the agency under a cloud, that he had sold information to the Soviets. Howard met Bosch several times in this period, boasting of his KGB contacts. He told Bosch how his vacation in Milan was a "cover for action," that he filled a dead drop for the Soviets and had taken secret CIA documents and buried them for later passage to the KGB. Howard tried at least once to recruit Bosch to join him and "go and see Boris my case officer." Bosch later expressed worry about Howard's mental stability and wasn't sure if Howard was joking—or serious. But Bosch, who had his own troubles with the CIA, never reported any of this to the authorities.[7]

With the information obtained from Howard, the KGB began to look for a spy inside a vast network of military research institutes, design bureaus, and factories spread across eleven time zones. Although the KGB had served as the cruel hammer of Soviet repression, they had become more legalistic and procedural over the decades. They would not make a move based on Howard's tip alone. They were seeking evidence, and they wanted to catch a spy in the act. Howard apparently described to the KGB some details about Tolkachev but did not, or could not, provide his name. Howard later claimed he didn't know the name.[8] The KGB was left with a vague description of the spy they were hunting for. Several participants later recalled that they began with a broad investigation that examined both aviation and electronics branches of the defense industry but then narrowed it down to one institute: Phazotron.[9]

Just as the KGB was learning more from Howard, another American intelligence officer stepped forward with new information. On April 16, 1985, Aldrich Ames went to the bar of the Mayflower Hotel in downtown Washington. A tall man, with a mustache and heavy eyeglasses, he was head of a counterintelligence branch inside the Soviet division at CIA headquarters. Ames was regarded by colleagues as a rather bland and mediocre intelligence officer. At the hotel bar, he waited for a Soviet diplomat to show up. When the man didn't come, Ames walked two blocks to the Soviet embassy on Sixteenth Street NW. He handed an envelope to the receptionist and motioned to the duty officer that he wanted it given to the KGB *rezident* upstairs. Inside the envelope, Ames offered to become an agent for the Soviet Union, describing two or three cases involving Soviets who had approached the CIA to offer their services, but not Tolkachev.

Ames also included a page from the CIA internal phone directory that identified him. He asked for $50,000. Ames returned to the embassy on May 15 and, meeting the KGB in a soundproof room, was told he would get the money. Two days later, the KGB gave it to him in hundred-dollar bills at a restaurant. Up to this point, Ames had given the Soviets some hints of his potential but not a large quantity of secret materials. He had not disclosed such operations as CKVANQUISH and CKELBOW. But he certainly offered the promise of more.[10]

In the spring and summer of 1985, CIA headquarters was confronted with a string of anomalies, all related to espionage against the Soviet Union. There was no single, credible explanation, and some of the events might not have been connected to Howard and Ames. At this point, the CIA did not know that either of them was committing treason. But the events of 1985 came quickly and sent a shudder through headquarters. What worried them most were the anomalies that they couldn't explain.

In May, Sergei Bokhan, a longtime CIA agent in Athens who was serving in the GRU, Soviet military intelligence, was unexpectedly summoned to Moscow. Bokhan was told his son was in trouble at a military academy, but he knew that was false. Had he been betrayed? Would he be arrested in Moscow? Bokhan consulted with the CIA, and in a decision approved by Gerber, the division chief, in just a matter of days Bokhan was exfiltrated by the CIA to the United States.[11]

Also in April, a case officer in the Moscow station, Michael Sellers, met a KGB source who called himself "Stas," whose real identity was not known to the CIA. He was a rough-cut officer with a guttural, street-jargon Russian that wasn't easy to understand, but Sellers managed to grasp it, and they walked around Moscow and talked for an hour and a half, undetected, as "Stas" provided a stream of valuable intelligence, including the disclosure that the Moscow station had made a major error in another operation.[12] Just as they were getting ready to part, "Stas" took out what looked like a small can and a plastic bag and sprayed something into it. He informed Sellers it was a sample of a mysterious powder the KGB used to track officers of the Moscow station. The invisible chemicals were sprinkled by the KGB on car door handles and other locations. A special light exposed the spy dust on a doorknob, a telephone, or a bus window. Sellers had seen the stuff before in his car, even on a child's car seat—it looked like yellow bee pollen—but now the United States had proof. Why had "Stas" volunteered? Who was he? It wasn't clear.[13]

In the spring, a case officer from the Moscow station made a run to the underground cable tap. With an electronic device, the case officer "interrogated" the recorder about tampering, and it responded with an alarm. The sensor wasn't perfect, and it could be a false alarm, but the case officer decided to abort the run. After a debate, the Moscow station decided to try again, figuring that an espionage machine that had cost tens of millions of dollars was worth the risk. The case officer returned to the site and safely retrieved the recorder, and it was sent back to the United States, but the valuable intelligence that had been picked up for years on the underground cable had completely dried up. No one knew why.[14]

Amid these jarring events and unanswered questions, the CIA decided not to bother Tolkachev until the next scheduled rendezvous, set for June. The summer months would bring more daylight, and the CIA might be able to give him new film or a better camera. The Moscow station and headquarters seemed optimistic that they could solve the photography problem, even if it meant urging Tolkachev to take pictures in the toilet only on sunny days.[15]

# 19

# WITHOUT WARNING

On the evening of March 10, 1985, the ailing Soviet leader, Konstantin Chernenko, passed away. The next day, the youngest member of the Politburo, Mikhail Gorbachev, became the fourth leader of the Soviet Union in three years. Tolkachev usually paid little attention to politics. At home, he was content to bury himself in his technical books, ignoring broadcasts and pronouncements of the party-state. He loathed them all and rarely even glanced at a television. He was not an optimist that the Soviet system would change. But when it did, he took notice. After the arrival of Gorbachev, he could not get enough of the television news. One day at home, he marveled, "Did you notice this concert on television, there were no propaganda songs?" Frequently, he read the newspapers—which he hadn't done for years. He was curious and excited about Gorbachev and the hints of new thinking. Could it be that their dashed hopes from the days of the thaw would be realized at last?[1]

On Wednesday, June 5, the next date for a planned meeting with Tolkachev, the Moscow station checked the *fortochka*. This time, the correct window was open, a signal that he was ready, but that evening the case officer had to abort, saying there was too much surveillance.[2]

Over the weekend of June 8 and 9, Tolkachev and his wife, Natasha, drove to their dacha north of Moscow. Their son, Oleg, no longer joined them for trips to the country. While Tolkachev and his wife were away, KGB officers secretly entered and searched their apartment. They discovered the fountain pen with the L-pill from the CIA. They might also have found the other CIA materials in the *entresol*, including the schedule and maps for upcoming meetings.[3]

A family friend recalled that at the dacha Adik often worked with wood, repairing window frames, while Natasha liked to cultivate the garden. They had plans on Sunday evening, June 9, to see old friends in Moscow, the Rozhanskys.[4] When they left the dacha, Adik put on a light sport coat, and his wife a black-and-white-check dress with trim at the sleeves, anticipating they would meet their friends soon after their return to the city. Natasha had only recently obtained a driver's license and was behind the wheel of the Zhiguli. The country had been cool for the weekend, and as they drove, it was drizzling. The Zhiguli's wipers were on.

On a narrow two-way road toward the city, which cut through a stand of pine and birch, they were stopped by a traffic policeman wearing a uniform and a rain cape who waved them over with a baton. A traffic police checkpoint was not unusual, although it was not often found so far out in the country. The ocher Zhiguli approached the checkpoint, pulled over as instructed, and braked jerkily behind a parked blue-and-white police van. The traffic policeman saluted and asked the owner of the car to get out.

Adik and Natasha sat inside quietly for a moment, and then

Adik climbed out on the passenger side. He was wearing his sport coat and appeared to slide something, perhaps his documents, into his left inside coat pocket after he got out of the car.

The policeman directed him to step forward of the blue-and-white van, toward other vehicles parked along the shoulder. Tolkachev took about ten strides in that direction, with the traffic policeman in front of him. Tolkachev raised his left hand and scratched the right side of his chin.

At that moment, a young man with black hair and a mustache briskly strode up behind him, holding a white rag in his left hand. The man threw his right arm around Tolkachev's neck, into a choke hold, and with his left hand stuffed the white rag into Tolkachev's mouth. Three others grabbed Tolkachev's arms and yanked them behind him, lifted his feet off the ground, and carried him back toward the van. The rag still in his mouth, Tolkachev was silent. The side doors to the blue-and-white van swung open, and Tolkachev was shoved inside.

His wife was escorted away from the Zhiguli into another car. As she prepared to climb into the other vehicle, she looked up, confused.

None of the men who stopped them were traffic police. They were all KGB.

In the van, still restrained by the KGB man's arm around his neck, Tolkachev was stripped of his clothing to make sure he was not carrying a suicide pill. The KGB remembered well how Ogorodnik tricked them years earlier with the poison concealed in a fountain pen. They put Tolkachev in a tracksuit. Tolkachev was then driven in the blue-and-white van to Lefortovo, the KGB's notorious prison in Moscow. Once there, he re-dressed in his street clothes, after they were checked again for a suicide pill.[5]

———

When the Tolkachevs did not telephone, and did not show up to see the Rozhanskys on Sunday, their friends began to call the apartment at Ploshchad Vosstaniya. There was no answer. They tried to call Natasha at work on Monday, no answer. On Monday morning, at the institute, Natasha's supervisor, Vladimir Libin, took note that she was absent. Libin was also a family friend who had visited the Tolkachevs at home and privately shared Natasha's deep antipathy toward the system. Libin gave her the benefit of the doubt and wrote "compensatory time" on her records, figuring there was a good reason she did not come to work. It could be that someone became ill, a car malfunctioned—anything. In the middle of the day, a woman telephoned Libin, saying she was a neighbor of the Tolkachevs at the dacha, that Adik was ill, he had been taken to the local hospital, and asked that his wife be given some time off. For two more days, Libin marked her down for more time off.

On Wednesday, frantic, the Rozhanskys drove to the Tolkachevs' dacha. It was locked. The village was very small, and everyone knew everything about each other; neighbors said they had seen nothing unusual. Tolkachev had left with his wife on Sunday, carrying flowers back to the city.

Did the car break down? The Rozhanskys went to the local auto shop. No, there were no incidents on Sunday, neither breakdowns nor accidents. They went to the local hospital. Again, nothing. The Rozhanskys returned to Moscow and went to the Tolkachevs' apartment building. The ocher Zhiguli was not in its usual parking space.

On Wednesday, June 12, Natasha telephoned Libin at work. She said Adik had been stricken with severe back pain, and she didn't know when she could return to work. Libin expressed his sympathy. Her voice sounded weak, less than cheerful.

With no word after days and days of calling friends, the Rozhanskys went back to the Tolkachev apartment. With relatives who had a key to the apartment, they opened the first of two doors to enter it. But they stopped on the inner door. It was marked with paper seals on which were visible three bold letters: KGB.[6]

Oleg had also been searching for his parents when they did not return from the dacha. He, too, went to their apartment and saw the KGB seal on their door.[7]

Tolkachev's next scheduled meeting with the CIA was to be June 13, the day after Natasha had called the institute to say Adik was sick.

In anticipation, the Moscow station drafted an ops note, which began "Dear Friend," and praised Tolkachev's material delivered in January, which was "considered to be extremely valuable by our national security experts." But the Moscow station informed Tolkachev the photographs of that "very important document" had not come out, "due to insufficient light levels ... caused by the extremely overcast weather" during the winter. The station said that headquarters was working on a new, more light-sensitive camera, but in the meantime they would give him five more Tropel cameras, like those he had used before. They urged him to "photograph on bright days" only.

"We remain extremely interested in the very important documents you photographed for our last meeting," the ops note said. Please take those pictures again, it added, "when you are certain conditions are absolutely secure."[8] The ops note for Tolkachev also raised the possibility of another CIA attempt to replicate Tolkachev's library permission sheet so he could replace it with the original, "as we did in 1980."[9]

The materials for Tolkachev this time were bulky. The station packaged everything carefully: the ops note; the cameras; four pages of original material he had provided to the CIA in January, being returned; twenty French drawing pens; twenty German drawing pens; two architecture books; eight boxes of dental medicine and instructions; eight bottles of fluoride; eight tubes of toothpaste; a book containing 250 pages of newspaper and magazine articles from the West; and 100,000 rubles toward interest on his escrow account.[10] But the CIA told Tolkachev they were reluctant to provide the English-language lessons he wanted for his son because of concern about how he would explain where he got them. The tapes were not in the package.[11]

Tolkachev's *fortochka* window was open on June 13 at the correct hour, signaling that he was ready for a meeting that evening. But KGB surveillance on the case officer selected for the meeting had been so heavy that the station picked an alternate case officer. There was always a primary and an alternate, and sometimes a third. In this case, the job fell to Paul "Skip" Stombaugh, a case officer who, before joining the CIA, had worked for the FBI. Stombaugh was well liked, a straight-arrow, hardworking type. His Russian-language skills weren't great, but his colleagues remembered his tenacity in studying. In Moscow, he became a sort of hybrid officer, undercover in the embassy's political section, but not strictly "deep cover." He had his own desk in the Moscow station and in 1985, having passed the initial period of KGB scrutiny, was spending about half his time in the station, a colleague recalled.[12]

That week in June, the Moscow station chief made a trip out of town, to the southern Caucasus Mountains region. The KGB would have been notified, and the station chief hoped to distract them from operations in Moscow.

On the evening of June 13 in Moscow, Stombaugh set out on a long surveillance detection run carrying two large Russian shopping bags with handles. He was wearing a white shirt and sport coat. While many case officers tried to disguise themselves to look Russian on the street at times like this, in drab clothes and with thick eyeglasses, Stombaugh did not. He looked very much like an American diplomat. He was driven on the first leg of the run by his wife, then proceeded on foot. Stombaugh reached the meeting site, code-named TRUBKA, or "pipe," about an hour early. It was located in a residential area of five-story apartment blocks in western Moscow, four and a half miles from Tolkachev's home, farther out than in the earlier days. The meeting was to be at two pay phones.[13]

Stombaugh walked past the meeting site, making an initial check, noticing nothing unusual.[14] He then waited on a park bench until 9:40 p.m.

Leading to the meeting place was a broad sidewalk under a canopy of trees, with apartment buildings on all sides. Puddles still remained on the sidewalk from recent thundershowers. As Stombaugh walked, slowly, toward the site, he noticed a young, red-haired woman talking on one of the pay phones. He thought it was odd that she was talking so loudly on an otherwise quiet street, but he did not change course or move away from her. Under his right arm, Stombaugh cradled one of the bags for Tolkachev and grasped the other, in his left hand, by the handle. He walked just beyond the woman on the phone, then turned on his heel and took a few steps back in the other direction, all the while looking up and around for Tolkachev. He saw what looked like Tolkachev's ocher Zhiguli car, parked a hundred to two hundred yards away.

Three plainclothes men ambushed Stombaugh, leaping out from a row of bushes. One pulled Stombaugh's arms behind him sharply, while the other two wrested free the packages. Five more men, all from the KGB, rushed to the scene. Stombaugh was hustled into a van, which drove off to the Lubyanka, the KGB headquarters building.

In the van, Stombaugh protested that he was an American diplomat. A KGB man told him to shut up, he didn't want to hear it.

Stombaugh was ushered into a holding room in the Lubyanka and searched. The KGB removed from his pockets his tape recorder, a plain plastic Tropel camera, some change, cryptic notes he had made before the meeting on possible dead drop sites for the future, his meeting agenda, some medicine for Tolkachev in his right-hand coat pocket, a black felt-tip pen, two pages of a Moscow map, and his watch, wallet, and belt. After an hour in the holding room, Stombaugh was taken to a conference room and told to sit down. Spread out in front of him were the items taken from his pockets and the two packages for Tolkachev, still unopened.

Rem Krasilnikov, the major general who led KGB counter-intelligence, declared, "You have been arrested for committing espionage. Who are you?"

Stombaugh: "American diplomat. I want to call the embassy. Now."

Krasilnikov: "You are not a diplomat, you are a spy."

Stombaugh: "I am a diplomat."

Krasilnikov: "You are a spy!"

Stombaugh, with his sport coat folded over his arm, flexed his shoulders, obviously sore. His arms had been pinned behind his back for the first hour of his detention. The KGB turned on a video camera. Krasilnikov then proceeded to open the two packages, carefully examining each item inside. When he opened the second package, those present in the room stared in awe at the bulging stack of rubles. Holding the brick of currency, sealed in plastic, Krasilnikov said, "A huge bundle of 50 ruble notes!" He asked Stombaugh about the plastic Tropel camera, and Stombaugh refused to answer. Krasilnikov then took out the ops note and read the first two lines aloud, thanking the agent for valuable information at the last meeting. Krasilnikov read the rest of the letter in silence until he reached a line about the CIA's reluctance to give the agent English-language training materials and read

it aloud. Krasilnikov also found the notes handwritten by Tolkachev containing intelligence information, the pages given to
the CIA in January that had been oddly numbered. The CIA
was returning them to Tolkachev at his request. Krasilnikov
commented that they were "most interesting."[15]

The Soviet Foreign Ministry notified the U.S. embassy that
an American had been detained by the KGB. When an embassy
duty officer came to the Lubyanka to get Stombaugh, a heated
confrontation erupted. Krasilnikov kept insisting Stombaugh
was a spy, and the embassy duty officer demanded they be
allowed to leave. The embassy officer was told by Krasilnikov
that Stombaugh had been detained "in the act of meeting with
a Soviet citizen for alleged espionage purposes" and "the Soviet
citizen in question had been arrested."

Just before the ambush, the KGB had put an impersonator on
the street to resemble Tolkachev, carrying the recognition signal,
a book with a white cover in his left hand. The KGB also opened
the *fortochka* in Tolkachev's window and parked Tolkachev's
car nearby as additional enticement. Stombaugh saw the car but
didn't see the fake Tolkachev. He thought he had been free from
surveillance, but the KGB was waiting.

A flash cable was sent to CIA headquarters reporting an
arrest. A longer cable was sent to headquarters after Stombaugh
was released, describing the ambush. Stombaugh was released
after midnight, Moscow time, declared persona non grata, and
expelled.[16]

The incident carried an ominous meaning for those who
knew of the Moscow station's most valued asset. The KGB had
the exact time and place where Stombaugh was to meet the agent.
It meant the Tolkachev operation was over.

He was already in the grip of the KGB.

That same afternoon, Aldrich Ames arrived at a small restaurant, Chadwicks, on the Georgetown waterfront in Washington. Ames had wrapped up a bundle of classified messages in his CIA office and carried them out of headquarters without being stopped. He brought the cables and documents in a plastic bag to the restaurant, where he was met by Sergei Chuvakhin from the Soviet embassy. Ames gave him the materials, a colossal breach that was just the beginning of his treachery. The KGB had already detained Tolkachev, but if they had any doubts, Ames gave them further confirmation.[17]

That evening, Gerber was at home on Connecticut Avenue in Washington. His wife, Rosalie, was cooking, expecting a guest for dinner, James Olson, who had worked with them in the Moscow station. Olson was the first case officer to climb into the manhole for CKELBOW and had also met Sheymov in Moscow and worked with Rolph on the CKUTOPIA exfiltration. After dinner, Gerber and Olson were scheduled to participate in an exercise on the streets of Washington, providing training in detecting, evading, and escaping surveillance to the next generation of CIA case officers. Gerber was to play the role of a spy, and the young trainees would attempt to find him while dodging or escaping the surveillance, provided by the FBI. On a warm summer evening, the exercise would require a few hours out on the streets, teaching the rookies the exacting, choreographed methods that Gerber had polished over a long career. Olson arrived with a grim face at Gerber's apartment. The first thing he said was, "Terrible news." The CIA had just received the message from the Moscow station that Stombaugh had been arrested.

Gerber realized instantly what that meant: Tolkachev had been lost. Gerber cared passionately about his country and about agents who risked their lives for it. A Roman Catholic, he often lit a candle at Mass for agents who had been killed in the line of duty. But after a career in espionage, he was also determined not to let setbacks slow him down. He often compared the work to that of a surgeon or a cancer doctor. He did everything he could to save the patient, but if and when a patient died, he moved on to save the next. Gerber always felt it necessary to soldier on, even with the burden of loss. He did not torment himself over whether he should have done something differently. He knew there would be all kinds of questions about Tolkachev in the morning; for now, he and Olson headed out to the street to prepare future CIA case officers in how to run a spy.[18]

In the weeks that followed, the Moscow station and headquarters attempted to puzzle out what might have compromised Tolkachev. The cables and messages were defensive and inconclusive. The reports and requirements branch in the division, responsible for sharing intelligence with the "customers," emphasized that "all of CKVANQUISH's material has been disseminated on an extremely limited basis" and that "all of the customers made a conscientious effort to keep down the number of people cleared."[19]

On July 8, headquarters wrote to the Moscow station, "We cannot state definitively what might have caused his compromise." One possibility, headquarters said, was that Tolkachev was "compromised at work through discovery of his intelligence gathering activities," and another was that he was discovered "as a result of a security investigation" at Phazotron. Perhaps the investigation in early 1983 that had so frightened Tolkachev was still going on in early 1985 and exposed him.

There was one more embarrassing possibility. Three pages of the master copy of a top secret Tolkachev document were lost in July 1984 when they were sent to the CIA's printing and photography division. The contents of the pages were "specific enough to compromise CKVANQUISH," headquarters noted. No one knew what happened to those three pages.

Did Tolkachev make a mistake with all his money from the CIA? Headquarters didn't think so. "Lavish spending does not seem to accord with what we know of CKVANQUISH's character and conservative lifestyle, or with his statements from time to time that he viewed the money we gave him as a nest egg, or insurance against adversity," headquarters told the station.

Was Tolkachev already under control by the KGB at the January 1985 meeting, when he turned over the cameras, with the end caps switched and the film blurred? Headquarters thought this was not likely, given the high value of the potential intelligence to the United States. The KGB didn't like to dangle agents who could relinquish really important secrets.

All of the headquarters messages at this point were speculative and largely wrong. None of them focused on the possibility that Tolkachev was betrayed from within the CIA. But one observation was very accurate. Because the KGB knew the time, date, and place of the June 13 meeting with Tolkachev, they must have discovered the materials the CIA gave Tolkachev in January, including the meeting sites, ops note, and schedule. All of it was terribly incriminating.

"The arrest, therefore, came without warning."[20]

# 20

# ON THE RUN

On August 1, 1985, Vitaly Yurchenko went for a stroll from the Soviet embassy in Rome and never returned. He had recently been named deputy director for the KGB department that ran Soviet spies in the United States and Canada. From the street, he called the U.S. embassy and said he wanted to defect to the United States. A quiet and dignified officer, Yurchenko was debriefed by the CIA before being flown from Naples, Italy, to Andrews Air Force Base outside Washington.

Alerted to the defection, Gerber remained late in his office at CIA headquarters, waiting for details. Sometime after 8:00 p.m., the cable secretariat called and said new messages had come in. Gerber walked down the stairs to get them, and as he climbed the stairs back to his office, he opened the envelope, found the most recent cable, and began to read.

He felt his throat tighten. The cable reported that Yurchenko told the debriefers that the KGB had a very good source, code-named ROBERT. Yurchenko did not know the true name of the source but identified him as a disgruntled former CIA trainee who was in the pipeline for the Moscow station and was subsequently fired.

Gerber suddenly felt overcome with emotion. He immediately put the pieces together: the KGB source was Edward Lee Howard, and he had betrayed Tolkachev. After all they had done to protect Tolkachev—after all the concealments, identity transfers, surveillance detection runs, electronic communications gear, Tropel cameras, and messages urging Tolkachev to be careful—the billion dollar spy had been destroyed by one of their own, by a failed trainee.[1]

Yurchenko's mention of the mystery agent ROBERT led to an internal meeting at the CIA. The CIA's quasi-independent security office wasn't yet convinced of the link and said there were several possible suspects. But Gerber was adamant. "This is undoubtedly Howard," he insisted. The clue was unambiguous; Yurchenko was talking about a trainee who had been fired and was in the pipeline for assignment to Moscow. That description fit Howard perfectly.[2]

More than two years had passed since Howard had been forced out of the CIA, and for a long time the agency's attitude was to keep its problems to itself. Now the CIA informed the FBI they had a problem. The person known as ROBERT was Edward Lee Howard. But the hour was late.[3]

Howard's next planned meeting with the Soviets was to be in Mexico City, but he sent them a signal, changing it to Vienna. He flew there on August 6, 1985. Howard took with him his own handwritten notes about CIA matters on water-soluble paper, a trick he had learned in training. According to his wife, Mary, he received $100,000 on this trip. On August 12, he opened a Swiss bank account in Zurich and made a large deposit. The Soviets had a word of caution for Howard: One of their own officers had defected to the United States. Howard was told if he ever felt he was in trouble, he should go to any Soviet consulate.[4] On his return to New Mexico, Howard bought a metal "ammo box" and put inside $3,100 in $100 bills, $900 in $50 bills, a dozen one-ounce Canadian maple leaf gold coins, a hundred-troy-ounce bar of fine silver, and two gold Krugerrands. Howard then drove to a wooded area about three miles away from his house and buried the box.[5]

The FBI began an investigation, opening a file titled "Unknown Subject, Known as Robert." The file was created on August 5 or 6, according to an FBI official directly involved. The title of the file was changed to "Howard" within days. But the FBI did not contact Howard right away. Rather, it asked the Justice Department whether there was probable cause to arrest Howard. The response came back: no. Meanwhile, the department sought a court order to wiretap Howard's phones, which took some time. The bureau decided not to interview Howard immediately because that might alert him and make further investigation more difficult.[6]

In early August, FBI headquarters directed special agents in Albuquerque to "conduct discreet inquiries" about Howard's whereabouts and activities. Surveillance was begun on August 29 and was "carried out in a discreet, intelligence gathering mode, attempting to determine his routines."[7] The surveillance consisted of special FBI teams of watchers who are trained to blend in and look like civilians, as well as regular FBI special agents. With court approval, Howard's phone was tapped, and fixed-wing airplanes were used to keep an eye on his movements. The "discreet" surveillance of Howard was carried out from 7:00 a.m. until he went to bed in the evening.

On September 3, Howard bought a $10,000 U.S. Treasury certificate. His annual salary at the Legislative Finance Committee in New Mexico was $30,000.[8]

On September 10, Howard drove out into the desert about three miles, stopped, and retraced his route, all the while being watched by the FBI. At one point, he pulled over to the side of the road and turned off his car lights, attempting to spot the surveillance. The FBI decided it was time to confront him. The FBI had obtained Howard's psychiatric evaluations and other evidence "which indicated that Howard would probably break in an interview and confess his espionage." The word came from Washington: go ahead. Howard was put under more intensive, twenty-four-hour FBI surveillance on September 18.

The next day, he was called at his office at 2:00 p.m. and asked to come to the lobby of the Hilton hotel in Santa Fe, where the FBI wanted to talk to him. On the phone, Howard sounded concerned, but fifteen minutes later he showed up at the hotel. The FBI agents took him to room 327. He was told that he was being questioned about working with the KGB and that he had been implicated by a defector "in London." Howard adamantly denied making contact with the Soviets and angrily accused the CIA of being out to get him. Asked about trips to Vienna, Howard quickly suggested that the FBI check the "paper trail," his American Express card receipts, and see that he had not been to Vienna, although he mentioned he had been elsewhere in Austria in 1984 on business. What Howard didn't say is that he had carefully avoided using the American Express card on the trip. About twenty minutes into the interview, Howard said the FBI was denying him his rights and he wanted to consult with an attorney. The FBI agents agreed; he was free to leave. Howard got up out of his seat and began to walk out of the room, but as he did, the FBI told him that if he did not cooperate, they would begin a full-scale investigation, interrogating his wife, relatives, employer, and associates. Howard reconsidered and sat down.

Then the FBI agents said Howard should take a polygraph examination at some later point, suggesting that if he were innocent, the lie detector would clear him and the FBI could look for the "true" suspect. Howard adamantly refused, saying he had been "screwed" by the polygraph in the past, reiterated that he was innocent, and again demanded time to consult a lawyer. The FBI then switched gears and said Howard would have to take a polygraph *before* seeing his lawyer. At that, Howard grew irate and said the FBI could do whatever it had to, including search his house. The FBI agents asked if he would sign a consent to be searched. Howard refused. The FBI agents said if he reconsidered, they would be around the next morning, and they gave him a phone number to call.[9]

The next day, a Friday, late in the day, Howard called the FBI agents in the hotel room, saying he had talked with a lawyer and suggested that, despite his fear of the polygraph test, he might agree to go through with it, to get the FBI "off his back" and to prove his innocence. His tone seemed cooperative, a sharp change from the day before. He told the FBI that on Sunday he was going to Austin, Texas, on business and would get back in touch when he returned on Monday afternoon.[10] After Howard's phone call, the FBI decided to revert to "discreet" surveillance, "in order to avoid antagonizing" him.[11]

The FBI had trouble keeping an eye on Howard's house at 108 Verano Loop, located in a desert area with wide open terrain. They couldn't find a neighboring house to use for a lookout, so they parked an empty van with a video camera across the street from Howard's low-slung single-story home. The video signal was transmitted by microwave to a trailer a short distance away and monitored by a single FBI special agent. FBI surveillance teams were also parked just outside the subdivision, to follow Howard in case he left, but they could not see the house or the exits of the subdivision. The entire watch depended on the video feed from the empty van to the trailer and on the lone agent to alert the others. The agent was assigned an eighteen-hour duty shift, from 3:00 p.m. on Saturday until 9:00 a.m. on Sunday.

Inside the trailer, he thought the video image from the van was poor.

On Saturday, in the early evening, Howard and his wife hired a babysitter and went out to a local restaurant, Alfonso's. They took their red Oldsmobile but left a second car, a Jeep, in the driveway. The lone agent in the trailer didn't see the Oldsmobile leave, so the surveillance teams were not dispatched to follow Howard. The babysitter made calls from Howard's home phone that were picked up by the FBI tap, but still the surveillance teams did not move. Mary even called the house from the restaurant and had a conversation with the babysitter, but this did not trigger the surveillance teams. About 7:30 p.m., the surveillance teams decided to conduct a drive-by of the house because so little had been seen or heard. Nothing unusual came from the drive-by, either.[12]

The FBI completely missed Edward Lee Howard and Mary Howard. On the way home from the restaurant, Mary was at the wheel and took the car on a winding route, a surveillance detection run like those they had practiced a few years before. At one point, the car stopped near downtown, her husband jumped out, and she flipped up a makeshift Jack-in-the-Box dummy in his place. It was made from a Styrofoam head on which Ed had drawn a face; a brown wig; an orange-and-white baseball cap with the word "Navajo" on the front; a two-foot-long stick; and a tan waist-length jacket. Before he departed, Howard told his wife to drive straight home with the dummy in the passenger seat, open the garage door with the remote control, pull in, and close the door.

The ruse was taught them by the CIA. But it wasn't necessary. No one was following them. The lone FBI agent in the trailer, supposedly watching a video feed from the van, never saw Mary Howard's return in the Oldsmobile with the dummy in the passenger seat. The surveillance teams never spotted the Oldsmobile either. When she was back home, Mary Howard dialed the phone number of her husband's psychiatrist and played a tape over the phone of Howard's voice, asking for an appointment. This was intended as a diversion. The voice was picked up by the FBI wiretap.[13]

After his jump from the Oldsmobile, Howard jogged to his office in Santa Fe, wrote out a resignation letter to his boss, and caught an airport shuttle to Albuquerque under the alias "J. Preston." He flew to Tucson, Arizona. In a motel room there, he dyed his hair but didn't like it and washed out the dye.[14] Early Sunday, he went to the airport and bought tickets for flights from Tucson to St. Louis, New York, London, and Copenhagen, arriving in Denmark on Monday morning. He paid for the $1,053 fare on his TWA credit card. He then flew on to Helsinki.[15]

While Howard was jetting off, the FBI knocked on his front door in Santa Fe. It was 3:05 p.m. on Sunday. The special agents had just received word from Texas of an interview the FBI conducted there with Howard's friend Bosch. The FBI agents felt that Bosch had corroborated the accusation that Howard gave information to the Soviets.[16]

The FBI special agents asked Mary where Howard was. Mary said he was out jogging and would return in half an hour.[17]

He never did.

On Monday, a federal warrant was issued for the arrest of Edward Lee Howard on charges of espionage.[18] But he had eluded the FBI, and they would never catch up. In Helsinki, Howard contacted the Soviets on Monday and crossed the border on Tuesday, smuggled in the trunk of a car. He was granted asylum by the Soviet Union in 1986, the first CIA officer ever to defect.

In the subsequent investigation, Mary Howard was interviewed repeatedly by the FBI. She gradually revealed what she knew about his trips to Vienna and contacts with the Soviets.

Mary "admitted her knowledge and participation in Ed's espionage activities" and passed two polygraph tests, the FBI records show. With her help, the FBI dug up Howard's buried ammo box in the desert, recovered the makeshift Jack-in-the-Box head and disguise, and learned of his Swiss bank account in Zurich. She eventually "disclosed all that could have been helpful" to the FBI. Mary continued to receive phone calls from Howard and visited him in Moscow. She was never prosecuted. They divorced in 1996.[19]

Howard published a memoir, *Safe House*, in 1995, that is full of deceptions, including a denial that he betrayed Tolkachev.[20]

He died at fifty years old in Moscow on July 12, 2002, as a result of a fall at his home.[21]

# 21

# "FOR FREEDOM"

**A**dolf Tolkachev fell into the dark place he feared most—the hands of the KGB. He was interrogated in prison and confessed to spying but steadfastly insisted his family did not know. The KGB found plenty of incriminating evidence, including stacks of rubles, the Tropel spy cameras, and the CIA's maps, sketches, and meeting schedules. The KGB also discovered the library sign-out sheet the CIA forged to cover Tolkachev's tracks and the pen with the L-pill inside.[1]

Tolkachev was convicted of espionage and sentenced to death by a three-member military tribunal. As the sentence was announced, Tolkachev stood straight upright, wearing a loose-fitting sport coat and open-collared shirt, eyeglasses in his breast pocket. Two guards flanked him, seated.

"Give your name correctly," the judge demanded.

"Tol-ka-chev," he replied firmly. "Adolf Georgievich." He gave his age, birthplace, and education.

Where did you work before the arrest, and in what position?

"Before my arrest, I had worked at the Research Institute of Radio Engineering, in the position of chief designer."

The judge read out the verdict: guilty of treason in the form of espionage, punishable by death.

Tolkachev looked straight ahead, emotionless. The two guards stood and grasped him by the elbows.

Later, his appeal for clemency was rejected.[2]

After the sentence was declared, Tolkachev was granted a farewell visit by his son, Oleg, for fifteen minutes in a crowded prison conference room. Tolkachev had worried about his son all the years of his spying. The moment was difficult for both of them. Oleg was just as scornful of the Soviet system as his parents. He remembered his mother and father reading the prohibited works of Solzhenitsyn. But he never asked where the Western rock music and the drawing pens had come from. He never knew of his father's spying.

Tolkachev told his son he was sorry. Oleg replied, "No, no, no"—that he shouldn't say it.[3]

President Reagan, who was briefed by Stansfield Turner on the eve of his first inaugural about the agent in Moscow, now got the whole story of how Tolkachev had been betrayed. The President's Foreign Intelligence Advisory Board laid out the details in a secret report that Reagan took to Camp David to read on September 26, 1986. Both the CIA and the FBI were sharply criticized in the report; the CIA was taken to task for not reporting sooner to the FBI that Howard could be a security risk.[4] The advisory board came to the Oval Office on October 2 to brief Reagan. In handwritten notes from the meeting, the White House chief of staff, Donald T. Regan, noted that "in one year" of training at CIA Howard "picked up quite a bit."[5] All of which was now lost.

On September 25, 1986, the Soviet Politburo met in Moscow.

The head of the KGB, Viktor Chebrikov, reported that Tol-kachev's death sentence had been carried out the previous day. Gorbachev noted that "American intelligence paid him gener-ously." Chebrikov told the Politburo, "This agent betrayed very important military-technical secrets." On October 22, the Soviet news agency Tass announced that Tolkachev had been executed for "high treason in the form of spying."[6]

Natasha was also prosecuted on grounds that she knew of Tol-kachev's espionage activity. Libin, her former supervisor and fam-ily friend, wrote later that she did not confess, but was betrayed to the KGB by an informer in prison. She was sentenced to three years. She served the first at Potma, a harsh labor camp 242 miles southeast of Moscow that had been part of the Soviet gulag. For the second year, she was transferred to a less severe penal colony, making bricks, in Ufa, 730 miles east of Moscow, where Oleg managed to visit her. She was released after two years under a broad amnesty and returned to Moscow in 1987. She could not resume her profession as an engineer, so she found work as a duty operator in a boiler room. She kept her head high, read books, and paid attention to the lively politics of the Gorbachev period. She went to Memorial, the group formed during the glasnost era to preserve the memory of those who perished in Stalin's camps, and wrote out the details of how her parents had been repressed, noting that both were rehabilitated after Stalin's death.[7]

In 1990, Natasha was stricken with ovarian cancer. She wrote to the American embassy saying she was seriously ill and asking for medical assistance. She said she was the wife of Adolf Tol-kachev, who "worked for the benefit of America and for freedom in our country for many years," according to Libin, who helped her draft the letter. Libin recalled that the embassy wrote back simply saying they got many requests and could not help every-one who asked. The embassy apparently did not recognize who she was. The CIA learned of her appeal only years later.[8]

Natasha remained angry about only one thing: Adik had misled her and continued his espionage after he promised to stop. It was not the spying that she objected to but the danger to the family. She died of cancer on March 31, 1991, just as the Soviet party-state that she and Adik had both loathed was about to expire. She was laid to rest alongside her father, Ivan Kuzmin, the newspaper editor, in Moscow's Donskoye Cemetery.[9]

On August 11, 2014, the CIA hung a portrait of Tolkachev at headquarters alongside other paintings that depict the agency's greatest operations. The portrait by the artist Kathy Krantz Fieramosca of New York shows Tolkachev in his apartment, his hands grasping the Pentax 35 mm camera, photographing a secret document illuminated by two desk lamps. A clock shows it is almost 12:30 p.m., the end of the lunch break. At the unveiling ceremony, a senior CIA official said that Tolkachev is portrayed in the painting with "fierce determination," "intense concentration," and, knowing his fate if caught, "a trace of fear."

# EPILOGUE

On January 19, 1991, the third day of Operation Desert Storm, Larry Pitts roused himself at 4:00 a.m. at the King Faisal Air Base at Tabuk, northwestern Saudi Arabia. He ate a breakfast of scrambled eggs and pita bread, listened to the intelligence briefing, suited up, fastened on his survival vest, grabbed his helmet bag, and headed out to the tarmac. In the predawn darkness stood an F-15C fighter, the most advanced warplane ever built by the United States and the most lethal air-to-air combatant in history. Sixty-four feet long, with a wingspan of forty-three feet, built of aluminum, titanium, steel, and fiberglass, the fighter had twin Pratt & Whitney turbofans that could send it straight up in the sky, like a rocket. Everything about the F-15 was the pinnacle of American technology, from a powerful pulse-Doppler lookdown radar, to wings that could survive battle damage, to sophisticated electronic jammers inside a black box tucked behind the pilot.

Pitts was preparing to fly a fighter that was designed, down to the smallest detail, to defeat Soviet MiGs. Saddam Hussein's air force possessed one of the largest fleets of MiG warplanes outside the Soviet Union. In the first two days of war, the aerial battles over Iraq followed the same scenario that had been written for the skies over Europe if hostilities broke out in the Cold War. Both the United States and the Soviet Union designed, built, and deployed air superiority fighters that, it was assumed, would face each other over Germany and Czechoslovakia. But the battles over Iraq showed they were not evenly matched. The American pilots and their warplanes had an edge, gained from intensive training and penetrating intelligence, especially the fruits of espionage by Adolf Tolkachev.

On this morning, Captain Pitts walked slowly around the aircraft for a visual check, scanned the logbook, then climbed into the cockpit. Once in the sky, he enjoyed stunning visibility in all directions. The plane sloped down from the pilot's shoulders. The sensation was like sitting on the end of a pencil.[1]

Pitts was airborne at 5:00 a.m., flying as the right wingman in a "four-ship," a formation of four F-15C aircraft. Operation Desert Storm was a military campaign to force Iraq out of Kuwait. The Fifty-Eighth Tactical Fighter Squadron of the U.S. Air Force Thirty-Third Tactical Fighter Wing, known informally as the Gorillas, had already flown three missions into Iraq. Pitts was thirty-four years old and had longed to fly since he was a boy growing up in Anchorage, Alaska.

In the U.S. Air Force, he had trained for hundreds of hours on the F-15C, but this was his first war—and his first days in combat.

Pitts and the plane he was flying embodied what the air force and the navy had learned from the debacle of Vietnam. Back then, F-4 Phantom pilots had often been outgunned by Soviet-built MiG fighters flown by the North Vietnamese. The Phantom pilots needed to flip twelve switches to fire a missile; they lost precious seconds to the more nimble MiGs. By contrast, in the F-15 cockpit a pilot could search for, detect, lock on, and fire at an approaching MiG without ever taking his hands off the throttle and stick or looking down from his heads-up display. He just had to move the fingers of his left and right hands on buttons, what pilots called playing the piccolo. The F-15C's chaff dispensers carried dielectric fibers that were cut to lengths designed precisely to blind MiG radars. The F-15C tactical electronic warfare suite was wired to thwart Soviet avionics. The F-15C could accurately target and fire a missile at an enemy MiG beyond visual range, or so far away that Pitts could not see it.

In Vietnam, American pilots used rigid tactics, flying in close formations that were easily outfoxed by the North Vietnamese fighters. After the war, the United States transformed pilot training, and a new generation was encouraged to be more flexible and make their own combat decisions. Soviet pilots had traditionally been told what to do from the ground; Americans were trained to know the enemy's capabilities and counter them on the fly. To help them react faster, data links were built to bring American pilots all the information they needed at high speed. Pitts was a product of this transformation in training. He had flown three "Red Flag" exercises, simulating possible dogfights against a Soviet bloc adversary. He had studied the threat manuals on the MiG-25 and the MiG-29, and his generation of pilots had benefited from information gleaned from CONSTANT PEG, a top secret operation in which air force pilots trained against older Soviet-built MiGs in the Nevada desert.

Pitts and the other three F-15C pilots refueled from an aerial tanker and then waited. A bombing mission they were assigned to accompany was canceled. For a while, they remained aloft because of intelligence that Saddam Hussein might flee Iraq. By midday, it appeared Hussein wasn't going anywhere, and the four-ship returned to their base in Saudi Arabia. Pitts was thinking about getting some sleep.

Just minutes after touchdown, the Gorillas were ordered to

refuel and take off again. The mission was to fly over Iraq to see if the Americans could goad the reluctant Iraqi air force into the sky. In the early days of the war, it was an important objective to win total air superiority. Saddam possessed twenty-five of the fast MiG-25 interceptors and thirty of the latest MiG-29 fighters, with look-down, shoot-down radar, as well as hundreds of older Soviet-built aircraft. Iraq had been at war with Iran for eight years in the previous decade, so it was safe to assume that Iraqi pilots were experienced. But the Iraqis were avoiding an air battle, and not many were flying.

During the aerial refueling over Saudi Arabia, Pitts and his four-ship got word that two groups of "bogies"—unidentified planes—had been spotted by the powerful U.S. airborne early warning and control system, the E-3 Sentry, or AWACS, another technological triumph that could scan the airspace for hundreds of miles around. The four-ship headed north toward Iraq at slightly over the speed of sound, with Pitts on the right side of the formation.

Then the bogies became "bandits," positively identified as Iraqi fighters. Two of them were MiG-29s, and two were MiG-25s. The more modern MiG-29s veered away. But the high-speed MiG-25s were barreling directly at Pitts.

The MiG-25 once inspired fear in the West, where some thought it was the fastest aerial fighter in the world. But after Belenko flew a MiG-25 to Japan in 1976, it was found to be an interceptor, not a maneuvering fighter. From his training, Pitts knew the MiG-25 was powered by mammoth engines, but he also knew its limitations. The plane was sluggish at low altitudes, and the cockpit set low in the fuselage, so the pilot could not easily see behind him. The turning radius was wide. The radar's scan was narrow. The MiG-25 was no longer the mystery it once was: the United States knew about every wire and rivet.[2]

Two of the F-15Cs peeled away from the four-ship, leaving Pitts and his lead, Captain Rick Tollini, to deal with the MiG-25s. The Iraqi planes circled and came back again, straight at the Americans, who were flying at about fifteen thousand feet.

Suddenly the MiG-25s turned at "beam," or ninety degrees away from the oncoming American fighters, and dived to the deck—almost to the ground—covered with a low-lying fog. The break toward the deck was a classic Soviet tactic; at ninety degrees, there was a "notch" where the Doppler radar was weakest and might not see a moving target against the ground clutter. Pitts lost the MiG-25s from his radar. He feared the MiGs would reappear and take a shot at him before he could shoot them down.

The MiG-25 was not a ballet dancer in the air; it was a hurtling bullet. One of them returned almost instantly. Pitts got a radar signal: the plane was five miles off his nose. He was now at about thirteen thousand feet, but the MiG-25 was barely five hundred feet off the ground, flying left to right in front of him. The MiG-25 rocketed at 700 knots, or 805 miles per hour, faster than the speed of sound. The pilot probably did not see Pitts above him and might not have cared; he was trying to outrun danger. The astounding speed of the MiG-25 "gimballed" the F15's radar: it zoomed across, left to right, and exited the screen.

Pitts did not give up. He had lost radar lock again but could visually see the MiG-25, and all his training and his reflexes kicked in.

"Engaged!" he called to Tollini.

"Press!" Tollini responded—which meant that Pitts was now the shooter and Tollini would support him.

Pitts threw the F-15C into an inverted roll, known as a split-S maneuver. The F-15C dived after the MiG-25. The force of the roll thrust Pitts deep into his seat, at twelve times the force of gravity, for several seconds. The F-15C was rated for about nine times gravity. In his headpiece, Pitts heard the onboard computer shout a warning, "Over G! Over G!" But it was too late, his adrenaline was pumping, his decision made. He needed to align his plane's nose with the fleeing MiG-25 so he could shoot. Pitts dived twelve thousand feet and pulled up a mile or so behind the MiG-25, just slightly higher, and in pursuit. In the old days, an American pilot might have tried to fly under his quarry for a better radar lock, but Pitts enjoyed superb radar coverage in the F-15C and could stay just above and behind. He was in the "six" of the MiG-25, meaning at six o'clock, right behind him, putting the Iraqi pilot in mortal danger.

If the MiG-25 had blasted straight ahead at full speed, he might have outrun Pitts. But he did not. The pilot banked to the right, an evasive move, realizing that Pitts was preparing to fire. The Soviet-built plane slowed as it turned in the thicker air near the ground. Pitts banked too, but his turning radius was tighter, and his plane far more nimble. Soon he was advancing inside the MiG's turning circle, closing the gap, slightly behind the wing line of the enemy plane, the most vulnerable position for the MiG.

Pitts had eight missiles under the F-15C's belly and wings. He saw a big heat plume behind the MiG-25, an afterburner, so with his left hand he selected a 150-pound AIM-9 Sidewinder heat-seeking missile. He fired the missile with his right hand by pressing a button on the piccolo. But the MiG-25 just as quickly emitted a curtain of flares, which decoyed the missile, and it missed.

Pitts selected a 500-pound, radar-guided AIM-7 Sparrow missile, and when it locked on the enemy plane, a cue on the heads-up display flashed: "SHOOT." Pitts fired. The missile was designed to detonate next to the target, but a fuse malfunctioned; it flew right over the cockpit of the fleeing MiG without exploding and fell away.

Pitts quickly selected another heat-seeking Sidewinder missile. Now six thousand feet behind the MiG, he fired, but flares again threw it off.

Pitts had never fired a missile in combat; now he had fired three without success. The two planes, their history wrapped up in the Cold War, were thundering across the Iraqi desert, the MiG-25 at three hundred feet and the F-15C just above and behind, both now slower than before, but still at 575 miles per hour.

On his fourth try, Pitts selected another radar-guided AIM-7 Sparrow missile. This time, it flew right up the exhaust pipe of the MiG and blew it up. The MiG pilot ejected, and Pitts saw the seat whiz by his window. Just as the MiG exploded, another missile pierced the cloud—it was fired by Tollini. The fate of the pilot was not known, but ejecting at such high speed and low altitude is often not survivable.

Minutes later, Tollini downed the other MiG-25.

Heading back toward Saudi Arabia, Pitts tried to relax. He was low on fuel. After the rush of the engagement, his hands were shaking. At the tanker refueling, he had to back off, calm himself, and try again.

The two MiG-29s that Pitts and Tollini had seen earlier were shot down later that day. Three MiG-29s and two MiG-21s were shot down on January 17. The Iraqi losses continued, day after day. By the end of the war, U.S. Air Force planes had shot down thirty-nine airborne enemy aircraft, without losing one.[3] Sixteen of the U.S. kills involved missile shots that were fired beyond visual range, at fighters the U.S. pilots could not even see, a remarkable new dimension in air combat, made possible because the U.S. fighters, guided by AWACS, could shoot with little risk of accidentally hitting friendly aircraft.[4]

In direct aerial combat over Iraq, the U.S. Air Force downed every Soviet-built tactical fighter that it confronted. The reasons were many: superior technology, finely honed tactics, and vastly improved pilot training. But all of these advantages were bolstered by something less visible. The United States had collected every scrap of information it could find about Soviet planes, pilots, and radars, every photograph, diagram, and circuit board that could be obtained—by any means.

And for this, there was a spy.

Adolf Tolkachev's espionage is a Cold War story, but one that still resonates today. Human source intelligence remains indispensable to national security. As long as it is necessary to know an adversary—to steal secrets, uncover intentions, and crack open safes—it will be essential to recruit agents who can conquer their fear and cross over to the other side. It will be necessary to look them in the eye, earn their trust, calm their anxiety, and share their peril.

Tolkachev, an engineer and designer, stood apart from others who betrayed the Soviet Union and became agents for the United States. He did not belong to the Communist Party or serve in the military or the security agencies. Most of the others came from either the KGB or the GRU, Soviet military intelligence, including Penkovsky, Popov, Sheymov, Polyakov, and Kulak. Kuklinski, the agent in Poland who passed revealing material about Warsaw Pact war plans, was a Polish army colonel. Ogorodnik was a Soviet diplomat.

What makes Tolkachev's espionage even more remarkable is that he passed materials to the CIA literally under the nose of the KGB. Most of the twenty-one meetings were held within three miles of the front entrance of the KGB headquarters. Yet the spy and his handlers were never detected by the KGB. The Moscow station's painstaking tradecraft—identity transfer, street disguises, surveillance detection runs, the SRR-100 radio monitors—paid off handsomely.

The nature of the material from Tolkachev—the complex

diagrams, specifications, blueprints, and circuit boards from airborne radars and the disclosure of Soviet military research and development plans stretching a decade into the future—was extraordinary. Two U.S. intelligence and military experts who examined thousands of pages of Tolkachev's documents over a period of years said they never found a single page contaminated with disinformation, and they cross-checked the intelligence as far as they could with other sources.[5]

Tolkachev opened a window on Soviet intentions and capabilities, which were at the core of the CIA's mission. For the leadership of the United States, it was vitally important to know Soviet priorities in military research and development, as well as capabilities—what they could do and could not do. For decades, there were holes and misjudgments in U.S. intelligence on Soviet intentions and capabilities.[6] But when it came to air defenses, Soviet tactical fighters, interceptors, radars, avionics, and guidance systems that would confront Americans in any hot war, Tolkachev delivered.

His intelligence arrived just as the U.S. Navy and the U.S. Air Force were undertaking the revolution in pilot training in classrooms at the navy's elite Fighter Weapons School, known as Top Gun, in Miramar, California, and the U.S. Air Force Weapons School at Nellis Air Force Base in Nevada. No scrap was too small for those preparing to fight the next American air war. Intelligence gleaned from Tolkachev's documents was briefed to Top Gun instructors and pilots.

As a result, the United States has enjoyed almost total air superiority over Soviet-built fighters for more than two decades: in the Persian Gulf War of 1991, in which Pitts downed the MiG-25 over Iraq; in 1995, when the U.S. and its allies forced the Serbs of the former Yugoslavia to recognize the independence of Bosnia-Herzegovina; and in 1999, in stopping an ethnic cleansing campaign in Kosovo. Both Iraq and Yugoslavia flew Soviet-made

MiG warplanes. There were American losses to ground fire, but the United States dominated the skies. The record is stark: for every six enemy aircraft air force pilots shot down in Korea, the United States lost one. In Vietnam, the United States lost one airplane for every two enemy planes shot down. Thus, the kill ratios went from six to one in Korea, and two to one in Vietnam, to forty-eight to zero for the air force in the wars in Iraq and the Balkans. The impressive advances in American technology and pilot training were essential to this achievement.[7] But Tolkachev's espionage also contributed; the United States possessed the blueprints of radar in every major Soviet fighter of the 1980s.

Tolkachev also provided the United States with renewed confidence in weapons systems that cost billions of dollars and took years to develop, especially those designed to strike the Soviet Union at low altitude. The terrain-hugging, winged cruise missile was flight-tested and deployed in the years of Tolkachev's espionage. The Soviet leaders knew it was a potent threat. In Moscow on June 4, 1984, Anatoly Chernyaev, who later became Mikhail Gorbachev's national security adviser, went to a military briefing at the Central Committee. The briefing was titled "The Characteristics of Modern Warfare," and Chernyaev wrote in his diary afterward that he saw films about American weapons systems.

"It was amazing," he wrote, "missiles homing in on their targets from hundreds and thousands of kilometers away; aircraft carriers, submarines that could do anything; winged missiles that, like in a cartoon, could be guided through a canyon and hit a target 10 meters in diameter from 2,500 kilometers away. An incredible breakthrough of modern technology. And, of course, unthinkably expensive."[8]

The "winged missiles" were not a cartoon; the U.S. cruise missile was a reality. The Soviet radars could not see them coming, and the CIA knew why.

# A NOTE ON THE INTELLIGENCE

Adolf Tolkachev's espionage produced intelligence so voluminous that the U.S. military and intelligence community continued to draw on it for valuable details well into the 1990s. The information became part of the finished intelligence reports of the era that were sent to the White House and policy makers, many of which are now declassified. The highest-level reports, National Intelligence Estimates, blend reporting and analysis and include details from many different sources. They do not mention Tolkachev by name. But they reflect the impact of his spying.

In March 1976, a year before Tolkachev first volunteered, a U.S. intelligence memorandum described Soviet air defenses as deficient, including the lack of a look-down, shoot-down radar and weapons capability.[1] That was the view of the CIA's in-house analysts, but in the summer and early autumn the CIA sought a second opinion about Soviet capabilities. In an unusual experiment, the CIA allowed an outside team of hawkish experts and analysts to critique its annual estimate of Soviet forces. Among other things, the critique examined Soviet air defenses.[2] The outside team, known as Team B, was quite uncertain. It found evidence that Soviet air defenses, measured by equipment, were becoming "formidable" but, given operational problems seen in troop exercises, could be "marginal," and the actual situation was unknown because "hard intelligence" was lacking.[3] Thus, the CIA had multiple answers to sort out: Soviet air defenses were weak, or strong and growing stronger.

The United States needed a better answer. The Soviet Union possessed the longest borders in the world, about thirty-seven thousand miles. To stop intruders, it needed weapons and radars both on land and in the air. If there were gaps in its air defenses, they could be exploited. Within a few years, Tolkachev provided the answer: the system was weak, and the vulnerability could be exploited.

In 1979, a National Intelligence Estimate reaffirmed the Soviets had "major technical deficiencies in their ability to intercept penetrators at low altitudes."[4] In 1981, a CIA internal memorandum noted that the Soviet Union had little capability against low-flying targets, Soviet air defenses were technically crude, and "they rarely practice low altitude air defense operations." Moreover, the command-and-control system for air defenses was poor, and its troops "are not among the best and often perform poorly in training exercises." The bottom line, the memo concluded, there is "a widely held feeling that the Soviets are really quite inept in this area."[5]

In 1983, a U.S. intelligence report asserted that low-flying U.S. cruise missiles and advanced bombers "have the potential to render obsolescent billions of rubles in Soviet investment" in air defenses—they could fly right under them.[6] In March 1984, the CIA's annual intelligence estimate on Soviet forces described how Moscow was struggling to improve air defenses, including the effort to build improved "data links" between the new Soviet fighter jets, radars, surface-to-air missiles, and airborne warning and control planes.[7]

The conclusions in all these reports came in part from thousands of pages of secret Soviet documents delivered by Tolkachev to the CIA.

By 1985, the CIA had a precise fix on Soviet capabilities for airborne radar. A 1985 report mentioned five major areas in which the Soviets were taking action "to enhance their air defense capabilities." Every one of them had been compromised by Tolkachev on his rolls of film and his notes, including the airborne warning and control plane and look-down, shoot-down radar.[8]

Separate from the finished intelligence, Tolkachev's material was also fed directly into U.S. military research and development programs. Often, Tolkachev's information would be most helpful to the technical wizards who were building black boxes and other advanced technology to defeat Soviet radars and avionics. One such project was a radar jammer. In the late 1970s, the U.S. Navy and the U.S. Air Force were collaborating on a jammer for their latest fighter planes. The project was in its early stages when Tolkachev reported on Soviet research into pulse-Doppler radar. For many years, the Soviets had lagged behind the West in the development of pulse-Doppler, which allows radar to effectively look down at very high speeds and discriminate a moving target against the ground clutter of the earth. The U.S. radar jammer, as originally planned, lacked a way to counter a pulse-Doppler radar. After a study by the U.S. Defense Science Board in 1980, the jammer design was modified to include a beam that would confuse pulse-Doppler radars, like the ZASLON. This change was made precisely at the time that Tolkachev was providing information about Soviet radars. The Airborne Self-Protection Jammer was an ambitious project, designed to deceive enemy radar into thinking a plane was at a different location. It might have been an important advantage, had the Cold War ever become hot.[9]

Tolkachev delivered to the United States a library of top secret documents about the design and capability of radars deployed on

Soviet fighters and interceptors, including the MiG-23 fighter, the MiG-25 high-altitude interceptor, the MiG-31 interceptor, and the MiG-29 and Su-27 multi-role fighters. In particular, Tolkachev compromised several versions of the SAPFIR radar and the ZASLON radar. Tolkachev also carted away Soviet secrets on surface-to-air missiles and the sensitive Soviet project called SHTORA, or "window blind," which was designed to conceal surface-to-air missiles from the radars of target aircraft.

In another intelligence windfall, Tolkachev was the first to alert the United States that the Soviet Union was starting to develop an advanced airborne warning and control system, or AWACS, a flying radar station. Once Tolkachev pointed it out, U.S. spy satellites confirmed it. The twenty-ton radar, named SHMEL, or "bumblebee," would be carried on a modified Ilyushin Il-76 military transport jet, with a flying disk for the radar dome, not unlike the advanced U.S. E-3 Sentry system, based on a modified Boeing 707, which was already flying. The new AWACS would be critical to Soviet efforts to deal with the low-altitude gap and the lack of look-down radar capability. A flying radar would provide much greater detection of threats and deliver data and instructions to airborne pilots.[10] The Tolkachev documents showed the SHMEL would have look-down capability. The radar could potentially track fifty or more targets simultaneously over land.[11]

Soviet national air defenses were stitched together from thousands of separate units. There were 1,250 ground-based radars, about 25 percent of them supporting ground control centers to direct pilots to their targets; about 1,000 surface-to-air complexes and 12,800 surface-to-air missile launchers; and 3,250 fighters capable of air intercept missions at some ninety airfields.[12] For the system to be effective, they would all have to be knitted together—and work. With a strong ethos of centralization, the Soviet Union had in the past relied on ground-controlled intercept, meaning that controllers in radar stations on the ground would give directions to fighters and interceptors—where to fly, when to shoot. Soviet pilots had little autonomy. This was slow and clumsy. Most of the radar operators on the ground couldn't see beyond their own unit's coverage. A modernized Soviet AWACS could change all that. Thanks to Tolkachev, the United States had a front-row seat to Soviet AWACS technology. A CIA memo written in 1981 noted that the Soviet AWACS was "still in the early stages of field testing" but said the radar "has detected targets over land as low as 300 meters," or 984 feet. That would help, but not entirely close the low-altitude radar gap. The U.S. bombers were planning to fly even lower, at 800 feet altitude or less, and cruise missiles would sneak in at just 50 feet above the ground. Moreover, the Soviets knew, and feared, that the cruise missiles were relatively inexpensive and thus the United States could send swarms of them racing to targets, undetected.[13] By September 1981, a secret twenty-three-page U.S. defense intelligence estimate on the Soviet AWACS had been prepared. The estimate had the express purpose of helping create countermeasures to the Soviet aircraft and noted that there would be gaps in the Soviet AWACS coverage—gaps that Western planes could sneak through—and that Moscow still faced serious difficulties in spotting cruise missiles and future U.S. stealth bombers.[14]

The Tolkachev documents also revealed that the MiG-31 fighter, equipped with the ZASLON radar, carried an air-to-air data link that would allow it to function as a mini-AWACS on its own, sharing radar information with other fighters. Previous attempts to break such a data link and "read" it had proven almost impossible for the United States. But now, with Tolkachev's documents identifying what each bit of information meant, the link could be cracked open, an incredible breakthrough. The United States could intercept Soviet AWACS signals, to detect—and deceive—the pilots who depended on them.[15]

The United States was reading the enemy's mail, in real time.

# ACKNOWLEDGMENTS

Two retired CIA officers, each with decades of experience in the clandestine service, generously contributed time and effort to this project. Burton Gerber, who served as both chief of the Moscow station and Soviet division chief, devoted hours to research into the original cables, with the agency's approval and clearance of the materials before release to me. He provided invaluable guidance and context for the Tolkachev story. Barry Royden, who authored an internal CIA monograph on the operation in the 1990s, was an early enthusiast for the book and a source of great insight. Both helped to navigate the declassification process and demystify the world of espionage.

I wish to express special thanks to Ron, chief of the CE division at the CIA when the project began, who provided critical support for declassification of the operational files. He remains in the clandestine service so cannot be further identified. I also benefited from the recollections of David Forden, Robert Fulton, Sandra Grimes, Gardner "Gus" Hathaway, Thomas Mills, Robert Morris, James Olson, Marti Peterson, William Plunkert, David Rolph, Michael Sellers, Haviland Smith, and Robert Wallace. Catherine Guilsher generously provided recollections of John's life and times. Karin Hathaway graciously helped with memories of Gus. John Ehrman provided an important link to the agency. My thanks also to several retired intelligence officers who agreed to share their knowledge and recollections without being identified.

In Moscow, I was assisted by Anna Masterova, who skillfully sifted archives, conducted interviews, and translated. I also am grateful to Irina Ostrovskaya of Memorial International for archival records on the repression of the Kuzmin family. Volodya Alexandrov and Sergei Belyakov were, as always, selfless and ready to help at every turn. Masha Lipman has been a peerless source of wisdom and insight about Russia for two decades, and provided perceptive and detailed comments on the draft manuscript.

Maryanne Warrick transcribed interviews and carried out research assignments, and I am grateful for her precision and tireless efforts. Charissa Ford and Julie Tate also contributed research.

At the *Washington Post*, I was fortunate to be part of a golden age of journalism built by Don Graham and Katharine Graham, and I am grateful to the executive editors Benjamin C. Bradlee and Leonard Downie for giving me the opportunity to contribute to it. I am particularly thankful for years of advice and support from Philip Bennett, a colleague and friend with whom I shared some of the best years in the newsroom and who gave me an important critique of the manuscript. Robert Kaiser has been a model and mentor, and Joby Warrick a valued friend and adviser. Peter Finn and Michael Birnbaum, talented Moscow bureau chiefs, offered their cooperation and help.

I am indebted to H. Keith Melton for sharing images from his collection and to Kathy Krantz Fieramosca for permission to reproduce her painting of Adolf Tolkachev. I wish to thank Jack

F. Matlock, Dick Combs, and James Schumaker for recollections of the 1977 fire at the Moscow embassy. For insights about radar and air defenses, I am grateful to David Kenneth Ellis, William Andrews, Robin Lee, and Larry Pitts. I also received valuable advice and help from Robert Berls, Benjamin Weiser, Fritz Ermarth, Charles Battaglia, Jerrold Schecter, Robert Monroe, Peter Earnest, George Little, Louis Denes, Matthew Aid, Joshua Pollack, and Jason Saltoun-Ebin. Cathy Cox of the Air Force Historical Research Agency at Maxwell Air Force Base fulfilled requests professionally and promptly. I am grateful for access to the collections of the National Security Archive, Washington, D.C.; the National Archives at College Park, Maryland; the U.S. Naval Institute Oral History Program, Annapolis, Maryland; the Ronald Reagan Presidential Library, Simi Valley, California; and the Russian State Archive of the Economy, Moscow.

Glenn Frankel has been a mentor on writing for years and once again gave me perceptive and valuable comments on the manuscript. I am also grateful to Svetlana Savranskaya for comments on a draft and sharing her knowledge about how to pry Cold War secrets out of the world's archives.

For the second time in a decade, the wise and patient editing of Kris Puopolo steered me from a hazy vision and a box full of loose documents to a finished narrative, and I am deeply appreciative. My thanks, too, to Bill Thomas for believing this book would be worthy of Doubleday. I thank Daniel Meyer for keeping the project on track. I'm grateful to Esther Newberg for being an extraordinary agent. Her first phone call upon reading the draft manuscript, full of enthusiasm, was a moment to cherish.

My deepest gratitude goes to my wife, Carole, who lovingly guided our own Moscow station, with our sons, Daniel and Benjamin, when I was a correspondent for the *Washington Post* in the late 1990s. She offered advice and insight at every stage of this project. More important, she endured the disruptions and unpredictable twists and turns that come with a life in journalism but never lost a conviction that discovering the world was a voyage worth taking. For as long as I can recall, a small scrap of paper has been fastened to our refrigerator door with a proverb from Saint Augustine: "The world is a book, and those who do not travel, read only a page." With her steadfast support and participation, the world is, once again, a book.

# NOTES

The Tolkachev story is based, in part, on 944 pages of declassified operational files, primarily cable traffic between CIA headquarters and the Moscow station from 1977 to 1985. The cables are cited individually in the notes below by sender, recipient, date, and time-date stamp. The time-date format is as follows: the first two digits are the date, the next four are the time in GMT that the cable was sent, followed by a Z, such as 131423Z for a cable sent on the thirteenth at 2:23 p.m. GMT. In some cables, this time-date information was redacted; they are identified by date where possible.

The CIA cables were often written in a clipped, minimalist style, with some words dropped. When quoting directly, the author has preserved this style, verbatim.

The documents were reviewed by the CIA for information considered sensitive, and that information was redacted prior to release to the author. The CIA placed no restrictions on the author's use of the documents it released, nor did the agency review the manuscript prior to publication. Selected CIA cables are posted at www.davidehoffman.com.

The FBI released records on the Howard investigation in response to a Freedom of Information Act (FOIA) request by the author.

The book is also based on interviews and additional documents obtained by the author from other sources.

## PROLOGUE

1. William Plunkert, correspondence with author, March 28, 2014; Moscow station to headquarters, Dec. 8, 1982, 081335Z.
2. Barry G. Royden, "Tolkachev, a Worthy Successor to Penkovsky," *Studies in Intelligence* 47, no. 3 (2003): 22. Also Robert Wallace and H. Keith Melton, *Spycraft: The Secret History of the CIA's Spytechs from Communism to al-Qaeda*, with Henry Robert Schlesinger (New York: Dutton, 2008), 130–31.

## 1: OUT OF THE WILDERNESS

1. Roberta Wohlstetter, *Pearl Harbor: Warning and Decision* (Stanford, Calif.: Stanford University Press, 1962), 48–49. Also see Joint Committee on the Investigation of the Pearl Harbor Attack, "Investigation of the Pearl Harbor Attack," U.S. Senate, 79th Cong., 2nd sess., Report no. 244, July 20, 1946, 257–58. In his memoirs, Truman wrote that he had "often thought that if there had been something like coordination of information in the government it would have been difficult, if not impossible, for the Japanese to succeed in the sneak attack at Pearl Harbor." Harry S. Truman, *Memoirs*, vol. 2, *Years of Trial and Hope* (Garden City, N.Y.: Doubleday, 1956), 56.
2. Woodrow J. Kuhns, ed., *Assessing the Soviet Threat: The Early Cold War Years* (Washington, D.C.: Center for the Study of Intelligence, CIA, 1997), 1, 3.
3. The agency toppled leaders in Iran and Guatemala, carried out the abortive landing at the Bay of Pigs, warned of Soviet missiles in Cuba, and was drawn deeply into the Vietnam War, eventually managing a full-scale ground war in Laos. U.S. Senate, "Final Report of the Select Committee to Study Governmental Operations with Respect to Intelligence Activities," 94th Cong., 2nd sess., bk. 1, "Foreign and Military Intelligence," pt. 6, "History of the Central Intelligence Agency," April 26, 1976, Report 94-755, 109.
4. Dmitri Volkogonov, *Stalin: Triumph and Tragedy*, trans. Harold Shukman (London: Weidenfeld & Nicolson, 1991), 502–24.

5. David E. Murphy, Sergei A. Kondrashev, and George Bailey, *Battleground Berlin: CIA vs. KGB in the Cold War* (New Haven, Conn.: Yale University Press, 1997), ix.

6. "Report on the Covert Activities of the Central Intelligence Agency," Special Study Group, J. H. Doolittle, chairman, Washington, D.C., Sept. 30, 1954, 7.

7. Richard Helms, *A Look over My Shoulder: A Life in the Central Intelligence Agency*, with William Hood (New York: Random House, 2003), 124.

8. Evan Thomas, *The Very Best Men: The Daring Early Years of the CIA* (New York: Simon & Schuster, 1995), 25, 30, 36, 142–52. Also, U.S. Senate, "Final Report," pt. 6, "History of the Central Intelligence Agency." Richard Immerman, "A Brief History of the CIA," in *The Central Intelligence Agency: Security Under Scrutiny*, ed. Athan Theoharis et al. (Westport, Conn.: Greenwood Press, 2006), 21.

9. Helms, *Look over My Shoulder*, 124, 127.

10. Gerald K. Haines and Robert E. Leggett, eds., *CIA's Analysis of the Soviet Union, 1947–1991: A Documentary Collection* (Washington, D.C.: Center for the Study of Intelligence, 2001), 35–41.

11. Kuhns, *Assessing the Soviet Threat*, 12.

12. Richard Helms, interview with Robert M. Hathaway, May 30, 1984, released by CIA in 2004. Hathaway is co-author of an internal monograph on Helms as director.

13. This account of the Popov case is based on five sources. William Hood, *Mole: The True Story of the First Russian Intelligence Officer Recruited by the CIA* (New York: W. W. Norton, 1982), is descriptive. Hood was an operations officer in Vienna at the time, but his account is fuzzy about some details. Clarence Ashley, *CIA Spymaster* (Grenta, La.: Pelican, 2004), is based on recorded interviews with George Kisevalter, and the author is a former CIA analyst. John Limond Hart, *The CIA's Russians* (Annapolis, Md.: Naval Institute Press, 2003) includes a chapter on Popov. More can also be found in Murphy, Kondrashev, and Bailey, *Battleground Berlin*. Lastly, for examples of the positive intelligence and its significance, see Joan Bird and John Bird, "CIA Analysis of the Warsaw Pact Forces: The Importance of Clandestine Reporting," a monograph and document collection, Central Intelligence Agency, Historical Review Program, 2013. On the farm journal, see Hood, *Mole*, 123.

14. Intelligence reports based on Popov's reporting are contained in Bird and Bird, "CIA Analysis."

15. He was Edward Ellis Smith, then thirty-two, who had served in Moscow as a military attaché during World War II. He went to Moscow posing as a low-level State Department official. His choices of dead drop sites were deemed unsatisfactory by Popov. See Richard Harris Smith, "The First Moscow Station: An Espionage Footnote to Cold War History," *International Journal of Intelligence and Counter-intelligence* 3, no. 3 (1989): 333–46. This article is based on an interview with Edward Smith, who died in an auto accident in 1982, and on his papers. There are conflicting accounts about Smith's role in the Popov case and whether Popov passed useful intelligence to the CIA while in Moscow. According to Hood in *Mole*, the CIA decided not to run Popov at all while in Moscow because of the risks. In contrast, Richard Harris Smith says Popov while in Moscow tipped off the CIA to the most momentous political event of the decade, Khrushchev's secret speech to the Twentieth Party Congress denouncing Stalin on February 25, 1956. Ashley reports that Smith never met Popov. That doesn't preclude operations, however; if he was just servicing dead drops, there would be no need for a meeting. Smith had an affair with his Russian maid, who was working for the KGB and who made surreptitious photographs. The KGB then showed Smith the photographs and tried to blackmail him into working for them. Smith refused and confessed to the U.S. ambassador, Charles "Chip" Bohlen. Smith was recalled to CIA headquarters in July 1956 and fired.

16. Jerrold L. Schecter and Peter S. Deriabin, *The Spy Who Saved the World: How a Soviet Colonel Changed the Course of the Cold War* (New York: Scribner's, 1992). This is the definitive work on Penkovsky, based on the CIA's files. Also see Richard Helms, "Essential Facts of the Penkovskiy Case," memo for the Director of Central Intelligence, May 31, 1963, and Oleg Penkovskiy, *The Penkovskiy Papers* (New York: Doubleday, 1965), which is based in large part on Penkovsky's meetings with the U.K.-U.S. team. A recent account is Gordon Corera, *The Art of Betrayal: The Secret History of MI6* (New York: Pegasus Books, 2012), 135–83. Also see Leonard McCoy, "The Penkovskiy Case," Studies in Intelligence, CIA, date unknown, declassified Sept. 10, 2014, and "Reflections on Handling Penkovsky," author and date unknown, Studies in Intelligence, CIA, declassified Sept. 3, 2014. Declassified CIA documents are available at www.foia.cia.gov, and documents older than twenty-five years via CREST, a CIA electronic search tool available at the National Archives, College Park, Md.

17. The officer code-named COMPASS arrived in Moscow in October 1960. His cover was to be the superintendent—basically, a glorified janitor—at America House, a dormitory-like building for U.S. embassy marine guards and others. Inexperienced, he found it rough going. In his letters to headquarters, he proposed that the prospective new agent toss packages of sensitive intelligence materials over the twelve-foot wall of America House at night, and he would be on the other side to catch them, a strange suggestion given that the building was under KGB surveillance. COMPASS could find no other dead drop sites in Moscow and complained about his personal misery. Two months after his arrival, he had failed to make contact. On February 5, 1961, he finally tried to telephone Penkovsky at home. It was a Sunday morning. His instructions were to call at 10:00 a.m. and speak in Russian; instead, he called at 11:00 a.m. and spoke in English. Penkovsky had little English and never used it at home; he told the caller he didn't understand and hung up. The whole COMPASS effort was a dead end.

18. Hart, *The CIA's Russians*, 59–60.

19. McCoy, "Penkovskiy Case," 3.

20. Ibid., 5.

21. Christopher Andrew, "Intelligence and Conspiracy Theory: The Case of James Angleton in Long-Term Perspective," keynote address at a conference, March 29, 2012, Washington, D.C., sponsored by the Woodrow Wilson Center and the Georgetown University Center for Security Studies. McCoy suggests that Penkovsky's arrest must have shaken the Soviet leadership in September–October 1962 because they did not know what he had passed to the United States. McCoy says the arrest might have undermined Khrushchev's confidence in his response to President Kennedy. "The timing of Penkovskiy's arrest gave Kennedy the upper hand," he wrote. McCoy, "Penkovskiy Case," 11.

22. Penkovsky moved about in high-level Moscow military circles, including the family of General Ivan Serov, the former KGB chief who now headed the GRU, and thus gave the West a sense of the thinking of Soviet military leaders.

23. Schecter and Deriabin, *Spy Who Saved the World*, 147. Examples of the positive intelligence that Penkovsky provided are in Bird and Bird, "CIA Analysis," 13–28, and the associated document collection. McCoy offers a detailed account of the positive intelligence gleaned from the operation. A more skeptical view of Penkovsky's contribu-

tion to the Cuba crisis is offered by Len Scott, "Espionage and the Cold War: Oleg Penkovsky and the Cuban Missile Crisis," *Intelligence and National Security* 14, no. 3 (Autumn 1999): 23–47.

24. Unknown author, "Reflections on Handling Penkovsky," Studies in Intelligence, CIA, date unknown, declassified by the CIA Sept. 3, 2014. This monograph was written by the CIA case officer who arrived in June 1962. See p. 53.

25. Wallace and Melton, *Spycraft*, 36–39.

26. Unknown author, "Reflections," 57; McCoy, "Penkovskiy Case," 9.

27. Wynne was sentenced to eight years in prison but released in a spy swap in 1964.

28. A large literature exists on Angleton. This account draws upon Tom Mangold, *Cold Warrior: James Jesus Angleton: The CIA's Master Spy Hunter* (New York: Simon & Schuster, 1991); David C. Martin, *Wilderness of Mirrors* (New York: Harper & Row, 1980); David Robarge, "Cunning Passages, Contrived Corridors: Wandering in the Angletonian Wilderness," *Studies in Intelligence* 53, no. 4 (2010); and Barry G. Royden, "James J. Angleton, Anatoliy Golitsyn, and the 'Monster Plot': Their Impact on CIA Personnel and Operations," *Studies in Intelligence* 55, no. 4 (2011), released via the National Security Archive, Washington, D.C. Also see "Moles, Defectors, and Deceptions: James Angleton and His Influence on U.S. Counterintelligence," report on a conference held at the Woodrow Wilson Center and co-sponsored by the Georgetown University Center for Security Studies, March 29, 2012, Washington, D.C. Also see Robert M. Hathaway and Russell Jack Smith, "Richard Helms as Director of Central Intelligence," Center for the Study of Intelligence, CIA, 1993, 103.

29. Robert M. Gates, *From the Shadows: The Ultimate Insider's Story of Five Presidents and How They Won the Cold War* (New York: Simon & Schuster, 1996), 34. Also see Robarge, "Cunning Passages."

30. Burton Gerber, interview with author, Oct. 25, 2012.

31. Although the tunnel had been compromised from the start by George Blake, the KGB's agent inside British intelligence, the Soviets apparently allowed use of it to proceed unhindered, wanting above all to protect their source. For an official account of the tunnel operation, see "The Berlin Tunnel Operation, 1952–1956," Clandestine Services History, Historical Paper No. 150, June 24, 1968, declassified in part by the CIA in 2012, included as doc. No. 001-034, chap. 1, in the document collection accompanying Bird and Bird, "CIA Analysis." Some previous accounts have claimed the intelligence take from the

tunnel was contaminated with disinformation. In an authoritative account, Murphy, Kondrashev, and Bailey, *Battleground Berlin*, say the operation "did in fact produce a large amount of badly needed and difficult to obtain military intelligence" in a period before such material became available from the U-2 overflights and satellite imagery. They also report that the KGB had its own, secure channels for communications, but the military and the GRU used lines that were tapped by the West.

32. Anne Applebaum, *Iron Curtain: The Crushing of Eastern Europe, 1944–1956* (New York: Doubleday, 2012), 64–87. Robarge, in "Cunning Passages," says "by fixating on the Soviets," Angleton "largely ignored" other adversaries, including the East German and Czech services.

33. Haviland Smith, correspondence with author, June 5, 2013. Smith's pioneering influence is also well described in Benjamin Weiser, *A Secret Life: The Polish Officer, His Covert Mission, and the Price He Paid to Save His Country* (New York: PublicAffairs, 2004), 74–78.

34. David Forden, interview with author, Feb. 6, 2013.

35. Bruce Berkowitz, "The Soviet Target—Highlights in the Intelligence Value of Gambit and Hexagon, 1963–1984," *National Reconnaissance: Journal of the Discipline and Practice*, no. 2012-UI (Spring 2012): 110–12. Much of this innovation was in response to the lack of good human intelligence inside the Soviet Union. In 1954, President Eisenhower established a panel to study the possibility of surprise attack, headed by James Killian of MIT. The panel concluded, "We *must* find ways to increase the number of hard facts upon which our intelligence estimates are based, to provide better strategic warning . . . we recommend adoption of a vigorous program for the extensive use, in many intelligence procedures, of the most advanced knowledge in science and technology." See National Security Policy, doc. 9, "Report by the Technological Capabilities Panel of the Science Advisory Committee," Feb. 14, 1955, in *Foreign Relations of the United States, 1955–1957, vol. XIX* (Washington, D.C.: Government Printing Office, 1990).

36. Martin L. Brabourne, "More on the Recruitment of Soviets," *Studies in Intelligence* 9 (Winter 1965): 39–60.

37. Paul Redmond, "Espionage and Counterintelligence," panel 3, at U.S. Intelligence and the End of the Cold War, a conference at the Bush School of Government and Public Service, Texas A&M University, College Station, Nov. 18–20, 1999.

38. Jerrold M. Post, "The Anatomy of Treason," *Studies in Intelligence* 19, no. 2 (1975): 35–37. A later effort is by William Marbes, "Psychology of Treason," *Studies in Intelligence* 30, no. 2 (1986): 1–11.
39. Milt Bearden and James Risen, *The Main Enemy: The Inside Story of the CIA's Final Showdown with the KGB* (New York: Random House, 2003), 22–24, discusses the Gerber study and its conclusions.
40. Ibid., 23–24. On Blee, see Weiser, *Secret Life*, 7–9.
41. Wallace and Melton, *Spycraft*, 87–102.
42. Ibid., 87–96. Wallace is the former director of the CIA's Office of Technical Service.

## 2: MOSCOW STATION

1. Martha Peterson, *The Widow Spy: My CIA Journey from the Jungles of Laos to Prison in Moscow* (Wilmington, N.C.: Red Canary Press, 2012). Also see Bob Fulton, *Reflections on a Life: From California to China* (Bloomington, Ind.: Authorhouse, 2008), 61.
2. Martha Peterson, interview with author, Oct. 12, 2012, and *Widow Spy*.
3. Fulton, *Reflections*, 72–76.
4. Peterson, *Widow Spy*, 174, and interview.
5. Robert Fulton, interview with author, May 12, 2012. The encounter at the gas station was January 12, 1977. Moscow station to headquarters, Jan. 13, 1977, 131150Z; Fulton, *Reflections*.
6. Royden, "Tolkachev," 5–33. This is an unclassified version of a larger, classified monograph about the case.
7. Ibid., 6. Royden reports the CIA had several other operations planned in Moscow in the months ahead and did not want to jeopardize them; moreover, the new administration of President Jimmy Carter was preparing to send Secretary of State–designate Cyrus Vance to Moscow for arms control talks and did not want a spy dustup to interfere.
8. Moscow station to headquarters, Feb. 18, 1977, 181010Z.
9. Royden, "Tolkachev," 6–7; Fulton, *Reflections*, 79.
10. James M. Olson, interview with author, Nov. 2, 2012.
11. Peterson, *Widow Spy*, 241–42.

## 3: A MAN CALLED SPHERE

1. After the arrests and Peterson's expulsion, the CIA carried out an internal review of the Ogorodnik compromise and that of the agent caught a few months later. The CIA official Duane R. Clarridge,

who participated in the internal review, says the panel concluded "the agents' own actions had brought about their downfall." See Clarridge, *A Spy for All Seasons: My Life in the CIA* (New York: Scribner, 1997), 167–68. Later, it was learned that Ogorodnik was betrayed by Karl Koecher, a Czech man who came to the United States in 1965 with his wife, saying they were fleeing communism but who was actually working for the Czech intelligence service and the KGB. Koecher attended Columbia University and obtained a job translating for the CIA. As part of his contract, he was given transcripts from telephone taps to translate. Some of the calls he translated pointed to a Soviet diplomat in Bogotá as a source for the CIA. This information led the KGB on a hunt that eventually pointed to Ogorodnik, who was probably arrested in the early summer, before Peterson was ambushed at the bridge. See Peterson, *Widow Spy*, 241. Koecher was arrested in 1984 and, with his wife, was included in a nine-person prisoner swap with the Soviet Union in 1986 that brought the release of the dissident Anatoly Shcharansky. Koecher received a life sentence that was reduced to time served on the condition he participate in the swap and never return to the United States.

2. John T. Mason Jr., *The Reminiscences of Admiral Stansfield Turner, U.S. Navy (Retired)* (Annapolis, Md.: U.S. Naval Institute, 2011). This is a set of twenty oral history interviews with Turner, courtesy the U.S. Naval Institute.

3. Loch K. Johnson, *A Season of Inquiry: Congress and Intelligence* (Chicago: Dorsey Press, 1988).

4. John Raneleagh, *The Agency: The Rise and Decline of the CIA* (New York: Simon & Schuster, 1987), 234, reports that Carter had asked General Bernard Rogers, but he declined and suggested Turner.

5. Stansfield Turner, address to the U.S. Naval Academy Class of 1947, Nov. 13, 1980, Washington, D.C. Also see Stansfield Turner, *Secrecy and Democracy: The CIA in Transition* (Boston: Houghton Mifflin, 1985), 15, and Mason, *Reminiscences*, 744–48. On Carter's mind-set, see Raneleagh, *Agency*, 634–35.

6. For details of the satellite programs, see F. C. E. Oder, J. C. Fitzpatrick, and P. E. Worthman, *The Gambit Story* (Chantilly, Va.: Center for the Study of National Reconnaissance, 2012), and R. J. Chester, *A History of the Hexagon Program: The Perkin-Elmer Involvement* (Chantilly, Va.: Center for the Study of National Reconnaissance, 2012). Also Stansfield Turner, *Burn Before Reading: Presidents, CIA Directors, and Secret Intelligence* (New York: Hyperion, 2005), 161.

7. Turner's insistence on this analytic approach to the military balance was highly unusual and triggered a major dispute in a 1980 intelligence estimate. See Gerald K. Haines and Robert E. Leggett, *Watching the Bear: Essays on CIA's Analysis of the Soviet Union* (Washington, D.C.: Center for the Study of Intelligence, 2003), 169.

8. Gates, *From the Shadows*, 138.

9. A month after taking office, Turner asked Williams to carry out a "thorough review" of how the espionage branch was operating. Turner recalls that Williams reported back that it was operating ethically and soundly, which he shared with Carter. Turner, *Secrecy and Democracy*, 197. But Williams was viewed with suspicion for his questions about personal behavior, CIA officials told the author. Williams had worked at the Naval War College with Turner.

10. Turner said, "Too many old-timers were hanging on." The directorate had done its own study in 1976, calling for a cut of 1,350 positions over five years, but no action was taken by Bush. Turner eliminated 820 positions over two years, with 17 persons fired, 147 forced into early retirement, and the remainder leaving by attrition as people were moved elsewhere. The decision was made in August 1977, but notices were given on October 31, 1977, in what became known as the Halloween Massacre. An abrupt, two-paragraph letter was sent to the employees being cut, which Turner later acknowledged was "unconscionable." Turner, *Secrecy and Democracy*, 195–205.

11. Jack F. Matlock Jr., correspondence with author, Dec. 2, 2012; Dick Combs, interview with author, Sept. 27, 2013; James Schumaker, correspondence with author, Sept. 23, 2013, and blog post in "Personal Recollections of the Moscow Fire," from MoscowVeteran.org. Schumaker was special assistant to the ambassador. Hathaway was decorated by the CIA with the Intelligence Star for his actions to protect the Moscow station.

12. Bearden and Risen, *Main Enemy*, 26.

13. Sandra Grimes and Jeanne Vertefeuille, *Circle of Treason: A CIA Account of Traitor Aldrich Ames and the Men He Betrayed* (Annapolis, Md.: Naval Institute Press, 2012), 59. The authors were both long-time staff members in the CIA's Soviet division.

14. Gardner "Gus" Hathaway, interview with author, June 10, 2011.

15. The Kulak case had a complex history involving both the FBI and the CIA. Under J. Edgar Hoover, the FBI regarded him as an authentic asset, while the CIA was skeptical, driven by Angleton's doubts. These positions changed after Angleton was removed and Hoover

died. The FBI began to doubt whether Kulak could be trusted. The suspicions stemmed from vague comments he made on a phone call between New York and Washington, on a phone line that had been tapped by the FBI, according to a source with direct knowledge. Meanwhile, the CIA conducted a study of the case and concluded that Kulak was genuine and could be run in Moscow. Grimes was one of those who carried out the study. See Grimes and Vertefeuille, *Circle of Treason*, 55–57.

16. Ibid., 55–61.

17. "Foxbat/Lt. Belenko Update," Oct. 12, 1976, released to author under FOIA, Air Combat Command, Department of the Air Force, Aug. 25, 2014; Pacific Air Forces, "History of the 475th Air Base Wing, CHO (AR) 7101, Vol. III, 1 July–31 Dec. 1976," 316, released to author under FOIA, June 12, 2014.

18. Hathaway, interview with author, June 10, 2011.

19. "Evaluation of Information Provided by CKSPHERE," memo, CIA, Dec. 29, 1977.

20. Moscow station to headquarters, Jan. 3, 1978, 031450Z.

21. Ibid.

22. "Memorandum for: Director of Central Intelligence," CIA, Jan. 3, 1978.

## 4: "FINALLY I HAVE REACHED YOU"

1. Hathaway, interview with author, June 10, 2011.

2. Royden, "Tolkachev," 8.

3. Moscow station to headquarters, March 2, 1978, 021500Z. This cable, a translation of Tolkachev's note, refers to the "faculty" in Kharkov but more precisely means the "department," which I have substituted.

4. Royden, "Tolkachev," 8.

5. Nina Guilsher Soldatenov, "Our Family History," unpublished, courtesy Catherine Guilsher, April 5, 2013.

6. Catherine Guilsher, interviews with author, March 30, 2011, and April 5, 2013.

7. President Ronald Reagan approved Operation GUNMAN in February 1984 to remove the bugged machines, and it was carried out by the National Security Agency. See Sharon Maneki, "Learning from the Enemy: The GUNMAN Project," *United States Cryptologic History, Series VI*, vol. 13, Center for Cryptologic History, National Security Agency, 2009. The bugged typewriters were in use by diplomats, not in the Moscow station, according to two CIA sources.

8. It was common to call Galina a colonel, but a source told the author that, while an informer, she probably did not hold the KGB rank.

9. Catherine Guilsher, interview with author, March 30, 2011.

10. Moscow station to headquarters, March 6, 1978, 060835Z. Guilsher's cable, sent the next morning, reconstructed the call.

11. The book that prompted the alarm was Edward Jay Epstein, *Legend: The Secret World of Lee Harvey Oswald* (New York: Reader's Digest Press, 1978), 20, 263. The leak is described in Grimes and Vertefeuille, *Circle of Treason*, 61.

12. Hathaway, interview with author, Aug. 28, 2013; Grimes and Vertefeuille, *Circle of Treason*, 60–62. Kulak was not discovered and later died of a heart attack.

13. Hathaway, interview with author, Aug. 28, 2013; Royden, "Tolkachev," 9.

14. Moscow station to headquarters, March 21, 1978, 210817Z.

15. Moscow station to headquarters, March 21, 1978, 211350Z.

16. Headquarters to Moscow station, March 24, 1978, 242036Z.

17. Moscow station to headquarters, April 11, 1978, 111215Z.

18. Royden, "Tolkachev," 10.

19. Headquarters to Moscow station, May 17, 1978, 170214Z.

20. Royden, "Tolkachev," 9.

21. Headquarters to Moscow station, June 13, 1978, 13000Z.

22. Moscow station to headquarters, Aug. 25, 1978, 251205Z.

23. Royden, "Tolkachev," 9.

24. Moscow station to headquarters, Nov. 1, 1978, 011315Z.

## 5: "A DISSIDENT AT HEART"

1. It is not possible to give a meaningful equivalent in dollars to such a sum. Although there was an official exchange rate of 0.60 ruble for $1.00, the Soviet ruble was not a freely convertible currency, and Tolkachev had no access to dollars. His rubles had a value based entirely on what could be bought or acquired inside the Soviet economy. A thousand rubles was about three times Tolkachev's monthly salary.

2. Moscow station to headquarters, Jan. 2, 1979, 020805Z, and a longer cable to headquarters that followed on Jan. 2, 1979, 021403Z. Also Catherine Guilsher, interview with author, March 30, 2011.

3. Draft of Moscow station ops note to agent, untitled and undated, in Tolkachev collection from the CIA.

4. Moscow station to headquarters, March 2, 1979, 021410Z, which contains Guilsher's draft ops note for the next meeting.

5. Moscow station to headquarters, April 5, 1979, 050859Z.

6. Royden, "Tolkachev," 9–10, and a confidential source.

7. Moscow station to headquarters, April 26, 1979, 261013Z, and April 30, 1979, 301033Z.

8. Headquarters to Moscow station, May 1, 1979, 012316Z.

9. Moscow station to headquarters, May 4, 1979, 041429Z.

10. Headquarters to Moscow station, May 7, 1979, 072329Z.

## 6: SIX FIGURES

1. For more about the Soviet economy of shortages, see David E. Hoffman, *The Oligarchs: Wealth and Power in the New Russia* (New York: PublicAffairs, 2002). On the gastronomes, David Hoffman, "Stalin's 'Seven Sisters': 'Wedding-Cake' Style 1950s Towers Define Moscow Skyline," *Washington Post*, July 29, 1997, 1.

2. Royden, "Tolkachev," 11.

3. Hathaway, interview with author, June 10, 2011.

4. Headquarters to Moscow station, May 1, 1979, 012316Z.

5. Ibid.

6. Headquarters to Moscow station, May 18, 1979, 182251Z.

7. Moscow station to headquarters, May 22, 1979, 221139Z.

8. Moscow station to headquarters, May 8, 1979, 081522Z.

9. For example, in the 1960s and early 1970s, the United States spoon-fed leaks to the GRU, Soviet military intelligence, about development of a "breakthrough" nerve gas, but it was a fabrication. The nerve gas wasn't in the U.S. arsenal. See David Wise, *Cassidy's Run: The Secret Spy War over Nerve Gas* (New York: Random House, 2000).

10. In the cable released to the author, the field of research at issue has been redacted.

11. Headquarters to Moscow station, June 1, 1979, 011954Z.

12. Moscow station to headquarters, May 8, 1979, 081522Z.

13. The CIA had used a similar procedure when it distributed intelligence from inside the Warsaw Pact through the agent Ryszard Kuklinski, a highly respected colonel in the Polish army. Confidential source.

14. Headquarters to Moscow station, April 12, 1979, 120107, and additional information from a confidential source.

15. The confusion might have been caused by Tolkachev. In his letter, he wrote "I have" the ailment. But then, after describing the treatment, he wrote, "If there are more effective means of treatment in this field, then it would be very beneficial for our family to know them." Moscow station to headquarters, April 30, 1979, 301033Z.

16. Moscow station to headquarters, June 7, 1979, 071342Z.

17. On the Ford discussion, see Erin R. Mahan, ed., *Foreign Relations of the United States, 1969–1976, vol. XXXIII, SALT II, 1972–1980* (Washington, D.C.: Government Printing Office, 2013), 452.

18. William Perry, deputy defense secretary for research and engineering in 1979, estimated that even if the Soviet Union invested in a massive catch-up effort, including fifty to a hundred airborne warning and control planes, two thousand advanced interceptors with lookdown, shoot-down radars and new air-to-air missiles, and five hundred to a thousand surface-to-air missiles, perhaps costing $30 billion to $50 billion and requiring five to ten years to deploy, it could destroy only half of any onslaught of American cruise missiles. Kenneth P. Werrell, *The Evolution of the Cruise Missile* (Maxwell Air Force Base, Ala.: Air University Press, 1985), 191.

19. David Binder, "George T. Kalaris, 73, Official Who Changed CIA's Direction," *New York Times*, Sept. 14, 1995.

20. George T. Kalaris to Director of Central Intelligence and deputy directors for operations and for intelligence, memo, June 25, 1979.

## 7: SPY CAMERA

1. Moscow station to headquarters, April 30, 1979, 301033Z.

2. Wallace and Melton, *Spycraft*, 37. On Minox characteristics, see http://www.subclub.org/shop/minoxa.htm.

3. Wallace and Melton, *Spycraft*, 37–40.

4. Ibid., 90–92, 233. Tropel Inc. of Fairport, New York, was established in 1953 by three professors from the Institute of Optics at the University of Rochester: Robert Hopkins, Jim Anderson, and Jack Evans. They were joined by a fourth, John Buzawa, who was president of the firm at the time of the CIA work. Tropel was later bought by Corning Inc. and was subsequently spun off again. Louis Denes (Corning Inc.), correspondence and telephone interview with author, Sept. 18, 2013.

5. Moscow station to headquarters, Feb. 15, 1979, 1513111.

6. The spy was Elyesa Bazna, code-named CICERO, who photographed documents taken from the British ambassador to Turkey and passed them to the German service, SD. H. Keith Melton, *Ultimate Spy*, 2nd ed. (New York: Dorling Kindersley, 2002), 34.

7. Moscow station to headquarters, undated but apparently written immediately after the meeting.

8. Moscow station to headquarters, Oct. 18, 1979, 181630Z.

9. Moscow station to headquarters, Nov. 16, 1979, 161426Z.

10. George T. Kalaris, memo for the Director, Dec. 12, 1979.

11. Charles Battaglia, interview with author, Feb. 7, 2013.

12. Headquarters to Moscow station, Dec. 15, 1979, 150019Z.

## 8: WINDFALLS AND HAZARDS

1. Moscow station to headquarters, Dec. 28, 1979, 281255Z.

2. Guilsher later admonished Tolkachev for running after him. "I was a little scared," he confessed. "In such a case it is simply better to leave the forgotten until next time." Guilsher wrote this in his draft ops note in February 1980, undated.

3. Moscow station to headquarters, Dec. 29, 1979, 290943Z.

4. Royden, "Tolkachev," 18. The $70 million estimate is contained in Moscow station to headquarters, March 20, 1980, 200825Z.

5. The nuclear-armed cruise missile was prominent in this new arms race. After the Soviet Union deployed SS-20 missiles aimed at Western Europe in the late 1970s, NATO responded with the "dual-track" approach, seeking talks but deploying new weapons, including the Pershing II missile and 484 cruise missiles.

6. Moscow station to headquarters, Jan. 9, 1980, 091410Z.

7. Headquarters to Moscow station, Jan. 16, 1980, 160052Z.

8. Moscow station to headquarters, Jan. 8, 1980, 081240Z.

9. "Memorandum for: Director of Central Intelligence," Jan. 17, 1980.

10. Moscow station to headquarters, Jan. 28, 1980, 281127Z.

11. Headquarters to Moscow station, Jan. 12, 1980, 120429Z. Headquarters proposed a cover story to the effect that "he has run into a certain problem in the design of a system he is now working on and wanted to check specifications on older systems to see if the same weakness was evident in them. It would obviously be best if the weakness CKSPHERE chooses is a true one."

12. Headquarters to Moscow station, Jan. 16, 1980, 160052Z.

13. Headquarters to Moscow station, Jan. 16, 1980, 160058Z.

14. Headquarters to Moscow station, Jan. 23, 1980, 231655Z. In this cable, headquarters wrote, "The feeling here is that at this juncture we simply must make every effort to try to dissuade CKSPHERE from taking unnecessary risks. This includes photographing at home . . . We recognize that CKSPHERE is a headstrong individual, bent on doing the greatest damage to the Soviet authorities in the shortest possible time. While we fully intend to live up to our commitment, we also feel that our commitment includes a moral obligation to protect our collabora-

tor to the best of our ability. We cannot let ourselves be carried along by the *Gotterdammerung* psychology which seems to drive this asset. While as an intelligence organization we are certainly in the business of collecting information, it is professionally incumbent upon us in the present situation to somehow slow CKSPHERE down."

15. Moscow station to headquarters, Jan. 18, 1980, 181453Z.

16. For reasons never clear, the identical red Tropel worked fine.

17. A foot-candle is a unit of illumination equal to the light cast by one candle onto one square foot. The Tropels probably would not work well at Tolkachev's office, if he could manage to use them covertly there; he measured only about fifteen to twenty foot-candles of light at his office desk with a meter the CIA had provided.

18. At the time, there was a major debate in U.S. intelligence and policy circles about Soviet emphasis on civil defense and whether it meant the Soviets were preparing for possible nuclear war.

19. Guilsher draft ops note, typewritten, undated.

20. Moscow station to headquarters, Jan. 28, 1980, 281135Z. The questions about the building pass are included in Guilsher's draft ops note for the February meeting, undated, typewritten.

21. Moscow station to headquarters, Feb. 12, 1980, 121358Z.

22. Moscow station to headquarters, Feb. 14, 1980, 141235Z.

23. Moscow station to headquarters, March 20, 1980, 200825Z.

24. Headquarters to Moscow station, March 26, 1980, 262244Z.

25. U.S. intelligence assessment quoted in cable, undated but believed to be March 27, 1980. The document has no time-date stamp.

26. Moscow station to headquarters, March 20, 1980, 200825Z.

27. Headquarters to Moscow station, April 12, 1980, 12184Z.

28. Headquarters to Moscow station, May 10, 1980, 100049Z.

29. Moscow station to headquarters, Feb. 14, 1980, 141235Z.

30. Moscow station to headquarters, March 20, 1980, 200825Z.

31. Headquarters to Moscow station, May 10, 1980, 100049Z.

32. Moscow station to headquarters, May 8, 1980, 081428Z.

33. Sakharov was arrested and sent to Gorky on January 22, 1980.

34. Guilsher reported to headquarters that apparently there were guests at home and Tolkachev could not leave, based on the call and unfamiliar voice. Later Tolkachev told him that his son, Oleg, had answered. In general, identity transfer required the case officer to have a "matched" partner of an embassy worker with similar build and appearance. Guilsher did not have such a partner; his efforts to don a workable disguise were more ad hoc and problematic, but they worked.

35. Moscow station to headquarters, May 23, 1980, 231415Z.
36. The Discus was ready some two decades before the first BlackBerry consumer device, which came along in 1999.
37. Headquarters to Moscow station, June 4, 1980, 042348Z.
38. Moscow station to headquarters, June 5, 1980, 051345Z.
39. Moscow station to headquarters, June 11, 1980, 111407Z.

## 9: THE BILLION DOLLAR SPY

1. Moscow station to headquarters, June 20, 1980, 201145Z.
2. Ibid.
3. Moscow station to headquarters, June 24, 1980, 241232Z.
4. In the spring of 1980, Guilsher struggled with his health and stamina. The Tolkachev meetings were draining him. His wife begged him to leave Moscow to seek medical attention. The U.S. embassy doctor examined him and said he should get on the next plane to Frankfurt for medical treatment. But Guilsher would not leave Moscow station until he was finished with Tolkachev. He insisted that he couldn't let him down. Later, when he got home, he underwent surgery to remove cancerous tumors on his thyroid gland (Catherine Guilsher, interview with author, Dec. 14, 2013). Guilsher, who passed away in 2008, was posthumously honored with the CIA's Trailblazer award in 2009, recognizing his "significant and enduring" contribution to U.S. national security in the Tolkachev operation.
5. Memo to the Director of Central Intelligence from chief, Soviet division, July 23, 1980.
6. Moscow station to headquarters, June 21, 1980, 210715Z.
7. Ibid.
8. Moscow station to headquarters, June 24, 1980, 241232Z.
9. Memo to the Director of Central Intelligence from chief, Soviet division, July 23, 1980.
10. Headquarters to Moscow station, July 11, 1980, 110003Z.

## 10: FLIGHT OF UTOPIA

1. David Rolph, interview with author, Feb. 3 and May 19, 2013.
2. Victor Sheymov, *Tower of Secrets: A Real Life Spy Thriller* (Annapolis, Md.: Naval Institute Press, 1993). In his memoir, Sheymov does not distinguish between different CIA case officers he met, and he describes one part of a meeting as a dream. This chapter is based in part on his memoir and on separate information from confidential sources.

## 11: GOING BLACK

1. Wallace and Melton, *Spycraft*, 108.
2. David Rolph, interview with author, May 6, 2012, and May 19, 2013. This chapter also includes material from interviews with confidential sources.
3. Moscow station to headquarters, Sept. 9, 1980, 091200Z, which includes Rolph's draft ops note.
4. Moscow station to headquarters, Sept. 17, 1980, 171047Z.
5. Headquarters to Moscow station, Sept. 29, 1980, 292348Z.
6. Moscow station to headquarters, Oct. 16, 1980, 161309Z.

## 12: DEVICES AND DESIRES

1. David Rolph, interview with author, May 6, 2012.
2. On the L-pill, two confidential sources familiar with the device.
3. Vasily Aksyonov's 1981 novel, *The Island of Crimea* (New York: Random House, 1983), depicts a fictional island that a journalist visits to see a prosperous Russian market democracy and is asked to bring back scarce goods to the communist Soviet Union. These are a sampling of items from the list, 113.
4. Moscow station to headquarters, Oct. 18, 1980, 180826Z.
5. Moscow station to headquarters, Nov. 21, 1980, 211118Z, and Nov. 28, 1980, 281231Z.
6. Moscow station to headquarters, Dec. 10, 1980, 101150Z. Tolkachev paid close attention to compensation. He wrote a long section in his ops note with mathematical formulas to calculate the interest and ruble exchange rate. He accepted the CIA offer, $300,000 a year, plus interest he put at the ruble equivalent of $43,000 a year. At the end of the note, he acknowledged the CIA might be justified in asking, if exfiltration plans were under way and "all the money I have received earlier has not been spent," why did he want so much more cash? "It happens that our exit is not being organized for today or tomorrow," he wrote. "During this time, anything can happen which can delay my exit or make it impossible altogether, for example I can have a car accident or become seriously ill and after that lose my ability to work." He wanted the money, he said, just in case something "unforeseen" would make it "impossible for me to get out of the USSR."
7. Moscow station to headquarters, Dec. 9, 1980, 090811Z and 091505Z; draft of ops note to Tolkachev, undated; Rolph interviews May 2, 2012, and Feb. 10, 2013.
8. William J. Casey, "Progress at the CIA," memo, May 6, 1981.

WHORM Subject Files: FG006-02, doc. No. 019195s, May 6, 1981, Ronald Reagan Presidential Library.

9. Bob Woodward, *Veil: The Secret Wars of the CIA, 1981–1987* (New York: Simon & Schuster, 1987), 86, 305.

10. Moscow station to headquarters, March 11, 1981, 110940Z.

11. Moscow station to headquarters, March 11, 1981, 111439Z.

12. Gerber wrote in a cable to headquarters on August 13, 1980, 131400Z, that "we do not think pace of operation and nature of product lend themselves" to electronic communications. "We have not suffered notably from lack of electronic commo in the past and see no real requirement for capability in the future." He added, "Requirements in CKSPHERE case have historically not been brief, specific, and urgent. Nor, based on our understanding of CKSPHERE's access, can we expect him to supply intelligence suitable for passage" with Discus. Gerber added that even with careful tradecraft, "some risk remains whenever agent is brought into proximity of case officer under surveillance. Slight error by station officer in casing, testing, or servicing or by agent in demeanor or servicing can be disastrous. With CKSPHERE, we have no opportunity for training or practice."

13. Weiser, *Secret Life*, 230–32. Also Hathaway, interview with author, Aug. 28, 2013.

14. Bob Wallace (former head of the CIA's Office of Technical Service), interview with author, Oct. 7, 2013.

15. Moscow station to headquarters, March 11, 1981, 111439Z. In this cable, Rolph said, "Although CKS did not mention his original production plan, we cannot help but recall that he may be reaching the limits of what he can reasonably and easily get his hands on in the way of desirable material."

16. Moscow station to headquarters, March 11, 1981, 111439Z.

17. Moscow station to headquarters, April 2, 1981, 020732Z.

18. Moscow station to headquarters, June 23, 1981, 231244Z.

19. Headquarters to Moscow station, June 26, 1981, 260019Z.

20. Moscow station to headquarters, June 26, 1981, 261440Z. Separately, two confidential sources said the device antenna was too small and Moscow was at the very outer limit of the Marisat satellite's workable footprint. Also see Moscow station to headquarters, July 2, 1981, 021348Z. About two years later, the device was returned to the Moscow station for testing. On Monday, March 7, 1983, the deputy chief of station, Richard Osborne, took it to an open field in Moscow known as Poklonnaya Gora. Osborne set up the device.

He was arrested on the spot by the KGB. The Soviet news agency Tass reported that Osborne, identified as a first secretary at the U.S. embassy, "was detained red-handed in Moscow on March 7, this year, while working with espionage radio apparatus. Confiscated from him was a set of portable intelligence special-purpose apparatus for the transmission of espionage information via the U.S. 'Marisat' communications satellites, and his own notes which were written in a pad made of paper quickly soluble in water, and which expose Osborne's espionage activities." Osborne was declared persona non grata and expelled from the Soviet Union. See John F. Burns, "Moscow Ousts a U.S. Diplomat, Calling Him a Spy," *New York Times*, March 11, 1983, 11.

21. Moscow station to headquarters, April 11, 1981, 110812Z.

22. Headquarters to Moscow station, Nov. 25, 1981, 251829Z. Some of these topics were also included in earlier rolls of film.

## 13: TORMENTED BY THE PAST

1. Except where otherwise noted, details of Tolkachev's family and work in this chapter are drawn from his letters and comments to the CIA, primarily three cables: Moscow station to headquarters, March 2, 1978, 021500Z, in which the station reports on Tolkachev's note revealing his identity; Moscow station to headquarters, April 26, 1979, 261013Z, transmitting Tolkachev's answers to questions from headquarters; and Moscow station to headquarters, Dec. 10, 1980, 101150Z, providing answers to questions concerning a possible exfiltration. The author also interviewed a confidential source close to the family.

2. It was the Church of the Nine Martyrs of Kizik, founded by a patriarch who had opposed Peter the Great's reforms of the seventeenth century.

3. The aviation and rocket elite who lived there are honored by stone tablets at the base of the tower.

4. Most Russian men his age were married by about age twenty-five. See Sergei Scherbov and Harrie van Vianen, "Marriage in Russia: A Reconstruction," *Demographic Research* 10, article 2 (2004): 27–60, www.demographic-research.org.

5. *Lyogkaya Industriya*, Jan. 1, 1937, 1, Russian State Archive of the Economy, Moscow.

6. *Lyogkaya Industriya*, Jan. 19–Feb. 1, 1937, Russian State Archive of the Economy.

7. Robert Conquest, *The Great Terror* (New York: Oxford University Press, 1990), 252.

8. Robert Conquest, *Stalin: Breaker of Nations* (New York: Viking, 1991), 206.

9. Conquest, *Great Terror*, 239. According to Orlando Figes, of the 139 members of the Central Committee elected at the Seventeenth Party Congress in 1934, 102 were arrested and shot, and 5 more killed themselves in 1937–38; in addition, 56 percent of the congress delegates were imprisoned in those years. Of the 767 members of the Red Army high command, 412 were executed, 29 died in prison, 3 committed suicide, and 59 remained in jail. See Figes, *The Whisperers: Private Life in Stalin's Russia* (New York: Metropolitan, 2007), 238–39.

10. An examination of a mass grave outside Moscow showed that blue-collar and white-collar workers were prominent among those who suffered. Together with the peasants, they were about two-thirds of the victims. See Karl Schlögel, *Moscow, 1937* (Malden, Mass.: Polity Press, 2012), 490.

11. Figes, *Whisperers*, 240; Schlögel, *Moscow, 1937*, 492–93.

12. Conquest, *Great Terror*, 240.

13. Ibid., 256–57.

14. The Pale of Settlement was a section of imperial Russia, in the west, to which permanent residency by Jews was confined. The Jews were often poor and concentrated in areas that made them targets for attacks, or pogroms.

15. Bamdas, S. E., fond 1, opis 1, delo 282, 1–2, Archives of Memorial International, Moscow.

16. Kuzmin, I. A., fond 1, opis 1, delo 2543, 1–2, Archives of Memorial International.

17. Conquest, *Great Terror*, 235.

18. Cathy A. Frierson and Semyon S. Vilensky, *Children of the Gulag* (New Haven, Conn.: Yale University Press, 2010), 167.

19. Confidential source close to the family. It is not known why Sofia's sister did not take in her daughter, but relatives were often fearful of accepting children of "enemies of the people." Sofia's sister, Esfir Bamdas, was married to Konstantin Starostin, a Moscow party leader, who was arrested in December 1937 for "anti-Soviet activity" and sentenced to ten years in prison. He died in 1939. Esfir, also a party member, was arrested in 1951 as a result of a denunciation and sentenced to five years but was released in 1953 under an amnesty.

20. Kuzmin, I. A., fond 1, opis 1, delo 2543, 1–2, Archives of Memorial International, Moscow.

21. Vladimir Libin, "Detained with Evidence," *Novoye Russkoye Slovo*, New York, June 27, 1997. Libin was a close family friend. A confidential source close to the family recalled Natasha reading Pasternak and Mandelstam.

22. Rodric Braithwaite, *Moscow, 1941: A City and Its People at War* (London: Profile Books, 2006), 184–207. Soviet engineers and scientists had been studying the new radar technology since the 1930s but lagged behind Britain and the United States, hampered by rivalries, indifference in the armed forces, and Stalin's purges. One of the country's most knowledgeable radar scientists, Pavel Oshchepkov, was arrested in 1937 and spent the next ten years in prison. John Erikson, "Radio-location and the Air Defence Problem: The Design and Development of Soviet Radar, 1934–40," *Social Studies of Science* 2 (1972): 241–68.

    Also see http://en.wikipedia.org/wiki/Radar_in_World_War_II for details on Factory No. 339.

23. Tolkachev was born in Aktyubinsk, a railroad town, the scene of a major battle in the civil war that followed the Bolshevik Revolution. The Bolsheviks captured the town from the White Army in 1919. Local archives show that in September 1919 a man named Tolkachev was chosen to be secretary of the local Bolshevik organizing bureau in Aktyubinsk. He was probably Tolkachev's father, Georgi. About a decade later, by 1928, Soviet authorities were attempting to turn the local government over to Kazakhs, and the Tolkachev family departed for Moscow. See "History of Aktyubinsk Oblast: A Historical Chronicle of the Region in Documents, Research, and Photographs," http://myaktobe.kz.

24. "Phazotron: From 20th to 21st Century," Phazotron-NIIR Corp., 2003. The author is grateful to Rustam Rahmatullin, a historian of Russian architecture, for context on the buildings.

25. In the early Cold War, the nuclear threat came from high-flying bombers. The United States planned a new, manned penetrating bomber, the XB-70 Valkyrie, that would reach altitudes of 77,000 feet and three times the speed of sound. See National Museum of the U.S. Air Force, "North American XB-70 Valkyrie," fact sheet, http://www.nationalmuseum.af.mil/factsheets/factsheet.asp?id=592. Also, starting in 1956, the CIA's U-2 spy plane was overflying the Soviet Union at altitudes of 68,000 feet and higher. In response to

these high-altitude threats, Soviet aircraft designers began work on what became the MiG-25 interceptor. The radar was designed at Phazotron. The Soviet Union also built improved surface-to-air missiles that could shoot down aircraft at high altitudes. On May 1, 1960, a Soviet surface-to-air missile exploded near the U-2 being piloted by Francis Gary Powers at 70,500 feet above Sverdlovsk, downing Powers and bringing the CIA's overflights of the Soviet Union to an end. Gregory W. Pedlow and Donald E. Welzenbach, "The Central Intelligence Agency and Overhead Reconnaissance: The U-2 and OXCART Programs, 1954–1974," Central Intelligence Agency, Washington D.C., 1992, declassified 2013. The United States canceled the XB-70 bomber in 1961, and the U.S. Air Force changed its strategy for threatening the Soviet Union. Instead of dropping bombs from very high altitudes, the air force decided to send in low-flying, penetrating bombers. The Soviet air defenses at low altitudes were weak. In fact, both superpowers had struggled with this problem; radars of the 1960s could not detect flying objects that were very low because of the uneven contours of the earth. But the radar gap was more of a threat to the Soviet Union because of its vast borders, the longest in the world, and because NATO was sitting on its western front in Europe. The European flash point for conflict was far away from the United States but near to the Soviet Union. The United States also sought to close the low-altitude gap with the E-3 airborne warning and control system (AWACS), able to spot low-flying targets for two hundred miles out, and the F-15 fighter, the first with lookdown, shoot-down capability.

26. Phazotron, "From 20th to 21st Century," notes that NIIP built the radar on parts from Phazotron. The handoff to NIIP is also described in "Overscan's Guide to Russian Avionics," http://aerospace.boopidoo.com/philez/Su-15TM%20PICTURES%20&%20DOCS/Overscan%27s%20guide%20to%20Russian%20Military%20Avionics.htm.

27. Lyudmila Alexeyeva and Paul Goldberg, *The Thaw Generation: Coming of Age in the Post-Stalin Era* (Boston: Little, Brown, 1990), 4.

28. Andrei Sakharov, *Memoirs* (New York: Knopf, 1990), 282–85.

29. Ibid., 292–93. Michael Scammell, *Solzhenitsyn* (New York: W. W. Norton, 1984), 640.

30. Joshua Rubenstein and Alexander Gribanov, eds., *The KGB File of Andrei Sakharov* (New Haven, Conn.: Yale University Press, 2005), 144.

31. Ibid., 150.

32. Sakharov describes his meeting with the correspondents in his *Memoirs*, 385–86, and reproduces some of the attacks on him, 631–40. Also, Robert G. Kaiser, *Russia: The People and the Power* (London: Martin Secker, 1976), 424–25.

33. Rubenstein and Gribanov, *KGB File of Andrei Sakharov*, 155.

34. Tolkachev wrote, "I would not begin to establish contact for any kind of money with, for example, the Chinese embassy. Why, the money does not smell? The money, yes. But societies, created by people, sometimes exude bad smells." Moscow station to headquarters, April 26, 1979, 261013Z.

35. Libin, "Detained with Evidence."

## 14: "EVERYTHING IS DANGEROUS"

1. Moscow station to headquarters, Nov. 12, 1981, 120858Z; Rolph interview with author, May 6, 2012.

2. "MASHINA," undated, map and description of signal site, given to Tolkachev, released to author by CIA.

3. On September 3, 1981, a CIA case officer had gone to meet an agent who was a Soviet citizen. The agent had been compromised. At the site, the case officer and the agent were detained. The newspaper *Izvestiya* identified the arrested man as Y. A. Kapustin. Dusko Doder, "Moscow Arrests Soviet Citizen as Agent of CIA," *Washington Post*, Sept. 4, 1981, A25.

4. Rolph, interview with author, May 6, 2012; Moscow station to headquarters, Nov. 12, 1981, 120858Z and 121233Z.

5. Royden, "Tolkachev," 21. Each broadcast lasted ten minutes, a burst of dummy messages with a genuine one mixed in. Tolkachev could later break out the genuine message by scrolling numbers on the demodulator. The first three digits of the message would indicate if it included a genuine message; if so, he could view the message, contained in five-digit groups, and then decode it using a onetime pad. He could receive up to four hundred five-digit groups in any one message. It was complex and cumbersome but a way to avoid the KGB.

6. Casey, "Progress at the CIA," memo, May 6, 1981.

7. Burton Gerber, interview with author, Jan. 30, 2013.

8. Gus Weiss, "The Farewell Dossier," *Studies in Intelligence* 39, no. 5 (1996). On the explosion, see Thomas C. Reed, *At the Abyss: An Insider's History of the Cold War* (New York: Ballantine Books, 2004). For more on Vetrov, see Sergei Kostin and Eric Raynaud, *Farewell: The*

*Greatest Spy Story of the Twentieth Century*, trans. Catherine Cauvin-Higgins (Las Vegas, Nev.: Amazon Crossing, 2011).

9. Moscow station to headquarters, Dec. 9, 1981, 091105Z.

10. Headquarters to Moscow station, Nov. 25, 1981, 251829Z.

11. Moscow station to headquarters, Feb. 16, 1982, 161100Z.

12. This description of deep cover is from confidential sources.

13. Moscow station to headquarters, Jan. 13, 1982, 130801Z, draft station ops note.

14. Moscow station to headquarters, Feb. 16, 1982, 161100Z.

15. Moscow station to headquarters, March 9, 1982, 091400Z.

16. Moscow station to headquarters, March 15, 1982, 150742Z.

17. Moscow station to headquarters, March 17, 1982, 171006Z.

18. Royden, "Tolkachev," 23.

19. Moscow station to headquarters, May 25, 1982, 250800Z, and confidential source.

20. William Plunkert, correspondence with author, March 28, 2014.

21. Moscow station to headquarters, Dec. 8, 1982, 081335Z.

22. Moscow station to headquarters, Dec. 10, 1982, 101400Z, and Dec. 22, 1982, 220940Z. Tolkachev had raised eyebrows at the CIA by suggesting in his ops note that he might use his money from the CIA to buy silence from a colleague at work if he was caught. The CIA thought this was alarming and unrealistic and told Tolkachev later that he had other options besides bribery. See headquarters to Moscow station, March 1, 1983, 010053Z.

23. Moscow station to headquarters, Dec. 10, 1982, 100945Z.

24. Thomas Mills, interview with author, Feb. 16, 2013, and correspondence, Dec. 19, 2013.

25. Headquarters to Moscow station, Feb. 19, 1983, 190143Z.

26. Headquarters to Moscow station, March 1, 1983, 010053Z.

27. Robert O. Morris, interviews with author, May 4, 2012, and Dec. 19, 2013; Robert O. Morris, *Fighting Windmills* (Virginia Beach, Va.: Legacy, 2012), 144.

28. Moscow station to headquarters, March 17, 1983, 171555Z.

29. Headquarters to Moscow station, March 22, 1983, 220128Z.

30. Moscow station to headquarters, March 22, 1983, 221210Z.

31. Headquarters to Moscow station, April 1, 1983, 010055Z.

32. Moscow station to headquarters, April 25, 1983, 250900Z.

33. Moscow station to headquarters, April 25, 1983, 251445Z.

34. Headquarters to Moscow station, June 13 and 23, 1983, no time-date stamp on either cable.

35. Headquarters to Moscow station, June 23, 1983, no time-date stamp.
36. Headquarters to Moscow station, July 6, 1983, no time-date stamp.

## 15: NOT CAUGHT ALIVE

1. Except where otherwise noted, this account is based on the translation of Tolkachev's ops note passed to the CIA describing the events in detail, contained in Moscow station to headquarters, Nov. 17, 1983, 171810Z. The cable translates the regime as a "procedures" department, but the author believes "security" better reflects the purpose and duties.

2. In these weeks of early 1983, there was a renewed campaign for "discipline and order" imposed by the new Soviet leader, Yuri Andropov, who used the KGB and the Interior Ministry to attack the problems of absenteeism and poor economic performance. People were "caught loafing" during working hours in subways, saunas, and shops. Tolkachev would certainly have known about the new climate, although it seems unlikely to have triggered the investigation. Andropov's campaign is described in R. G. Pikhoia, *Soviet Union: History of Power, 1945–1991* [in Russian] (Novosibirsk: Sibersky Khronograf, 2000), 377–79, and in Mikhail Gorbachev, *Memoirs* (New York: Doubleday, 1995), 147.

3. Tolkachev was named as the inheritor of the house by the owner but had no explicit title, and a dishonest owner could change it at any time. Libin, "Detained with Evidence." Other sources confirmed to the author this was a common technique.

4. Ibid.

5. For details about CKELBOW, see Wallace and Melton, *Spycraft*, 138–56; Bearden and Risen, *Main Enemy*, 28–29; and Rem Krasilnikov, *Prizraki s ulitsy Chaikovskogo* [The ghosts of Tchaikovsky Street] (Moscow: Gei Iterum, 1999), 179–88.

6. Moscow station to headquarters, Nov. 17, 1983, 171007Z.

7. Moscow station to headquarters, Nov. 17, 1983, 171810Z.

8. Moscow station to headquarters, Nov. 22, 1983, 221400Z, on the suggestion to bury the cameras.

9. Headquarters to Moscow station, Nov. 30, 1983, time-date stamp redacted. Headquarters said Tolkachev's handwritten materials had never left the division. When his material was translated, it was disseminated only in top secret, blue-bordered memorandums. The material was marked at a level of sensitivity above top secret, and the blue borders were a control system indicating it was extremely sensi-

tive. No defense contractors ever saw it. When sent to the government "customers," it was kept in secure vaults at each agency dedicated to such blue-border sensitive reporting, and only a select few had access to it. "This, unfortunately, would not preclude loose talk," headquarters said in a cable to Moscow. But "we are aware of no leak, verbal or written, of No. 19 material."

10. "Expanding Navy's Global Power," *Aviation Week and Space Technology*, Aug. 31, 1981, 48.

11. Headquarters to Moscow station, Nov. 23, 1983, time-date stamp redacted. The identity of the officer is not known.

## 16: SEEDS OF BETRAYAL

1. Thomas Mills, interview with author, Feb. 16, 2013.

2. "Edward L. Howard," résumé, contained in Federal Bureau of Investigation, "Prosecutive Report of Investigation Concerning Edward Lee Howard; Espionage-Russia," Nov. 26, 1986, Albuquerque, N.M., file No. 65A-590, sec. 2, 201–2, released in part under FOIA, hereafter cited as FBI report. Also see Edward Lee Howard, *Safe House: The Compelling Memoirs of the Only CIA Spy to Seek Asylum in Russia* (Bethesda, Md.: National Press Books, 1995), 15–32, and David Wise, *The Spy Who Got Away* (New York: Random House, 1988), 22–31.

3. On Howard's dream of Switzerland, see *Safe House*, 38; on drinking, Wise, *Spy Who Got Away*, 31.

4. Wise, *Spy Who Got Away*, 54.

5. Howard, *Safe House*, 39.

6. The dates of Howard's service are from a briefing by the President's Foreign Intelligence Advisory Board to President Reagan and White House officials on October 2, 1986. See "USSR" folder, President's Foreign Intelligence Advisory Board, box 7, Donald T. Regan files, Ronald Reagan Presidential Library.

7. On training regimen for CKELBOW, two confidential sources; FBI report, 273; also on overall training, see Wise, *Spy Who Got Away*, 58–63.

8. Howard, *Safe House*, 40–42; Wise, *Spy Who Got Away*, 64–75.

9. Mary told the FBI that Howard attempted to "beat the second polygraph by keeping his muscles tense," and when he admitted that to the examiner during the third test, the examiner got so upset he demanded the fourth test. FBI report, 353. For Howard's account of the polygraphs, see *Safe House*, 43–50; Wise, *Spy Who Got Away*, 76–86. David Forden, interview with author, Feb. 6, 2013.

10. Wise, *Spy Who Got Away*, 85, quoting Howard. Howard's version of the events is in *Safe House*, 46–47.

11. FBI report, 306, reporting on an Oct. 28, 1985, interview of Mary C. Howard; although her name is redacted, the context indicates it is Howard's wife.

12. Wise, *Spy Who Got Away*, 87; Howard, *Safe House*, 51.

13. "Edward L. Howard," résumé, in FBI report, 201.

14. Wise, *Spy Who Got Away*, 85; Howard, *Safe House*, 51.

15. FBI report, sec. 5, 1316, and FBI interviews with Legislative Finance Committee personnel in sec. 4.

16. FBI report, 285.

17. The CIA's insular approach was described to the author by CIA officials. It was also the focus of the later investigation by the President's Foreign Intelligence Advisory Board and is discussed in Wise, *Spy Who Got Away*, 87–93. A former CIA official told the author there wasn't enough hard evidence at this point to compel the FBI to do anything.

18. FBI report, 306.

19. Ibid., 286, quoting Mary. Howard, *Safe House*, 54, says he pondered, "What would happen if I walked through that door and told them everything I know?" He says he did not enter but omits any mention of his letter.

20. Victor Cherkashin, *Spy Handler: Memoir of a KGB Officer*, with Gregory Feifer (New York: Basic Books, 2005), 146.

21. FBI report, 307.

22. Howard, *Safe House*, 49.

23. FBI report, 285–86.

24. Ibid., 2, 23; also see Wise, *Spy Who Got Away*, 108–17; Howard, *Safe House*, 55.

25. FBI report, 285.

26. On the meeting in Santa Fe, Mills told the author he could not recall the trip. Other sources include Gerber, interview with author; FBI report, 401; Wise, *Spy Who Got Away*, 137–40; Howard, *Safe House*, 56–57.

27. FBI report, 308.

28. Ibid., 11, 287.

29. Ibid., 10, 286.

30. Cherkashin, *Spy Handler*, 148.

31. FBI report, 287. Cherkashin also says there was a system of using postcards sent to the consulate in San Francisco.

32. Ibid., 277. This appears to be an FBI interview with Mary Howard on the day it was confirmed that Ed had defected.

## 17: VANQUISH

1. Headquarters to Moscow station, April 27, 1984, no time-date stamp.
2. Moscow station to headquarters, April 20, 1984, 201316Z.
3. Headquarters to Moscow station, Feb. 22 and 23 and April 27, 1984, no time-date stamps.
4. Headquarters to Moscow station, April 27, 1984, no time-date stamp.
5. Ibid. This cable includes the translation of the Tolkachev ops note from the April meeting.
6. Headquarters to Moscow station, May 25, 1984, no time-date stamp.
7. Moscow station to headquarters, Oct. 12, 1984, 121213Z.
8. Headquarters to Moscow station, Oct. 31, 1984, no time-date stamp.
9. Ibid.
10. A confidential source close to the family.
11. Headquarters to Moscow station, Nov. 1, 1984, 010133Z.
12. Moscow station to headquarters, Nov. 27, 1984, 271314Z, the draft ops note for the next meeting.
13. Moscow station to headquarters, Jan. 19, 1985, 191038Z; Royden, "Tolkachev," 30.
14. Moscow station to headquarters, Nov. 27, 1984, 271314Z, which includes the draft ops note for delivery to Tolkachev in January 1985.
15. Moscow station to headquarters, Jan. 19, 1985, 191038Z.
16. Headquarters to Moscow station, Jan. 31, 1985, 311535Z.
17. Headquarters to Moscow station, Feb. 4, 1985, no time-date stamp.
18. Ibid.
19. Headquarters to Moscow station, Feb. 6, 1985, no time-date stamp.
20. On the wrong *fortochka*, see Royden, "Tolkachev," 30.

## 18: SELLING OUT

1. FBI report, 10. Records of the Legislative Finance Committee in Santa Fe, New Mexico, showed that Howard was absent only one morning, on the ninth, for an illness. He apparently went to Vienna over a weekend. Later, one week of his desk calendar was found missing.
2. FBI report, 285, Mary Howard's interview with the FBI on Oct. 17, 1985. Mary's name is redacted but her identity is clear from the context.
3. FBI report, 10.

4. Ibid., 287, 399.

5. Ibid., 1390. The FBI interviewed someone at the UN agency and reported that the interview was set for April 25, but "shortly before that interview was to take place, Mr. Howard called a representative of the UNRWA and cancelled the employment" application. Howard's letter to the UN is at FBI report, 1086. The FBI's chronology suggests that Mary told them that Howard opened a Swiss bank account at this time, but the details are not clear, and she also told the FBI that he received payment for his information only later, in August 1985.

6. Howard, *Safe House*, 59. Mary gave conflicting accounts to the FBI about a side trip to Zurich. At one point, she said he made such a trip to open a Swiss bank account. But later she said he went to open that account in August when he was alone.

7. FBI report, 11, 100–101, 112–17. Bosch is not directly identified, but context makes it clear. For more on Bosch, see Wise, *Spy Who Got Away*, 103–8, 118–23, 160–64.

8. Howard, *Safe House*, 141, 143.

9. This is reported in *Ampule with Poison*, Vakhtang Mikeladze, writer and director, a film made for Russian television, 1997. Mikeladze told the author the film was based on original materials and interviews provided by the Federal Security Service, a successor to the KGB. Not all assertions about KGB counterintelligence in this film are plausible or believable, but original footage and interviews provide interesting additions to what is known about the case. Vakhtang Mikeladze, interview with author, Sept. 19, 2011.

10. Senate Select Committee on Intelligence, "An Assessment of the Aldrich H. Ames Espionage Case and Its Implications for U.S. Intelligence," Nov. 1, 1994, pts. 1 and 2, U.S. Senate, 103rd Cong., 2nd sess. Also see Cherkashin, *Spy Handler*.

11. The exfil was in late May. See Grimes and Vertefeuille, *Circle of Treason*, 72–75; Bearden and Risen, *Main Enemy*, 29.

12. In 1981, the CIA received an envelope from an anonymous scientist that contained extremely detailed and valuable information about Soviet strategic weapons but left some questions unanswered. For several years, the Moscow station attempted without success to locate the scientist to fill in the gaps. In early 1985, the CIA thought it had identified a possible source and made an approach in Moscow with a letter carrying instructions on how to contact the CIA. But the letter somehow fell into the hands of the KGB. The original scientist was

never identified. "Stas" informed Sellers that the approach had gone awry and the KGB knew of the CIA letter. See Bearden and Risen, *Main Enemy*, 50–59.

13. Sellers, interview with author, Jan. 28, 2014. Also see Bearden and Risen, *Main Enemy*, 59. Also Sellers's Web site, http://mdsauthor.the johncarterfiles.com, and Antonio Mendez and Jonna Mendez, *Spy Dust: Two Masters of Disguise Reveal the Tools and Operations That Helped Win the Cold War*, with Bruce Henderson (New York: Atria Books, 2002), 120.

14. This account is from a source with direct knowledge. Bearden and Risen, *Main Enemy*, 29, says "the tapes were blank," but the situation was more complex; the cable had stopped transmitting useful information.

15. Headquarters to Moscow station, April 1, 1985, no time-date stamp.

## 19: WITHOUT WARNING

1. A confidential source close to the family.
2. Moscow station to headquarters, June 6, 1985, no time-date stamp.
3. Mikeladze, *Ampule with Poison*.
4. Libin, "Detained with Evidence." Libin was a close family friend.
5. Mikeladze, *Ampule with Poison*.
6. Libin, "Detained with Evidence."
7. A confidential source close to the family.
8. Headquarters to Moscow station, April 26, 1985, no time-date stamp.
9. Royden, "Tolkachev," 31.
10. Moscow station to headquarters, May 23, 1985, 231358Z.
11. Royden, "Tolkachev," 31.
12. Sellers, interview with author, Jan. 28, 2014. Sellers was a case officer in the Moscow station at the time.
13. Wallace and Melton, *Spycraft*, 124, reproduces the CIA drawing of TRUBKA.
14. Moscow station to headquarters, June 13, 1985, 132347Z. Stombaugh is not identified by name in the cables but was identified in Bearden and Risen, *Main Enemy*, 11.
15. Moscow station to headquarters, June 13, 1985, 132347Z, and June 14, 1985, 141518Z.
16. Moscow station to headquarters, June 13, 1985, 132305Z.
17. Ames was asked as part of his duties at the CIA to review the file on Tolkachev and the arrest of Stombaugh and to prepare an analysis of what had gone wrong but never finished it, according to Grimes and

Vertefeuille, *Circle of Treason*, 77. The CIA continued to suffer major compromises in what became known as "the 1985 losses," which extended into 1986 and beyond. Howard could not have accounted for all of them. Who or what had caused it? For a while, the CIA believed there might be a leak in communications. Headquarters and the Moscow station put in place new, strict precautions and compartmentation. But communications were not the problem. What the CIA did not know then is that Ames continued to sell out its agents and operations. Ames not only provided confirmation about Tolkachev and CKELBOW but also betrayed a U.S. intelligence report on the ZASLON radar and compromised the "Gerber rules" for vetting volunteers. He betrayed Dmitri Polyakov, the general in Soviet military intelligence who had been the first to experiment with Buster, the handheld communications device, and "Stas," the guttural KGB officer who provided the sample of "spy dust," later identified as Sergei Vorontsov. Both were executed. According to a damage assessment by the CIA, nine of the agents whom Ames identified on June 13 were executed. The Senate Select Committee on Intelligence said Ames admitted compromising over a hundred U.S. intelligence operations of the CIA, FBI, military, and allied governments. The committee said "his betrayal stands as the most egregious in American history." Still more damage was caused by Robert Hanssen, an FBI specialist on counterintelligence, who offered his services to the KGB in October 1985. Hanssen and Ames remained Soviet agents for years to come. On Ames, see Senate Select Committee on Intelligence, "Assessment of the Aldrich H. Ames Espionage Case and Its Implications for U.S. Intelligence," 53; also statement by the director of Central Intelligence, John Deutch, Dec. 7, 1995; and Grimes and Vertefeuille, *Circle of Treason*. For details on Hanssen, see "Statement of Facts," *United States of America v. Robert Philip Hanssen*, July 3, 2001, Criminal Case No. 01-188-A, U.S. District Court for the Eastern District of Virginia, Alexandria Division.

18. Gerber, interview with author, Jan. 30, 2013.
19. Headquarters to Moscow station, July 12, 1985, no time-date stamp.
20. Headquarters to Moscow station, July 8, 1985, no time-date stamp.

## 20: ON THE RUN

1. Gerber, interview with author, Jan. 30, 2013.
2. In one of the truly bizarre moments of the Cold War, the CIA sent Ames—already secretly carrying out espionage for the KGB—to

greet Yurchenko at Andrews Air Force Base, ride in the car with him, and begin the debriefing. Yurchenko was spilling KGB secrets in front of a CIA man who was most certainly playing them back to the KGB. Within months, Yurchenko grew disillusioned. He wanted his arrival in the United States to be kept secret, but it had leaked. An attempt to rekindle an old romance failed. On November 2, while at a restaurant in Georgetown, he walked away from his inexperienced CIA handler. On November 4, at a press conference at the Soviet embassy, he claimed he had been abducted in Rome, drugged, and held against his will. Then he flew back to Moscow. There has been speculation that Yurchenko was a diversion to distract attention from the Ames operation, but CIA officials discount this, saying his information was too sensitive. CIA officials believe Yurchenko was a genuine defector but simply changed his mind. CIA officials, interviews with author; transcript of Yurchenko news conference, via CREST, CIA-RDP88-01070R000301930005-9.

3. In a memoir, Milton Bearden, who was Gerber's deputy at the time, recalled that he and Gerber informed the FBI about Howard on Saturday, August 3, 1985, at a meeting in a parking lot in Virginia with James Geer, head of the FBI's intelligence division. Bearden and Risen, *Main Enemy*, 83. Gerber also recalls the meeting in the parking lot and that he told the FBI who Howard was and why he believed that Howard was ROBERT. Geer said he did not have such a meeting that day in the parking lot with Gerber and Bearden but recalled meeting CIA officials somewhat later in a parking lot en route to being introduced to Yurchenko at a safe house. However, Geer said he does not recall discussing Howard then. Geer's deputy, Phil Parker, said he recalled no such meeting and Geer had never mentioned it to him. Geer, telephone interview with author, Sept. 10, 2014. Parker, correspondence with author, Sept. 12, 2014.

4. FBI report, 12; on the Swiss bank account, ibid., 289–90.

5. Ibid., 309–12, reports on contents of the box that was excavated by the FBI on October 17, 1985.

6. This account of the early FBI response is from Phil Parker, who was deputy assistant director for operations in the bureau's intelligence division, responsible for counterintelligence and counterespionage investigations at the time. Parker, correspondence with author, Sept. 12, 2014.

7. FBI, "Disappearance of Edward Lee Howard," Albuquerque Division, administrative inquiry, Dec. 5, 1985, 3–4, released to author

under FOIA. This report, on the actions of the FBI in monitoring Howard, is separate from the FBI investigation into Howard's espionage.

8. FBI report, 12.

9. Ibid., 4, 17–18.

10. Ibid., 20.

11. FBI, "Disappearance of Edward Lee Howard," 3–4.

12. Ibid., 6–8.

13. FBI report, 6. Howard claims in his memoir, *Safe House*, 91, that they had been watched since they were at the restaurant, but the FBI reports do not support this. Mary Howard later told the FBI that the Jack-in-the-Box worked because the FBI was following the Oldsmobile so far behind, but this is at odds with the FBI record, which shows the surveillance team did not follow them and only deployed later in the neighborhood. Howard said the taped call to his psychiatrist was his idea to put the FBI off his trail.

14. Wise, *Spy Who Got Away*, 223.

15. Details of the ticket, FBI report, 38.

16. Ibid., 318.

17. FBI, "Disappearance of Edward Lee Howard," 7.

18. FBI report, 7.

19. Ibid. The FBI report has redacted Mary's name, but her identity is clear from the context. See ibid., 285–447. Mary reported the divorce, ibid., 57, sec. 1, loose papers.

20. Howard, *Safe House,* 140, 141, 144–45.

21. State Department, Office of the Spokesman, Washington, D.C., Aug. 19, 2002. The department said, "According to Russian police authorities, Edward Lee Howard died in Moscow on July 12, 2002, as a result of a fall in his residence. His body was cremated privately at the instructions of his next of kin."

## 21: "FOR FREEDOM"

1. Mikeladze, *Ampule with Poison*. The Tropel cameras, library permission sheets, and L-pill are displayed in the film, which includes original KGB archival footage provided to Mikeladze and interviews with KGB officers who worked on the case, including Rem Krasilnikov, then head of counterintelligence, and Colonel Oleg Dobrovolsky, head of the investigation department of the KGB. Mikeladze, interview with author, Sept. 19, 2011, Moscow. Mikeladze said the film was created in 1997 and broadcast that year on Russian television.

2. A video clip of the sentencing is seen in *Ampule with Poison*. The date is not known.

3. A confidential source close to the family.

4. This point figured prominently in the President's Foreign Intelligence Advisory Board investigation of the Howard case. John M. Poindexter, then the White House national security adviser, told Reagan in a cover note for the briefing, "I would invite your attention particularly to the need to ensure that future cases are referred to the FBI on a timely basis for investigation." John M. Poindexter, "Memo to the President," Oct. 1, 1986, contained in Regan files, Ronald Reagan Presidential Library. Also see Wise, *Spy Who Got Away*, 87–93.

5. "USSR" folder, President's Foreign Intelligence Advisory Board, Oct. 2, 1986, box 7, Regan files, Ronald Reagan Presidential Library.

6. Politburo minutes, Sept. 25, 1986, READ-RADD collection, National Security Archive, Washington, D.C. Tass announcement, AP, Oct. 22, 1986.

7. Libin, "Detained with Evidence," and a confidential source close to the family. The data on the Kuzmin repressions, prepared by Natasha, are contained at the archive of Memorial International, Moscow.

8. An informed official said the CIA learned of her appeal only from Libin's 1997 article. Tolkachev's substantial earnings remained in escrow and would have been given to Natasha had the CIA known of her request at the time, the official said. The existence of the letter was also confirmed by a confidential source close to the family.

9. A confidential source close to the family.

## EPILOGUE

1. This account is based on Larry Pitts, interview with author, Sept. 10, 2013, Colorado Springs, and the following: "Dogfights of Desert Storm," History Channel, Nov. 5, 2007; Craig Brown, *Debrief: A Complete History of U.S. Aerial Engagements, 1981 to the Present* (Atglen, Pa.: Schiffer Military History, 2007), 51–59; Steve Davies and Doug Dildy, *F-15 Eagle Engaged: The World's Most Successful Jet Fighter* (New York: Osprey, 2007); Steve Davies, *Red Eagles: America's Secret MiGs* (2008; Oxford: Osprey, 2012). The author is also grateful to correspondence with David Kenneth Ellis and Robin Lee.

2. Lieutenant Colonel James W. Doyle (ret.), "1967 Soviet Air Show: Naming the Planes," U.S. Air Force, National Air and Space Intelligence Center, Wright-Patterson Air Force Base, Ohio. The MiG-25

was given the NATO designation "Foxbat." Details about the plane were revealed in the Belenko defection. See U.S. Fifth Air Force, "The MiG Incident," 1976 command history, vol. 3 of 13, obtained under FOIA.

3. Daniel L. Haulman, "No Contest: Aerial Combat in the 1990s," Air Force Historical Research Agency, presented at the Society for Military History, University of Calgary, Calgary, Alberta, May 2001, and updated July 8, 2002. For the most part, the Iraqi air force decided not to fight; 137 Iraqi pilots fled with their aircraft to Iran. These tallies do not include ground fire; Iraq shot down fourteen U.S. Air Force planes in the Gulf War. The tallies also do not include a navy loss, the downing of Lieutenant Commander Michael Scott Speicher in an F/A-18 Hornet fighter on January 17, 1991, the first combat casualty of the war. It is not known exactly how the plane was downed. His remains were discovered in Iraq in 2009.

4. Thomas A. Keaney and Eliot Cohen, *Gulf War Air Power Survey: Summary Report* (Washington, D.C.: Government Printing Office, 1993), 58–62.

5. The two experts, interviewed by the author, asked not to be identified by name. They had direct access to the Tolkachev positive intelligence for many years.

6. For example, the CIA overestimated the pace of modernization of Soviet strategic forces in every National Intelligence Estimate between 1974 and 1986. Haines and Leggett, *CIA's Analysis of the Soviet Union*, 291, from "Intelligence Forecasts of Soviet Intercontinental Attack Forces: An Evaluation of the Record," SOV 89-10031, March 1, 1989.

7. Haulman, "No Contest." These kill ratios refer to aerial combat and the air force, not losses from ground fire, nor losses by the other U.S. military services, but the larger point holds true.

8. Anatoly Chernyaev, *My Six Years with Gorbachev* (University Park, Pa.: Pennsylvania State University Press, 2000), 9.

## A NOTE ON THE INTELLIGENCE

1. Interagency Intelligence Memorandum 76-010, "Prospects for Improvement in Soviet Low-Altitude Air Defense," March 1976, top secret, declassified in part, Oct. 1999.

2. The CIA had long struggled with this topic. Howard Stoertz Jr., "Observations on the Content and Accuracy of Recent National Intelligence Estimates of Soviet Strategic Forces (NIE 11/3-8),"

July 25, 1978, 5–6, 45–50, Anne H. Cahn Collection, National Security Archive, Washington, D.C.

3. The Team A–Team B experiment came in late 1976, at a time when support in the United States for the Nixon-era détente with the Soviet Union was crumbling. Hawkish conservatives in the United States, including Paul Nitze, charged the Soviet Union was striving for military superiority and claimed the CIA had missed the threat. The CIA director, George H. W. Bush, consented to an experiment in competitive analysis. The group of outside experts, led by Professor Richard Pipes and largely drawn from the conservatives, were given access to the same raw intelligence used by the CIA's staff analysts for the annual estimate on strategic forces. Three panels were created, one of them to look at Soviet air defenses. The Team B air defense panel concluded Soviet air defenses were "formidable" and bristling with equipment. "There are 30 Soviet fighters and 100 surface-to-air missiles for each U.S. bomber which will arrive over the coastline," they declared. "The system is still growing, both in size and performance." This alarming conclusion suggested the Soviets might be capable of stopping American bombers from reaching their targets, meaning one-third of the U.S. strategic deterrent—the air leg of the triad of land-sea-air forces—could be obsolete. But the outsiders in Team B also saw evidence that the Soviet system didn't work very well, because the ground-based radar units and the communications networks were slow. The bottom line, Team B insisted, was the CIA just didn't know. The Team B air defense panel concluded, "Sufficient hard intelligence which would resolve or narrow all of the uncertainties, current and future, is not likely to be forthcoming for some time." The overall Team A–Team B experiment is described well in Anne Hessing Cahn, *Killing Detente: The Right Attacks the CIA* (University Park: Pennsylvania State University Press, 1998). Also see "Competitive Analysis Experiment: Soviet Low Altitude Air Defense Capabilities," Feb. 24, 1977, top secret; "Summary of B Team Findings—Low Altitude Air Defense," no date; "Soviet Low Altitude Air Defense: A Team Briefing to PFIAB, Outline," no date; and memo for the record, Joint Meeting of "B" Teams, Sept. 9, 1976, all courtesy of Cahn Collection, National Security Archive, Washington, D.C.

4. Director of Central Intelligence, National Intelligence Estimate NIE 11/3-8/78, "Soviet Capabilities for Strategic Nuclear Conflict Through the Late 1980s," Jan. 16, 1979, 1:19–23.

5. National Intelligence Officer for Strategic Programs to Director of Central Intelligence, "Assessments of Soviet Strategic Air Defenses," memo, Oct. 30, 1981, via CREST.

6. Director of Central Intelligence and Secretary of Defense, "US and Soviet Strategic Forces: Joint Net Assessment," Executive version, NI 83-10002X, Nov. 14, 1983.

7. "Soviet Capabilities for Strategic Nuclear Conflict, 1983-93," National Intelligence Estimate 11/3-8/83, March 6, 1984, vol. 1, "Key Judgments and Summary," 9-10. A version of this report provided to the president contains the handwritten notation "Pres has seen 3/8/84."

8. Director of Central Intelligence, "Air Defense of the USSR," Interagency Intelligence memo No. 85-10008, Summary, Dec. 1985. Also see Special National Intelligence Estimate 11/7-9/85/L, "Soviet Reactions to Stealth," Aug. 1985.

9. Alfred Price, *The History of Electronic Warfare, Vol. 3: Rolling Thunder Through Allied Force, 1964–2000* (Alexandria, Va.: Association of Old Crows, 2000), 339–47. A CIA cable, Moscow station to headquarters, March 20, 1980, 200825Z, and Royden, "Tolkachev," both say Tolkachev's information prompted the air force to completely change direction on a $70 million avionics package for the most modern U.S. fighter. Details remain classified. This may refer to a fighter's tactical electronic warfare suite or to the Airborne Self-Protection Jammer, which came to be known as the ALQ-165. In later years, the jammer project turned out to have a number of technical problems that could not be overcome and was never built or deployed in quantity.

10. Until then, the Soviets had been relying on an aging, propeller-driven aircraft, known as MOSS, for airborne radar. There were only nine of them, two of which had been disassembled. The MOSS system could only track a few targets at a time, could not look down, and was largely outdated.

11. See "A-50," *Ugolok neba* (Corner of heaven), an online aviation encyclopedia, in Russian, http://www.airwar.ru/enc/spy/a50.html.

12. Director of Central Intelligence, "Air Defense of the USSR." Also see Douglas D. Mitchell, "Bomber Options for Replacing B-52s," Issue Brief No. IB1107, Congressional Research Service, May 3, 1982.

13. "Relative Concern of Soviets About B-1 and Cruise Missiles," memo, June 24, 1977, via CREST, declassified in 2005.

14. Defense Intelligence Agency, "Prospects for the Soviet Union's Airborne Warning and Control System (SUAWACS)," Special Defense Intelligence Estimate, Aug. 6, 1981, released in part via CREST. Also

see John McMahon, director, National Foreign Assessment Center, "Note for: Deputy Director of Central Intelligence," Sept. 22, 1981, via CREST. Also Interagency Intelligence Memorandum, "Prospects for Improvement in Soviet Low-Altitude Air Defense," NIO IIM 76-010 J, March 1976, declassified in part by CIA, Oct. 1999, 4.

15. The data link is reported in Director of Central Intelligence, "Air Defense of the USSR," 14.

# INDEX